ASK
Arthur Frommer
& **travel** better, cheaper, **smarter**

W9-BLM-407

by Arthur Frommer

WILEY

Wiley Publishing, Inc.

Published by:

WILEY PUBLISHING, INC.

111 River St.
Hoboken, NJ 07030-5774

ISBN 978-0-470-41849-9
Editor: Michael Spring
Production Editor: Heather Wilcox
Photo Editor: Richard Fox
Production by Wiley Indianapolis Composition Services

For information on our other products and services or to obtain technical support, please contact our Customer Care Department within the U.S. at 800/762-2974, outside the U.S. at 317/572-3993 or fax 317/572-4002.

Wiley also publishes its books in a variety of electronic formats. Some content that appears in print may not be available in electronic formats.

Manufactured in the United States of America

5   4   3

ABOUT THE AUTHOR

Arthur Frommer is widely regarded as the nation's foremost travel authority. His books, articles, and speeches have profoundly changed the travel habits of Americans and the products of the travel industry.

He is the author of *Europe on $5 a Day,* which set off a torrent of transatlantic travel; the author of *The New World of Travel,* which brought awareness to new forms of alternative, meaningful travel; the founder of Frommer's travel guides, consisting of more than 340 yearly volumes of realistic, value-conscious travel; and the founder of *Arthur Frommer's Budget Travel* magazine, the first glossy designed for average-income travelers. His weekly newspaper columns on travel are syndicated nationally by King Features; his weekly radio program on travel is broadcast nationwide by the W.O.R. Radio Network; his influential daily blog on travel appears on Frommers.com; and he has also written scores of other travel guides and magazine articles on destinations and modes of travel.

Millions of Americans have learned to ASK ARTHUR FROMMER!

DISCLAIMER

Although the prices and other details in this book were accurate as of the time the book was produced, it should be stressed that this is a period of unusual turbulence in travel. The reader should expect revisions in those prices or details, the imposition or withdrawal of fuel surcharges, and even the occasional bankruptcy or disappearance of both small travel firms and large airlines.

ACKNOWLEDGMENTS

I am grateful, first and foremost, to Mike Spring, who rejuvenated Frommer's travel guides when he became publisher of them in 1994 and soon built them into the nation's leading series of travel guides. Though he retired from that position in mid-2008, he agreed later that year to edit the manuscript of *Ask Arthur Frommer,* and I am deeply indebted to him for shaping and greatly improving the book in a myriad of ways. To my daughter Pauline, for making hundreds of helpful suggestions, and always alerting me to the travel discoveries for which she has developed an awesome reputation, I am as always lovingly appreciative. I am so very proud that she will now carry on the Frommer name and bring our kind of advice to a new generation of travelers.

This book began as a daily blog on Frommers.com, and for launching that diary with such skill and imagination, I owe a great debt to Bob Bosch, David Lytle, and Jason Clampet. In addition to editing my daily entries, Jason also rounded up the photographs illustrating this book and did so with great talent. But although he also discussed with me a great many of the assertions in this book, the responsibility for them is solely mine.

This book is for
ROBERTA
whose values, love, and wisdom
have so improved the journey of my life

CONTENTS

2: "ALL I WANT IS A ROOM SOMEWHERE . . ."
Sleeping better & cheaper at hotels, hostels & homes............28

4: "Get Your Kicks on Route 66 . . ."
Trains, buses, bicycles, light cars & RVs have it all over planes 100

5: In the Footsteps of Indiana Jones
Adventure tours, safaris, camping, trekking & yoga 122

6: "THIS LAND IS YOUR LAND, THIS LAND IS MY LAND . . ."
Affordable travel & vacations in the United States 140

7: A NEW WAY TO VISIT THE OLD WORLD

Offsetting that dramatic decline in the U.S. dollar. 153

8: TRIPS THAT CATER TO YOUR MIND

Learning vacations, brainy tours, cerebral cruises 164

9: SPECIAL INTERESTS & SPECIAL PEOPLE

From students to seniors to singles, from nudists to vegans, there's travel for everyone **178**

10: The Preparations You Make, the Products You Buy

11: THE PEOPLE WHO ASSIST YOU
To separate the talented from the not so, get references. 225

12: THESE ARE A FEW OF MY FAVORITE PLACES
The cities, islands & nations to consider for your next trip 236

13: YOU'LL NEED MONEY

14: PROBLEMS, PITFALLS & CONTROVERSIES

15: TIPS, RULES & PREDICTIONS
We pontificate a bit about the general art of travel. 412

APPENDIX: LATE DEVELOPMENTS
New websites, tactics, destinations, travel trends & choices 428

INTRODUCTION

A BOOK OF ANSWERS TO MOST TRAVEL QUESTIONS: HERE'S WHY IT WAS WRITTEN

In a time of crowded airports, tense security lines, jam-packed flights, fuel-inflated airfares, and poor exchange rates, it is harder than ever to travel.

But it has never been more important to travel.

Despite all the problems, we cannot permit ourselves to live stunted, stay-at-home lives. We need to travel if we are to enjoy the fullness of life. Through travel, we experience different lifestyles and cultures, different philosophies and theologies, different responses to personal, social, and economic challenges—and in that jolting contact with the new and the different, we grow and develop.

It's possible, of course, to seek those goals in ways other than travel. But there is something about actually experiencing the world that cannot be duplicated. You can read endlessly about other countries, regions, and people, but nothing has the lasting impact of actually being there.

It is the purpose of this book to overcome the problems of travel. And though this task can sometimes require discussing a great many tedious facts, the overall goal is important, as I can testify from my own life.

If I had never traveled, I would never have witnessed all the many startling ways—some that work, some that don't—in which other cultures respond to their social, urban, and personal problems. I would never have fully understood all the enormous variety of solutions.

I would never have spoken with a European conservative defending the laws that prevent an employer from firing a long-time employee for insubstantial reasons. I would have gone through life assuming such a right to be God-ordained. I would never have met an Indonesian lawyer who ridiculed the idea of submitting lawsuits to a jury of one's peers. I would regard the jury principle as sacrosanct.

In other words, I would have remained limited in my mind's ability to consider other solutions.

If I had never traveled, I would never have understood that all people, no matter how exotic their appearance, have basically the same concerns, the same desires. I would never have spoken with an African woman in a dung hut about theories of child upbringing. I would never have heard the reactions of an Egyptian laborer to recent films.

If I had never traveled, I would never have felt physically sick when I read about the oppression or misfortune of peoples I had met in the course of my journeys. I would never have remembered them as fellow human beings instead of abstract news items. In short, I would have remained—despite all the reading I could do, all the lectures I could hear—a person who fundamentally was without humility, subconsciously believing in the constant superiority of his own nation or tribe.

Travel, in short, is a life-changing experience, a positive and joyous activity. So why am I so troubled by the current state of travel in America? It is because travel is not simply hampered by current economic conditions. Travel is also under attack.

It is under attack, first, through ignorance. It has been trivialized by media executives of superficial culture and attitudes. Barely a handful of American newspapers devote serious attention to travel, or keep up with major travel trends, or perform any real service to the traveler of average income. Nearly all the others treat travel as a mere recreation, and cover it in the most frivolous fashion. People who have never traveled extensively or given a moment's thought to the deeper implications of travel are appointed to the travel desk, if there is a travel desk. Several of the few impressive newspaper travel editors have recently been dropped from staff for reasons of economy, and persons with other responsibilities have been asked, part-time, to throw together a travel section from wire services and canned features.

And even the more serious newspaper travel sections are today devoted almost exclusively to travel facilities that no normal American can afford. One of the newspaper travel sections, felt to be the best of them, never fails to announce the opening of yet another absurdly expensive boutique hotel. In defending that choice, its editor has claimed he is required to report the news. But he remains silent over the fact that his travel section has never once reported on the really newsworthy opening of moderately priced 300-room hotels in the center of Paris, while never failing to gush over a tiny, new, deluxe 48-room lodging for the jet set.

Even worse than the newspapers are the glossy travel magazines, all worshippers of wealth without exception. Written in the main by young people dazzled by millionaire celebrities, the travel magazines rhapsodize about $700 hotel rooms and $150 meals. Not one of them any longer provides real service to the thoughtful American traveler.

If the travel magazines are atrocious, the travel TV programs are even worse. With minor exceptions, they are hosted by giddy starlets who gush about familiar sights and provide not a single fact of genuine usefulness to would-be travelers.

So in addition to world economic problems, the current sorry state of the travel media is another reason for this book. I have thus tried to deal with both the content of travel and the price of travel. I have discussed the current obstacles to serious travel and the ways to travel affordably. And I have tried to answer the questions that almost always occur to persons contemplating a trip.

I hope this book will encourage you to continue traveling—and to enjoy the full rewards of travel. And I hope we will always pause to appreciate the great privilege of travel. We are the first generation in human history to be able to go to other continents as easily as people once boarded a trolley to a nearby town. It is a precious right we enjoy, and we should not squander it by failing to acquire the skills to travel. Bon Voyage!

—Arthur Frommer

Chapter One

"INTO THE WILD BLUE YONDER..."

ALL ABOUT AIRFARES, AIRLINES & AIRPORTS

For years, we have all exulted over the low cost of airfares. While every other expense of travel went up, up, and up, airfares remained stable or even declined.

No longer. Not simply the high cost of fuel but the poor financial condition of the airlines has caused carriers to cut flights, eliminate destinations, end the discounts (or made them harder to get), and hike the average cost of transportation to really serious levels, making it a big and growing part of our total vacation expenses.

So it has become utterly necessary to learn how to find the occasional bargains. And that's what I've attempted to do in this chapter. In alphabetical order, from "A" to "F," I've grouped all the sources of those lower fares and all the methods for finding and obtaining them. And then, under "P," I've discussed the question of passenger rights, which relates to the quality of the flight experience.

AGGREGATORS

NEXT TIME YOU'RE DETERMINED TO FIND THE LOWEST POSSIBLE AIRFARE, USE AN AGGREGATOR

Aggregators are like Google—they search everything in sight. But unlike Google, which "orders" (that is, tampers with) its results, aggregators list the fares they find in an untouched and strictly logical order. They also claim to be totally comprehensive. When you use an aggregator (I'll name several prominent ones below) to find an airfare for your next trip, they search not only the big airlines but the little ones; not just the established airlines but the upstarts, too; not just the airlines but the consolidators (discounters) of travel. They peer not only at the American booking engines (Orbitz, Travelocity, Expedia) but at the British (www.ebookers.com, for example), French (such as www.anyway.com), and Asian (such as Ctrip.com) varieties, too.

It may come as a surprise that none of the famous U.S. booking engines— Orbitz, Travelocity, Expedia—are nearly as comprehensive in the searching they do for you. None of them list fares of all the cost-cutting, upstart airlines, and some list only a few. None of them reach out overseas to pick up the special deals enjoyed, on occasion, by the foreign booking engines. None, as far as I know, go to the companies that operate only as consolidators (taking risk positions on blocs of seats and thus enjoying lower fares).

The reason aggregators can go to so many additional sources of fares is rooted in their cost structure. Instead of taking a hefty commission on the fares they offer, they ask only a modest "per click" referral fee. They do not book the

Previous page: Upstart airlines, such as Britain's easyJet, offer savings in exchange for some-times-casual service and harsh conditions.

airfares they show, but simply direct their customers to "click through" to the airlines (or other sources of airfares) for the actual issuance of tickets. Fewer airlines or other airfare companies are thus reluctant to deal with the aggregators.

Kayak is one of several aggregators claiming to ferret out the best possible fare from a welter of choices.

Some typical aggregators? Try www.kayak.com, www.sidestep.com, www.farechase.com, or www.cheapflights.com, then www.mobissimo.com (the latter for international flights primarily) and www.momondo.com. The big one is Kayak; among the 10 largest airfare search engines recently ranked by the prestigious trade newspaper *Travel Weekly*, Kayak was number seven in popularity.

What other advantages do they offer? Many of the aggregators present their results in a form that can be customized to your needs, allowing you, say, to choose to see only those flights that don't require a transfer, or leave only from certain airports in your area. You can also usually limit the results to certain airlines, or search for fares leaving or returning within a several-day window (often, if you leave a day earlier or later you can save big). It's like having a virtual assistant perform 50-or-so individual Web searches on your behalf—a powerful tool indeed in the hunt for the cheapest airfare.

Most important, the aggregators search the low-cost and no-frills airlines (the Southwests and Ryanairs of the world) that most other booking sites ignore. They frequently find the same route being offered for drastically different prices, saving you up to 40%. They won't book the ticket for you; they merely ferret out all the going rates. It is then up to you to click over to the appropriate site and commence the booking process.

EVEN FOR FLIGHTS WITHIN THE UNITED STATES, A DANISH-BASED SEARCH ENGINE (YES, A DANISH SEARCH ENGINE!) SEEMS TO COME UP WITH THE BEST FARES

I've tried every search engine there is in the eternal search for the best airfares. And after testing the wares of the top American firms (Kayak, SideStep, FareChase, and others), I recently concluded that the European website known as Mobissimo (see below) was more likely to do the best job.

But that was before I ran tests on a Danish service called Momondo (www.momondo.com). It claims to search more than 500 airfare sources (upstart airlines, budget airlines, big and little airlines, other airfare websites, consolidators, and aggregators), which is two to three times the number scanned by most of its competitors.

Since claims are one thing, results another, I ran several of the best-known search engines through a series of tests of popular routes: a domestic flight (New York to Los Angeles), a transatlantic flight (New York to London), and an inter-European flight (London to Rome).

And would you believe—Momondo saved the most! I won't bore you with every pricing detail, but suffice to say, the little Danish-based Momondo was the clear winner every single time, finding fares that were from 20% to 40% less.

To use a firm headquartered in Copenhagen may seem an odd tactic for finding air bargains between New York and California, or between Atlanta and Chicago. But there it is—those canny Danes are something else!

MOBISSIMO IS ALSO COMING ON STRONG (FOR INTERNATIONAL AIRFARES), A MAJOR PLAYER AMONG THE AIRFARE SEARCH ENGINES

It isn't just my imagination. On several recent instances—too many to be ignored—Mobissimo (www.mobissimo.com) has occasionally produced the best airfare for international itineraries.

Mobissimo, as I've pointed out, is an aggregator. It reveals all the many options for reaching a particular destination, but then leaves it to you to access the winning fare, by going directly to the website of the airline or consolidator with the lowest price. A search engine with strong European roots (though it maintains a major office in the United States), Mobissimo is obviously best used for international itineraries, not domestic ones, such as New York to Zagreb, Croatia.

The lesson: Include Mobissimo when you search for advantageous international airfares.

AIRFARES (& FLIGHTS)

STAY ALERT TO AIRFARE "DEALS" LEAVING FROM YOUR OWN HOME CITY

Most airfare websites do a terrible job of alerting you to information that's relevant to your own particular needs. Even when they send you periodic e-mails containing the latest "deals," the offers are often so varied and geographically scattered that it's difficult to find anything of real value from your own home airport.

Half the time, when you open up a "deals e-mail" from the likes of American Airlines, there won't be a single airfare you can use. You'll have wasted your time.

But that confusing situation is improving, and some websites are doing better than others. The current champ is Kayak.

Of all the travel websites, Kayak is, in my experience, the best at tailoring its flight information to your home airport. While Kayak's deals may not be exactly last minute (many of them are for travel a month or two in the future), most of them are certainly late breaking, making it necessary for travelers to book sooner than later if they want to lock in the savings. Once users set their home city, Kayak produces its list of the "top 25" (the criteria are uncertain) deals. And once the Kayak website knows your home city, it comes up with helpful links to deals specific to your location, such as late-breaking fares. Kayak also gives you the option of receiving e-mail fare alerts to the destination of your choice.

Kayak's RSS feed (called Recent Kayak Deals) is less helpful; it's an unsorted mix of deals to and from everywhere, and thumbing through it will waste your time.

Yapta—which tracks the price after you've bought the ticket—is something else!

You can now take advantage of a subsequent airfare sale on a ticket you've already purchased by going to www.yapta.com. Yapta is a fab new website whose initials stand for "Your Amazing Personal Travel Assistant." It tracks prices on specific flights of major U.S. carriers. If the price goes down after you have bought your ticket, Yapta alerts you and you can then contact the airline and demand either cash back or a voucher for the difference in price, good for future transportation. Although all airlines other than Southwest now charge change fees of from $75 to $100, the savings from an airfare sale will frequently exceed that amount, justifying the use of Yapta. Note that the service is valid only for tickets purchased directly from the airline and not from such intermediaries as Expedia or Orbitz. I think Yapta has a future, and you might want to look at it.

In terms of its practical benefits, a website called FlightStats has become rather valuable

Because of the hub-and-spoke system used by most airlines, the great majority of flights require a connection to reach the ultimate destination. You change planes in Minneapolis, let's say, to reach Billings, Montana. You have an hour in which to walk from the gate of one plane to another, often in a different and far-away terminal.

Now let's assume that the flight you've chosen to Minneapolis has a record of arriving 40 minutes late at least 50% of the time. Or that the

DEPARTING TO	SCHED	FLIGHT		GATE	REMARK
ATLANTA	6:33PM	DELTA	664	C40	ON TIME
CHICAGO MIDWAY	8:00PM	SOUTHWEST	1135	C45	ON TIME
DALLAS/FT WORTH	6:18PM	AMERICAN	1272	C37	ON TIME
DETROIT	9:21PM	AMERICA WEST	98	C32	ON TIME
LAS VEGAS	6:40PM	SOUTHWEST	1371	C43	ON TIME
LAS VEGAS	9:21PM	AMERICA WEST	98	C32	ON TIME
LOS ANGELES	7:25PM	SOUTHWEST	1300	C43	AT 7:55
LOS ANGELES	7:57PM	AMERICAN	2261	C39	ON TIME
LOS ANGELES	7:57PM	EVA AIRWAYS	9004	C39	ON TIME
MINN/ST PAUL	6:46PM	NORTHWEST	562	C38	ON TIME
PHOENIX	5:55PM	AMERICA WEST	687	C30	ON TIME
PHOENIX	7:53PM	AMERICA WEST	6633	C31	ON TIME
PHOENIX	7:25PM	SOUTHWEST	1300	C43	AT 7:55
PHOENIX	8:45PM	SOUTHWEST	1616	C43	ON TIME
SACRAMENTO	7:53PM	AMERICA WEST	6633	C31	ON TIME
SALT LAKE CITY	6:53PM	DELTA	1737	C44	ON TIME

Monday April 17 2006 5:53PM

A system of flight times and connections that once ran like clockwork is now full of traps and snares.

"median delay" is 40 minutes, leaving you (and your luggage) unable to reach the other terminal in time. How wise is it to take the flight to Minneapolis in order to make a 1-hour connection to Billings? Wouldn't it be smart to book a flight whose arrival is more reliable, even if that flight is not at the most convenient time?

Before scheduling a flight that involves a connection, it has now become prudent to check the on-time record of that flight. FlightStats (www.flightstats.com) does just that. And though none of us enjoys complicating our lives, the conditions of air traffic in America require this extra bit of caution. In a country whose airlines all want to leave at the same popular times of day, requiring far more takeoffs than the airport or the air controllers can handle, delays are rampant.

We shouldn't book these habitually late flights if by doing so we lessen our chance of making a connection. FlightStats tells you what's likely to happen.

AS AIR TRAVEL WITHIN THE UNITED STATES GROWS COSTLIER & COSTLIER, EIGHT BASIC TACTICS REMAIN FOR REDUCING YOUR OVERALL TRAVEL COSTS

Recent months have been among the gloomiest in the history of U.S. travel. Everything has gone wrong. The dollar plummeted in value, the cost of oil skyrocketed to over $140 per barrel, and major airlines—including American, United, and Continental—all announced they will be reducing flights by 10% to 15%, thus causing airfares to climb, by amounts that I predict will be shocking.

So what can you do about it? Several solutions come to mind:

♦ **You can use alternative forms of transportation.** On trips to nearby cities, you can seek to substitute less expensive buses or trains for air travel, especially the new "cheap" buses ($10–$25 each way) that travel the eastern seaboard and crisscross the Midwestern states to and from Chicago: BoltBus (owned by Greyhound), Megabus.com (in the Midwest and on the East Coast), Fung Wah Bus (the pioneering Chinese-American company operating between Chinatowns in Boston; New York; Philadelphia; Washington, D.C.; and Richmond), and DC2NY (operated as a side business by an executive of Marriott Hotels).

To cities that aren't serviced by these remarkable cost-cutting god-sends, you can take good old Greyhound. People who once turned up their noses at Greyhound should think again (that premiere bus line is engaged in upgrading the quality of its terminals and vehicles). And in those instances where Amtrak is cheaper than air, you ought now to consider taking Amtrak (as so many Americans are now doing).

♦ **You can purchase your plane tickets well in advance.** Though airfares will obviously climb, they may be a little cheaper if purchased long in advance. They will not be cheaper at the last moment, since more and more flights are taking off totally full—and with big waiting lists, too.

♦ **You can use cost-cutting, cheaper airlines.** Because of its brilliant policy of hedging its fuel costs, Southwest Airlines will undoubtedly remain cheaper than the others in 2009 and early 2010. And though some of Southwest's hub cities (Islip, Long Island; Providence, Rhode Island; Oakland, California) may be less than convenient, you should grin and bear their awkward locations. You should also look long and hard at feisty Spirit Airlines and AirTran.

♦ **You can offset the higher cost of air transportation by lowering the price of lodgings at the destination.** You will want to consider staying at a Comfort Inn. You may even (gulp!) consider booking a Motel 6. (It's a good idea to scan the Motel 6 website for properties identified as having interior corridors—meaning that they are relatively "new builds." I recently stayed at a brand-new, fresh, and modern $59-a-night Motel 6 near Dallas/Fort Worth Airport, and it was just as good as many higher-category motels charging twice the price.)

♦ **You can cut your air costs by taking public transportation to the airport** (there always is a public bus used by airport personnel), and by bringing sandwiches along to escape the need to buy one of those overpriced, tasteless snacks at an airport eatery or—heaven forbid!—on the flight itself.

◆ **You can cut your total travel costs by renting an apartment or vacation home** at the destination instead of booking a room in a standard hotel. You can turn to Vacation Rentals by Owner (www.vrbo.com), HomeAway (www.homeaway.com), or various local rental agencies listed in guidebooks; or you can go (cautiously) to Craigslist (www.craigslist.com) or Kijiji (www.kijiji.com) to find a low-cost rental apartment or vacation home.

◆ **You can join a hospitality club,** such as Servas (www.usservas.org) or Evergreen (www.evergreenclub.com), or a hospitality service, such as Couch Surfing (www.couchsurfing.com) or GlobalFreeloaders.com. Contrary to the common perception, those organizations are not limited to foreign destinations but have copious listings within the United States. You might also consider using a vacation exchange club, such as HomeExchange.com or Intervac (www.intervac.com), swapping your own house or apartment for someone else's in the United States or Canada.

◆ **You can become politically active and work** for the defeat of those several U.S. senators who have thwarted the development of an adequate and inexpensive U.S. system of rail transportation. You can retire those servants of the oil industry so that we Americans can once again travel our beautiful country at affordable costs.

SOME REFLECTIONS ON THE RISE IN AIRFARES & OUR OWN RESPONSES TO THOSE INCREASINGLY HEAVY COSTS

Most of us have now experienced, firsthand, the practice of a la carte pricing for air transportation in the United States—the imposition of all sorts of extra fees and charges for services that used to be included in the cost of the ticket. Nearly every airline now charges at least $15 to check aboard the first suitcase per person and $25 to check a second suitcase. Some of the carriers now charge $2 for a small plastic bottle of water or a soft drink. I haven't yet learned how costly the peanuts will be.

These fees are part of a frantic effort to raise money. One analyst has predicted that if oil rises again to more than $130 a barrel, one or more major carriers will be forced into bankruptcy. So they are panic stricken and we probably haven't seen an end to additional charges.

You can gain a glimpse of America's airline future by noting the tactics of the low-cost airlines that fly within Europe. The biggest of them, Ryanair, goes well beyond charging for each suitcase checked aboard. They now also

Ryanair, Europe's largest cut-rate carrier, often charges as much for your luggage as it asks for the fare.

charge 5€ ($7.50) for simply checking in at the airport rather than online. Because you have to check in at the airport if you want to check aboard luggage, people with luggage to check always have to pay that extra fee.

Ryanair also charges $6 for using a credit card to pay for your ticket. And it imposes unusually harsh charges for overly heavy luggage, which it defines as more than 33 pounds. It charges $22—think about that—for each 2 pounds above the weight limit. And that's each way. In some instances, passengers have paid more than 98€ ($150) in total extra charges, which in some cases is higher than the cost of the Ryanair ticket itself. (Another European airline, the Hungarian/Polish carrier called Wizzair, is charging 1€/$1.50 per minute simply to phone them.)

Within the United States, we haven't yet experienced the congestion, delays, and fistfights that these luggage fees will inevitably bring about. But because so many people will attempt to limit their baggage to carry-ons stowed in the racks above their seats, it's obvious that rack space will soon be at a premium, that passengers will battle for that space, and that carry-ons will be strictly limited to small sizes. It's been reported that airlines are preparing to hire personnel to hang around the luggage belts, and at the gates leading into planes, spying on the carry-ons taken aboard, to ensure that persons do not attempt to smuggle on overly large suitcases.

And because many persons will limit themselves to carry-ons, they will also have to ensure that their liquid, gel, or aerosol containers are no greater in size than 3 ounces apiece, all enclosed in a medium-size, transparent Ziploc bag. What a mess!

To worsen matters, scarcely a week goes by that the airlines don't increase their ticket prices. Those increases will gain momentum as many airlines exhaust their "hedge" contracts limiting the cost of aviation fuel—and indeed, most such contracts will soon expire. Already, the cost of fuel surcharges across the Atlantic is approaching $250 round-trip, on top of increased security charges, government taxes, and baggage fees. The days when you could cross the Atlantic, or the United States, for $299 each way are over. I'm expecting many one-way fares (and additional charges) to total (including fuel surcharge, taxes, fees, baggage, and other added charges) $700 to $800 each way, at least $1,200 round-trip. A couple going to Europe, or from New York to California, will often need to budget $2,400 (and possibly more) for round-trip transportation.

Unless you are among a small group of high earners, the only way you will be able to travel in the future is to become increasingly cost-conscious about lodgings and other land expenditures. I used to be looked on as an eccentric for constantly stressing the need to consider alternative low-cost accommodations: hostels and hostales, *pensiones* and B&Bs, apartments and vacation homes, convents and monasteries, private homes and house-boats. May I suggest that for many travelers these will now become necessities? May I advise that for most of us the glossy pages and upscale recommendations of *Condé Nast Traveler* and *Travel & Leisure* will now become crushingly irrelevant? Most American travelers, if they are to continue to travel extensively, will have to seek out economical approaches that offset the high cost of getting there.

AIRFARE CONSOLIDATORS

DON'T FORGET THE SAVINGS YOU CAN ACHIEVE BY SIMPLY PHONING AN AIRFARE CONSOLIDATOR

Wholly apart from using aggregators or airfare search engines for your tickets, booking the flight via an airfare consolidator can also occasionally save you anywhere from 20% to 40% off the published fares (though it is usually much closer to the 20% end of that spectrum). How is this possible?

Consolidators—not to be confused with their similar but shadier cousins known as "bucket shops" (thinly financed fly-by-nights)—use their buying power to negotiate directly with various airlines to purchase seats in bulk at a wholesale price. Some of them then sell these seats exclusively to travel agents, but increasingly most consolidators are turning around and reselling their discounted plane tickets directly to consumers—naturally, at a slightly smaller discount than they were purchased for, pocketing the difference as their fee.

Chief among reputable consolidators specializing in Europe is 1-800-FlyEurope (its name is, conveniently, also its phone number and website: ☎ 800/359-3876; www.1800flyeurope.com). Others that go to destinations other than Europe include AirfarePlanet.com (☎ 503/429-1811), based in Salem, Oregon; the Chicago-based CheapTickets (www.cheaptickets.com); Dallas-based D-FW Tours (☎ 800/780-5733; www.dfwtours.com); Los Angeles–based Picasso Travel (☎ 800/742-2776; www.picassotravel.net); and Atlanta-based Economy Travel (☎ 888/222-2110; www.economytravel.com).

All these providers have good track records based on years of reputable service, but there are many others, as well as smaller, regional consolidators and so-called "ethnic consolidators." The latter are travel agencies located in ethnic neighborhoods, specializing in airfares between the city in which they're located and the country of origin of most of their customers (in other words, your local Chinatown is a good resource for cheap tickets to China).

Just make sure you check out any company first with the Better Business Bureau (www.bbb.org). Added layers of protection are afforded if the company is a member of any or all of the following trade guilds: the American Society of Travel Agents (www.travelsense.org, a site maintained by the travel agents' organization), the International Air Transport Association (www.iata.org), or the Airlines Reporting Corporation (www.arccorp.com).

Some tips: Consolidator fares are usually locked in by about 6 to 8 weeks before departure; waiting until the last minute only makes it more likely the consolidator will have sold out its bloc of seats.

Most people think air tickets consist of three categories: first class, business class, and steerage (otherwise known as coach or economy class), but in reality there are dozens of gradations. The arcana of how these degrees of tickets work varies from airline to airline, but one thing holds true across the board in the airfare game: The less you pay for the fare, the more rules and conditions are imposed on the ticket.

Consolidator tickets tend to hang around the bottom rungs of this regulations hierarchy, boasting the most restrictions and stiffest penalties for any changes—if, indeed, changes are allowed at all.

Still, when you consider an airfare to Europe can easily be $1,100 or more round-trip, the prospects of slicing 20% or more off that expense can easily be worth the mild extra layer of restrictions.

WE SHOULD BE ENTHUSIASTIC ABOUT THE AIRFARE CONSOLIDATORS, BUT WARY OF THE CONDITIONS THEY OFTEN IMPOSE

Most smart travelers know that any dirt-cheap plane ticket is going to come with some standard restrictions: no refunds or exchanges without incurring a penalty of $200 or more, requirements that you purchase the ticket 2 weeks in advance, that your trip straddle a Saturday, and that you stay a minimum of 7 and maximum of 30 days. But some discounted fares come with restrictions you might not even notice until they come into play.

A friend recently reported that, after years of purchasing discounted plane tickets to Europe from the noted and excellent consolidator 1-800-Fly-Europe (www.1800flyeurope.com), he ran into an unexpected snag on a recent trip to Italy. The tickets—on which he saved nearly $100 over other advertised fares by using 1-800-Fly-Europe—routed him through Amsterdam on Northwest/KLM. Weather delays caused his outgoing flight from New York to Amsterdam to be canceled. A helpful Northwest agent at the airport obligingly rebooked him on a new flight with a partner airline that had an added benefit: It would fly direct to Rome and get him in even earlier than planned!

His relief was short-lived. As he walked away from the desk, the agent called him back with an apology and some bad news. His discounted fare had come with restrictions on flying any airline other than Northwest/KLM and on flying any route other than the one scheduled. In short, he had to wait to be rebooked on a KLM plane, and he had to fly via Amsterdam.

He ended up flying a ridiculous new routing via Detroit, where he had to dash through the airport, barely making a connection to Amsterdam, where again he had to run to catch the plane to Rome. He also arrived in Rome about 8 hours after he was originally scheduled to do so, in effect losing an entire day of his trip. In a stroke of sheer luck, his luggage actually managed to make all the connections.

The moral: The consolidators of discount fares, and the budget airlines themselves, continue to be a reliable source for discounted airfares, but be prepared to ride out any potentially bigger bumps in the road that come with the fare rules. Also, make sure you read the fine print on any discounted ticket, as the savings may come with more restrictions than you realize.

AIRFARE SEARCH ENGINES

WHEN YOU GO TO AN AIRFARE SEARCH ENGINE SEEKING A BARGAIN, ALWAYS KEEP IN MIND THAT SCARCELY ANY OF THEM LIST THE REALLY CHEAP AIRLINES

I'm indebted to my colleague, George Hobica of Airfarewatchdog, for recently reminding us that scarcely any of the airfare search engines (such as Travelocity, Expedia, and that ilk) ever list the fares or flights of the really cheap airlines, such as Southwest and Skybus. Most of them fail to list Virgin America or Allegiant, and only a handful list cost-cutting Spirit Airlines.

Some of them list low-fare airlines but never show the sales fares offered by those carriers. It's all a reminder that there's really no shortcut for obtaining airfare bargains. After you consult the search engines and the results of the aggregators (Sidestep, Kayak, and the like), it's wise then to go directly to the airline websites (especially those of Southwest, JetBlue, Spirit, and AirTran), and compare fares. And don't forget to consider some of the foreign airfare aggregators, such as Denmark's Momondo or the increasingly popular Mobissimo.

AFTER YEARS OF WITHHOLDING ITS FARES FROM THE MAJOR AIRFARE SEARCH ENGINES, JETBLUE HAS FINALLY AGREED TO APPEAR. HOORAY!

The first benefit of the new arrangement is a practical one. Consumers can now find out what JetBlue (www.jetblue.com) is charging at the same time as they're checking with dozens of other airlines. That makes shopping for airfare much easier, with fewer steps.

Second, it steps up the competition between airlines. Now, with all the big players' fares appearing in the same Web window (JetBlue is now the eighth-largest airline in America), head-to-head price competition becomes a very real thing, with the marketplace deciding the victor.

JetBlue's agreement to appear in the major search matrixes does not mean, however, that the airline has completely joined the ranks. It still lacks baggage-handling agreements with the major carriers, meaning that if you intend to transfer from JetBlue to another airline, you still have to pick up your bags after the JetBlue leg and recheck them in for the leg on the other airline (or vice versa). That's an important scheduling consideration if you're planning on using JetBlue to connect with an expensive, infrequent flight—say, to Europe via JFK in New York.

Given a choice, I'd still book my JetBlue flights on JetBlue's corporate-owned website, because the airline's own site often grants booking bonuses (such as frequent-flier points) and slight discounts that aren't available elsewhere.

The JetBlue agreement leaves Southwest as the only major airline that declines to participate on the major Internet search engines. With Southwest as profitable as it is, the airline has little incentive to transfer control over its bookings to other websites, so on routes where Southwest is a player, you still have to troop over to its website to complete your price-comparison research.

IN LOOKING FOR A CHEAP AIRFARE, HOTEL, OR CAR RENTAL, IT ALWAYS PAYS TO SEEK OUT THE FOREIGN VERSIONS OF SEVERAL AIRFARE SEARCH ENGINES

When you use an Internet search engine, it pays to look not simply at the U.S./international version—the one that ends in ".com," such as www.expedia.com or www.hertz.com—but also at the foreign versions of those websites set up for residents of the country to which you're traveling, such as www.expedia.fr in France, www.hertz.es in Spain, or www.travelocity.com.au in Australia.

Because travel is priced differently in different markets, the savings can be substantial over what you would need to pay on the ".com" version of the site. The technique is fraught with difficulties, however, as some sites have a built-in blocker that keeps anyone who is not a resident of a particular country from buying through that country's version of the site (they usually verify this by the mailing address for your credit card).

Still, shopping around never hurts, and it always pays to know the lowest price out there. In some cases, you may discover that it would behoove you to wait until you arrive in a country, visit a travel agent (often clustered in and around major train stations), and have them book for you at the lower price available only in that country. The marginal fee they might charge may be more than worth it.

TELLING YOUR AIRFARE SEARCH ENGINE THAT YOU WANT TO LOOK AT FLEXIBLE DATES IS A POWERFUL WAY OF SECURING THE LOWEST AIRFARE

Such airlines as American, Delta, Continental, and more all permit you to look at airfares over a range of dates—you simply click on a feature called "flexible dates" or perhaps a link that says "more options." Trouble is, they will then search only their own flights—and not those of other airlines.

So go to an aggregator offering flexible searches. Although such services as Kayak (www.kayak.com) require customers to register before doing flexible data searches, the 30 seconds it takes to register is well worth the trouble. Once you're signed in, the website gives you the option of searching fares up to 3 days before or after the dates selected. I recently plugged in a Chicago-London round-trip in September with a Friday departure, returning the following Sunday. Within seconds, Kayak retrieved prices from more than a dozen airlines and revealed that by shifting the trip around and leaving a day earlier and returning 2 days later, I could save nearly $175.

Travelocity and Orbitz also offer flexible date searches. But each site has its own glitches. On Travelocity, the website sometimes retrieves prices only for the exact dates plugged in, never producing the better fares resulting from slight shifts in dates. Orbitz is better at finding a range of fares, but its grid only shows prices—information regarding airlines, flight times, and stopovers doesn't appear unless you click on a price and the website does a separate search. And, of course, always remember that Travelocity and Orbitz add fees of $5 to $10 onto the flights they sell.

Whatever you decide, flexible technology permits you to see more—and see it faster—than ever before.

AIRLINES

SPIRIT AIRLINES HAS BECOME A MIGHTY FORCE IN LOW-COST TRAVEL—ALWAYS GO DIRECTLY TO ITS WEBSITE FOR THE BEST OF ITS BARGAINS

Spirit Airlines began as an oddity, pure and simple, a cut-rate airline flying mainly to Myrtle Beach, South Carolina, of all places. And then it caught on. Today, it has countless flights each day all up and down the East Coast (from Boston, New York, Atlantic City, Washington, and even Atlanta) to and from Florida (mainly Fort Lauderdale, where it is now the largest airline using that airport), with onward flights to the Caribbean, Mexico, and Central America, and still other flights from Detroit to Las Vegas and Los Angeles. (It has still more flights from Chicago to Cancun and Florida.)

On each of those routes, it is a big-time price leader. Its fares

Though it's not as well-known as some of its competitors, Spirit Airlines is often the source of unmatched travel bargains.

sometimes boggle the mind ($9 is one offering) and almost always undercut the rates of other airlines flying the same routes (Delta, American, even JetBlue). How do you spot those bargains? By going direct to the Spirit Airways website (www.spiritair.com). Too many of the airfare search engines do not list Spirit's flights, and often you must simply ferret them out yourself.

In early 2008, Spirit announced plans for a major expansion of its fleet and labor force (a 40% jump). It's hoped that those additional personnel will eliminate the lines that often snake from Spirit check-in counters in Florida.

THERE'S TROUBLE BREWING AMONG THE CUT-RATE CARRIERS OF BRITAIN & EUROPE, WHICH CALLS FOR GREAT CAUTION (ALWAYS USING A CREDIT CARD) ON YOUR PART

Ryanair (www.ryanair.com) is the Southwest Airlines (the budget champion) of Great Britain, and so is easyJet (www.easyjet.com). Both fly at absurdly low prices from British cities to locations throughout western and eastern Europe. They siphon off so much business from domestic British transportation (that is, they cause the English population to vacation on the Continent rather than in England, Scotland, or Wales) that they have recently come in for violent criticism from Travelodge (www.travelodge.co.uk), which is the Motel 6 chain of Great Britain (offering ultracheap lodgings). Travelodge claims that Ryanair and easyJet are destroying the British hotel industry by causing more and more Brits to fly outside of Britain for their holidays and vacations. Got it?

Now why is this of interest to us Yanks? Well, there's trouble in the British/European industry of ultra-low-cost carriers. Because of an incipient recession in Britain, and the skyrocketing cost of fuel costs raising the price of air tickets, bookings are down on the budget airlines, and Ryanair and easyJet are enjoying load factors not of 95% (on which they rely for their rock-bottom pricing) but of 80%, which doesn't produce a profit at the rates they're charging. When the president of Ryanair announced that he expects a sharp drop in results for 2009, his competitors grew alarmed.

The various British newsletters dealing with the "LCCs" (low-cost carriers) are growing alarmist, too. One such publication openly predicts that two or three of the European low-cost carriers must either merge or go under. It all means that you should exercise extreme caution in booking one of these services in the months to come. If you can, make your purchase via credit card and try to pay as late as possible.

Airports

THE NEW PROTOCOL FOR GOING TO AIRPORTS

They may seem obvious, but special precautions need to be taken nowadays when you head to an airport for a flight. First, bring reading matter for those long periods when you'll be cooling your heels because you followed the advice to check in 2 hours in advance and then unexpectedly whizzed through security in record time. Bring the tastiest sandwich of which your kitchen is capable—for those flights on which nothing edible is provided. Bring those sandwiches even if your flight is supposed to include food. A meal supplied by an airline in bankruptcy—and two of the big ones recently were—is unlike any you've enjoyed in your earlier life. Bring nothing really valuable to the airport, such as your best watch or heavy expensive jewelry that you'll need to place in a plastic tray at the security gates; there's been an uptick in airport thefts. And finally, don't argue with the one bit of advice that should be heeded by every traveler: Do arrive at the airport much earlier than usual. The security procedures can cause long lines, and some overconfident flyers have missed their planes because of security delays.

THE GROWING PROBLEM OF THE PREMATURE PLANE

We sat chatting over coffee in a cafe no more than 40 yards from the gate at which our plane would depart. At 15 minutes before the flight's scheduled departure time, we casually strolled to the gate, only to find that the plane had already closed its doors, pulled away from the gate, and was now

Make peace with the fact that you'll be spending a lot of time at the airport—and prepare accordingly.

taxiing to the runway. Having fully checked in, and holding valid boarding cards, my wife and I had missed our flight despite having appeared where the plane was to leave, a full 15 minutes ahead! Hell-bent to achieve a record of on-time performance by departing in advance of schedule, some airlines are apparently forcing even prudent passengers to appear in the boarding area—not the check-in counters—as many as 20 minutes ahead of time.

I have now placed four phone calls to the public relations departments of major airlines in a fruitless attempt to determine whether these jump-the-gun departures are sanctioned by airline policies. Each time I encountered a runaround ("We'll call you back," "The person who knows is on vacation," "Give us a few minutes to ask around") worthy of a CIA press conference. And meantime, it behooves all of us to pass up the temptations of airport cafes or newsstands in favor of rushing to the gate.

1 HOUR OF CONNECTION TIME JUST WON'T WORK ANY LONGER AT TODAY'S AIRPORTS

It's become painfully obvious, based on more dreadful experiences than I choose to recall, that the "legal connection time" of 1 hour between flights is no longer sufficient in today's world. The number of flights arriving half an hour late, and the distances that one must often cover from one terminal to another to board a connecting flight, ensure that you will often be left behind. And when that happens, you can say goodbye to all your other scheduled activities.

Sad to say, split-second timing and efficient scheduling are no longer realistically available to the airline passenger. If only we had a decent railroad system for our transportation needs!

FOR THOSE WITH AN INCONVENIENTLY LONG LAYOVER, THERE IS A WEBSITE DEVOTED TO THE FINE ART OF SLEEPING IN AIRPORTS

On a recent edition of my weekly radio call-in show, I received a call from a man who would be spending a 13-hour layover in Beijing en route from Vietnam back to the United States. Normally I would have said it would be worth the hassle and fee to obtain a visa to visit China's capital, even for just the 1 day. Unfortunately, most of his layover would be taking place during the overnight hours, and he was desperate for information on where he could get some sleep between his flights.

Although airline schedules for the transatlantic market have largely evolved to the point where long layovers, let alone overnight ones, are

Parking, eating, and sleeping at airports are skills that every smart traveler will try to acquire.

uncommon, for other long-haul flights (and for many people attempting to link up a transatlantic flight with a connection to a no-frills or low-cost carrier in Europe), layovers of 8 to 12 hours or longer are a surprisingly common occurrence. If a quick trip into town isn't a real possibility, as with this gentleman's Beijing flight, and you just want to catch some shut-eye, there now exists a website just for you.

The Budget Traveller's Guide to Sleeping in Airports (www.sleeping inairports.com) is essentially a bulletin-board database detailing the best places to sleep in airports around the world. It is a clearinghouse where travelers share all the best tips for catching some Zs between flights. These can range from some quiet gate that is tucked out of the way, to a list of terminals with seats without armrests (allowing you to lie across them), to various nooks and crannies where you can cozy up to your carry-on luggage (here used as a pillow) and airport security will not bother you. Contributors are invited to rate their sleeping arrangements into one of three categories: "Hell," "Tolerable," and "Excellent, considering it's an airport."

If you access this site, you'll discover that, in Beijing, the best places to nap are in the main terminal (comfy benches, with armrests only every three seats) and in the dimly lit Irish Bar one flight above the check-in counters. On the downside, you will apparently have to contend with security personnel waking you up every 15 minutes to check your ticket.

ESPECIALLY IN HOLIDAY PERIODS (BUT OTHER TIMES, TOO), PRINT YOUR BOARDING PASS AT HOME BEFORE GOING TO THE AIRPORT TO AVOID BEING OVERBOOKED & BUMPED

I can't absolutely guarantee you'll avoid those consequences by printing out your boarding pass before you leave for the airport, as many airlines permit you to do so. The various carriers have a strange tendency to bump those passengers who have paid the lowest price for their tickets, regardless of whether they already have a boarding pass and assigned seat. But expert after expert has told me that in a period when airports will be jammed, and overbooking widespread, it's smart to do as I've suggested above (within 24 hr. of your flight). And how can it hurt?

Other tips for the airport around holidays times, when the airports are packed: Key the toll-free number of your airline into your mobile phone so that you can quickly phone reservations and get another seat if your flight is canceled. Reserve a parking space at the airport through Airportparking. com—those places will also be jammed. Ascertain the average waiting time to clear security at your airport, and then add another half-hour in planning your arrival at the airport—go to www.waittime.tsa.dhs.gov/index. html for that information. And for your Thanksgiving or Christmas travels, give some thought to flying on Thanksgiving and Christmas day themselves, early in the morning, when the airports and the planes are empty.

NUTRITION FOR TRAVELERS—MAKING WISE CHOICES AT THE AIRPORT ITSELF

How can you eat better when flying by air? A group of doctors recently reported that the meat-stuffed, cheese-stuffed sandwiches on a big roll that most airlines are now serving, are, healthwise, the worst possible repast. One so-called airline snack, of ham, salami, and provolone cheese on a huge and doughy slab, brings you a big 800 calories and 40 grams of fat. They suggest, instead, that you order in advance a vegetarian sandwich. Since many airlines are no longer responding to such requests, the doctors recommend that you eat in the airport before you take off: Veggie burgers are widely sold, the popular Sbarro's has pasta primavera, and amazingly enough some of the Starbucks at airports sell vegetable panini sandwiches to accompany your coffee. Plus, some airports offer healthy salads and sandwiches to take on the plane.

Six websites help to reduce the discomfort of airport check-ins & waits

Often unusual, sometimes quirky, but always useful, these online resources can greatly improve the preflight portion of the trip:

◆ **Finding the airport:** Perhaps the best—but often overlooked—resources available to air travelers are the websites of the actual airports they will be using. Airport sites, which are listed at www.atlasnavigator.com/directory/airports.html, are treasure troves of information covering everything from maps of the terminals, with shopping and dining options, to real-time arrival and departure information. You can find direct phone numbers for various airport services and, perhaps most useful of all, details (and links) on every means of getting to and from the airport, from private limo services to taxis to shuttle bus services, regional rail lines that link to the airport, and the frequently missed (but potentially cost-saving) local city bus lines.

◆ **Picking the perfect seat on the plane:** To help you select the best seat available on any flight on any carrier, visit www.seatguru.com.

◆ **Tracking your flight:** The www.flighttracker.com service from Orbitz offers current weather and delay conditions at airports across the country, wait times for security lines, and links to track the flight status of any flight.

◆ **Finding a parking space:** There's an effective solution to the high fees and often full airport parking lots at airports: parking at discount, off-site lots near the airports. They may add from 5 to 15 minutes of extra time on a shuttle bus to the terminal, but off-site lots have the benefits of a) costing several dollars less per day and b) allowing you to reserve a spot ahead of time—often a crucial service during holidays and other busy travel periods. The two biggest networks and booking services are www.airportparkingreservations.com and www.parknflynetwork.com.

◆ **Killing time at the airport:** Booking engine Expedia has thoughtfully posted selections from Harriet Baskas's book *Stuck at the Airport*, detailing survival tips, hints, and insider secrets to getting the most out of your waiting time at each of 65 major airports around the world. You can find it at www.expedia.com/daily/airports.

◆ **Catching some Zs:** For truly long layovers and unexpected flight delays, the funky www.sleepinginairports.com rates various airport terminals on how easy it is to catch 40 winks and lists the prime spots for snoozing without being bothered.

IT'S THOSE SHORT-HAUL FLIGHTS THAT ARE
JAMMING UP OUR AIRPORTS & AIRWAYS

My wife and I flew to Sanibel, Florida (reached via the Fort Myers airport), on JetBlue, boarding at what is probably the busiest and most crowded terminal building in all of America. JetBlue at JFK Airport is a scene from an all-year-'round New Year's Eve, crammed with hordes of people standing patiently in line to pass through security, looking for empty seats in which to rest, surging to the gates when a flight is announced. And why is JetBlue so busy? A glance at the departures board tells the story.

Flights from New York City to Rochester, New York, less than 350 miles away. Flights to Buffalo, New York. To Syracuse, New York. To Portland, Maine. To Burlington, Vermont. To Richmond, Virginia. All of them short, under-1-hour flights, each scheduled for several departures a day, and using up a large percentage of JetBlue's total takeoffs and landings.

Not one of these nearby places should be reached by airplane from New York. They should be serviced by train—by trains on high-speed tracks. If we had such trains, we could radically reduce congestion in the skies. We could return to an efficient, comfortable aviation system, and conserve giant amounts of fuel at the same time.

We urgently need to increase the appropriations for Amtrak and permit that system to grow and get faster.

CUT-RATE CARRIERS (EUROPE & TRANSATLANTIC)

CUT-RATE CARRIERS—& THREE FOREIGN WEBSITES
IDENTIFYING THEM—WILL WHISK YOU AROUND EUROPE,
FOR SUMS YOU CAN AFFORD

It's important that first-time visitors to Europe be aware of some 20 low-cost airlines that have created a fast and remarkably cheap way to travel between famous European capitals and resorts.

To see all the possibilities, go to a website called WhichBudget (www. whichbudget.com), which lists all the relevant budget airlines. Or go to a website called Dohop.com, on which you plug in a pair of airports and within seconds discover the cut-rate airlines that connect them. Or you can go to a site called Attitude Travel (www.attitudetravel.com), which lets travelers search for low-cost airlines in other parts of the world. The cut-rate airlines have revolutionized travel.

It's important to know how to approach the new low-cost airlines of Europe

A score of low-cost airlines now crisscross the continent of Europe, enabling you to visit all sorts of remote locations for peanuts—but they present you with a number of novel challenges. Bear in mind the following:

1. The baggage allowance on such tightwad firms as Ryanair, Air Berlin, easyJet, and others may be considerably less than on airlines that fly transatlantic. So reduce the weight of your load and leave part of your wardrobe at home.

2. Low-cost airlines keep their prices down by using out-of-the-way airports, such as Charleroi for Brussels.

3. All secondary airports have cheap and direct bus service into town, whatever airport taxi drivers tell you to the contrary.

4. The cheapest airfares on the cut-rate carriers are sold on the Internet.

5. Book well in advance; prices increase as the departure date approaches.

6. The cheap airlines will "close the gate" at the advertised time, and no amount of pleading will get you on if you're late. And finally:

7. Once aloft, don't expect more service than you'd get on a bus. Some will sell you coffee and a snack.

But used wisely, these low-cost carriers have opened up a new world of travel opportunities in Europe.

Upstarts are flying the Atlantic— go directly to their websites

Other European upstart airlines fly across the Atlantic. A long-experienced Italian company called Eurofly (www.euroflyusa.com) has low-cost flights between New York City and several cities in Italy (Naples, Palermo, Bologna, Rome, and others). A carrier called Air Plus Comet (www.airpluscomet. com) flies to Spain. Condor Airlines (www8.condor.com) goes to Germany from Orlando and Las Vegas. Martinair (www.martinair.com) flies from Florida to Holland. Britain's Flyglobespan (www.flyglobespan.com) flies from Orlando to Edinburgh. Because these flights aren't always listed by the big airfare search engines, you'd do well to access the airlines' own websites when you next consider a transatlantic trip.

The German airline known as Condor has a 50-year record of operating low-cost flights transatlantic and within Europe.

FREQUENT-FLIER PROGRAMS

ATTENTION, FREQUENT FLIERS: YOU HAVE BIG PROBLEMS

If you're a collector of frequent-flier privileges and enjoy the periodic pleasure of using your "miles" to fly for free to some attractive place, then steel yourself, have a drink, beware of darkening clouds. United Airlines and US Airways have cut in half the amount of time for miles in "inactive" accounts to expire, from 3 years to just 18 months. In doing so, they have adopted a similar policy announced by Delta Airlines (miles are canceled in accounts remaining "inactive"—that is, without additions or redemptions—for 2 years).

Obviously, the airlines are out to reduce the "free" travel privileges you thought you safely possessed. And persons who are infrequent fliers and need more than 18 months to accumulate the necessary numbers are out of luck. What you can do about it?

First, you can transfer your allegiance to the more generous airlines. On Continental Airlines, miles never expire (at least for now)—and you might keep that in mind when you book your next flight. On American Airlines, miles expire only after 3 years. What's more, American is known as the airline that gives away the most frequent-flier seats each year, and gets the highest marks in consumer surveys for its frequent-flier program.

Second, make use of a mileage credit card issued by your favorite airline for virtually all purposes, including flights. Downside of that tactic: These are usually expensive cards with high interest and fierce late-payment penalties.

Third, periodically "spend" your miles for purchases other than a flight, such as a hotel room or rental car—this, too, extends the life of your mileage. Downside of that tactic: You're depleting your miles and making it more difficult to amass the number needed for a flight.

All in all, the average U.S. flier has taken a big hit. It will now be necessary to pay careful attention to the status of your frequent-flier account, and to redeem your miles earlier than you may have wanted.

At least one airline is compounding its actions with greed. A friend, who a few months ago saw more than 50,000 miles evaporate from her long-established US Airways account simply because she hadn't used them or earned more in the past 18 months, recently received an email from US Airways offering to reinstate those miles . . . for a price. It was entitled "Get your Dividend Miles back" and gave her three options:

◆ Sign up for a US Airways credit or debit card, all but one of which carry an annual fee (and with the caveat that she would have to make a purchase with the card to get her miles back).

◆ Pay a service charge of $300.

◆ Purchase a ticket to fly first class or envoy class on US Airways.

The kicker? The fine print on these offers to "reinstate" her miles carried yet another 18-month deadline.

Is this how airlines now reward loyalty? By taking away the rights and privileges their frequent fliers have earned and then holding them hostage with the promise to return them only in exchange for a cash payment or for further shows of "loyalty"? That's not customer appreciation. That's an abusive relationship. The airlines can do better.

WHEN YOUR FAVORITE AIRLINE TURNS YOU DOWN ON THE USE OF FREQUENT-FLIER MILEAGE, TURN TO ITS ALLIANCE PARTNERS

A potent travel secret: When one of the four major U.S. air carriers—Delta, United, American, or Northwest—turns down your request to use the frequent-flier mileage you've earned on that carrier (because of "blackout periods," "exhaustion of space," a half-dozen other phony reasons)—you can often use the same mileage on flights of one of its alliance partners. All four belong to groups whose other members honor one another's mileage. American Airlines' One World Alliance is with Aer Lingus, British Airways, Cathay Pacific, Finnair, Iberia, Lan Chile, and Qantas; every one of these airlines pledges to honor AA's frequent-flier mileage. Delta's Sky Team consists of Aeromexico, Air France, Alitalia, Czech Airlines, and Korean. Northwest's partners are Continental, KLM, Alaska Airlines, Horizon, and US Airways. United's Star Alliance includes Air Canada, British Midlands, Lufthansa, Mexicana, ANA, Air New Zealand, Austrian Airlines, Varig,

SAS, Singapore, Thai, and Asiana. Although miles from one carrier can't be combined with miles from another, they can be used on carriers other than the one on which they were earned. And thus, a turndown by the airlines operating your program shouldn't end the quest; simply call the others.

PASSENGER RIGHTS

AN ORGANIZATION FORMED TO PROMOTE AIRLINE PASSENGERS' RIGHTS HAS GAINED NEW CLOUT

Whatever happened to the Airline Passengers' Bill of Rights? Various versions of it have been introduced into Congress and are awaiting committee approvals. In the meantime, various states have either passed or are considering legislation of their own to compel the airlines to respond to passenger health issues when planes are left stranded on the tarmac for several hours. Pushing back against such efforts, the airlines have filed lawsuits to prevent state legislation from going into effect, claiming that only the federal government has the right to regulate airline behavior.

The situation is untenable. Almost a decade after the first widely publicized, 8-hour stranding of passengers by Northwest Airlines, no law exists compelling the airlines either to return to the gate after an extended delay in takeoff, or to ensure that passengers receive food, water, ventilation, and clean toilet facilities during such delays.

When these delays reoccurred last winter, a frustrated airline passenger named Kate Hanni of California decided to form the Coalition for an Airline Passengers' Bill of Rights and began soliciting members and funds. Today, more than 22,000 Americans have signed up with her, and her efforts are beginning to attract national attention. Among other things, she has now set up and staffed a telephone hot line—☎ 877/FLYERS6 (359-3776)—to receive reports of passenger hardships, so that her group may then use such reports to publicize the problem and pressure the Congress into action.

Though the airlines continue to proclaim, "Trust us," it's increasingly apparent that none of them has yet agreed to return planes to the gate after a delay on the tarmac of, say, 4 hours. Not one has issued instructions to its staff requiring them to return the plane and permit passengers to get off because of an overly extended delay. And though various state legislators are currently making noises about requirements that the airlines provide stranded planes with food, water, and clean toilets, it is increasingly obvious that the only adequate remedy will be a single, clear, unambiguous legal mandate to limit the number of hours passengers can be involuntarily confined on the tarmac.

Other remedies are also badly needed, and those include requirements of "Truth in Scheduling," as the coalition puts it. Flights are "deceptively scheduled," they say, if they "are late more than 70% of the time or . . . are cancelled more than 8% of the time."

Go to www.strandedpassengers.blogspot.com for further information or to join the coalition. You can also listen to a Frommers.com podcast with Kate Hanni.

Chapter Two

"ALL I WANT IS A ROOM SOMEWHERE . . ."

SLEEPING BETTER & CHEAPER AT HOTELS, HOSTELS & HOMES

In a great many famous cities all over the world, average hotel room rates are now more than $300 a night; in others, rooms that once cost $100 are now $200 and $250. In addition to using hotels of a category far below what they were previously accustomed to, cost-conscious American vacationers will now have to seek out the far-less-expensive "alternative accommodations": apartments and vacation homes, rooms in private homes and apartments, hostels, convents and monasteries, B&Bs and farmstays. Others will engage in vacation exchanges or will join "hospitality clubs" that put them up free of charge (or almost so).

And surprisingly enough, the persons who make use of these cheaper alternatives will often find that their vacations have been improved, made far more interesting, profound, and authentic. In this chapter, I review all the lodgings possibilities. And along the way, I also examine the many services that claim to cut your costs in standard hotels.

American Accommodations

If the Motel 6 has "interior corridors," it is probably a "new build" & therefore a stunning value for the price

It's a closely guarded secret among savvy travelers: There are two types of Motel 6, the original (and occasionally shabby) versions with outdoor corridors, and the "new builds" with interior corridors and modern, comfortable amenities. And while the older versions may not be to your liking, the newer kinds (designed by the chain's innovative French owners, the Accor hotel corporation) are the full equivalent of motel chains charging considerably more. While most Motel 6s ask a uniform $50 or $59 per room ($40 in low-season periods), regardless of whether they are older motels or "new builds," the newer models are a tremendous, comfortable value at that price (even though they are probably the cheapest lodgings in their communities). In advance of a road trip through the United States, go to the company's website—www.motel6.com—and take a look at the description of each motel you're considering. If it lists "interior corridors," book it! There are now

New additions to the rock-bottom-priced Motel 6 chain are equal in comfort and modernity to many higher-priced motels.

Previous page: The immense, 140-year-old Mohonk Mountain House in the Hudson Valley is a remarkable resort with every form of recreation.

nearly 400 of these newly built Motel 6s. You'll stay in modern, clean, comfortable surroundings and enjoy all the traditional Motel 6 extras: free local phone calls, no surcharge on long-distance calls, free morning coffee, dataports, no charge for kids 17 and under occupying their parent's room, and free HBO and ESPN.

Wanna go deep-water scuba diving in America, with lodgings at $25 a night?

It is beyond a doubt the world's top underwater bargain. Olympus Dive Center of North Carolina (☎ 252/726-9432; www.olympusdiving.com) is a 2,000-square-foot facility (renting all the equipment you'll need and providing air and nitrox fills) in the midst of the docks at Morehead City, on the southernmost tip of the Outer Banks; out front, at a pier, are its two premier dive boats, the 65-foot Olympus and the 48-foot Midnight Express. And only 2 blocks away is the Olympus Divers' Lodge with 32 bunks in five separate rooms, for men and women. The price, believe it or not: $25 a night per person. Each bunk has its own lockable storage area. If you'd like a low-cost alternative to diving off the Caribbean island of Bonaire or in the Red Sea, this is it. If you'd like low-cost training in scuba, this has it. Dives are conducted daily throughout the year, even in the (generally mild) winter.

If you haven't been to Mohonk Mountain House in upstate New York, you're missing a national treasure

Mohonk Mountain House (☎ 845/255-1000; www.mohonk.com) in New Paltz, New York, 90 miles north of New York City in the Hudson Valley, is handed down to us directly from the Victorian era, a vast, sprawling, castle-like structure of 261 rooms and the oldest continuously operated large resort in America, dating back to 1869. It sits amidst thousands of acres of totally unspoiled scenery, atop a high ridge of the Shawangunk Mountains, directly alongside the half-mile-long Lake Mohonk, a mountain lake thousands of feet up.

From a porch at the front of the building, you feed fish in the lake; from a boat-side dock, you take out rowboats and canoes for paddling across the vast, high-altitude lake; on numerous trails you hike or go horseback riding. Cuisine: classic American, extremely well done. Rates are based on the Full American Plan (that is, they include all three meals daily) and range year-around from $300 per single, and from $240 per person double, in standard rooms.

THREE BIG RESORTS IN THE WESTERN STATES OFFER MAJOR DISCOUNTS IN OCTOBER & NOVEMBER & THUS EXCEPTIONAL VACATION OPPORTUNITIES. TAKE A LOOK!

Our country is dotted with some 30 large historic, self-contained, inland resorts, each operated for nearly 100 years. And during the months of October and November, most of them go into an off-season or shoulder-season mode of relatively inexpensive prices. Though none is dirt cheap at any time, they provide such glorious travel experiences that I want to recommend them.

I like three giant Western resorts in particular. The Bishop's Lodge (☎ 800/732-2240 or 505/983-6377; www.bishopslodge.com), on Bishop's Lodge Road, 3 miles from downtown Santa Fe, New Mexico, was first the 19th-century hillside retreat and chapel of Jean Baptiste Lamy, the first archbishop of Santa Fe, New Mexico, and hero of Willa Cather's 1927 novel, *Death Comes for the Archbishop;* his original buildings are well preserved and a popular site for weddings. The complex was later expanded to over a thousand acres, with an additional 88 rooms and suites in 11 guest buildings faced with adobe, earth-colored, and stunningly decorated with Southwestern furnishings. The chief activity is horseback riding along multiple trails through the canyons and foothills of the Sangre de Cristos mountains (trained cowboys accompany you and prepare cookouts); but there are also four tennis courts, skeet and trap shooting, a heated outdoor pool, indoor whirlpool and saunas, exercise room, children's play area, and numerous hiking opportunities. From early October through the end of

Surrounded by trails for hiking and horseback-riding, Bishop's Lodge in Santa Fe, New Mexico, is a distinguished ranch resort.

November, standard rooms (there are also suites and deluxe rooms) rent for about $210 on weekdays, $230 weekends. Sun Valley Resort (☎ 800/786-8259 or 208/622-4111; www.sunvalley.com), in Sun Valley, Idaho, isn't a single resort hotel but rather a "vacation village" of multiple structures. It is one of the great ski resorts of America, but recent efforts have accelerated to enliven and enhance its spring, summer, and fall use as an all-year resort. In addition to a Robert Trent Jones, Jr., golf course, it has 18 tennis courts, ice skating at two rinks throughout the year, a movie theater, multiple indoor and outdoor pools, trap and skeet shooting, day camps and play schools for children, family-style river trips, bicycle riding, fishing, hunting, and horseback riding. Approximate shoulder-season autumn rates (Oct 23–Dec 17) are $149 to $179 per room in the Inn, $179 for most standard condos. Tanque Verde Ranch in Tucson, Arizona (☎ 800/234-DUDE [234-3833] or 520/296-6275; www.tanqueverderanch.com), is perhaps the nation's most luxurious dude ranch, on 640 spectacular acres in the desert foothills (2,800 ft. up) of the Rincon Mountains next to Saguaro National Park and Coronado National Forest; you are 40 minutes by car from Tucson International Airport. The stable here has 120 well-trained horses (they provide walking rides for beginners, loping rides for the more experienced); and you stay in 1 of 74 large and well-furnished ranch rooms (most with adobe fireplaces), with private patios and air-conditioning. Price includes three meals a day, horseback riding, tennis, swimming, guided hikes, mountain biking, nature programs, spa facilities, indoor and outdoor pools, a Jacuzzi, men's and ladies' saunas, exercise room, and a fully supervised children's program. Shoulder-season (Oct 1–Dec 15) prices are $270 to $350 per single, but only $370 to $515 double (that is, for two persons).

THOUGH SUMMER IS THEIR HIGH SEASON, A NUMBER OF COLORADO DUDE RANCHES OFFER ATTRACTIVE RATES FOR COST-CONSCIOUS, WOULD-BE COWHANDS

The dude ranch season in Colorado enters high gear in late spring (most ranches open in May), and close to 30 of these cowboy-staffed resorts offer reasonable all-inclusive rates (not including airfare to Denver or Grand Junction) for 6 nights in a rustic lodge, with three meals (including campfire cookouts) daily, and your own steed for the length of your stay. If you've never been to a Colorado ranch, you're missing an exhilarating experience (riding instruction, trail riding, outdoor barbecues, songfests). For a list of the properties that charge as little as $1,295 to $1,595 per person per week in summer for adults, $995 for children 5 to 12, log on to www.colorado ranch.com or contact the Colorado Dude Ranch Association, P.O. Box D, Shawnee, CO 80475 (☎ 970/641-4701).

More than a dozen inexpensive, western dude ranches stay open throughout autumn and winter in other areas

Keep in mind that though the majority of low-cost western dude ranches are in the high-altitude Colorado Rockies, a number of them are found in sunnier states (such as Arizona) or in low-altitude locations of Colorado, and these stay open throughout the year. If you'll request a copy of the publication, "The Dude Rancher," published by the Dude Ranchers Association of Cody, Wyoming (P.O. Box 2307, Cody, WY 82414; ☎ 866/399-2339), you'll learn about the several big dude ranches that remain open November through March. These charge less than $1,100 per person for 7 fall/winter nights of accommodations, all three meals daily, and 1 week's use of a horse.

B&Bs

WERE YOU AWARE THAT TEACHERS (& THEIR SPOUSES) CAN STAY AT MORE THAN 6,000 B&Bs AROUND THE WORLD FOR ONLY $40 A NIGHT?

Every teacher should know about Educators Bed & Breakfast Travel Network (☎ 800/956-4822; www.educatorstravel.com), an association run by teachers for teachers that guarantees all its member a flat fee of just $40 per night (plus a $5 booking fee) for a double room at any of more than 6,000 homes in 50 countries. That rate applies to a teacher's entire family (spouses/partners and children under 18). This is essentially a hospitality network that is limited to current, former, or retired teachers. You search the database of available cities, send a request (at last 2 weeks in advance) listing the top four homes in which you wish to be hosted, and then are notified if any are available. The lion's share of members is in the United States, but there are also opportunities from Bangkok, Thailand, to Naples, Italy, to São Paulo, Brazil. By joining ($36 annual fee, plus a $10 initiation fee), you do agree to be a host yourself, but are under no obligation to do so if a request comes along for an inconvenient time. Cleverly, the organization encourages members to host by granting a $10 credit for every night you serve as a host—or $20 a night for allowing a homestay of 5 nights or more. A homestay is essentially like getting a house sitter for free when you go away on your own vacation (members doing the homestay pay $50 a night). Incidentally, teachers should ask about "teacher discounts" anywhere and anytime they travel. Frequently, your school ID will be enough to grant you reduced or free admission to many museums. A quick Google search of the phrase "teacher discount B&B" reveals savings of 10% to 20%

at inns and hotels in Tennessee; Arizona; Texas; New York City; Walt Disney World; Newfoundland, Canada; and Mazatlan, Mexico—and those are just on the first page.

Inhabit a Norman Rockwell postcard for $79 at an old New England B&B this winter

Starting in December, anywhere in New England that doesn't happen to have a ski mountain is in low season. This means virtually no crowds plus low prices on lodgings in picture-perfect towns of church steeples and antique shops snuggled around village squares frosted with snow. The low prices rule is particularly true of the B&Bs, inns, and chain hotels (Comfort Inn, Holiday Inn, Best Western, and so forth) of Massachusetts, which offer rooms from Cape Cod to the Berkshires starting at $79 per night for two people—including breakfast—though March 31. You can search through some 215 offers at the state tourism office's website in its "Warm Winter Specials" section. You then contact each property directly by phone to make a booking, mentioning the promotion code listed on that hotel's info page on the tourism site. When I last looked, a full 61 properties were charging $79, with another 77 in the $99 category. To round things out, there were 43 hotels for $139, 18 for $179, just 7 charging $209, and 9 at the high end of $229.

Book a guesthouse from London Bed & Breakfast Agency & you'll pay as little as $36 per person per night

I've now made the acquaintance of a superb website for finding inexpensive rooms in private London homes, many of them extremely well located. It strikes me as one of the best organized and easily used services of this sort. London Bed & Breakfast Agency (www.londonbb.com) provides lodgings in a range of private homes and guesthouses for rates that run as follows: in category C houses, £25 ($36) per person per night; in category B houses, £28 ($40) per person per night; in category B+, £33 ($47) per person per night; in category A houses, £47 ($68) per person per night. A sizable number of rooms in private homes are now being offered in Britain's capital, in response to the sharp rise in the value of the British pound (£1 now equals about $1.45—and more than that when you add commissions tacked on by the money changers). Spend a few moments with www.londonbb.com, and you'll find the solution to that problem, provided you're willing to stay in category C homes. Many of them have posted photographs of their rooms and facilities, and look quite suitable. It's reassuring to find a website for B&Bs that doesn't greatly favor its upscale properties and pass off the less expensive ones as oddities, gives equal treatment to the C category option, and provides a highly descriptive write-up of each one—accompanied in many cases by a descriptive photograph.

BRITISH LODGINGS

IN AMERICA, IT'S MOTEL 6. IN BRITAIN, IT'S TRAVELODGE (NOT TO BE CONFUSED WITH THE U.S.'S TRAVELODGE). BRITAIN'S VERSION IS THE CHEAPEST IN ALL THE LAND.

For Yanks on vacation in the U.K., even hotels that were once passably affordable are now quite expensive. Even family-run B&Bs, which were once the most reliable low-cost standby for cheap travel to Great Britain, can cost upwards of $175 a night under the current exchange. The solution? One of them, if you're headed to Britain, is to base yourself at a Travelodge (which has no connection with the Travelodge chain in the United States)—they are now the cheapest standard accommodation in the U.K. The company's policy is to keep its room prices low as long as its properties aren't full. So if you book online far in advance, or if you make reservations at one of its business-oriented properties on a quiet weekend, you can find some of the lowest prices in town. If you book far enough in advance, room rates

Cheap but comfortable, Britain's Travelodge hotels are the fastest-growing chain of lodgings in Europe.

Britain's Wolsey Lodges are stately homes that accept paying guests, a unique but affordable experience.

at Travelodge properties across Britain cost as little as £34 a night. (Typical last-minute rates shoot up to around £80 in London, which is a market rate.) A friend was recently in a bind for Sunday night accommodations in London, and by turning to a Travelodge that is quiet on the weekends, he was able to secure a perfectly comfortable business-class motel-style room in the center of the city, near the Liverpool Street train station, for just £50 ($73) a night. Meanwhile, rival hotels in the same district were charging three times that. If you're planning a U.K. vacation, book now at a Travelodge while the pickings are lush and the advance-purchase deals are available, and you're likely to pay prices as low as £26 ($38) a night. What you'll miss in style and coziness, you'll gain in savings. Just go to www.travelodge.co.uk.

At stately homes throughout England, you can enjoy bed and break-fast—and the company of extraordinary Brits—for £40 to £44 ($58–$64) per person per night.

A "luxury B&B" may sound like an oxymoron, but that's exactly what's offered by a British company called Wolsey Lodges that puts you up in assorted mansions, small palaces, and amazingly lavish carriage houses. And there you'll meet a remarkable range of English and Scottish home-owners: a retired don of Oxford University; a real estate broker who once served with the Tenth Hussars Regiment of the British Army; the business manager for a renowned duchess; an intensely contemporary theatrical agent spending weekdays in London's West End, but weekends at his Dorset home. Most of these people are land rich but cash poor, which is why they take paying guests into their homes. Whatever the reason, they regard their own company and conversation as part of the quid pro quo for your payment, and nearly all of them also offer you the extra-charge option of taking dinner in their homes. You'll find all the information at www.wolseylodges.com, which runs long lists with photos and descriptions of the stately homes in which lodging is available through their auspices and in every major area of the British Isles. As you scan them, you'll occasionally find a particularly grand mansion whose charges are higher than £40 or £44 ($58–$64) per person per night, but the great majority are exactly that much and occasionally a little less, always including a colossal, traditional English breakfast. You can make your bookings by phoning Wolsey Lodges at ☎ 1473/822058 or by phoning the individual stately homes at the numbers listed for each one.

ADD SMARTCITYHOSTELS TO THE INCREASING LIST OF BRITAIN'S ENORMOUS NEW LODGINGS FOR ECONOMICAL LIVING

Another smart new lodgings chain has appeared in Britain, operated by people eager to take the concept international. It's called SmartCityHostels (www.smartcityhostels.com), and its first enormous 620-bed facility has opened in Edinburgh, Scotland. The location is peerless: in Old Town on a short street long known for its hostels and proximity to charming pubs. Like earlier versions of the same concept, SmartCity offers a women-only section for female travelers—a new and welcome idea for hostels. It also promises one private bathroom per room, which houses between 2 and 12 people. Most of the year, Edinburgh's tourist traffic won't keep every bed full, but during the summer festival period, you can bet that reservations will be jammed for weeks. Unlike many independent hostels, this one has been designed and built by people who know that even money-saving tourists want a stylish environment. Interior rock walls, Jetsons-inspired carpeting, free Wi-Fi, a roof terrace done in woods and metals, and designer furniture are part of the deal, as is an in-house cafe (serving actual cooked food!) that puts the festering self-catering kitchens of its rivals to shame. Nightly rates start at about £14 ($20). Anytime a budget accommodation choice gives its guests more than hand-me-down furniture and bored service, I'm in full support. Backpackers deserve respect, too, and as long as new ideas such as SmartCity do well, budget travelers will be well served.

CLUB MED

FOR INTERGENERATIONAL TRAVEL, THE NEWLY REOPENED & REFURBISHED CLUB MED IXTAPA IS A TOP CHOICE. IT'S ALSO EXCELLENT FOR PARENTS TRAVELING WITH VERY YOUNG CHILDREN.

Of the Club Meds marketed to a North American audience, only six—Ixtapa Pacific, Punta Cana, Cancun Yucatan, Sandpiper, Buccaneer's Creek, and La Caravelle—are intended primarily for an audience of families with children aged 4 months to 18 years. And of these six, the newest (because it has recently reopened after an extensive period of rebuilding and improvement) is the Club Med Ixtapa (on the Pacific Coast of Mexico), thoroughly redesigned and now equipped with 298 enlarged rooms and attractive furnishings. Despite its orientation towards families, it also accepts persons of all ages, and ends up with a mix of age groups that I find extremely attractive.

Several years ago on a trip to Ixtapa-Zihuatanejo, I had a look at the Club Med Ixtapa (☎ 888/WEB-CLUB [932-2582]; www.clubmed.us) and was impressed by its almost unique melding of age groups. There were vacationers of all ages (20-somethings to middle-aged and elderly people) all dining exuberantly at the same tables, and there was a substantial percentage of families staying there with very young children. It was unusual at

Rooms at the intergenerational Club Med Ixtapa, Mexico, are designed for family use, a current theme of the French resort chain.

that time to find a Club Med that wasn't dominated by singles in their 20s and 30s. Now, I have nothing against the Club Meds catering to the 20- and 30-year-old set; they are perhaps the predominant clientele of Club Med, and all power to them. But for older vacationers, and for families, it was exciting to find a Club Med that permitted everyone to enjoy all the classic pleasures and policies of a Club Med without feeling out of place. And it was fascinating to find a resort where all the generational differences seemed unimportant. Greatly improved and as comfortable as any upscale resort, the newly reopened, family-friendly Club Med Ixtapa deserves a look.

EVERY YEAR, CLUB MED PROVIDES A FINE, QUICK GETAWAY TO THE TROPICS, PROVIDED YOU DON'T CARE WHERE YOU'RE GOING

You won't always find these deals on the Club Med website (www.clubmed. us), which is notoriously difficult to use. But if you phone ☎ 888/932-2582 and tell the Club Med reservationist that you're looking for a bargain-priced 3- or 4-night package anywhere in the Caribbean or other warm-weather destination, you'll be amazed by the number of cost-saving packages and prices, mainly in the autumn. Recently, last-minute, 3-night all-inclusive getaways (but without airfare) to Punta Cana and Turks and Caicos were priced at $249 and $339 per person, respectively. Last-minute 4-night all-inclusive packages to the deluxe Club Med resort on the Bahamas' Columbus Isle were priced at $799 per person, with airfare from Fort Lauderdale included. Just tell them you want to get away and don't care where. And if you are traveling with children, ask about the "Kids Stay Free" program at several of Club Med's family villages for children up to age 15 (one for each accompanying parent). As for your airfare (if it's not included), look to the smaller carriers that aren't usually associated with the Tropics. Spirit Airlines (☎ 800/772-7117; www.spiritair.com) flies to all-inclusive capitals, such as Punta Cana, Cancun, and Montego Bay, Jamaica. The always-growing JetBlue (☎ 800/538-2583; www.jetblue.com) now has service to Cancun, Aruba, Nassau, the Dominican Republic (two air-ports), and Puerto Rico (three airports). Frontier Airlines (☎ 800/432-1359; www.frontierairlines.com) and USA 3000 (☎ 877/872-3000; www. usa3000.com) offer flights from widely scattered cities in the Midwest, Northeast, and mountain states to such warm destinations as Cancun, Montego Bay, Punta Cana, Puerto Vallarta, Cozumel, and several resort areas of Florida.

Condo Rentals

Some rueful observations
about a recent condo rental

Last winter (Jan 2008), my wife and I became snowbirds for 2 weeks by renting a one-bedroom condo on the west coast of Florida. And although we had a wonderful time, we learned a few things about vacation condos. We found out, first, that facilities at a condo can break down. The loo fails to flush, the dishwasher goes dead, the ceiling fan breaks from its moorings and crashes down onto the dining room table. Unless the owner has given you the name and number of a maintenance person whom you can instantly summon for repairs paid by the owner, you'll find the occasional mishap somewhat unsettling. And though there are reasons for renting directly from the condo owner, I felt relieved that we had made our own arrangements through a management company that retained 24-hour responsibility for repairs. Remember, too, that vacation condos don't usually permit you to make long-distance phone calls. Nearly every owner who rents for short periods has disabled the phone to permit only local calls to be made. You'll need phone cards to make those out-of-town calls, and better yet you'll need to bring a cellphone. Keep in mind that condo kitchens rarely have the utensils for elaborate cooking. Condo owners provide you with the minimum: a tiny skillet, no tea kettle, no vegetable peelers or other such devices. Ask in advance for proper utensils. If you're a serious cook, you'll grit your teeth at having to purchase them for 1 or 2 weeks' use. And, finally, remember that some condos can look swell in the pictures, but are awkwardly located. In our case, the condo was exactly 1 mile from a big general store down the road. That meant that every morning, to pick up the newspaper, a bagel, and a coffee, I had a reason to make a healthy 2-mile walk. We visited other condos too far for easy walking and requiring a 10-minute drive. Don't get me wrong; I loved our condo vacation. It was dreamlike to sip cocktails on our screened-in porch and watch the sun set over the beach and sea. We'll rent a winter condo again next year, but we'll take some of the precautions I've described.

Convents & Monasteries

See "European Accommodations."

EUROPEAN ACCOMMODATIONS

EUROPE & THE VOLATILE DOLLAR: WHAT DO WE DO NOW?

I'm not sure that the full impact of volatile exchange rates—as we went to press, a British pound was worth $1.40, and a single euro was worth $1.30—has yet sunk into the psyche of Americans planning a European trip. Or that they've considered the radical new tactics that a cost-conscious trip there will require. Because the average guesthouse room—I'm talking a modest guesthouse and a double room—is currently renting for £100 in London and for at least 100€ on the Continent, the cost for lodgings is therefore some $145 a night per couple in London and $140 in Europe. Multiply those costs by 14 nights, and for a pair of Americans traveling together, the average 2-week trip can start off with a $2,100 tab for lodgings alone. So what's to be done? It's clear to me that the cost-conscious American must, from now on, seek out not hotel accommodations, not even guesthouse accommodations, but so-called "private homestays"—a low-cost, $40-per-person room in a residence whose owners are supplementing their income by renting out an occasional room. If you'll go to www.happy-homes.com or www.athomeinlondon.co.uk, you'll find such $40 per person accommodations in London. You'll find the same for Paris at www.good morningparis.fr or www.bed-and-breakfast-in-paris.com, and in Rome at www.b-b.rm.it.

THE BASIC TIPS FOR LIVING CHEAP IN EUROPEAN HOTELS ARE SO IMPORTANT IN THESE DAYS OF A WEAK DOLLAR THAT I'LL REPEAT THEM AGAIN

Here are 10 tried-and-true formulas for an affordable trip overseas:

1. **Ask for a room without private bath.** At more modest tourist-class hotels, this is the quickest and easiest way to get a room at a bargain. If you don't insist on having a private bathroom and are willing to make do with one down the hall (usually shared with two or three other rooms), you can often save 20% to 30%. Almost all "bathless" rooms in Europe have at least a sink in the room, and some even have a shower (just no toilet).

2. **Bargain.** European hotels always post the highest rate they can legally charge, even though that peak charge is asked only during the high season, or when holidays, major festivals, or trade fairs book the city solid. At any other time of year, you can get the room for much

less—and if things are particularly slow, you can even get a discount on the going rate in low season. After all, they'd rather rent you a room for 20% less than their asking price than let it stay empty.

3. **Opt out of breakfast.** Hotels in Europe routinely add 5€ to 10€ per person to room rates to cover the cost of a breakfast that usually consists of little more than croissants or rolls, butter and jam, coffee, and juice. You can often get the same thing—and freshly made, not packaged—from a corner cafe for half that amount and get the benefit of rubbing elbows with locals on their way to work. Ask if you can opt out of breakfast for a reduced rate.

4. **Check the hotel website.** Many hotels will post Web specials, last-minute sales, or discount packages on their sites, especially in low season. It's always worth Googling your intended hotel's name and city to find its website; even if there are no discounts listed there, at least you'll get to see photographs of the place and a locator map.

5. **Try an online booking service.** Even if a hotel doesn't bother posting Web specials on its own site, there's a good chance you can get a room for less than the advertised rack rate by going through an online booking service and taking advantage of its bulk discount. Two in particular stand out: www.venere.com and www.booking.com. Both specialize in Europe and, unlike the bigger booking engines, tend to include a lot of smaller, family-run, two- and three-star hotels.

6. **Lodge the whole family in one room.** Asking the hotel to place an extra cot or two in your room for the kids will usually add only 15% per bed to the rate—far less than booking a second room.

7. **Pay cash.** Many hotels, especially the cheaper mom-and-pop joints, will shave 3% to 5% off the price if you pay in cash. Essentially, they build the fee the credit card companies charge them into the room rates, and may agree not to charge it when they won't be paying that fee.

8. **Pick a "matrimonial" bed.** This tactic is admittedly getting a bit hoary, as it only applies in some small, generally one-star hotels where they still charge a higher fee for a room with two twin beds than one with a single "matrimonial" bed (of a size ranging somewhere between an American double and a queen).

9. **Stay in residential neighborhoods.** In Europe, inexpensive hotels tend to cluster around major train stations, but these are often bland, dirty, unappealing locales, whereas if you were to stay in a hotel that's in a pleasant residential area, you could save money while also experiencing a living, breathing, genuine side to the city few tourists get to see. Just be sure you're near a subway stop or major bus line and are no more than a 15-minute ride from the sights you came all this way to see.

10. **Consider a different lodging option.** There are many alternatives to hotels these days, from B&Bs to rental villas, most of which cost less than a traditional hotel while often offering a more interesting cultural experience (such as staying on a working farm or living in someone's home through a house-swapping deal).

IF YOU WILL FOREGO THE SECURITY OF ADVANCE RESERVATIONS, YOU CAN FAIRLY EASILY OBTAIN A CHEAP PRIVATE HOMESTAY ON ARRIVAL IN EUROPEAN CITIES

Private homestays are usually available on arrival in a European city, from lists maintained by city tourist offices. You can assume with fair certainty that every local tourist office—and every European city, large and small, has a local tourist office—maintains lists of private families with inexpensive rooms to rent. You simply show up and ask. Or else you look for those ubiquitous signs reading *zimmer* (in German-speaking countries), *camere* (Italian-speaking), or *chambres* (French), affixed to the walls of homes offering such lodgings. Unfortunately, very few of the city tourist offices will respond to an e-mail request for an advance reservation in a private home. The more casual tourist, willing to travel about without advance reservations, is the person who benefits from the lists maintained by such offices.

YOU CAN SLEEP & EAT AFFORDABLY IN EUROPE BY STAYING IN SMALL TOWNS WITHIN AN HOUR (OR LESS) OF THE FAMOUS, EXPENSIVE TOWNS

Here's a strategy that will let you thumb your nose at the mighty euro and survive the increasingly weak level of the U.S. dollar: By staying in towns within an easy radius of the major European cities you wish to visit, you can often cut your hotel costs—and even some of your meal costs—by two-thirds. You simply need to find a neighboring city that lies within about an hour's commute by public transportation—a city where prices are significantly lower. For example, rather than paying through the nose for a room in crowded and costly Venice, try staying instead in the lovely university town of Padua (Padova in Italian), a half-hour away. Padua boasts a fresco cycle by Giotto arguably greater than that in Assisi, and the famed Basilica of St. Anthony (complete with Donatello sculptures)—and it's just 30 minutes by train from Venice herself, so you can visit the city of palaces and canals on a day trip or two but leave behind the high prices of its hotels and dinners each evening. As a bonus, Padua is less than an hour by train from other Veneto highlights, including the Palladian villas of Vicenza and Verona (the city of Romeo and Juliet, which has an ancient Roman amphitheater hosting outdoor opera performances). Now, it helps if the neighboring inexpensive town has attractions in its own right that make it an interesting place to explore—for example, I would never recommend staying in dull and dreary Mestre rather than Venice, even though it lies closer to Venice than does Padua. Here are a few other cities where this tactic works well: Stay in Haarlem rather than Amsterdam, Prato instead of Florence, Avila instead of Madrid, Chartres instead of Paris, and just about anywhere instead of London (I suggest Oxford). Will this entail a different trip from one on which you stay in the big city and experience everything it has to offer, from hotels to nightlife? Yes. But it will also be a cheaper trip and, in its way, more rewarding since you will get to know two cities for less than the price of one.

HIP HOSTELS ARE OPENING ALL OVER EUROPE & RESEMBLING BOUTIQUE-STYLE HOTELS— BUT AT BACKPACKER PRICES

Hostels were once the almost-exclusive domain of penny-pinching backpackers in their late teens willing to put up with rough sheets, noisy cot springs, crowded dorms, inadequate shared bathrooms, and an avalanche of rules in exchange for a cheap bed. But over the past 15 years or so, hostels have been giving themselves a makeover and appealing more to young families, seniors, and budget-minded 30-somethings looking for a bargain. The European standouts include two chains; one of them, Meininger (www.meininger-hostels.com), currently runs six European hostels, most in Germany (Cologne, Munich, and three in Berlin) plus one each in London and Vienna. The newest one features so many amenities—each room comes with a private bathroom, TV, and telephone, and there's a lounge with free high-speed Internet access—it actually qualifies as a three-star hotel. The rates, though, remain at hostel level, starting at 18€ ($29) per person, including breakfast, in a room sleeping six to eight. You can choose to share a room with fewer strangers, but the price will go up: 19€ ($29) for a bed in a room sleeping four to five, 23€ ($35) in a triple, 28€ ($42) in a twin, or 45€ ($68) in a single. (Rates are roughly similar at the other continental Meininger hostels; the one in London charges a bit more, on a similar sliding scale from £15–£45/$21–$65.) A rival to Meininger, in London and Berlin, is Generator (www.generatorhostels.com), which clearly lives by the maxim that bigger is better. The self-billed "party king" of London hostels, Generator London sleeps an astounding 800 people (in rooms bunking from 4–14 for £15–£20/$21–$29), a 5-minute walk from the British

Museum. There are afternoon movies, 24-hour services including Internet and laundry, a travel agency, and a pub that stays open until 2am—long after most London bars must close by law. The Berlin branch sleeps 900 near Alexanderplatz, with its own beer garden (naturally), a disco, pool tables, laundry, restaurant, and karaoke bar; beds run 21€ to 25€ ($32–$38).

EuroCheapo has just dramatically improved its ability to find ultracheap lodgings for your next European trip

It's been around for quite some time. But prior to now, its hotel search engine was limited to surveying the prices offered by various individual low-cost hotels. Now, EuroCheapo (www.eurocheapo.com) has been modified to search other hotel search engines as well (such as Venere.com, Booking.com, and Hostelworld.com). After doing so, it sends you to the particular source—either the hotel itself or another comprehensive search engine—that has the best rates for the dates of your stay. When I last tested EuroCheapo for Rome, I found 266 vacancies starting at $56 a night for a hostel and $101 a night for a B&B (both near Termini rail station). For the same nights in Paris, a search turned up 142 possibilities, leading with a $61 hostel between the Opera and Montmartre and an $82 room in a hotel in the Latin Quarter. You'll still want to compare EuroCheapo's results with price searches on the established aggregators—notably Kayak, Mobissimo, SideStep, and Travelaxe. However, its focus on the value-for-your-money end of the lodging market and honest editorial take on each property make EuroCheapo and its new price search feature a welcome addition to the online hotel hunt.

Private homestays are also abundant in Ireland & on the Continent

I've already listed organizations for London and Paris that would enable you to stay for about $40 per person per night in private residences. How about the rest of Europe?

Here are some leads for low-cost lodgings in Germany and Ireland, and the cities of Florence and Venice. In Germany, the Germany tourism website (www.germany-tourism.de/ENG/infocenter/bed_and_breakfast.htm) maintains important links to regional tourism sites, which often provide details on private homestays. For example, at the Berlin site (www.berlin-tourist-information.de) you can download a 38-page PDF titled "Vacation Homes" or "Holiday Homes" (same document, two names), which lists hundreds of private rooms for rent. In Ireland. the national tourist board has a searchable database (www.discoverireland.ie, then click on "accommodation," then "types," then "bed & breakfast") full of photos and detailed descriptions of private homestays. Among the private websites, Town and Country (www.townandcountry.ie) describes one of the largest private B&B networks, representing thousands of properties in the Republic and Northern Ireland. In Florence and Venice, the official Florence website (www.firenzeturismo.it) lists a staggering 341 "B&B-Rooms to Rent" in that city (plus another 277 in the province of Florence), while the official Venice site (www.turismovenezia.it) offers 235 "Rooms to Rent" and another 187 "Bed & Breakfasts." Average price: around 75€ ($113)—still quite a savings when midrange Venetian hotels routinely top 200€ ($300).

STAYING ON YOUR OWN IN A EUROPEAN HOME OR APARTMENT IS WHAT UNTOURS REGARDS AS AN "UNTOUR"—A UNIQUE & REWARDING EXPERIENCE

A great many Americans dream of renting an apartment in a tiny Greek town or a house in the Tuscan countryside but are intimidated by the details, worried about getting a lemon, or concerned about throwing themselves into an independent vacation where they don't speak the language or understand the local customs. That's where Untours fits in (☎ 888/868-6871; www.untours. com). Founded in 1975, it supplies you with a private home or apartment in Europe for 2 weeks (usually in a small town, such as an Alpine village), throws in a self-drive car (or train pass) as well—and, most important, provides you with a nearby local contact to show you the ropes. It's a far easier business than working with an international real estate broker to rent such a property, especially since most of the latter will require a lease of more than 2 weeks. Untours's local rep will meet you at the airport to drive you to your new temporary home, show you the good local shops so you can start cooking in your kitchen, and give you guidebooklike literature to the region. The rest of your time, you're on your own, though your local "guide" remains on call to answer questions and overcome emergencies. Rentals are available in any of two dozen of Europe's most popular cities and regions—Provence (2 weeks for $1,799, including the home/apartment and a self-drive car) or Prague ($1,459 for 2 weeks of the same), Andalusia ($1,669 for 2 weeks) or Greece ($1,299 for 2 weeks), Switzerland ($1,399 for 2 weeks) or Sicily ($1,949 for 2 weeks). Also on tap are the slightly more expensive Barcelona ($2,269), Salzburg ($1,599), Tuscany (from $1,889), Paris ($2,169), Venice ($2,089), Leiden (from $1,369), and more. Those prices are per person based on double occupancy (though most of the rental units can easily accommodate three to six people) and do not include airfare to Europe, which is for you to arrange (best done by consulting an airfare aggregator, such as Kayak, SideStep, or Mobissimo). Untours has also recently started offering "Sampler" trips that allow you to split the stay between two destinations, spending 1 week in each—take 1 week in Umbria and another in Rome ($2,189), or spend a week in a 14th-century Bavarian castle followed by one on the Rhine River (from $1,792). I've been following Untours for quite some time, have frequently met with its founder Hal Taussig, and have the highest regard for the organization and its program. They offer a sensible and popular method of living like a European resident, and thousands of loyal customers have repeated the experience time after time.

WONDERS NEVER CEASE! WERE YOU AWARE YOU COULD USE PRICELINE TO OBTAIN CUT-RATE HOTEL ROOMS IN EUROPE?

High-class hotel rooms in such cities as London, Paris, Amsterdam, and Rome can be obtained by bidding as little as $100 a room on Priceline, the famous opaque search engine. But you may want to try www.biddingfor travel.com and www.betterbidding.com first; they alert you to the prices that Priceline has accepted on previous and recent bids, thus aiding you to make a successful bid on Priceline.

Obviously, Priceline won't work for those popular high-season dates when hotels are heavily booked in major European cities—the hotels offer discounted rates to Priceline only when they're in trouble. And on those much-in-demand dates, you'll still need to search out a private homestay (room in a resident's apartment or home in London, and so forth) if you're to enjoy affordable rates.

AN ENTIRE APARTMENT, FOR A PROLONGED LENGTH OF TIME, MAY BE THE SOLUTION TO THE HIGH COST OF EUROPEAN LODGINGS

Many of the European websites for finding hotels—I'm talking about www. venere.com, www.octopustravel.com, and www.eurocheapo.com—also list apartments for rent in major European cities, which can be had for less than the cost of a hotel room if they are rented for 1 or 2 weeks. With Europe as expensive as it now is, such apartment rentals may be the antidote to budget-busting costs. You may have to lessen the number of European cities you visit in the course of a trip, in favor of longer apartment stays in fewer cities. If you're willing or able to do that, then you'll want to click the "apartment" button on the three websites mentioned above.

THE CONVENTS & MONASTERIES OF WESTERN EUROPE SUPPLY COMFORTABLE & AFFORDABLE LODGINGS

How realistic is the advice of some travel writers to use the convents and monasteries of Europe for your lodgings? Very real, indeed. A great many monastic orders in Europe take vows of hospitality in place of poverty, and accommodate visitors for a token fee of $10 to $40 a night—sometimes even for free. The freebies, of course, are found at only a small number of monasteries, traditionally the more isolated ones in the countryside, where you stay in a monastic cell on a kind of personal religious retreat. At one of these retreatlike places, you are expected to stay for at least 3 days, following the monastery's rules, eating with the monks, and attending Mass several times a day. More to the speed of most tourists are the religious hospices run by convents. These are often set up as guesthouses for pilgrims and, as a result, are concentrated in such pilgrimage locations as Rome, Assisi, and Lourdes—though you can find hospices associated with major churches in most other big cities. Here, the rules tend to be less rigid (at most there might be a curfew), though showing a healthy amount of respect is always expected. Decor is monastically simple: a plain bed, perhaps a desk, and a crucifix on the wall. Rates range from $20 to $40, but can be higher at a few places. How do you find them? They're occasionally (but only very occasionally) found on the Internet. The American church of Santa Susanna in Rome maintains an excellent Italian list at www.santasusanna.org/coming ToRome/convents.html. The religious tour operator Zefiro World will

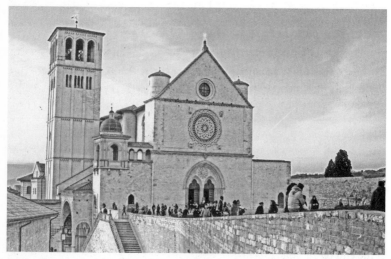

Staying in a monastery (such as this one in Assisi, Italy) is an effective way to cut the cost of lodgings in Europe.

reserve a spot at a few dozen other religious guesthouses (www.go-to-italy. com/English/Religious.htm), though these tend to fall toward the pricier end of the scale. There is also an excellent series of guidebooks by Eileen Barrish that includes these titles: *Lodging in Italy's Monasteries, Lodging in Spain's Monasteries,* and *Lodging in France's Monasteries* (they're in most big bookstores, and online). Two similar and helpful books are *Bed and Blessings Italy* by Anne and June Walsh, and *Europe's Monastery and Convent Guesthouses: A Pilgrim's Travel Guide* by Kevin J. Wright.

EUROPEAN FARM VACATIONS

EUROPEAN FARMHOUSES ARE A LAST ALTERNATIVE TO THOSE OVERPRICED HOTELS

You can stay at a working European farm for far less than the cost of a hotel. The practice is called agritourism, and it's a booming part of the European scene that is, sadly, seldom used by Americans. For as little as $30 to $70, two persons can get a comfortably rustic room in the farmhouse itself or in a converted outbuilding. Breakfast—of the heartiest, freshest farmers' variety—is almost always included, and you can often get inexpensive, rib-sticking dinners as well. Some agritourisms invite guests to try their hand at agriculture. A highlight of my (then-5-year-old) granddaughter Veronica's farm-stay trip to Ireland a few years ago was getting to gather the eggs from the chicken coop each morning.

While there are only a few central sources of *agriturismi,* the website of the European Federation for Farm and Village Tourism (www.eurogites.org) links to about 20 official agritourism organizations around Europe, and the independent website BeyondHotels.net has a section on agritourism with more than 50 links to resources in various European countries. Among these are www.bienvenue-a-la-ferme.com (France); www.irishfarmholidays.com (Ireland); www.terranostra.it, www.turismoverde.it, and www.agriturist.it (all Italy); and www.farmstayuk.co.uk (the United Kingdom).

HOME EXCHANGES

IT'S IMPOSSIBLE TO OVERESTIMATE THE IMPORTANCE OF THE HOME EXCHANGE

Friends of mine—he's a college professor, she's a psychotherapist—left town at the end of the college semester to spend 3 weeks in Tuscany living in the home of a Tuscan couple while the Italians occupied my friends' apartment in New York City. Later this year, in July, my friends will swap their New York apartment for a 1-month stay in the city of Victoria in British Columbia. They are enjoying these two remarkable vacations without any expense for accommodations, by doing a home exchange. While I have several times mentioned this brilliant method of vacationing, it can never be cited too often. The top names for arranging such exchanges are www.homeexchange.com, www.ihen.com, and www.intervac.com. There are many more, and much to discuss about them—see "Vacation Apartments" and "Vacation Homes" later in this book.

CRAIGSLIST HAS GROWN INTO A MIGHTY INSTRUMENT FOR EXCHANGING HOMES—WITHOUT EXPENSE OR FINANCIAL COMMITMENT

If you have recently glanced at the "housing swap" notices in Craigslist (www.craigslist.org), you've seen that there has been a startling increase in the use of these free-of-charge, electronic classified ads for vacation purposes. Though Craigslist will rarely propose "housing swaps" for small towns, it now nearly always offers an impressive number of homes for people living in, say, the hundred largest cities of the United States. Simply pick your home city from the main city page at craigslist.org/about/cities.html, then click on "housing swap." Up will come offers from a great many persons in other cities, offering a temporary swap of their home or apartment for yours. Craigslist is not as extensive in its inventory of overseas homes as are the well-established home-exchange clubs, such as HomeExchange.com, Intervac (www.intervac.com), or HomeLink (www.homelink.org). But each of these clubs charges a hefty yearly fee (as much as $100) for the right to use their services, and charges that fee even if you are unsuccessful in your quest for an exchange. Craigslist permits you to see what's offered, and to suggest an exchange, without committing yourself to a penny's expense. As such, it's a major advance in vacation planning, too often overlooked by Americans considering a home exchange—the single most sensible, logical, intelligent method of vacationing there is.

A HOLIDAY CHICK FLICK HAS CAUSED UPWARDS OF 20,000 PEOPLE TO JOIN HOMEEXCHANGE.COM

Not long ago, a travel company called HomeExchange.com was simply one of several firms working in the field of vacation and home exchanges ("you stay in their home while they stay in yours"). Then some folks in Hollywood produced an utterly unrealistic but wildly enthusiastic film about a home exchange (*The Holiday,* starring Cameron Diaz and Kate Winslet) in which

This clean, spacious, and comfortable apartment, available for a "home exchange," was discovered on Craigslist.

the owner of a palatial mansion in Southern California swaps (for a time) her gigantic residence with swimming pool and extensive grounds for a cozy cottage in Great Britain. And reference was made in the film to HomeExchange.com, which is portrayed as bringing about the fictitious swap. The entire transaction, as depicted in the film, took less than 24 hours to arrange. When *The Holiday* was released, a firestorm of bookings occurred. The phones rang off the hook, and thousands of persons all over the world rushed to add their homes or apartments to the vacation inventory of HomeExchange.com. At the *Los Angeles Times* Travel Show, the owner of HomeExchange.com was in attendance, along with his expanded staff and a recently hired public relations representative. Since then, his firm has skyrocketed in size, and charges a fee of $99 a year for its assistance. If you don't snare an exchange the first year, you get the second year free. HomeExchange.com now has more than 20,000 listings—repeat, 20,000 homes and apartments around the world. While HomeExchange.com may not be the largest such exchange firm, it's obviously contending for the top spot, and should be considered for your own next vacation.

HOSPITALITY

MEET GLOBALFREELOADERS & COUCHSURFING

There may be no such thing as a free lunch, but free beds are increasingly available all over the world. And one of the reasons is the explosive growth of two hospitality organizations called GlobalFreeloaders.com and Couch-Surfing International (www.couchsurfing.com). Both of them sign up people who enjoy having or being a foreign guest and allow them to use a spare room or a spare couch for overnight stays—totally free of charge. And both organizations have elaborate systems for screening out the wrong type of person. Some of them require references and elaborate personal statements. You'll get a kick out of reading their funky websites, and if you're the right kind of person, you may want to use their services either as a guest or as a host.

DESPITE COMPETITION FROM NEWLY FORMED YOUTH NETWORKS, SERVAS REMAINS KING OF THE FREE HOSPITALITY CLUBS—BUT IT'S NOT FOR CRASH PADS

Though other sources of free hospitality may currently enjoy a vogue (see above), the organization known as U.S. Servas (☎ 707/825-1714; www.usservas.org) remains a leader in the field. Its origins date back to 1948, when an American pacifist living in Denmark created a network to enable world travelers to stay for free in the homes of idealistic people around the world. Using volunteers to gather the names of respectable persons who enjoyed having foreign visitors as guests, he quickly accumulated the names of as many as 10,000 persons living in hundreds of cities who would offer such free hospitality. When members embark on a trip, they receive the names of dozens of other Servas members residing in the cities they plan to visit—and they then request a free stay of 2 nights or so with those generous souls. Members of Servas sign up as either "hosts" or "travelers," or both. They agree to be interviewed by screeners delving into their bona fides; Servas is not a budget travel service, and seeks to exclude persons who are simply looking for a free crash pad. The goal is for people to meet and exchange ideas. The application process, including the interview, takes about 3 weeks. As a nongovernmental organization affiliated with the U.N., Servas believes that the cause of world peace is furthered by such interchanges among people. Currently headquartered in Arcata, California, and no longer maintaining a New York City office, Servas is a cause as much as a hospitality service, and stresses that "hosts and travelers share their lives, interests and concerns about social issues." It charges a membership fee of $85 a year for international travelers, $50 for domestic travelers. A major effort is underway to attract younger persons to an organization whose average member, because of the long history of Servas, is obviously of mature age. Why not look them up?

WOMEN WELCOME WOMEN HAS BEEN O...
SUCCESSFULLY & EFFECTIVELY FOR 25

The gender-specific hospitality club Women Welcome Women (www.women welcomewomen.org.uk) is celebrating its 25th anniversary. Second only in longevity to the free-housing services of U.S. Servas, it was founded in Great Britain (where many of its members live) and is especially active as well in Australia, New Zealand, Germany, Japan, and the United States. Women Welcome Women doesn't always guarantee that its members will provide a free room to other members passing through; some members specify that they will (at least initially) simply meet female travelers for a drink or take them on a tour of their home city. Others are almost always willing to provide a spare room or cot to any member. The recommended length of stay is 3 nights, but members often accommodate visitors for much longer than that. The yearly membership fee is £35 ($50), which screens out persons unwilling to make a sincere offer of hospitality, and successful visits are almost always enjoyed. A prominent U.S. member of the club, Kim Giovacco, told me she would be more than happy to take phone calls (☎ 774/269-6558) from persons interested in further information about Women Welcome Women.

HOSTELS

THE ERUPTION OF LOW-COST, PRIVATE HOSTELS
ALL OVER THE WORLD IS AMONG THE BIGGEST
DEVELOPMENTS IN BUDGET TRAVEL

Their founders are among the most active entrepreneurs in travel today. They find a building—any building—where they're able to install dormlike rooms with bunk beds, from four to eight such beds per room. Their facilities include multiple bathrooms for communal use, a bar or lounge, an office. And in such small, improvised lodging establishments, they're able to charge from $20 to $35 per person per night—and thus defeat the high cost of travel.

The eruption of hostels—hostels by the scores—all over the world, is probably the single biggest news in the world of low-cost travel. They accommodate travelers of all ages, and have greatly expanded the capacity of the large, impersonal dormitories that used to make up the "official" international hostel movement.

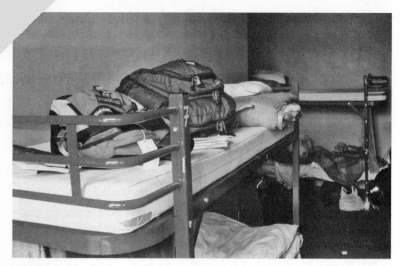

Hostels by the hundreds—some from the nonprofit hostel organization, some commercial—are today found all over the world.

Most of them belong to chains (for marketing purposes). Hostel Management (www.hostelmanagement.com), a new website dealing with the phenomenon, tracks the current state of expansion, hosts a message board for hostel operators, and provides listings for hostels by city, country, and name. The most heavily used websites for finding hostels are Hostelworld.com, Hostels.com, HostelBookers (www.hostelbookers.com), hostelmania (www.hostelmania.com), Hostels247.com, HostelsClub.com, GOMIO.COM, and VIP Backpackers (www.vipbackpackers.com).

You can also go to Google, inserting such terms as "New York hostels" or "Sydney hostels." Next time you take a trip to anywhere in America or abroad, consider the use of a hostel.

TAKE A LOOK AT HOSTELBOOKERS FOR AN IMPORTANT NEW SOURCE OF CHEAP DIGS

A British-managed website called HostelBookers (www.hostelbookers.com) is a revelation—a collection of more hostels (40 or so in New York City alone) in more cities than you would ever have thought possible, with excellent write-ups of each and an efficient method for making reservations at them. HostelBookers lists not only the "official" hostels belonging to Hostelling International but the many recent modest hotels converting double rooms into low-cost dorms and calling themselves "hostels."

Their rates in even the most expensive cities average about $25 to $35 a night, and thus permit budget travelers to cut their costs for lodgings below the price of even private homestays. And the extra reward of staying in a hostel (there's no maximum age limit for doing so) is the camaraderie of other dynamic travelers and the easy access to information on interesting, low-cost activities in the cities you're visiting.

BEFORE YOU REJECT THE IDEA OF STAYING IN A EUROPEAN HOSTEL, YOU SHOULD KNOW THAT THEY'VE CHANGED CONSIDERABLY IN RECENT YEARS

Most travelers who haven't peeked into a hostel in 10 or 15 years probably harbor a lingering image of the "youth hostels" of yesteryear: dreary institutional structures featuring cavernous dorm rooms of 50 or more beds, ridiculously early curfews, midday lockout periods, and lamentable locations on the outskirts of town.

The good news is that hostels have dropped the "youth" requirement and are now used by everyone from traveling families with young children to peripatetic grandparents on quirky retirement trips. Though you still get a bunk in a shared room, most of those rooms now average four to six beds each; a few are doubles and triples; and many have bathrooms "en suite" (with private baths) rather than down the hall. Prices average 16€ to 22€ per bed, a bit more for a private room sleeping two to three people.

In addition to the older hostels affiliated with Hostelling International, most European cities also now feature a score of private hostels, often with excellent locations in the historic center or near the rail stations; frequently with laundry rooms, cheap (or free) Internet stations, dining rooms, and in-house pubs or discos; and few, if any, of those old school-marm rules (which do, unfortunately, survive at most HI-affiliated hostels).

But be warned that even if they have dropped "youth" from the name, hostels still tend to draw a youthful backpacker crowd, which means a convivial atmosphere that can often verge on one big party—wonderful if that's what you came for, not so great if you expected to get any sleep before the thumping beat from the basement disco ceases at 3am.

There is an official HI site (www.hihostels.com), but if you want to peruse private hostels alongside HI-affiliated ones you'll find far better resources at the independent sites www.hostels.com, www.hostels.net, www.hostelbookers.com, and www.europehostels.org, of which the last named includes a primer on hostel travel and direct links to hostelling sites in 34 European countries.

Though you may be determined never to stay in a hostel, you should nevertheless consult HostelBookers

When HostelBookers (www.hostelbookers.com) announced that it was listing tens of thousands of hostels in 2,500 locations, it was understood that the word "hostel" was now being used in a broader sense than ever before. The world does not possess tens of thousands of traditional hostels.

And yet the assertion by HostelBookers is a truthful one. If you will play around with that impressive website, you will quickly see that it does not confine its coverage to traditional hostels (older buildings with dormitory accommodations, mainly for backpackers), but includes a great many traditional budget hotels that are now calling themselves hostels to broaden their appeal to an older, wider audience (the average age of guests has increased from 24 to 32). Many of these properties consist mainly of private rooms, often with private bath (although many of them also place four, six, or even more beds in a room). They are more likely to have flocked wallpaper, free Wi-Fi, rainfall showers, and a rooftop bar, than bedbugs and bad plumbing.

If you're at all interested in ultracheap accommodations around the world, including in ultracostly London and New York, you might want to look at the well-presented website. You'll quickly discover that a great many budget hotels are now taking steps to redesignate themselves as hostels.

Add Base Backpackers of Australia & New Zealand to the increasing list of trendy new lodgings for economical living

A top new chain of hostels, one of the best for digs "down under," is Base Backpackers (www.basebackpackers.com), supplying perks that few other hostels do, including Egyptian cotton sheets, women-only floors, and in one property, a rock-climbing wall. Base Backpackers began life a few years ago as a single outpost in St. Kilda, in Melbourne, Australia, and judging from its quick growth rate—there are now eight properties in Australia and New Zealand—budget travelers are grateful to be treated with respect. Earlier in this chapter (see "British Lodgings"), I've also alerted you to the enormous, 620-bed SmartCityHostels of Edinburgh, Scotland, still another in the big movement to cheap-but-comfortable hostels.

ADD EUROPEANHOSTELS.COM TO THE LIST OF WEBSITES DIRECTING YOU TO THE FASTEST-GROWING TYPE OF ACCOMMODATIONS IN TRAVEL

To support this explosion in the number and size of hostels, the founders of EuroCheapo (www.eurocheapo.com) have created a new website called EuropeanHostels.com. Whereas EuroCheapo describes budget-priced hotels and guesthouses, EuropeanHostels.com will be more tightly focused on true hostels—that is, those in which most accommodations are dormlike in nature, and where the nightly rate is sensationally low. (But there is an overlap between the two sites; many of the "hostels" also offer single and double rooms, and all of them accept people of all ages.) The website's new search tools also include sorting and filtering by "Editor's Picks," "Price," "Distance to City Center," and "Highest Rating."

ALL AVID TRAVELERS SHOULD EQUIP THEMSELVES WITH A 1-OUNCE MAP OF THE "OFFICIAL" HOSTELS OF THE UNITED STATES

Rather than supply you with another bulky guidebook, Hostelling International USA has published a four-color, fold-out map identifying and locating (with addresses and phone numbers) the 150 major youth hostels of the United States. It's a remarkably handy publication that every avid traveler should have, as each of these hostels is now available to travelers of all ages and to families. The most expensive of them—the New York City Hostel—charges as little as $29 per person per night, while most others start at $18.

"Official" hostels are inexpensive dormitory-style accommodations for travelers of all ages. They provide separate facilities for males and females, fully equipped self-service kitchens, dining areas, and common rooms for relaxing and socializing. And many hostels also have private family/couples rooms which can be reserved in advance.

In addition, most hostels offer a variety of special programs and activities, providing hostel guests with more than just a "cheap sleep."

Within the United States, there are presently hostels in New York City; Boston; Nantucket; Washington, D.C.; seven different locations in Florida; Los Angeles/Santa Monica; San Francisco (one near Fisherman's Wharf, the other downtown on Union Square); on a former dude ranch—the H1-H-Bar-G Ranch—in Estes Park, Colorado; near Rocky Mountain National Park; Taos, New Mexico; and in dozens of other key locations. They are a precious national resource, and you ought to know more about them.

You can obtain a free copy of HI-USA's "Hostelling Map of the USA" by going to the shopping section of the HI website (www.hiayh.org) and adding the hostel map to your shopping cart.

HOTELS IN GENERAL

I HOLD THIS TRUTH TO BE SELF-EVIDENT, THAT BY ECONOMIZING ON YOUR HOTEL CHOICE, YOU DO NOT GIVE UP A GOOD NIGHT'S SLEEP

Do you sacrifice physical comfort when you stay at an inexpensive hotel? I've never believed that. The difference between categories of hotels is usually psychological in nature, not physical. What you are giving up is giant lobbies, arcades of chic boutiques, barber shops, and beauty parlors, but not physical comfort. At night, when you go to bed and turn off the lights and shut your eyes, it doesn't matter whether you are in a first-class hotel or a budget one. What matters at that time is whether the mattress is firm and whether the sheets are clean smelling and fresh. I've tossed and turned in deluxe hotels and fallen blissfully asleep in budget ones. Save the money.

IT STILL PAYS TO CALL A HOTEL DIRECTLY WHEN BOOKING A ROOM

It turns out that one old chestnut of a travel rule—you will always get the best price by calling a hotel directly to book a room—still holds true, even in this era of Web specials and so-called "lowest price guarantees" by online booking engines.

In an excellent piece of gumshoe travel journalism by Dion Lefler of the *Wichita Eagle,* Dion has compiled the data to prove that hotel booking engines—from Travelocity to Orbitz to CheapTickets.com—often add questionably high fees to the prices they charge for hotels.

Lefler found that even the booking engine's pretax "basic rates" were around $4.50 above the hotels' own "rack rates," the highest price you'd pay to book directly, before taking into account any discounts, low-season price drops, or sales. What's more, according to Lefler's research, taxes and fees pushed the booking engine's prices up to as much as $22 above the going rate. Add to this the fact that some booking engines charge taxes based on their total price of base rate plus fees, not on the base rate alone, which is all that is taxable by law.

Lefler also points out that when a booking engine shows a hotel as being "sold out," it doesn't mean there are no vacancies. It just means the booking engine has sold out its share of rooms.

In other words: caveat emptor. Online booking engines may make finding and booking a hotel easy, but they won't always be the cheapest way to get that room. Ever since chain hotels introduced toll-free numbers, I've counseled that you almost always get a better rate by calling the hotel directly. It seems that advice hasn't changed, even in the dot.com age.

A FEW NEW HOTELS WITH TINY CRUISE-SHIP-LIKE ROOMS ARE PRESENTLY OPERATING & MIGHT SUIT YOUR COST-CONSCIOUS NEEDS

Four chains of "tiny hotels" are presently operating in Europe and New York—easyHotel, YOTEL, Pod Hotels, and Qbic—but they have so few branches at the moment that they are unlikely to provide lodgings to a great many travelers. Still, for that odd occasion when you might stumble across one, I'm attempting this brief survey.

easyHotel, from the people who gave us easyJet and easyCruise, operates three easyHotels in London; one in Basel, Switzerland; and another in Budapest. Rooms—which you can reserve only through www.easyhotel. com—are miniscule and bathrooms have been compared in size to those on airplanes. The cheapest rooms are without windows and rent in winter for £25 ($36), going up in warmer seasons to £38 to £50 ($55–$73) a night, all phenomenal bargain rates for high-priced London.

YOTEL, which has its lone property at London's Gatwick airport, rents its compact, 7-sq.-m (75-sq.-ft) "cabins" for as little as 4 hours at a time (for about £25/$36). A full night costs at least double that. Units are equipped with 20-inch flatscreen TVs (no extra charge), iPod docking stations, and work areas. The company has plans to open a dozen more properties, though where and when remains up in the air. Call ☎ 020/7100-1100, or go to www.yotel.com for reservations.

Based in the Netherlands, Qbic opened the first of its futuristic properties in Amsterdam this past July. Rooms are an interesting, cube-shaped design, and the lobby has vending machines for checking in and accessing snacks. Room rates start as low as $53, though the price a guest pays is partly based on when the reservation is made—the earlier you book, the less you pay. Other Qbic hotels are opening in Antwerp, Belgium, and the Dutch city of Maastricht. Contact the company at ☎ 31/433211111 or www.qbichotels.com.

Finally, New York City's Pod Hotel opened earlier this year with rooms—that yes, many people have compared to ship cabins—starting at just $89. The least expensive units are singles with shared bathroom, and during peak travel months even those can set the traveler back $159; $89 is a winter rate for the same room. In pricey New York—and especially at such a great midtown location, on East 51st Street a few blocks from Fifth Avenue—these rates are a bargain (☎ 800/742-5945; www.thepodhotel.com).

DON'T EVER BOOK A LARGE HOTEL WITHOUT INQUIRING WHETHER THEY CHARGE A "RESORT FEE"—IF THEY DO, REFUSE TO BOOK UNLESS THEY ELIMINATE IT

It's a practice, shamefully enough, of some of the most prominent chain hotels—and it needs to be stopped. You check out of your room and discover that they've added from $15 to $20 a day as a "resort fee" supposedly meant to cover the cost of the hotel's fitness room, large swimming pool towels, and business center. And you're charged that added fee despite the fact that you didn't use the fitness room, large swimming pool towels, or business center. Some hotels even mention that the "resort fee" covers the in-room coffeemaker perched on the bathroom ledge, even though you never used it.

That ubiquitous "resort fee" is an outrageous scam meant to raise the hotel's income (and its room rates) without telling you. It's a shameful, deceptive practice on the part of hotel executives who should know better; and yet it seems to be spreading all over the world of hotels, or at least to the larger ones.

Never get tricked into paying it. When confirming your reservation, ask whether there are extra charges such as a "resort fee" (or other similar scam). And if there are, refuse to book unless they remove them.

HIDDEN FEES ARE ERUPTING THROUGHOUT THE HOTEL & CRUISE INDUSTRIES. INQUIRE IN ADVANCE & TELL THEM YOU WON'T BOOK IF EXTRA CHARGES ARE ASSESSED.

You check out of an urban property and learn that $20 a day has been added to your bill for a fitness room you never entered, an in-room safe that remained untouched, a coffeemaker you never used. It's becoming more and more important to inquire as to whether the hotel plans such unanticipated fees, and then to demand that they not be charged as a condition of your rental.

Note, too, that cancellation charges have recently skyrocketed. Time was when you could cancel without penalty up until 24 hours in advance of arrival. At many hotels, that right will now require a full week's advance notice. Again, inquire in advance, and get some written proof—such as an e-mail sent to your home address—that reasonable cancellation penalties will be in effect.

And then there's the most recent ploy: fuel surcharges. Not long ago, hotels in Jamaica (other than the Sandals properties, which have publicly and adamantly refused to impose them) began charging guests up to $10 more per night. The reason given is—you got it—because of rising energy costs.

Unless tourists are bringing their electric cars to Jamaica and charging them up using the bathroom outlets, there is little chance that anyone could use the equivalent of an additional $10 of electricity in a day's vacation.

And it gets worse. Recently, many of the major cruise lines tacked on their own fuel surcharges of $5 to $7 per passenger per day. If a ship carries 2,500 passengers on a week's cruise, the fee comes to an additional $123,000 for the line, which seems greatly excessive.

Extra fees are usually a major sign of disrespect that a company has for its customers. They are an indication that the company you're dealing with sees you as a walking dollar sign and not as someone to be pleased by a superior product.

Such disrespectful treatment of consumers will bounce back to haunt the companies that deploy surcharges lightly.

I ACCIDENTALLY STRUCK A NERVE IN MY RECENT ESSAY ABOUT HIDDEN HOTEL & CRUISE CHARGES; THEY'RE MORE PREVALENT THAN I THOUGHT

Readers are outraged by these hidden fees. One wrote to tell me he was charged $10 a night for an extra person (his wife) staying in his room; when he called another telephone reservationist at the hotel, she agreed to eliminate the charge. Another staying at a well-known hotel in New York City was charged a "service fee" for Wi-Fi he had never used and for the availability of a telephone that didn't work. At the fanciest hotel of Atlantic City, a reader was charged for nonreturn of a pool towel, for which he had a return receipt.

In these economically challenging times, you've got to be a sharp-eyed sleuth, worried about becoming a potential victim of people who see you as a cash register and not as a guest.

WHY DON'T U.S. HOTELS COPY EUROPEAN ONES & TAKE ONE EASY STEP TO SAVE ON ENERGY COSTS?

In many European hotels, the key to your room is a plastic card with magnetic stripe that not only unlocks your hotel room door but then permits you to turn on the room lights. You first stick the card into a slot to open the door, and then stick it into another slot inside the room to turn the lights on.

Later, when you leave the room, you need to remove the card from the slot. That immediately turns off every light in the room. Instead of lights remaining on in millions of hotel rooms—as they often are in America—they have to be turned off when the room is not used.

Why hasn't this energy-efficient device been adopted by American hotels? It would save a massive amount of electric energy. I wish a U.S. hotel executive would explain why the U.S. hotel industry has not adopted this sensible European system.

I GOT THE STRANGEST REACTION WHEN I RECENTLY SUGGESTED THE ADOPTION OF A SYSTEM FOR TURNING OUT LIGHTS IN A HOTEL ROOM

When I recently discussed the European systems for turning off hotel room lights, I expected to receive broad expressions of approval from our hip readers. I thought they would applaud my suggestion that American hotels adopt the very same procedures.

Would you believe the typical response was critical? If the electricity was shut off, I was told, mobile phones and laptop computers could not be recharged while we were out of the room. Unthinkable! If the electricity was shut off, the air-conditioning wouldn't continue while we were outside and the room would be hot when we came back, and would remain hot for a couple of minutes while the room was recooled. What a hardship! If the electricity were shut off in winter, the room would be cold when we came back, and would take a couple of minutes to warm up. What a bummer!

And there you find the attitudes that presently prevent us from achieving a real reduction in the burning of fossil fuels to create energy. These are the same people who object to the elimination of SUVs to improve gasoline mileage. Americans are apparently willing to accept all sorts of purely cosmetic touches in energy conservation (leave hotel towels unwashed, recycle plastic cutlery), but are unwilling to turn off all lights in millions of unused hotel rooms.

HOTEL SEARCH ENGINES

LET'S GIVE A CHEER FOR A HOTEL SEARCH ENGINE THAT'S MAINLY FOR LEISURE TRAVELERS

The problem with many online hotel booking engines is that they tend to list the same properties, heavily favoring cookie-cutter international chains and four-star hotels that, frankly, appeal more to business travelers than leisure tourists. Tourist-class (two- and three-star) hotels that offer far more value for your money are in short supply. Even more rare is the inclusion of the kind of small, family-run hotels that not only cost less than the big hotels but also give you the kind of friendly welcome and local charm that no chain can provide.

The Italy-based booking engine Venere.com (www.venere.com), however, does provide just those sorts of lodging options all across Europe. (It has listings for major U.S. cities as well, but these are far from complete and not nearly as useful.) Venere.com is a booking engine for those of us who prefer a mix of tourist-class chains, mom-and-pop hotels, and B&Bs, along with rental apartments, farmstays, short-stay residence hotels, and even villas. Rarely have so many different types of lodging options been available in one place.

A LOT OF SAVVY, ENGLISH-SPEAKING TRAVELERS BOOK THEIR CUT-RATE HOTEL ROOMS THROUGH A SERVICE CALLED WOTIF ("WHAT IF?")

It's not nearly as well known in the United States as it is in Australia, but smart travelers are making increasing use of an Australian-owned website called Wotif (www.wotif.com). Although it deals with hotels all over the world, its chief strength is in enabling its users to obtain spectacular, last-minute bargains at a large number of hotels in English-speaking locations: England especially, but also Ireland, Australia, New Zealand, and Hong Kong. If you'll access Wotif and then click on England, and then London, you'll find bargains for the immediate days ahead, reducing rates by as much as 60% at a wide range of distinguished hotels, including budget properties. One recent offer was for a £40 ($58) double room with two continental breakfasts at a Comfort Inn normally charging £100 ($145). Don't be discouraged by the high rates at deluxe hotels; scroll down below the first-class levels, and you'll find encouraging deals.

FROM NOW ON, YOU'LL NEED TO CONSULT BOOKING. COM—EUROPE'S BIGGEST HOTEL SEARCH ENGINE— WHEN YOU'RE LOOKING FOR A HOTEL ROOM

In the United States, hotels.com and Quikbook (www.quikbook.com) almost monopolize the field of hotel searches. In Europe, they run a remote second to a website called Booking.com (www.booking.com). And now, Booking.com has opened offices in New York and San Francisco and is greatly supplementing its list of available properties with American hotels, often naming unbeatable discount prices for their rooms. From now on, you'd do well to access Booking.com (an attractive, well-organized site listing many bargains) after you've first searched the offerings of hotels.com and Quikbook.

THERE'S NOW AN AGGREGATOR FOR FINDING INEXPENSIVE HOTEL ROOMS ANYWHERE IN THE WORLD & ITS RESULTS SEEM PHENOMENAL

The Australians have done it. They've created a website called HotelsCombined.com that searches every hotel search engine and every hotel chain, in popular cities throughout the United States and abroad, and then impartially sorts the results by price. Although it also tells you whether the hotel in question has vacancies for the dates in which you're interested, it does not then proceed to book the room for you. Instead—and I like this feature—it advises you to go directly to the hotel and request a reservation. You pay the hotel directly and do not incur a penny's expense for using HotelsCombined.com.

I have found some of the best hotel deals imaginable through the use of HotelsCombined.com. Example: I requested a room in New York for a 2-night stay. Would you believe that HotelsCombined.com proceeded to name New York hotels where I could get a room (in properties ranging

A large number of hotel search engines carry photographs of the actual rooms and public facilities available to you.

from cheap hostels to decent tourist-class establishments) for $29 to $118—in what has to be one of the most expensive hotel cities on earth?

The Australian service not only surveys hotels directly—including numerous properties that aren't handled by any of the better-known hotel search engines—but also surveys such hotel-finding websites as www.venere.com, www.hotelbook.com, www.laterooms.com, www.hotelclub.com, www.lastminute.com, www.orbitz.com, www.expedia.com, www.travelocity.com, www.booking.com, www.asiarooms.com, and others.

For the life of me, I can't find any drawback to this service, any overlooked condition, any reason not to use it exclusively for hotel searches; since it surveys every other hotel-finding website, in the same way that an airfare aggregator surveys every other source of airfares, there's no need to go anywhere else.

RESORTS

PSSST! I'M REVEALING THE NAME OF THAT MONEY-SAVING WEBSITE FOR LUXURY RESORTS THAT INSIDERS CONFIDE TO ONE ANOTHER IN WHISPERS.

Periodically, I receive letters referring to a mysterious website that allows you to book luxury resorts in the Tropics for about a third of what is normally charged. The website is www.saveonresorts.com, which does in fact list such resorts at prices that low, and makes no secret of how it does so. It sends you to resorts at radically low prices provided you're willing to attend a 90-minute timeshare presentation. And the reference to those sessions is plainly and clearly stated, without any effort to deceive.

A great many travel insiders will advise you to attend the presentation with closed minds, endure the 90 minutes, and then walk out to enjoy your cut-rate stay. I'm troubled by the ethics of that advice. Though I'm not an admirer of timeshares, I feel there's something underhanded about accepting these offers without the slightest intention of honestly considering the purchase proposals that are made to you.

It's your call.

CONFINED TO ALL-INCLUSIVE RESORTS, A NEW INTERNET SERVICE CALLED RESORTCOMPETE WILL NOW DUPLICATE THE METHOD OF CRUISECOMPETE

I've written about CruiseCompete (www.cruisecompete.com), which invites the entire travel industry to bid for your business. You list a cruise you want to take, and then various discount cruise brokers and cruise travel agencies submit different bids (prices).

The founders of CruiseCompete have now created ResortCompete (www.resortcompete.com). You fill out a form describing your ideal all-inclusive resort: the general area in which it is found, the kind of sports and entertainment facilities it has to have, the price you're looking for. ResortCompete passes on your request to no fewer than 630 all-inclusive resorts around the world, as well as to numerous tour operators and travel agents. They, in turn, submit the price at which they're willing to supply your vacation and the specific resort at which the price will be honored. It's then up to you to decide whether they've made you an offer you can't turn down.

Requesting such bids does not require that you give up your privacy. If you turn down the bid, nothing happens. As the site states: "There is no obligation to buy, and sellers will not have your contact information unless you give it to them."

I think it's all quite interesting. Among other things, the site's list of islands and their all-inclusive resorts includes vacation destinations of which you might otherwise be unaware. (Many travelers are under the impression that only the Dominican Republic has all-inclusive resorts.) And note how the new service will be particularly appealing to families or small groups, forcing the resorts to negotiate hard for their business by offering special rates.

Vacation Apartments

An entire apartment, for a prolonged length of time, may be the solution to Europe's high costs of hotel lodgings

Most of the European websites for finding hotels—I'm talking about www.venere.com, www.octopustravel.com, and www.eurocheapo.com—also list apartments for rent in major European cities. These flats can be had for less than hotel rooms cost, if they are rented for 1 or 2 weeks. The downside is that you may have to lessen the number of European cities you visit in the course of a trip, in favor of longer apartment stays in fewer cities.

SACRE BLEU! THE DOLLAR HAS FALLEN EVEN FARTHER THAN BEFORE! THE SOLUTION: A RENTAL APARTMENT COSTING FAR LESS THAN A HOTEL.

On the currency markets when we went to press, the euro was exchanged for $1.40, and the British pound for $1.45. But that's only the start of our misery. Since all money changers (banks, currency kiosks, ATMs) charge at least—at least—5% for changing your dollars into euros or pounds, you actually pay $1.47 for a euro and $1.52 for a pound. And at those rates, Europe becomes very expensive indeed.

So what's to be done?

If you're hellbent on vacationing in western Europe, you may need to opt for alternatives to standard hotel accommodations: apartment rentals, rooms in private homes, hostels, convents and monasteries, student residences. All throughout Britain and the Continent, these alternative accommodation remains reasonable in price, and bring you not only savings on your lodgings but more spacious rooms, with a kitchen or kitchenette in which to prepare meals. By making a trip out of 1-week stays in successive cities, you can obtain a quite decent apartment almost everywhere for as little as $100 a day (and that's for two to four persons).

A growing number of vacationers believe that rental homes or apartments are superior in comfort and price to hotels.

The apartment-renting agencies to use are Vacation Rentals by Owner (www.vrbo.com), HomeAway (www.homeaway.com), Zonder (www.zonder.com), Endless Vacation Rentals (www.evrentals.com), and Rentalo.com. As a further alternative, consider the many local agencies that have emerged to rent you a bed in someone's private home or apartment ("hosted" stays while the owners are still in residence).

The use of apartment rentals, or rooms in private homes, is probably the single most effective way to continue visiting Europe affordably. It's the course that a great many Americans will need to follow as long as the dollar remains as weak as it presently is.

HomeAway has emerged as a leading source of inexpensive vacation homes & apartments

The mightiest of the vacation rental companies turns out be a firm of which you may not have heard: HomeAway (www.homeaway.com) of Austin, Texas. Formed in 2005, but not really operating until late 2006, it has recently scooped up the big VRBO, merged with it, and today offers far more than 100,000 vacation rentals in the United States and abroad. Part of its appeal is an unusually attractive website that's one of the most logical and informative of any in the field (take a look even if you're not presently in the market for such a rental).

Rentalo.com is currently listing one-bedroom apartments in Paris, capable of housing up to six persons, for under $175 a night

Rentalo.com, which I mentioned above, is a Florida-based outfit that lists thousands of apartments and home rentals throughout the world. Here are a few examples:

In a 17th-century building on the Rue Jean Jacques Rousseau, 2 blocks from the Louvre and the Seine, a one-bedroom apartment (with kitchen and living room, and with cable TV capable of receiving CNN and high-speed Internet) goes for under $160 a night (plus a small cleaning fee, if you want a maid). Why so cheap? The apartment is in a five-flight walk-up, and therefore only for vigorous people, who will be thrilled once upstairs to look out *sur les toits de Paris* ("over the rooftops of Paris"). Your landlord will usually require at least a 1-week stay, but has been known to rent in slow periods for as few as 4 nights.

Elsewhere in Paris, rent a one-bedroom apartment sleeping six (there's a king bed in the bedroom and two double sofa beds in the living room) on a quiet street near the Place de la Republique, a 3-minute walk from the

Métro (subway) and a supermarket. The kitchen includes a washing machine and dishwasher, and the price is, again, under $160, with a 3-night minimum.

KIJIJI IS ONE OF THE LATEST SOURCES OF VACATION RENTALS IN AMERICA—& DON'T PASS IT UP BECAUSE OF ITS FUNNY NAME

Kijiji (www.kijiji.com) is a relatively recent site with a collection of free classified ads, which is already receiving more and more visitors each month. A great many of those users go to it for its information on vacation rentals, which you find under the "Housing" category. Click on the U.S. city to which you're going, scroll down to "Housing," and you'll find a surprising number of notices alerting you to major bargains in vacation apartments and vacation homes for a short-term stay you've planned in that city. While those notices aren't any different in quality from those you'd find on Craigslist, they are just plain different in many cases, and therefore an important source of additional listings.

The reason why Kijiji is growing so fast has something to do with its owner: eBay. Though eBay also owns a minority share of Craigslist, it has apparently decided to strike out on its own in the world of free classified ads, and it obviously knows a thing or two about establishing a website.

As for that ridiculous name, keep in mind that "Google" also sounded pretty ridiculous when first introduced. I predict that Kijiji will henceforth be used for a growing number of travel services.

LOCAL FIRMS DESCRIBED IN GUIDEBOOKS ARE PERHAPS YOUR BEST SOURCE FOR VACATION HOMES & APARTMENTS

It's obvious that the big, global booking companies, some of which carry listings for more than 60,000 homes, can't be familiar with all the properties they represent. How could they have personally visited every one of them?

Clearly, the best informed of the rental agents are the ones that limit their services to a single destination, such as Orlando or London or Vegas, and are located in that destination. These are the hometown firms with names of which you've never heard, but with impressive knowledge of the conditions and neighborhoods in their community.

And where do you find these firms? Apart from hunting them up on the Web, using Google and then inserting the name of the city or area in which you'll be vacationing, you can use a guidebook that contains names of the top local rental agencies. And so help me, I'm being entirely objective when I suggest that the new series of Pauline Frommer budget guides performs that function extremely well. Pauline realized that the skyrocketing cost of hotel rooms would compel many travelers to substitute homes or apartments for hotels, and therefore, in the lodgings sections of her guidebooks, she has made it a point to describe the work of local rental agencies whose premises she has visited and whose owners she has interviewed.

VACATION HOMES

A WHOPPING BIG DEVELOPMENT: THE "BIG BOY" HOTEL CHAINS ARE NOW RENTING NONHOTEL ACCOMMODATIONS IN COMPETITION WITH THEMSELVES

It's obvious, as I've said, that more and more travelers have discovered that they can pay far less than hotels charge, and yet enjoy more spacious surroundings and more privacy, by electing to stay on vacation in apartments, condos, cottages, villas, and vacation homes.

Not long ago, the giant Wyndham Hotels (at least 7,000 properties marketed under several brands) launched a website called Endless Vacation Rentals (www.evrentals.com or www.wyndham-vacations.com) to represent no fewer than 60,000 apartments, condos, vacation homes, villas, and cottages in America and around the world—the largest inventory of that sort on the Internet. I interviewed the chairman and CEO of that new Wyndham operation on one of my broadcasts last summer, and unsuccessfully tried to get him to reveal his reasons for doing this. It's quickly became clear that the big boys in hotels have now decided that nonhotel lodgings are going to play an increasing role in vacation travel.

So now there's a humongous website from which to obtain such nonhotel lodgings—a site larger than VRBO, larger than Rentalo.com, larger probably than many of the others put together. You book a nonhotel on that site exactly as you would a hotel, giving them your credit card number. And thereafter your contact is with, not the individual owner of a condo, bungalow, or cottage, but the enormous Wyndham megalith. Will wonders never cease?

Chapter Three

"OVER THE BOUNDING MAIN . . ."

CUT-RATE CRUISES ON OCEANS & RIVERS—WITH GRIPES AS WELL

As many as 12 million Americans are now vacationing each year on the high seas—or along famous rivers and canals—on vessels that range from humongous, 3,000-passenger cruise ships to smaller, "premium" ships to freighters to riverboats and self-drive boats and barges. Some of these travelers take "shore excursions" on most days or ride a bike alongside a slow-moving canal boat.

The range of costs for these watery vacations can be enormous, and the possibilities are great for savings that do not sacrifice comfort. And so I examine all the options for a maritime trip and express my own personal opinions about the kind of experience that each offers.

BARGES & SELF-DRIVE BOATS

FLOATING THROUGH EUROPE—IN A SELF-SKIPPERED BOAT THAT EVEN A CHILD CAN STEER

The waterways of western Europe used to be traversed by thousands of barges loaded with farm products. About a hundred of these have now been replaced by hotel barges filled with comfortable rooms and staffed by skilled chefs and waiters. They drift along at, say, 3 or 4 miles an hour, while you sometimes walk or bicycle alongside, enjoying an enthralling view of the European countryside and of the villages found alongside the canals. At the top end are hotel barges charging as much as $500 a night per person, for superb service and cuisine. And if you'd like to consider that level of luxury, you simply go to www.bargesinfrance.com.

But a number of more moderately priced firms provide river and canal cruises that are still quite luxurious and in modern riverboats, for considerably less. Their cruises are 7 nights in length, preceded or followed by stays in key river cities, and yet cost as little as $250 or $300 a night per person, including elegant meals and lodgings. If you'd like to know more, log on to either www.amawaterways.com or to www.gate1travel.com (and click on "European river cruises"), and soon you'll be floating through France, Germany, Austria, Hungary, or Holland, on the most relaxing and comfortable trips in all of Europe.

Most discussions of cruises along European waterways deal with the so-called "riverboats" I've described, staffed by cooks, waiters, and chambermaids supplying the utmost in luxury. But you can cruise the canals of Europe for infinitely less in a boat you "drive yourself," stopping wherever you wish, dropping in at charming little country inns for lunch or dinner, letting even your children or grandchildren steer the vessel. The 9-year-old grandson of the initial owner of Le Boat, Inc., a leader in canal cruising, actually took the helm of one of that company's many barges, and nobody worried—because you can't go wrong on the calm and narrow waterways of Burgundy, or in any of the other areas Le Boat serves.

For the smallest and oldest crafts carrying up to three persons, you'll pay as little as $1,075 to $1,280 for 7 off-season nights (late Mar or late Oct). The same boat in higher seasons will run from a still-affordable $1,735 to $2,130 for 7 nights—and that's per boat, not per person. Or, you can rent a popular six-person boat costing about $1,800 in low season, $3,000 in high season. Rates include boat, license and tax, gas for cooking, canal tolls and instruction, and technical support. You pay extra for the fuel you use, food and drink, personal and trip cancellation insurance, and getting to the boatyard. You can rent bicycles and park your car, too. You can even have someone drive your rental car to your final destination, where it will be waiting for you. Phone Le Boat at ☎ 888/355-9491 or log on to www. crownblueline.com (affiliated with Le Boat) for online bookings.

Or consider the similar offerings of European Boating Holidays. This British firm, whose boats are moored in several European countries, has a booking office in Lake Placid, New York, staffed by an American enthusiast. She's at ☎ 866/606-5278, and for further details, go to www.locaboat.com (containing descriptions of the boats that European Boating Holidays offers) or www.europeanboatingholidays.co.uk (for prices and conditions).

For 2009, European Boating Holidays will be inaugurating a new base facility at Mikolajki, Poland, between two major lakes in the northeastern part of that country—an untouched and spectacular natural area—for self-skippered journeys in a historic land that is only lightly touristed. It will open another base in Terherne, Holland, for boating holidays on an extensive network of canals and lakes in the Friesland province of northern Holland. And finally, it will inaugurate a new base at Redon, France, in Brittany, for sailing between ancient and historic towns.

CRUISES

WHAT'S IT LIKE TO CRUISE ON ONE OF THOSE NEW SHIPS CARRYING 3,000 PASSENGERS & MORE?

I've now sailed on two of these giant vessels, and here's my report: With their 14 and more decks and vast expanse, the cruise lines have created a new type of entertainment center for vacationing Americans. The ships have not one, but three open-air swimming pools, each with its own large hot tub supplemented by a fourth within the ship. The casino is the size you'd find in a large Las Vegas hotel, and strategically situated to require

To escape the smothering crowds of the giant ships, you pay high prices for smaller premium ships, such as the *Crystal Symphony,* shown here.

that you walk through it to reach many other important facilities. The main theater (there is more than one) has two balconies, and surpasses in size the big movie houses that you'd find in a large town. The fitness center, with its many rooms for individual massage, is larger than the overwhelming percentage of gyms patronized by most Americans.

Everywhere you look are movielike sets operated by professional photographers who offer their services to commemorate the sailing. One of them features a giant background photograph of the railing of a ship with the sea behind it; thus, you needn't even step outside to have a picture of yourself and your traveling companion taken on an open deck. Earlier, as you boarded the ship, you were photographed standing in front of the street of a fake Mexican village, obviating the need to leave the ship for real-life scenes in Puerto Vallarta, Cabo San Lucas, or Mazatlán.

The main restaurant (there are several of them) seats 1,100 persons, and operates with two sittings for dinner. A crowd gathers and stands in line at the start of every evening meal. But the crowd control of diners is an accomplished feat on the part of the ship's staff, and rarely do you have to wait more than 5 minutes to enter and be seated. At other points of the cruise—entering the ship, leaving it in port, entering the theater, getting breakfast at different cafeteria-like setups—lines are also encountered, but they move quickly. Still, the constant sensation is that you are part of a crowd, an experience similar to waiting for the popcorn in a movie theater. The ship is so vast, and stable, and so totally enclosed without windows in many areas, that you have the feeling you are on land and not at sea.

Crowds, crowds everywhere, a constant pedestrian movement of persons passing through the atrium floor and gathering around the fake photographs to choose a likeness for the folks back home. This is not cruising as I have grown to love cruising. It is not a quiet, contemplative week at sea, gazing at the vastness of the water-covered earth, quietly conversing with other passengers, catching up on your reading, listening to music, having a quiet meal. It is something else. And although this new world of cruising is obviously popular among many, its very popularity is a sad commentary on the restless, rootless condition of so many of our fellow citizens. In all the many lectures I heard on board on subjects ranging from makeup to stomach flatness and cooking, there was not a single subject appealing to an intellectually curious person.

Let me, in fairness, compliment the cruise lines on providing a considerable degree of comfort—indeed, luxury—at an extremely reasonable price. The cruises I took were not of a premium level, but among the lower-cost offerings, something like the Walmart of cruises. But they were not cruises as I have known them. They were something entirely different—and somewhat troubling, too.

THE CRUISE SHIP BECOMES AN AMUSEMENT PARK—DO THOSE SHIP-LINE EXECS KNOW WHAT THEY ARE DOING?

On a recent broadcast of my Sunday radio show, a guest expert described all the new gimmicks to be expected on the dozen or so large cruise ships that will be debuting in 2009. "They will be like nothing you have ever seen before," she announced, and with enthusiasm in her voice, she ticked off the advances:

The Celebrity *Solstice* will have "circus training programs," "bungee jumping," "clown acts." These will be added, presumably, to the rock-climbing walls, boxing rings, bowling alleys, and vertiginous Jacuzzis jutting out from the top deck and hanging perilously over the sea.

On a new ship of Costa Cruises, expect every conceivable game, sport, and competition. What's more, Costa will introduce new, extra-charge "spa cabins" so close to fitness rooms that persons staying in them can walk to the showers in their bathrobes. People booking the new spa digs will have exclusive access to that spa, and to their own spa restaurant.

On some of the new ships, the democratic, one-class policies of cruising will be jettisoned. There will be a "ship within the ship," an area enjoyed solely by persons paying higher fares, a number of restaurants to which they alone will be admitted, lounges set aside for the elite. On a new ship of Norwegian Cruise Lines, elite passengers will have special suites, special sun deck areas, and luxury swimming pools for them alone.

These are cruise ships? They're more like gigantic, metallic, orgone boxes of the sort envisioned in the 1920s by hallucinating psychologists.

So why must they ever leave the dock? Shouldn't they simply remain immobile and thus save the considerable expense of going to sea?

Imagine the savings. By keeping one of those new 4,000-passenger ships tied to the dock, the fuel cost would approach zero. Highly skilled personnel would no longer be needed to navigate the vessel and attend to its motors. There would be no fees assessed by foreign ports, no charges for radio transmissions, no wear and tear on the engines. With the money that could be saved, the cruise lines could lower their fares to, say, $25 a day per passenger. A 7-day cruise would cost $175—affordable to nearly every American.

And could anyone tell the difference? With their boxing rings and multi-lane bowling alleys, their theaters resembling New York's Radio City Music Hall, their classes in flower arranging and better investments, and their Vegas-size casinos, the 4,000-passenger ships are already a largely indoor experience. You seldom leave the gym, the multiple dining facilities, or even venture onto the two outdoor decks so filled with crowds that you will quickly retreat indoors.

The constantly commercial atmosphere aboard many of the giant cruise ships will inevitably drive the more discriminating cruise passengers away

I have written before about how some of the popularly priced cruise lines—not all, but some—have pushed the pursuit of profit, through onboard sales, to ridiculous extremes. They surround you with commercial pitches, with mindless activities meant to promote shopping, with lectures and events designed for cretins. And there has never been a better summary of that trend than in the letter I received from a woman on an Alaskan cruise:

> The daily activities were lectures about makeup use, the joys of massage, how to value jewels, and ever-new ways to shop. The one serious lecturer was totally inept, had sparse attendance at his talks, and I can no longer remember his topic. Planets, I think. Most of the activities were for shopping, both on the ship and the ports of call.

Things were constantly hawked about the ship. Any gathering produced waiters with buckets of beer or trays of tropical drinks that you first thought were free. Before the shows they hawked raffle tickets. Seldom, outside your own cabin or in the library, was there ever peace or quiet.

Would I ever take another cruise with that company? Only if it were free! We have grown attached to small boat (100-passenger) river cruises, such as those run by Uniworld. We have been on three of theirs and cannot say enough good things about them.

FOR THOSE WEBSITES THAT WARN TRAVELERS ABOUT CRUISE-SHIP CABINS, I'LL SET ASIDE MY USUAL IRE ABOUT USER-GENERATED CONTENT

I am usually an ardent critic of user-generated websites supplying opinions from amateur travelers based on exactly one visit to one hotel on their trip to a foreign or unfamiliar city. I am not only put off by the amateur basis of those opinions, but by the ease with which opinions can be fabricated by biased supporters or competitors.

But a user-generated message which points out that Cabin E-902 on cruise ship ABC is located next to the motors or underneath a dance floor—that's something else. Such an opinion isn't the kind that is often fabricated, and it's unaffected by the amateur status of the source. Which brings me to information about cabins on cruise ships:

When it comes time to book your cruise cabin, you should never assume that every stateroom in the same category will have the same proportions. No, as with homes and apartments, cruise-ship cabins can vary slightly even within the same price category. Someone in the cabin right next door to yours—the one with the larger balcony, and the bigger bathroom—could be paying the same that you are. The difference between them and you is that they came into the booking process armed with information about which cabin number was the better deal.

Where do you get such information? Not from the cruise lines, which publish maps of their ships that are not to scale and would rather you didn't know which cabins are worth less than others. Not from travel agents, who deal with so many ships and price categories that they are unlikely to be able to tell you which cabins are best on any given ship. Instead, you turn to the Internet, where passionate cruise lovers post their findings for the benefit of everyone.

The user-generated websites provide a good photographic description of actual cruise-ship cabins.

The people posting on the message boards are very specific about which cabin numbers are the best value for the price—which have more space, or slightly bigger balconies for their class, and so on. It's always a smart idea to check here before paying for a stateroom that could end up being less of a value than one just 10 feet away. Head to Cruise Critic (www.cruisecritic.com) and CruiseMates (www.cruisemates.com), and search first by the name of the ship you'd like to take. If you don't find any advice, take a moment to post a request for information. Cruise-ship fans are a vocal bunch, and you'll be surprised how many come out of the woodwork to aid in your request. Other valuable message boards can be found at CruiseReviews.com.

CruiseDeckplans.com posts piles of maps of ships, along with some scoops about which cabins are preferable to others, but if you'd like nitty-gritty information about which cabin numbers are best, you'll have to pay a $12 lifetime membership to CruiseStateroom.com, its sister site.

Condé Nast Traveler, which normally revels in over-the-top luxury travel, published a list of excellent cabin values in a special issue that was mailed to subscribers. The article, which was so useful that it was appropriated without credit by innumerable webmasters, can be found for free on the magazine's online home, Concierge.com.

SO MANY GIANT CRUISE SHIPS ARE SCHEDULED TO BEGIN SAILING THAT THE DISCOUNTS WILL BE HUMONGOUS, ALMOST BEYOND IMAGINING

If there is any travel prediction we can make with confidence for 2009, it concerns the cruise-ship industry. After a 2-year slowdown in the construction of ships, the building frenzy has started up again, and a full dozen new ships—most of them enormous vessels—will go into operation in 2009, adding well over 20,000 berths a week to the industry's capacity. That means 1,000,000 new passengers must be induced to book these ships in the course of the year, and at a time of a slowing economy, that doesn't seem likely.

So what will happen? Discounts. We'll again see a rash of week-long Caribbean cruises selling for $499 a person. We'll see Mediterranean cruises reduced in price to below $1,000 a week per person. We'll see $599 cruises of Alaskan waters (a week in length), and cruises along the coast of South America for $899 per person for a week. It behooves you to become accustomed to the many services on the Internet into which the cruise companies dump their cabins for distress sale, such as www.onlinevacationcenter. com, www.vacationstogo.com, www.cruisesonly.com, www.cruisewizard. com, and many others.

The new ships include: the MSC *Fantasia* (3,900 passengers; that isn't a typo); the *Independence of the Seas* (3,600 passengers); the *Ruby Princess of Princess Cruises* (3,100 passengers); the *Carnival Splendor* (3,000 passengers); the *Celebrity Solstice* (2,900 passengers); the MSC *Poesia* (2,600 passengers); the *Norwegian Gem* (2,500 passengers); the *Eurodam* of Holland America Cruises (2,000 passengers); and the *Queen Victoria* of the Cunard Line (2,000 passengers). In addition to these nine giants, at least three "premium" ships carrying from 400 to 800 passengers apiece will begin sailing in 2009.

That's quite a list. And it makes up the only segment of the travel industry whose prices are obviously going to drop, not rise, in 2009—albeit for a very special experience that isn't quite cruising but also isn't quite travel. As I've said, these will be enormous entertainment complexes, floating gymnasiums, and theaters, for which the mind of man hasn't yet coined a name.

THE NEW AZAMARA CRUISE LINE IS LUXURIOUS IN LEVEL BUT PRICED RATHER MODERATELY FOR THE ELEGANCE IT OFFERS (AS LITTLE AS $1,500 FOR A 2-WEEK CRUISE)

The cruise industry has recently witnessed the launch of Azamara Cruises (☎ 877/999-9553; www.azamaracruises.com), the upscale offshoot of Celebrity Cruises that aims to lure passengers hungry for small-port itineraries and luxury-level staff attentions. Its first ship, the *Journey,* made Bermuda runs to fulfill old obligations, but now it and its twin, the *Quest,* are following the itineraries for which they were intended.

Prices for 2-week (14-day) trips are impressively reasonable for an intimate ship that purports to provide lavish attention to its guests (the crew-to-passenger ratio is nearly two to one). Rates are around $1,500 to $2,500 per person for those extended, 2-week itineraries. For that, you'll get a manageable ship (about 700 passengers, as opposed to Celebrity's usual load of 1,700 or so). Many of the cabins have private balconies.

The cruise line won't repeat the same itinerary more than a few times a season, which makes it easy to see some of the world's great smaller ports—the ones the giant cruise ships can't handle. When's the last time you saw Osaka, Shanghai, and Hong Kong on the same itinerary? Or how about an itinerary combining Amsterdam, Copenhagen, Edinburgh, Dublin, and Inverness?

Azamara is not a budget cruise line, to be sure. But its rates are reasonable enough to afford a whole new set of travelers the chance to experience offbeat ports without paying ridiculously for the privilege. Besides, any opportunity to cruise beyond the standard Cancun–Key West–Bahamas roster should be a cause for celebration.

THOSE MATURE GENTLEMEN WHO EARN A FREE CRUISE BY DANCING WITH THE OLDER WOMEN ARE STILL FOUND ON SOME—BUT A DIMINISHED NUMBER OF—CRUISES

On cruise ships, a "gentleman host" is a man between the ages of 45 and 72, who is a good conversationalist and an excellent ballroom dancer, a kindly human being, and a person of strict moral character. Numbering as many as six per cruise ship, they are dressed in blue blazers or white dinner jackets bearing a decal identifying them as employees of the line. They are carried free of charge aboard the cruise, and given a daily allowance for a reasonable number of drinks and substantial laundry privileges.

The gentlemen hosts dance with unaccompanied women of senior age, and are expected to go immediately from dinner to the ship's ballroom and to stay there, asking women to dance, during the evening hours. Earlier, they have dinner at tables with four or five unaccompanied women, engaging in pleasant conversation on noncontroversial topics.

What ships and lines continue to offer gentleman hosts? Although no guarantees can be given, and policies appear to fluctuate from season to season (and even from sailing to sailing), it has been reported to me that the two biggest of the lower-cost lines—Carnival Cruises and Royal Caribbean Cruises—no longer do so. The other low-cost line, Norwegian Cruise Line, appears to offer gentlemen hosts only on their cruises of longer than 1 week; a number of women have told me of encountering gentlemen hosts on 10-day-and-longer cruises of the *Norwegian Dawn.*

All three major ships of the Cunard Line—the *Queen Mary 2,* the *Queen Victoria,* and the *Caronia*—have offered gentlemen hosts on their sailings, even those of only a week's duration. Some female callers to my Sunday radio program have mentioned how eagerly they were looking forward to a 6-day crossing of the Atlantic on the *Queen Mary 2,* where they fully expected to be able to dance with gentlemen hosts.

Celebrity and Holland America, upscale lines charging slightly more than Carnival or Royal Caribbean, appear to offer gentlemen hosts on their longer-duration sailings and occasionally even on a 1-week sailing. Two of the costly, premium lines—Silversea Cruises and Seabourne Cruises—appear to offer gentlemen hosts on all their sailings. Both of them obviously attract a large number of older women. I thought that some of our readers might appreciate the information.

THERE ACTUALLY ARE ELDERLY PEOPLE WHO LIVE ABOARD A CRUISE SHIP IN PREFERENCE TO A HOME FOR ASSISTED LIVING

I thought you'd enjoy a reader's letter on the use of cruise ships as an economical alternative to senior citizen housing:

> About two years ago, my wife and I were on a cruise through the Western Mediterranean aboard a Princess liner. At dinner we noticed an elderly lady sitting alone along the rail of the grand stairway in the main dining room. I also noticed that all the staff, ships officers, waiters, busboys, etc., all seemed very familiar with this lady. I asked our waiter who she was, expecting to be told that she owned the line, but he said he only knew that she had been on board for the last four cruises, back-to-back. As we left the dining room I caught her eye and stopped to say hello.
>
> We chatted and I said, "I understand you've been on the ship for the last four cruises." She replied, "Yes, that's true." I stated, "I don't understand," and she replied without a pause, "It's cheaper than a nursing home."

So there will be no nursing home in my future. When I grow old and feeble, I am going to get on a Princess Cruise Ship. The average cost for a nursing home is $200 a day. I've checked on reservations for a Princess cruise and I can get a long term discount and senior discount price of $165 a day. I will have as many as 10 meals a day if I can waddle to the restaurant or I can have room service (which means I can have breakfast-in-bed every day of the week). I will meet new people every 7 or 14 days.

TELL YOUR GRANDMOTHER—QUICK!

I am now told by several travel agents that they occasionally receive inquiries from retired Americans about staying on a ship for several months. And travel professionals insist that there's one such elderly lady who, several years ago, lived aboard the *QE2*, paying for her cabin on a continuous basis. To check the possibilities, go to any cruise website and you'll find numerous successive 1-week cruises selling for $499, $549, $599, and so on—and then compare that cost to what a senior citizen residence now charges.

Some cruise-ship sailings are discounted so heavily that they can substitute as "homes for assisted living."

YOU WILL NEVER GUESS WHAT THE LATEST CRUISE SHIP ACTIVITY WILL BE. ARE YOU READY FOR THIS?

Glass blowing. You heard it right: glass blowing. Though I myself have no particular interest in glass blowing (I don't even go to see it in Venice), it appears that the public has been yearning to add glass blowing to the other cruise-ship distractions. And therefore, the new Celebrity *Solstice,* a giant passenger vessel, will maintain a glass-blowing shed on an upper deck, staffed by no fewer than three resident glass-blowing "gaffers" giving expert classes and lectures on the subject.

Apparently, the Corning Museum of Glass will be associated with the venture, the latest effort by the maritime industry to lure away Americans from land-based vacations. Also on the Solstice cruise ship will be a new bar containing "an ice-filled table where guests can participate in caviar and vodka tastings" (undoubtedly for an extra fee).

I'm so tongue-tied about this latest cruise-ship innovation—topping the rock-climbing walls, bowling alleys, boxing rings, and Jacuzzis angled perilously over the sea—that I'll refrain from further comment.

THE NEWEST REMEDY FOR SEASICKNESS ABOARD CRUISE SHIPS IS JUST PLAIN GINGER

We have none other than the respected British medical journal *Lancet* to cite for the claim that ginger—just plain ginger—is an effective remedy for seasickness. In a controlled experiment headlined in the *New York Times,* subjects were given (a) ginger, (b) various anti-motion-sickness medications (Antivert, Bonine, or Dramamine), or (c) a placebo. The persons receiving ginger did the best in terms of avoiding dizziness or nausea.

The same results have been noted by researchers in several other medical and scientific institutions. And presumably, taking ginger does not set off the drowsiness that anti-motion-sickness medications often create.

According to most of the literature, ginger for controlling seasickness can be taken either raw, powdered in pill form, or as tea. It can even be ingested via a glass or two of ginger ale, provided only that real ginger is used in the beverage. And if you think I'm making this up, go to Google and insert the words "ginger and seasickness."

IF YOU'VE GOT THE TIME BUT VERY LITTLE MONEY, CONSIDER A REPOSITIONING CRUISE

The "repositioning cruise"—shifting a ship from Europe to the Caribbean, or vice versa—is unpopular with the American public because it spends too many days simply at sea, without stopping at ports. The vessel undertakes a long sailing across the sunny south Atlantic, after heading down the coast of Africa (if it's a westbound repositioning cruise) or dipping to the southern Caribbean before crossing the south Atlantic to Africa and then Europe (if it's an eastbound repositioning cruise). Our anxious, stressed-out population apparently can't stand the thought of such a leisurely stint at sea, and the cruise lines need to charge breathtakingly low prices—as little as $34 a day—to fill their repositioning cruises.

Which makes for a superb vacation opportunity. If you're among the lucky few who can devote 16 or 17 days or so to simply luxuriating at sea, taking a "slow boat" to another continent, spending long hours with a paperback book, getting to know your fellow passengers, you'll carefully consider the repositioning offers, which carry the lowest price tags of any vacation around. Keep in mind that though the ship may not be entirely full, its cuisine is identical to the offerings on shorter cruises.

I went to a noted cruise broker for his choice of the most attractive repositioning cruises. He suggested several and gave me their dates of sailing. The details may change, but the dates and itineraries are typical of what's offered around the same time every year. Port charges, taxes, and airfare are extra.

1. November: Fifteen days from Genoa, Italy, to Fort Lauderdale, Florida, aboard the Costa *Fortuna* (one of Costa's newest ships), for $549 per person in inside cabins—that's $36 a day. The itinerary goes to Savona (the port of Genoa), Barcelona, Tenerife (the Canary Islands), Guadeloupe, St. Maarten, Nassau, and Fort Lauderdale (and includes 8 days simply at sea).

2. November: Sixteen nights from Genoa to Fort Lauderdale, Florida, aboard the Costa *Mediterranea,* for $899 per person in inside cabins—that's $56 a day. You sail from Savona (Genoa) to Barcelona, Casablanca (Morocco), Tenerife (Canary Islands of Spain), Barbados, Antigua, St. Maarten, Nassau, and Fort Lauderdale, spending 8 days simply at sea.

3. December: Nine nights from Barcelona to Boston aboard the Norwegian Gem of Norwegian Cruise Line, for $399 per person in inside cabins—that's $44 a day. You sail from Barcelona, to Madeira (Portugal) and Boston, spending 8 days simply at sea.

4. March 29: Seventeen nights from Fort Lauderdale to Dover, England, aboard the MSC *Lirica,* for $749 per person in inside cabins—that's $44 a day. You sail from Fort Lauderdale to San Juan, Antigua, Martinique, Madeira, Vigo (Spain), LeHavre (France), and Dover, England.

5. November: Seventeen nights on the *Lirica* sailing from Genoa to Fort Lauderdale, for $749 per person in inside cabins—that's $44 a day. Sailing is from Genoa to Barcelona, Casablanca (Morocco), Tenerife (Canary Islands of Spain), Barbados, Grenada, Martinique, Dominican Republic, and Fort Lauderdale. In between those stops, you spend a total of 9 days simply at sea (the hallmark of a repositioning cruise).

6. October 9: Sixteen nights on the *Norwegian Dream* of Norwegian Cruise Line sailing from Barcelona to Miami, for $539 per person in inside cabins (which is a remarkable $34 a day). You sail from Barcelona to Majorca, Alicante (Spain), Celita (Spain), Madeira, St. Thomas, and Miami, and spend 9 days at sea scattered between those stops.

7. October: Fifteen nights on the *Norwegian Jewel* of Norwegian Cruise Line sailing from Barcelona to Miami, for only $999 per person in inside cabins (which amounts to $66 a day). Departure is from Barcelona to Nice, Livorno, Civitavecchia (the port of Rome), Corsica, Majorca, Gibraltar, Madeira, and Miami.

Are there any such comparable bargains, anywhere? You'll find them at www.vacationstogo.com (register, then click on "90-Day Ticker" or "Find a Bargain," then click on "repositioning" in the list of destinations at the top of the page). You'll also see them at the websites of Cruises Only (www.cruisesonly.com), Cruise 411 (www.cruise411.com), White Travel Services (www.cruisewizard.com), and many others.

AN AFTERNOON WITH SOPHIA LOREN (CRUISE-RELATED)

How's that for a travel headline? Recently, attracted by the identity of the ship's "godmother," I accepted a junket to attend the christening of a new 3,000-passenger liner in Civitavecchia, the port of Rome, Italy. Rushing to Kennedy Airport from my Sunday afternoon radio program, I boarded an overnight flight to Rome, grabbed a bus to the Italian coast, boarded the giant vessel, took a fast shower, and staggered to a front seat at a 4pm press conference, where I sat 4 feet away from a national treasure of Italy. The sacrifices I make for Frommer's!

Sophia Loren makes an extraordinary impression. She is much taller than you might have thought, an imposing public celebrity totally at ease in the most hectic setting imaginable. In addition to about 30 journalists from all over the world, she was surrounded (and yet seemed totally nonplussed) by at least 30 frantic paparazzi taking flashbulb shots without a second's let-up, throughout the entire hour-long conference.

Two or three other persons and I were the only travel writers there, the remainder being celebrity journalists and movie magazine types who asked the most inane questions you can possibly imagine, such as: "Ms. Loren, will you ever do a film in Buenos Aires?" (This question from an Argentine journalist.) To which she would answer in fluent English: "I have a high regard for the film industry of Argentina." "Ms. Loren: Do you ever plan to make a film in Oslo?" (This, of course, from an Oslo newspaperman.) Answer: "I have the highest regard for the film industry of Norway." And then, from a journalist of Mexico City putting his question in high-speed Spanish, does she ever plan to make a Mexican film? And she, with no need for a translation, answered in Italian this time about how much she admired Mexico, and yes, she would love to do a film there.

In the course of the press conference, this celebrated actress with the body of a 20 year old pointed out that she was 72 years of age, and that she had made more than 100 films, starting with one when she was 15. And when someone asked whether there was a current love in her life, she answered that it was the first of her grandchildren, a little girl 1 year of age, with more on the way.

I plan to remain in the travel field, resisting any further temptation to write about the movies.

BELIEVE IT OR NOT, I WENT TO THE CHRISTENING OF A 3,000-PASSENGER CRUISE SHIP

From the afternoon press conference with Sophia Loren, I rushed back to my cabin to change into a blue suit and accompany my wife, Roberta (in her best cocktail dress), down to the pier alongside the ship for the actual christening ceremonies in a temporary amphitheater seating several thousand people. That ritual began in late afternoon and lasted for 3 hours into darkness.

We had front row seats for an event that was televised throughout Italy by multiple networks. Their camera crews were flanked by dozens of additional paparazzi aiming their flashbulbs at the beautiful people of Rome, who very solemnly made their entrances, the women in stunning dresses and the men in sleek Armani suits holding their heads high. Roberta leaned over and whispered that she felt as if she were in a Fellini movie.

The christening ceremony was of national significance because it involved one of the major companies of the Italian economy. MSC, the Mediterranean Shipping Corporation, is not that well known in the United States, but it is a household word throughout Europe. The single largest maritime firm, with over 200 container ships, it is rapidly becoming one of the world's largest cruise lines, with all sorts of 3,000- and 4,000-passenger vessels under construction.

The program began with speeches, then with introductions of European soccer stars, and then the entire symphony orchestra of Rome walked onto the vast outdoor stage accompanied by three of the largest choruses of Rome, and the famous Italian composer Ennio Morricone stepped to the podium to conduct a 1-hour concert of his own compositions while the entire crowd sat hushed and respectful.

After the concert Sophia Loren made her second entrance of the day. She emerged from a hundred yards away in a stunning evening gown, marching along to ecstatic applause, and then she cut the ribbon that made a bottle of champagne smash against the hull, while the owner of MSC Cruises solemnly announced that "*in nomine Deo*"—"in the name of God"—they were launching this ship. The orchestra produced an ear-splitting crescendo, a long line of ship's officers dressed in white marched onto the stage, fireworks went off, Sophia broke out into an ecstatic smile, and the audience went crazy. It was quite a thing to see.

FOR A CHANGE OF PACE (TO PUT IT MILDLY), YOU MIGHT CONSIDER A PEACEFUL MISSISSIPPI RIVERBOAT FOR YOUR NEXT VACATION

Under new ownership, the 432-passenger paddle-wheeler *American Queen* has resumed operating its stately 7-day, 4 mph cruises of the Mississippi River from New Orleans to Memphis, slightly longer than the 4-day cruise that my wife and I enjoyed several years ago. Should you consider it?

The positive points, first. A Mississippi River cruise encounters no waves or unsettling movements; the floor beneath you is as steady as a rock and you are never seasick. Seated in a comfy deckchair outside your cabin (nearly every cabin faces outdoors), you gaze on the shore and activities of the Mississippi (barges with freight and produce, shore-side plantations, industrial plants along the stretch between New Orleans and Baton Rouge, but no further north), while reading Mark Twain's classic *Life on the Mississippi*. The atmosphere is peaceful, relaxing, full of meaning.

As for your accommodations, they are as comfortable as you'd want, the staterooms twice the size of the average cruise-ship cabin, the bathrooms also. Meals are quite good, always copious, and served by a sensitive and attentive waitstaff. Southern hospitality is the standard.

Most surprising, the evening entertainment is clearly superior, in my view, to what you'd enjoy on most seagoing cruise ships. Because the *American Queen* cruises up and down the river, stopping in towns along the way, it usually picks up a city's very best entertainers for a single night's performance, and then drops them off the next morning (in contrast to the practice of employing less talented jacks-of-all-trade to present an entire week's entertainment on an ocean cruise ship).

So what are the drawbacks of a Mississippi River cruise? Up to a third of all passengers (more, in my experience, than on most cruises) are on the far edge of middle age, which won't be to everyone's liking. This is largely a traditional, unsophisticated crowd from the American heartland. Outspoken opinions, counterculture viewpoints, and flirtatious matchmaking are not what you find on the Mississippi.

I didn't find it dull; I thoroughly enjoyed this respite from a harsher, faster life. But don't say I didn't warn you. And for more information, log on to www.majesticamericaline.com. Seven days cost as little as $1,800 per person, double occupancy, though some trips will cost $2,689.

ON A CRUISE, IT'S THOSE EXTRAS THAT ADD UP

It's an obvious point, but it bears repeating, that you must develop a conditioned reflex against extra-charge activities while aboard a cruise ship. The cruise lines are able to charge remarkably low prices for a 7-night cruise— as little as $599 or $699—by pushing a host of expensive purchases on unsuspecting passengers.

Alcoholic drinks, that once used to cost $1.50 in the glory days of cruising, are now uniformly $4.50 and up. Shore excursions—a 2-hour ride in a 45-passenger bus—are as much as $40 and $50. And have you noted how seldom you win at the slots aboard a cruise ship?

The solution for you, the smart cruiser? Debark on your own, and either tour independently or hire a taxi driver to show you the sights. Avoid onboard casinos (an important profit center under new cruise policies) like the plague. Keep your wits about you, and don't ever open those bottles of mineral water already placed on the coffee table when you first enter your cabin. They're not gifts, they're an attempt by the line to earn another $5 per bottle in the opening moments of your cruise. Sadly, the cruise experience has been marred by these small but infuriating ploys.

THE LARGE NEW CRUISE SHIPS HAVE OPTED TO BE MERCHANDISE MARTS OF PRODUCTS & SERVICES

What is the general level of culture aboard the giant new cruise ships designed to house from 2,500 to 3,000 passengers? In a word: dismal.

The largest single area on the megaships—a vast expanse—is the casino, where various thousand-dollar jackpots and other windfalls are marketed to pitiable addicts of the slots and tables; they're found there, glassy eyed and silent, at 3am and later. The runners-up for space are the shops—not simply a few of them but whole arcades duplicating a suburban mall. Every day at sea, leaflets are slipped under your cabin door advertising various sales and markdowns, and tables of bargain-priced merchandise are placed in the public corridors, under signs urging you to buy, buy, buy! Most afternoons, heavily marketed art auctions (more leaflets slipped under your door) are scheduled to fool various innocents into believing they can pick up a genuine work of art.

In marketing and sales, no one matches the ocean spas. Their leaflets are found everywhere on the vast ship, promising through cellulite treatments to reduce your waist size by an inch. Aboard one of the megaships, the most heavily promoted treatment is a $175 massage using large, heated stones placed atop your back. Not to be outdone, the managers of various optional, extra-charge restaurants stand at the entrance to the main dining room displaying menus and exhibits of the gourmet delights that can be yours by agreeing to a $30-per-person cover charge at their snooty eating places.

I'm sorry to have burdened you with this detailed listing of pricey vulgarity, but the massive marketing aboard these megaships would hardly be believable without an actual inventory of excess. That astonishing commercialism is totally at odds with the better traditions of ocean travel, and a vast disappointment to those of us with cherished memories of previous trips at sea. As to the lectures and other presentations aboard, they have been limited—in my experience—to the most trivial of topics that mostly consist of diet discussions ("a flatter stomach in 2 weeks"), cooking demonstrations, and beauty and makeup advice.

How to escape mega–cruise ship vulgarity without breaking the bank

The smaller, quieter ships with open decks suitable for reading and repose, scholarly guest speakers, and itineraries that feature the less developed port cities, are generally the upscale "premium" ships (operated by such lines as Seabourn, Regent Seven Seas, Silversea, SeaDream Yacht Club, Crystal Cruises, Windstar, others) charging forbidding rates of often $600 to $1,000 per person per day.

But the premium lines have occasional vacancies. And in a slowing economy, they will periodically discount their unsold cabins through such cruise brokers (some specializing in upscale cruise ships) as www.cruiseweb.com, www.cruisecompete.com, www.mustcruise.com, www.cruise.com, www.vacationstogo.com, www.cruisewizard.com, and www.cruisesonly.com. If you will carefully scrutinize those sites, you will quite often find an opportunity to book an upscale smaller ship at rates of as little as $300 a day (low season) or $400 a day (high season) per person—a high price, but perhaps justified by the joy of real seagoing cruise.

ADD A NEW WEBSITE TO YOUR
LIST OF CRUISE DISCOUNTERS

Despite the claim by the largest cruise lines that they have wiped out the discounting of their prices, all sorts of cruise discounters remain in business and offer whopping big discounts; the prohibition is obviously being violated. Among the discounters whose websites you might visit is a rapidly expanding firm called BestPrice (www.bestpricecruises.com). The clearest evidence of their success is an eruption of bitter complaints by travel agents in the trade press saying that clients have been won away by BestPrice's lower prices. From this moment forward, when you look for a low-priced cruise, try such sites as www.cruisewizard.com, www.vacationstogo.com, or www.cruisesonly.com, and then look at www.bestpricecruises.com.

IF YOU'RE AN AVID CRUISER, YOU'LL
WANT TO KNOW ABOUT CRUISECOMPETE

Another site to visit is CruiseCompete (www.cruisecompete.com), which does for cruises what LendingTree.com does for bank loans, letting hundreds of travel agents compete for your business.

You designate the name of the ship and sailing date you want (along with the type and number of cabins, home state, and a few other details), and CruiseCompete shops it around on your behalf to 276 major agencies and discounters. Then it's up to those companies to try to undersell one another and offer you the best deal and lowest price. A quick perusal of the long list of agencies shows that it contains all the major discounters, such as iCruise. com, CruiseDirect, Cruise 411, and others I have long recommended.

You are notified by email whenever a new price quote is available to view in your CruiseCompete account, which you can peruse at your leisure. Once you've chosen a cruise broker or travel agent, you contact them directly to book the vacation.

A MAJOR CRUISE BROKER—CRUISEDIRECT—LISTS
"CRUISES TO NOWHERE" OF 1 AND 2 NIGHTS' DURATION,
COSTING $119 A NIGHT & LESS

It's a frequent dilemma: You like to cruise; your spouse, partner, friend, or companion doesn't, usually because he or she has never done it. Solution: Go on a 1- or 2-night "cruise to nowhere" that simply leaves a port, sails over the horizon, and then lazily circles around until it's time to come back. Because the ship is moving so slowly, it hardly ever leans or pitches, and the entire ride is usually smooth as silk. Your friend's apprehensions are often completely overcome. And the cost of the whole exercise is not much more than you would have spent on dinner and an evening out.

But where do you find these "cruises to nowhere"? Because they cost so little, offering such a small return to the broker selling them, most cruise websites fail to mention a single example. But one does—and gives prominence to the offer. Go to www.cruisedirect.com, look for "Select a destination," scroll down, and click on "Cruise To Nowhere." Last October (as one example), you would have found 1-night cruises from Los Angeles selling for $129; 1-night cruises from New York selling for $119; 2-night cruises from Norfolk, Virginia, selling for $329; 2-night cruises from New York selling for $329; and so on. These are opportunities known to very few travelers—even though they're cheaper than most dates!

LOOKING FOR A BARGAIN AT SEA? YOU'LL FIND IT FROM SOUTHWEST AIRLINES!

It may be my imagination, but I'm beginning to think that Southwest Airlines, one of the cheapest of all carriers, has wheedled some of the major ship lines into offering up the cheapest of all cruise rates. Time after time, the Southwest website seems to be quoting rates or discounts that are just plain awesome.

Go to www.southwest.com, click on "Special Offers," and then, when a list appears in a vertical column on the left-hand side of the page, click on "Cruise Specials." Up will come "Cruise of the Week"—an assortment of bargains—supplemented by a direction to "Find other cruise offers" by clicking on those words at the bottom of the page.

As I write this, "Cruise of the Week" is offering the following on sailings aboard ships of Royal Caribbean:

3-Night Bahamas: from $219 plus $100 onboard credit
4-Night Baja California: from $289 plus $75 onboard credit
5-Night Western Caribbean: from $399 plus $100 onboard credit
7-Night Mexican Riviera: from $499 plus $100 onboard credit
7-Night Eastern Caribbean: from $599 plus $100 onboard credit
7-Night Mediterranean: from $699 plus $100 onboard credit

While I can't confirm that these prices are lower than those offered by other cruise discounters, they seem awfully good. It is entirely possible that those bargain-conscious folks at our cheapest airline are also working hard to excel—pricewise—on the high seas. For information on current cruise bargains offered by Southwest Airlines, call ☎ 888/SHIP-SWA (744-7792).

FREIGHTERS

PASSENGER-CARRYING FREIGHTERS ARE PLENTIFUL FOR RELAXED TRAVELERS WITH TIME TO BURN

What's going on with passenger-carrying freighters? Are they still around? Answer: more than ever. The increasing use of computer-operated, automated equipment has reduced the size of crews, opening up more cabins for use by passengers. And the additional revenue is highly valued by the freighter companies, which now offer numerous sailings each month of these lengthy, 30-day-and-longer itineraries to exotic ports of the world.

The major recent change has been in price. Since tariffs are usually calculated (by the freighter companies) in euros, the dollar price has risen sharply over the years. While once there were some cabins available for about $100 per person per day, the usual minimum rate—based on my own review of recent charges—is about $140 a day. For that, you get the run of the ship, you dine with the officers, and wander about through long, lazy days, perhaps writing that novel you always had within you.

The best way to obtain a partial glimpse of the options is by accessing www.freighterworld.com and then filling out a form to receive a free copy of the biweekly, glossy, six-page newsletter ("Freighter Space Advisory") published by Freighter World Cruises, Inc. (180 S. Lake Ave., Pasadena, CA 91101-2655; ☎ 800/531-7774 or 626/449-3106), one of the largest of the passenger brokers for the 21 largest lines operating freighters. Although the newsletter writes up only three or four sample opportunities out of the dozens available (see the website for many more), its photographs and maps are tremendously instructive. Keep in mind that most passengers (except for that occasional novelist) are in their 60s and 70s, and that departure dates are only estimates, requiring you to board the ship on a day of their choosing (obviously, you must have time to burn). Twelve are the maximum number of passengers taken aboard each ship.

RIVER CRUISES (& RIVERBOATS)

THE EUROPEAN RIVER CRUISE IS ENJOYING MASSIVE POPULARITY AS A MEANS OF OFFSETTING THE WEAKNESS OF THE U.S. DOLLAR

At a typical price of $1,999 per person (off season), $2,699 (high season) for 7 nights, including round-trip airfare from the United States, the all-inclusive

European river cruise along the Rhine or the Danube is fast becoming the year's top travel hit. My own recent Rhine cruise, starting in Amsterdam (at the Rhine canal) and going to Cologne, Cochem, Rüdesheim, Heidelberg, and Strasbourg, ending in Basel, Switzerland, was sold out by American travelers looking for ways to combat the shrinking dollar.

All river cruise lines—Lueftner Cruises chartered by Gate 1 Travel, Ama Waterways, Peter Deilmann, Uniworld, and others—are reporting equally high sales.

Although we needed to change some dollars into euros for tips to the riverboat staff, there were few expenses beyond the basic cost of the cruise and airfare. Lodgings were in comfortable cabins aboard the ship, and two of the

Cruising the rivers of Europe—the Rhine, the Danube, the Elbe, and the Mosel—has become a popular, cost-effective form of vacationing.

daily meals consisted of a giant buffet breakfast aboard the ship and an equally massive sit-down dinner of near-gourmet level prepared by a surprisingly accomplished ship chef and his staff.

I will not pretend that seeing Europe in this fashion is a fully satisfying alternative to the kind of trips we used to enjoy when the dollar was king. But the European river cruise has some plus points.

You stop every day, usually for the entire day, in a historic European city. The river boat ties up very near to the center of town, and not—as on some ocean cruises—far out to sea or miles from the city. Although the riverboat tries hard to sell you optional land excursions by motorcoach, and many passengers buy them, you will have no difficulty simply wandering into the center of town just a short walk away.

Unlike an ocean cruise aboard one of those new, 3,000-passenger sea monsters, the river cruise ships do not inundate the cities at which they stop. The typical river ship carries 140 passengers—scarcely ever more than that—and its presence in town is scarcely noticed by inhabitants.

The cities visited on a European river cruise are never the major capitals (except, perhaps, for the starting or ending cities) but—in the case of my own Rhine cruise—historic and well-preserved examples of traditional, midsize European life, such as Cologne, Heidelberg, or Rudesheim.

The riverboats of Europe take you through a gentler scene of old-world life—they are soothing and instructive.

There are no casinos on board the European river ships—and passengers aren't the kind who crave casino life. There are no lip-synched, Las Vegas–style evening shows on the river ships. On my cruise, entertainment was by a pianist and singer, and most passengers never heard them, preferring to remain on shore to sample the local nightlife.

There were no bingo games, art auctions, wet T-shirt contests, rock-climbing walls, bowling alleys. There were no children's games (and no children). There was a bar, two computer monitors for e-mail, a tiny shop, an equally tiny fitness room with one treadmill, and a beauty parlor. That was it. The ship did not cater to people who rely on outside distractions for their entertainment. Most passengers looked forward to the port visits, and attended late-evening talks on the next day's stop in the ship's lounge.

On board the river ships, the staff was international—French, German, and Dutch officers; usually younger people from Hungary, Romania, and Bulgaria in the middle positions. Although the majority of passengers were middle-aged, a quarter of them were young people interested in the life and history of Europe.

How did the cabins compare to those on an ocean-going cruise ship? As best I could see, they were exactly the same size, but the bathrooms were somewhat larger. The cabins had all the furnishings and amenities of a cruise-ship cabin, and indeed the mattresses, feather blankets, and down-filled pillows were superior to those I remember. The cabin also had a large, flatscreen television able to get all the channels of a land-based TV system:

We not only received a full-length, English-language movie each night, but also BBC Television, Sky Television, CNN, CNBC, and four other German-language, Dutch-language, or French-language channels.

How was the food? Better than on the average, popularly priced cruise ship. It was thoroughly European, and reflected all the glories of the European cuisine and the care and attention that Europeans devote to meals. At a final-night party when the entire crew was paraded before us, we were surprised to discover that the ship had six cooks for its 140 passengers, and all of them were either Dutch or German chefs, well accomplished at making all the complementary sauces that Europeans pour over meats and fish. Wine was free and unlimited and good; in fact, the ship apparently picked up supplies of Mosel whites when we took a detour over a stretch of the Mosel River, and that night we all had mild, midsweet Mosel wine with our meal. Beer—good European beer—was also available and free at all meals. Breakfast was a giant buffet of endless dishes, including an omelet station at which a member of the crew prepared whatever kind of omelet you desired.

Readers, I share your sorrow over the drastic drop in the value of the dollar and the group-oriented travels to which we've all been condemned by that decline. My way to overcome the problem is to dramatically lower the category of my accommodations.

But if you're determined to enjoy all the creature comforts on your travels in Europe, you couldn't do better than on a European river cruise.

WERE YOU AWARE THAT A RIVERBOAT RESEMBLING THOSE THAT SAIL THE RHINE & THE DANUBE IS ALSO MAKING PROPELLER-DRIVEN (NOT PADDLE-WHEEL) RIVER CRUISES IN THE UNITED STATES?

River cruises are not limited to Europe; we also have river cruises in the United States. And these are not limited to the quaint, antebellum-like *American Queen* and *Mississippi Queen* paddle-wheelers with calliopes, but to a giant modern boat the length of a football field known as the R/B *River Explorer*. It sails on the upper and lower Mississippi, on the Ohio River, the Cumberland River, and the Texas/Louisiana Intracoastal Waterway, among others, and services such major ports as St. Louis, Cincinnati, Nashville, Pittsburgh, New Orleans, Galveston and Brownsville, Memphis and Louisville, at rates averaging around $300 a day per person for all-inclusive arrangements and large cabins.

The cruises are generally of 7, 8, and 12 days' duration; to book them, go to www.riverbarge.com.

Shore Excursions

At last! A company that will book your shore excursions for less than you'd pay to a cruise line—& for a better tour.

"Should I buy my shore excursions in advance? From the cruise line? Or should I take my chances once at the port? What if the ship docks at a pier far from town?"

On our Sunday radio show (noon to 2pm, streaming live on www.wor710.com), my daughter Pauline and I receive more calls about cruise-ship shore excursions than on any other topic. To all these callers we loudly respond: No! Don't buy those overpriced tours from the cruise line. Those canned and artificial experiences! Don't squeeze into a 45-passenger bus. Wander on your own. Enjoy the authentic aspects of the ports you visit.

But though this advice is politely received by our callers, it's obvious that they would still like to tour with a guide, and possibly as part of a small group.

Recently, help arrived, in the form of a website called ShoreTrips (www.shoretrips.com), administered from a small town in Wisconsin. Its founders, former travel agents, have apparently toured all the major ports in the Caribbean, Mexico, and Europe, interviewed scores of local tour companies, and made arrangements with the best of them to handle the shore excursions of the clients of ShoreTrips for prices that average 50% of what the cruise lines charge. And the tours in question usually run with four to eight persons, far fewer than the depressing groups of 45, squeezed into a giant motorcoach and operated by the cruise lines.

ShoreTrips looks for unusual, unique, memorable tour experiences, and not for the canned sights of the standard cruise ship–sponsored tours.

To share the cost of shore excursions with other passengers on your cruise, use the "Roll Call" feature of Cruise Critic

Rather than go to a tour operator, you can also create your own, form-it-yourself group of four to six persons by using a facility called Cruise Critic (www.cruisecritic.com). More and more cruise passengers would obviously prefer to hire a taxi or van to conduct a more private tour, sharing the cost and thus reducing the price to far below what the cruise-sponsored motorcoach tours cost.

Cruise Critic helps you to seek out other like-minded would-be tour participants. You first register for the use of message boards; you then use a

"Roll-Call" feature limited to the ship (and departure date) on which you're about to cruise. Entering those roll calls and reaching only the other passengers on your cruise, you list the ports you plan to tour and ask others to indicate whether they'd like to share the costs with you. In this manner, you quickly round up three, four, or five other people, and form a small group. You arrange to meet aboard the ship at a given place and time. And then, arriving at the port, you jointly hire a taxi or make arrangements with larger vehicles to transport your group to the places you wish to see or experience.

TWO MORE INTERNET-BASED SERVICES—PORT PROMOTIONS & PORTCOMPASS—OFFER PORT EXCURSIONS FOR LESS THAN THE CRUISE LINES CHARGE

I am writing now to identify two other companies—Port Promotions (www.portpromotions.com) and PortCompass (www.portcompass.com)—that claim to do the same as ShoreTrips. And although I have no way to judge their worth, their websites are impressive. On them, you simply enter the name of a port and up come various tours you can book, along with the exact price for each tour, almost always at a savings. The cruise lines will be gnashing their teeth!

Having said that, I again submit that do-it-yourself sightseeing, on your own two feet, is infinitely superior to any of these canned excursions. I can't imagine joining a group of others, no matter how small, after I have emerged from a cruise ship with 2,000 or more other passengers. The traveler, as opposed to a tourist, values the opportunity to join the authentic life of a foreign port city and have the kind of discourse with local residents that no group can ever experience.

An analogy: When, living at home, you decide to attend a play or visit a local museum or enjoy a park, what do you do? Do you call a tour company and arrange to join a group visiting these places? Or do you simply make your own way downtown and participate in the life and culture of your city? Which way is the right way? And why should it be any different on a cruise?

A special word about shore excursions in the Russian city of St. Petersburg. When you book a Baltic cruise which includes a stop in that historic metropolis, you are immediately notified that you will be permitted to disembark onto Russian soil only as part of a cruise-ship group using a group visa. Naturally, the cost of a land tour to St. Petersburg operated by the cruise line, under such a group visa, is quite substantial, and I don't even want to frighten you by revealing the cost (try $200–$225 and more, per day).

But it isn't true that you don't have alternatives. Two St. Petersburg tour operators—DenRus, Ltd., and Red October—operate independent shore excursions of St. Petersburg for far less money, using group visa arrangements which they obtain from the Russian authorities. On a 2-day stay in St. Petersburg, which many cruise lines schedule, the price works out to around $250. But DenRus also advertises that as many as six passengers can arrange for the rental of a van, driver and guide for a full-day tour of St. Petersburg for a total of $472, bringing the per-person cost down to about $78 a day. For information, go to www.denrus-us.com or to www.red october.us. They spare you the task of applying for your own individual visa, which is a burdensome process.

A READER'S WORDS OF WISDOM ON SIGHT- SEEING FAMOUS PORT CITIES WITHOUT PAYING FOR CRUISE SHIP–SPONSORED TOURS

Reader David Berger, of Wauwatosa, Wisconsin, has supplied us with a detailed formula for sightseeing the port cities of the Mediterranean on your own two feet:

In Athens, the port of Piraeus (where the cruise ships dock) is a distance from the city center, but the subway from the port goes straight into town and has a stop right at the foot of the Acropolis, for only 1.50€, as opposed to the horrendous charge for the cruise line's tour there. Admission to the Acropolis itself is 12€. Imagine the savings and the pleasure of pursuing your own timetable.

In Naples, it's a 5-minute walk from ship to train depot and then 11€ for a train to the very gates of Pompeii. You can even ride to Sorrento if you wish. After I got back to Naples, I stopped for a pizza, that city's most famous export. You can't do that on an escorted tour.

In Rome, the ship docks at Civitavecchia about 72km (45 miles) north of the city, but a train is available near the port dock that takes you right into the heart of Rome, including a stop next to Vatican City.

At Venice, the ship offered a 12€ ride by boat to St. Mark's Square, with a return every hour. But if you read up just a bit, you'll learn that Venice has a fantastic water bus system and a stop right next to the ship, and an all-day, unlimited-transportation pass (for 11€) on the canal boats lets you ride round and round, in and out of canals, on and off as you please.

I think I've made my point. You can have a great time in ports of call if you simply take the time to consult a travel guide, and check out the options ahead of time. Consulting the street maps in those guides can save you hundreds of dollars as well.

NEXT TIME A CRUISE LINE TRIES TO SELL YOU A $110 SIGHTSEEING EXCURSION TO THE MENDENHALL GLACIER IN JUNEAU, ALASKA, TELL THEM ABOUT THE PUBLIC BUS

The most startling example of mendacious cruise-line marketing is the effort by cruise ships visiting the port of Juneau, Alaska, to sell you a $110 excursion to the Mendenhall Glacier. As anyone who has spent even 10 minutes in Juneau will tell you, there is a public bus from downtown Juneau that takes you the 12 miles to the Mendenhall Glacier for a charge of $1.50. Once there, you can walk about viewing the glacier, or pay $3 to enter the Mendenhall Glacier Visitor Center for a number of exhibits and films.

Never buy a cruise-ship port excursion in advance of taking the cruise. Wait to make your decision until the ship docks. Then ask yourself: Do I really want to stuff myself into a tour bus with 45 of my fellow cruise passengers? Haven't I spent enough time with them already? Would I rather simply wander about the town on my own two feet, stopping to speak with Alaskans? Or would I perhaps like to split the cost of a taxi with a few of my fellow passengers, and tour the area in that manner? Cruise-ship port excursions are among the worst and most unnecessary rip-offs in travel.

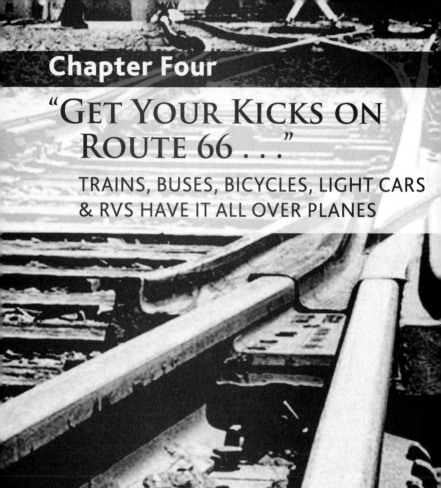

Chapter Four

"GET YOUR KICKS ON ROUTE 66 . . ."

TRAINS, BUSES, BICYCLES, LIGHT CARS & RVS HAVE IT ALL OVER PLANES

In the same alphabetical approach I've used throughout this book, I've tried to point out some of the ways you can enjoy affordable ground transportation within the United States (or via a self-guided bike tour of Europe). Whether it's a cut-rate bus or a rental RV, a remarkable website for learning about a hungry car-rental firm that has slashed the rates for the very weekend you'll be driving, or an organization for self-guided bicycle touring in New England or California, you'll find them all here.

AMTRAK

OUR TOONERVILLE TROLLEYS VS. THEIR 250-MPH TRAINS

The French *train de grande vitesse* ("train of great speed") has now begun daily operations between Paris and Strasbourg on the easternmost border of France, eliminating the need to take polluting airplane flights from Paris to parts of Germany. You may recall that in a test run, this train achieved a speed of 357 mph on the new track leading from Paris to Strasbourg. In its actual operation, it is now maintaining a standard speed of 199 mph.

In another part of the world, the Chinese have announced that they are currently operating 86 "bullet trains" that travel at a rate of more than 125 mph, cutting most train travel times in half. And all the while, the powers that be condemn Americans to the use of "Toonerville Trolleys" that barely function on the tracks set aside for Amtrak.

The Chinese have recently spent more than $4 billion on high-speed trains. We allocate only slightly more than $1 billion a year to the operation of the entire Amtrak system. Let us all dedicate ourselves to the fight to upgrade Amtrak, and to the defeat of those politicians whose allegiance to the oil and automobile industries is more important to them than sensible, environmental forms of land transportation in the United States.

DESPITE THE ENERGY CRISIS & THE URGENT NEED FOR MASS TRANSIT, THE ANTI-AMTRAK PEOPLE ARE AGAIN ON THE MARCH

Not long ago, efforts were made in the House of Representatives to cut back next year's appropriation for Amtrak from $1.4 billion to $800 million, barely enough to fund a greatly reduced operation of the trains. Though the anti-Amtrak forces failed to achieve that reduction, it is feared that the same battle will reoccur when the next Congress again considers our national passenger rail system.

Previous page: Recent action by Congress may lead to a shift away from the policy of "starve Amtrak" to a program of "expand and improve Amtrak."

Modern, high-speed trains at a European railroad terminal; only in America would antiquated, trolleylike cars still provide almost all rail service.

That controversy takes place at a time when our nation faces dreadful consequences from our dependence on foreign oil. We are currently studying every frantic way—subsidies for hybrid cars, ethanol, and switch grass—to reduce the gas consumption and gas emissions of our automobile-based way of life and its contribution to global warming and dependence on unstable nations in the Middle East. And yet the single most effective method of reducing oil use—mass transit through the increased use of trains—is deliberately starved and thwarted.

The same pro-oil, pro-automobile policies are being pushed on a state level. Just a few years ago, Florida repealed a measure to mandate the construction of a high-speed rail line along its heavily populated coasts. Other initiatives to encourage the development of mass-transit light rail have gone nowhere. Last winter, I spent nearly 3 hours traveling the 60 miles between Fort Myers and Naples, Florida, on a highway that resembled a continuous parking lot jammed with thousands of cars barely inching along. In a vacation area (the southwest coast of Florida) that is today populated by millions of Americans, there is no passenger rail transportation.

We need to persuade our representatives in Congress of the importance of providing adequate financial support for our trains. And beyond this yearly appropriation, we should urge them to support a bipartisan measure to place the funding of Amtrak on a long-term basis, allocating $19 billion over 6 years to the improvement and expansion of our passenger railways.

THE OPPONENTS OF AMTRAK HAVE RESPONDED TO MY DEFENSE OF THE NATIONAL RAILWAY SYSTEM WITH WHOLLY IDEOLOGICAL ARGUMENTS HARD TO UNDERSTAND

I am constantly surprised by the responses to my pleas for support of Amtrak. At a time when we are all so painfully aware of the need to limit the use of oil and reduce emissions of hothouse gases, I would have thought it self-evident that expansion of our railroads—the single most energy-efficient form of transportation—would receive broad approval.

At a time, too, when our air-transport system is literally falling apart—when planes wait for hours on airport runways and airports are crowded beyond belief—I would have thought it self-evident that we should expand the capacity of our railroads. If the tens of thousands of people who use Amtrak each day were forced instead to fly by air, their numbers would add chaos to our airports.

And yet whenever I write about the need to support Amtrak, I provoke angry dissents that are wholly ideological in nature. Most of them cite, as their chief argument, that Amtrak makes no money. Without explaining why that argument is relevant to the operation of a public utility—and Amtrak is an essential, increasingly important public utility—they repeat almost endlessly and without supporting explanation that Amtrak must make a profit—or else be abandoned.

What's strange is that no one makes the same argument with respect to cars and planes. The interstate highway system does not run at a profit. Yet every 2 years, Congress appropriates literally tens of billions of dollars for the maintenance and expansion of our interstate highways, so that more people can make long-distance trips by car. (Is it possible the oil industry has something to do with that funding?) Operating those highways at a profit would require that each U.S. interstate become a toll road, demanding ruinous fees from motorists, and not one of the responders to my argument would be in favor of that.

The air traffic control system does not operate at a profit. Each year, Congress appropriates at least $3 billion for air traffic controls, air traffic towers, and FAA safety operations. If the airlines themselves had to pay for the immense cost of air traffic control not covered by taxes and fees, most of those airlines would be forced to shut down. Yet none of my responders would deny the need to keep funding the air traffic control system.

And there are countless other government functions that do not operate at a profit. Our fire departments do not operate at a profit. When firefighters put out a blaze in a private home, they do not send a bill to the homeowner. Our police departments, public schools, municipal hospitals, sanitation departments, and downtown streets do not operate at a profit.

And neither should Amtrak. Fares on Amtrak should enable low-income and middle-income Americans to travel affordably to their work or to meetings and for many other purposes vital to our economy and society.

All over the world, major national railway systems, such as those in France, Germany, Spain, Scandinavia, and the Baltic states, are subsidized from general tax revenues and do not operate at a profit. They perform brilliantly for their public. In the few instances where passenger rail has been privatized, fares have often skyrocketed and grave safety concerns arisen. Even the private railway companies (such as Eurostar) depend, to a considerable extent, on partial government funding.

AMTRAK HAS JUST RECEIVED A SHOW OF SUPPORT IN THE U.S. SENATE, FOLLOWING DEFEAT OF MEASURES TO EMASCULATE IT

The enemies of Amtrak are unrelenting. Just shortly before a vote by the Senate on a proposal to set aside nearly $12 billion for the national passenger railway system over the next 6 years (an improvement on recent funding, though still inadequate), Senator John E. Sununu of New Hampshire introduced an amendment to require that Amtrak discontinue all its long-distance services in the West. He and another senator later introduced other amendments to limit, hamper, or discredit Amtrak. All such amendments were overwhelmingly defeated and the appropriation was then approved, 70–22, with Sununu among the 22 no votes. The same proposed appropriation will now be brought to the House of Representatives. As I write this, we can only hope for the best.

READ IT & WEEP: EUROPEANS CAN NOW TRAVEL BY TRAIN BETWEEN LONDON & PARIS IN JUST ABOUT 2 HOURS FLAT

Last year, on the new high-speed train tracks installed into London's St. Pancras Station, the Eurostar made the trip between Paris and London in only 3 minutes more than 2 hours. When, shortly thereafter, the train began regular daily service between St. Pancras Station and Paris, it usually made the trip in a more leisurely 2 hours and 15 minutes. It goes between London and Brussels in 1 hour and 51 minutes. For all practical purposes, it is no longer necessary—ever—to fly between London and Paris or between London and Brussels. It would be foolish to do so.

In Europe, the popularity of high-speed rail has virtually eliminated the use of airplanes between nearby cities, an environmental triumph.

It should also be noted that persons vacationing in London can now make easy day trips to Paris, leaving early in the morning from London, returning evenings from Paris, and having the greater part of the day to spend in Paris. That's an important expansion of travel opportunities.

WE ARE A NATION WEDDED TO THE AIRPLANE & THUS UNABLE TO COPE WHEN THE WEATHER PREVENTS AIRPLANES FROM FLYING

If you're like me, you've heard dozens of stories from relatives and friends about the nightmares of flying, particularly before and after major holidays.

Flights canceled by the hundreds. Flight delays causing missed connections. New York airports busing passengers to less crowded airports in Philadelphia. Chicago airports desperately seeking to accommodate stranded passengers in nearby hotels. Infants squealing, toddlers screaming. Snowstorms causing hundreds of canceled flights in Chicago, and thus backing up traffic all over the nation. Similar crises at a dozen other major cities in the Midwest.

Note that most of these problems are weather related and therefore won't ever be fixed by adjusting flight schedules, improving air traffic controls, using larger airplanes, or adopting all the other measures that earnest pundits propose. They are problems that arise from our decision to move people almost entirely by air—thus putting all our eggs in one basket. And they are problems that other, wiser nations avoid by maintaining an adequate rail system.

As I've argued before, unless and until Amtrak is expanded and turned into a high-speed system, we will continue to experience periodic nightmares at our airports.

U.S. POPULATION GROWTH DEFIES THE ARGUMENTS PUT FORTH BY AMTRAK OPPONENTS

The enemies of Amtrak are constantly arguing that the United States is different from Europe, that we do not possess the population density that would make a widespread rail system sensible. They are apparently unaware that we are now a nation of some 303 million people, the vast majority of whom are concentrated in the eastern half of the country, along the southernmost strip of the Sunbelt, and along the West Coast. In these areas, a use of train transportation is just as sensible and feasible as anywhere in Europe.

Take out a map of the United States. Starting at the northernmost tip of the Midwest, draw a somewhat jagged north/south line starting at Duluth, Minnesota, and then proceeding downwards through Minneapolis, Des Moines, Omaha, Kansas City, Joplin, Tulsa, Oklahoma City, Fort Worth, Austin, and San Antonio. Everything to the east of that line—nearly half the United States—is a place of intense population density growing "thicker" by the day.

Now add to that vast swath of the United States the southernmost area of the Sunbelt, going across the bottom of the United States to San Diego, and then up the entire West Coast to Seattle. That, too, is a place of population density that can well support an efficient rail system.

THE LATEST ATTACK ON AMTRAK IS BASED ON THE ASSUMPTION—A PURE FLIGHT OF FANTASY—THAT VARIOUS RAILROADS ARE ANXIOUS TO COMPETE WITH AMTRAK

Some Americans believe that the United States should end subsidies to Amtrak and privatize passenger rail transportation so that "competition can spur innovation."

According to this reasoning, if public funding for Amtrak is ended and the passenger railroad industry is privatized, "competitors" will magically appear to bring the benefits of free enterprise to the rails.

Competitors? Who? From where? Since no national rail system makes a profit, no one is standing in line to operate rail service in the United States. No purely private company has asked either to take over from Amtrak, or to compete with it, especially if they don't receive a public subsidy for doing so. As with any other public utility (the police department, the fire department, the air traffic control system), no commercial company would ever volunteer to enter these fields in the hope of making a profit without receiving public assistance.

I find that the arguments against Amtrak are taken from the world of fantasy. No train system anywhere in the world—including the private companies now operating in England—operates without government support.

I'll say it again: At a time when our reliance on overpriced foreign oil is among the most serious problems we face, it is absurd to favor highways and starve Amtrak.

AN INTERESTING FACT ABOUT THE STRUCTURAL ADVANTAGE THAT CONGRESS GIVES TO APPROPRIATIONS FOR HIGHWAYS OVER RAIL TRANSPORTATION

Were you aware that state governments have to pay far more of the cost of light-rail transit than of highways? An online edition of *The New Republic* carried this remarkable revelation from Bradford Plumer:

> It's no secret that Congress has always spent far more to promote driving than it's spent on public transit—note that the White House requested $40 billion for the federal highway budget in 2008, versus $1.08 billion for railroad funding. But that's only the beginning. While doing some searching around, I came across an old Brookings report from 2003, which usefully compared the funding process for highway and mass transit projects, and laid out some glaring differences.
>
> Under current law, the federal government usually covers about 80–90 percent of the costs for a new highway project, compared with only 50 percent of the costs for a transit system. Local communities have to pick up most of the rest of the tab for public transportation, with state governments chipping in what's left. Since doing that usually requires raising property taxes, most local governments just prefer to build highways. (Indeed, some 30 states restrict their gas-tax revenues to highway purposes only.)
>
> Moreover, transit projects have to undergo intensive scrutiny: a cost-benefit analysis, a land-use analysis, an environmental-impact analysis, and, usually, a detailed comparison among

various alternatives. That all sounds pretty reasonable, except that highway projects don't have to undergo any of this—save for a (considerably less strict) environmental analysis—federal oversight is rather minimal. Highway money is basically a gift to states and local governments.

Not surprisingly, most communities find it far easier to build new highways than to set up, say, a light-rail system, no matter how popular the latter might be. (The Brookings report gives an example of a popular light-rail proposal in Milwaukee going down in flames for exactly this reason.) So, sure, any decent plan for reducing emissions and curbing gasoline use should include more money for public transit. But it also seems like a lot of funding rules need to be changed, so that transit and highway projects can compete on a more level playing field.

AUTO RENTALS

ALWAYS INQUIRE WHETHER THE LOW BIDDER FOR YOUR AIRPORT AUTO RENTAL HAS A LOCATION AT THE AIRPORT

My daughter Pauline was stunned by a price of only $27 a day (including all taxes) for an auto rental commencing in high season at Fort Lauderdale Airport, and therefore made the booking and flew off to Florida in good spirits. When she arrived, she discovered that the company in question was nowhere to be found and that it was able to offer such a low price only by maintaining a difficult-to-reach off-airport location.

A number of highly effective Internet services, such as Breezenet.com, help savvy travelers find the lowest rates for auto rentals.

Now if Pauline had planned a stay of several days, she probably would have gone through the involved procedure of getting to the remote garage of that low-ball bidder. But time was important, and the rental was only for 1 day. After losing nearly an hour in a search for the little-known company's rental desk, she phoned them and indignantly canceled the rental.

I have nothing against off-airport car-rental firms. All power to them. But it's important to learn, before you commit, whether the firm is in a location requiring a fair bit of time and effort to reach.

ZIPCAR, RENTING AUTOS BY THE HOUR, IS A NEW SERVICE THAT YOU REALLY MIGHT CONSIDER

There's a great car-rental service available for urban dwellers who have given up their cars in exchange for public transport yet still relish the thought of short-duration escapes and for frequent travelers who are tired of spending more on their rental cars than on their hotels when they visit major North American cities.

It's called Zipcar (www.zipcar.com) and it can end up costing you far, far less than a traditional car rental. Rates run $7 to $10 per hour, and incredibly that includes gas and all insurances. (If you do need to top off the tank, you do so using the fuel card provided at no charge to you.)

Unlike a traditional rental, you are not gong to be stuck with a "Pontiac Grand Prix or similar." There are dozens of makes and models available, and you get precisely the car you reserve, from a staid Honda Civic to a trendy Scion xB, from a Cooper MINI to a BMW 328, or from an SUV to a hybrid Prius.

There's no rental counter, so you can pick up and drop off a car anywhere at any time. You simply sign in and reserve a car for a specific time and place—the site gives you a Google map flagged with locations showing where parked Zipcars are available in the city of your choice (I typed in a zip code for midtown Manhattan and there were nearly 300 vehicles between 23rd and 65th streets alone; Minneapolis, on the other hand, had five).

When you join the service you are issued a personal Zipcard, which looks a bit like a credit card. Wave this card over a sensor on the car door and it will automatically unlock for you (and only you at your reserved time; even another Zipcar user couldn't take the car you have reserved). The card also unlocks the ignition, allowing you to use the keys left hidden in the car.

This service is not really intended for the occasional traveler, but for people who either live in or regularly visit the big cities. I say this because there is a one-time application fee of $25 and an annual fee of $50. However, once those costs are absorbed, the rates were remarkably low when we went to press: $7 to $10 per hour, or $55 to $69 per day, depending on the city and whether you'll drive just occasionally or several times a month (the latter is cheaper). There are other benefits as well, ranging from discounts at rock-climbing gyms, bookstores, theme parks, and concert venues to free door-side parking spaces at some IKEA stores.

There is one limit no longer found on most traditional rentals: no unlimited mileage. You only get 180 miles on any reservation, whether it's for an hour or a full day. Still, 180 miles is enough to drive into town or anywhere about an hour away by highway. Drive farther than that and you'll pay a fee per mile.

You sign up for a specific city, but once a member you can use a Zipcar in any city where the service is offered. That list currently includes New York and northern New Jersey; the greater Washington, D.C., area; 10 locations in New England (including Boston, Providence, New Haven, and Lewiston, Maine); Chicago; Chapel Hill and Elon in North Carolina; Ann Arbor; Minneapolis; San Francisco and Santa Cruz in California; Canada (Toronto and Vancouver); and even London, England.

ALL OF AMERICA SEEMS EAGER TO OUTWIT THE CAR-RENTAL COMPANIES

A number of our readers have suggested excellent tactics for checking the rise in car-rental costs and thus outmaneuvering Messrs. Hertz, Avis, National, and Budget. Here are some of the best ideas:

◆ **Rent the smallest available compact car.** Since these are in limited quantity, the chances are good that the compact category will be sold out and you'll be upgraded without extra charge. Though you won't save money, you'll at least get more value for money spent.

◆ **Try to pick up the ultrasmall car you've rented as late in the day as possible.** That way, the chances are enhanced that all the compact cars will have been rented and you'll be furnished with a larger car for no extra charge.

◆ **If you're planning a hotel stay in a city where you need a car, arrange to pick it up at your hotel the day after your arrival.** This will save a day's rental.

◆ **Don't forget that large car-rental companies often place ads in the travel sections** of major newspapers, offering special discounted rates to persons who mention a certain combination of letters or numbers at the time of making their reservations. If you can't find them in your local paper, go online to a website, such as FatWallet (www.fatwallet. com), where people share coupon codes. Additionally, the "majors" place ads in the AARP magazine or in publications associated with

AAA. Most AAA offices even have car-rental discount coupons available to anyone who walks in.

IF YOU'RE RENTING A CAR IN THE UNITED STATES & NOT USING BREEZENET.COM, YOU'RE PROBABLY PAYING TOO MUCH

Surprising how such a superlative Internet service is so little known, even among the most intensely cost-conscious travelers. BreezeNet.com (www.bnm.com) is a comparison service that searches the prices of up to 20 car-rental companies (including purely local ones) and then tells you where you can get the best deal for the dates when you need wheels.

Since BreezeNet.com sometimes lists obscure local firms, they will tell you which of their recommendations have pick-up desks in the airport terminal and which require that you go outside the terminal (or into town) to procure your car.

BreezeNet.com surveys not only the car-rental companies, but the other car-rental search engines (such as Priceline). It's so very comprehensive it merits inclusion in any list you maintain of valuable websites. You ought to write it down and keep it in mind for your next trip.

AUTO TOURING

TAKING THE ROAD LESS TRAVELED REVEALS AMERICA AT ITS MOST SCENIC

If, like me, you're bored to tears by the sheer monotony of driving the nation's interstate highways—every exit encrusted with a nearly identical cluster of fast-food outlets, chain motels, and gas stations—you might want to consider taking a different route. When it comes time for a long holiday weekend or a simple road trip to visit family, try the back roads instead. They can make the process of getting there nearly as much fun as the destination itself and are often well worth the extra hour or two of travel time.

Finding the most scenic and historic roads less traveled has never been easier, thanks to the revamped website of the National Scenic Byways Program (www.byways.org). Part of the U.S. Department of Transportation, the Byways Program bills itself as a "collaborative effort established to help recognize, preserve and enhance selected roads throughout the United States." In conjunction with state authorities and organizations, it has since 1992 designated 126 roads (at least one in every state, plus D.C. and Puerto Rico) as scenic byways, and funded more than 2,000 projects to help preserve and promote them.

Some of these officially designated byways are famous, including the Blue Ridge Parkway along the spine of the Appalachian's Blue Ridge Mountains in Virginia and North Carolina; Historic Route 66 from Chicago to Los Angeles; and the Big Sur Coastal Highway (Rte. 1) in California. Others deserve to be better known, such as the Great River Road following 2,069 miles of the Mississippi River from Minnesota to Mississippi, or the gorgeous Natchez Trace extending from Nashville, Tennessee, to Natchez, Mississippi, following a trail that's been in continuous use for more than 8,000 years: first by ancient Indians, later by colonial traders, soldiers, and settlers.

Though it can—and probably will—be improved by additional information in future updates, www.byways.org is an invaluable resource: a free, one-stop guidebook to some of the prettiest and most historic roads in America.

THREE FUNKY GUIDES WILL AID ANYONE ON A DRIVE ALONG THE TWO MAJOR ROUTES BETWEEN THE NORTHEAST & FLORIDA

Anyone planning a long car trip in the eastern United States—or contemplating a drive to Florida at any time—should pick up a copy of three quirky guides to the major interstates. These spiral-bound books—one to I-95, from Cape Cod to the Florida border (www.drivei95.com); one to I-75, from Detroit to the Florida Border (www.i75online.com); and one titled *Along Florida's Expressways* (also at www.i75online.com/FLABookInfo. html)—have a homespun quality, and each is crammed with useful information and interesting historic tidbits.

The guides are divided into two main sections. First are pages of simplified, annotated maps, each covering 15 or 30 miles of the interstate and listing the facilities at each exit. When I say "the facilities" I mean all the facilities, not just the half dozen for which there is room on the highway's exit signs.

Refreshingly, in addition to the expected chains of service stations, fast-food joints, and motels, there are also listings of independent diners, restaurants, and B&Bs that are close to the exit. This is a cornucopia of travel info: a mix of practical tips, interesting sights at each exit, and a delightful collection of historical trivia that manage to take 1,500 miles and four lanes of unrelenting asphalt and make them interesting.

Where do you get these books? From any major bookstore, or by consulting the websites listed above.

Though it's not for everyone, an inexpensive, self-drive auto tour of Europe, using motels for lodgings, is entirely possible

Some families regard the self-drive automobile tour, staying in highway motels, as an excellent way to see the country. Not surprisingly, a great many Europeans feel the same way about their own highways and motels. At strategic autobahn and autostrada exits across Europe are modern roadside motels waiting to welcome them with standardized comforts, few frills, and rock-bottom rates: 29€ to 75€ for a double room.

I've written before about Travelodge (www.travelodge.co.uk), a British chain of 330 motels where Web sales can bring the price of a double room to as low as £19, but that is far from the only motel chain operating in Europe. Travelodge rival Premier Inn (www.premierinn.com) boasts 500 hotels in the U.K. and Ireland—and there are motels beyond the British Isles, from Berlin to Budapest.

Accor, the vast French-owned hotel group, may be more famous for its higher-end hotel brands Novotel and Sofitel (and, in the United States, Red Roof Inn and Motel 6), but at the other, lower end of the lodging spectrum it runs the famously basic Formule 1 (www.hotelformule1.com), a chain of some 380 motels in 14 European countries. These utterly bare-bones motels are fully automated (aside from a few hours each morning and evening), the "receptionist" consisting of an ATM-like machine you use to check yourself in.

One step up in the Accor family is Etap (roughly 369 motels in 11 countries; www.etaphotel.com), with a live receptionist all day, rooms with a double bed and a lofted bunk for a child, and a free breakfast buffet (breakfast at Formule 1 costs extra).

Other French motel chains include Campanile (more than 300 properties in nine countries; www.campanile.com) and Kyriad (200 motels, all in France; www.kyriad.com). Europe even boasts familiar roadside signs for such American chains as Holiday Inn Express (www.hiexpress.com) and Days Inn (www.daysinn.com), where rates start around 55€ to 75€ for roadside properties, rising to 130€ to 210€ for hotels closer in to city centers.

This brings up an important point. European motels are increasingly no longer limited to highway interchanges, airport approaches, and ring roads. A surprising number of these bland but reliable chains are opening up along the outskirts of, and sometimes even within, the historic city centers of Europe's major cities.

BICYCLING

BIKE TOURS DIRECT HAS ANNOUNCED ITS LATEST PROGRAM & IT'S AN ISLAND OF REASONABLE COSTS IN A SEA OF BIG-TIME EXPENSE

The high cost of bicycle tours is a problem that has caused much anguish. Despite the fact that it is your own two legs that provide the transportation, a bicycle tour—as offered by U.S. companies—invariably costs far more than an escorted motorcoach tour of the same areas. For some inexplicable reason, the bicycle tour companies take an elitist tack, making use of the most upscale lodgings and meals on the tours they operate. Even when they don't, they claim that the need to supply two tour leaders (one to cycle ahead of the pack, the other to cycle at the rear) and one "sag wagon" (carrying luggage, as well as exhausted participants who don't want to continue cycling) elevates their costs to lofty heights. The result is that most of the leading bicycle tour companies are as elegant as they come, charging $500 and $600 a day.

Coming to the rescue is the improbable Tennessee-based company Bike Tours Direct (www.biketoursdirect.com), which represents dozens of local European bike operators offering "self-guided" bicycle tours of Europe. Its prices often are 60% less than what most other American bike operators charge. For the equivalent of about $1,200 a week it provides you with accommodations with private facilities in two-star hotels each night, two meals a day (breakfast and dinner), shipment of your luggage from town to town, and detailed instructions on following the itineraries you're given. They take care of all the reservations and every one of your needs other than airfare to Europe, a bicycle—rentable for about $125 for 2 weeks—and daily lunch.

While most of their tours run for a week, you can combine them into either a 2- or 3-week itinerary. When you do that, the results are magical. My own "dream itinerary" starts in Orleans, France, and follows the Loire through the awesomely beautiful, historic Loire Valley to the Atlantic Ocean, from which you take a train back to Paris. For a 15-day, 14-night tour in 2009 (leave any day), the cost is around $2,400—and by bicycling standards (the major U.S. operators often charge $600 a day!), that's a remarkable price.

Bike Tours Direct has now incorporated all its 2009 tours into its website, and some of them are even cheaper than the Loire itinerary, including its most popular tour of 2008 called the "Danube Bike Path." Poland is a new destination for 2009, including five different weeklong tours that begin or end in Cracow. Among other new itineraries are Dubrovnik and the

Dalmatian Coast, Amsterdam to Bruges, and tours of the Mosel and Rhine rivers.

I wish I could announce a lower price for this year's Bike Tours Direct European programs, but the exchange rate for the euro has risen to around $1.50 for every euro. As long as that exchange prevails, Europe will be a pricey place. For now, Bike Tours Direct is one of the most effective ways to experience the highlights of Europe's countryside and historic villages at a reasonable cost.

To Burgundy, Provence & the Dordogne, self-guided (nongroup, nonescorted) bicycle tours start at $175 to $190 a day

On a self-guided bicycle tour, you, as a cyclist, together with a friend or companion, ride your bikes from town to town following an itinerary provided by the tour company. You have a confirmed reservation for a modest guesthouse each night, your luggage is sent by car from one town to the next, and you receive a stipulated number of meals, which are included in the price.

France—especially its provinces of Burgundy, Dordogne, and Provence—is the classic nation for self-guided, independent bicycling. These regions are so well supplied with B&B accommodations that your total costs can easily be kept within a $175- to $190-a-day limit.

By eliminating groups and escorts, new easy-to-use programs have slashed the cost of biking along the rural roads of France.

In addition to Bike Tours Direct, discussed above, you can go to the long-experienced firm of Randonée Tours (☎ **800/242-1825** or 604/730-1247; www.randonneetours.com).

A Canadian company with a loyal following for its independent, non-group biking tours, Randonée gives you a predesigned itinerary through France which you follow entirely on your own, without guide or escort, but with your luggage carted for you from town to town. Prices include accommodations at B&Bs, all breakfasts, some dinners, and high-quality bikes. Averaging about 8 to 11 days in length, tours run year around (but mainly between May and Oct).

Randonée also offers self-guided bike tours in Canada, Ireland, Italy, Spain, and the United States; but because they make use of good-quality hotels in those countries, not B&Bs, their prices creep towards $300 and even $400 per day in non-French locations. For the lower rates, confine your trip to France's Burgundy, the Dordogne, or Provence, where Randonée's long relationship with outstanding B&Bs enables a price that no one else in the industry seems to match.

BUSES

SUDDENLY, THE BUSINESS OF OPERATING LOW-COST BUSES IS EXPANDING ACROSS THE UNITED STATES

At the airports, the delays are worse than ever, the flights are fewer and costlier, the conditions just plain dismal. At the railroad stations, die-hard train enthusiasts put up with the limited service of an Amtrak that's been starved of adequate operating funds.

But who's saving the day? Buses! And though you've been alerted to some of them, you ain't seen nothing yet! With the announcement that Megabus (www.megabus.com) was connecting New York with six other cities (Philadelphia; Baltimore; Boston; Washington, D.C.; Buffalo; and Toronto) and charging only $1 per seat for the first several seats on each departure ($20 for the others), the rock-bottom, low-cost bus business takes on a new dimension.

You should also be aware of the new $1 a seat (and up from there) Bolt (www.boltbus.com), operating between New York and Boston. Turns out that Bolt is owned by none other than Greyhound; it was obviously formed to compete with Fung Wah (www.fungwahbus.com) and other Chinatown bus companies, such as DC2NY.com (www.dc2ny.com), that have revolutionized long-distance bus transportation. (In addition to charging remarkably low rates, the new transports provide electric outlets at each seat, mineral water, and free Wi-Fi.)

Megabus is currently doing business out of its two initial hubs: Chicago (connecting to several cities in the Midwest) and New York. By now establishing itself in Manhattan (from a pick-up spot at Eighth Ave. and 31st St.), Megabus has begun to resemble a nationwide line, and you'd be well advised to frequently check in at its website to learn of further developments.

It's exciting that bus transportation between major U.S. cities is now available for prices from $10 (such as Chicago to Milwaukee) or $20 (such as New York to Washington, D.C.) or $27 (such as Chicago to Detroit) each way; it would be more exciting still if comfortable, fuel-efficient trains made the same trips.

THE CHEAP BUS MOVEMENT—FORMERLY, THE "CHINATOWN BUS" MOVEMENT—IS SPREADING RAPIDLY ACROSS THE UNITED STATES

They started up about 7 years ago as "Chinatown buses" operated by various Chinese-American entrepreneurs from addresses in New York's Chinatown to various other street addresses (never an actual terminal) in Philadelphia; Washington, D.C.; and Boston. For about $20 each way, you booked passage on a shabby but workable bus, and saved a ton of money.

Then, in a little-noticed trend, other non-Chinese entrepreneurs bought their own buses and began operating along the Boston–New York–Philadelphia–Washington, D.C. circuit, at comparable bargain rates of $20 one-way to Washington, D.C., $35 round-trip.

Then the British entered the act, starting Megabus to service cities in the Midwest, especially Chicago, for an average of $20 or so per trip.

And now, in the latest development, a website called GotoBus.com has started to publicize a whole host of non-Chinese, but Chinatown-like, buses that take you everywhere up and down the entire East Coast of the United States (especially to and within Florida) and to a variety of other destinations. You'll learn all about their schedules and rock-bottom rates by going to GotoBus.com, but you won't always learn the name of the bus line. Though occasionally one is actually listed (such as AllStates Buses), often they remain anonymous until you actually book.

Sample prices? They're breathtaking. Los Angeles to Phoenix, $45 one-way; New York to Albany, $30 one-way; Orlando to Miami, $23 one-way. Cry your heart out, Greyhound!

GotoBus.com takes reservations for over 100 bus lines. Though I'm not prepared to comment on the quality of their vehicles or drivers, I am saying that a competitive marketplace has now created a new, money-saving travel opportunity for Americans.

GPS DEVICES

IF YOU HAVEN'T YET EQUIPPED YOUR CAR WITH A GPS DEVICE, YOU'RE MISSING OUT ON THE GREATEST MOTORING (& TRAVEL) ADVANCE SINCE AUTOMATIC TRANSMISSION

I still remember the first time I used a GPS (Global Positioning Satellite) device while driving. And I am still exhilarated by what it did.

We had landed at night, my daughter and I, at the airport of Fort Lauderdale, Florida, and rented a car to reach our downtown hotel. When she slid behind the driver's wheel, Pauline whipped out her Garmin (a 3×4-inch little navigational box) and affixed it to the windshield. Quickly, the Garmin accessed a high-altitude satellite, figured out where we were, superimposed our position over a map of the confusing crisscross of airport-area highways, and directed us by arrow and spoken commands along the correct route to our hotel.

When a right turn or left turn or U-turn was needed, the arrow indicated that turn and a female-mimicking robotic voice advised us that the turn was coming up in such-and-such a distance. When we were within a few hundred feet of the correct turn, the voice again reminded us to make the turn.

In the midst of frightening traffic whizzing along an absolute jumble of parallel highways and crossing highways, we found our way effortlessly to our hotel. The next morning, when Pauline had to appear on various TV programs broadcast from the Fort Lauderdale area, she used the Garmin to get correctly and almost effortlessly to all three stations.

Pauline and her husband had bought the device (which is simply one of the many brands of GPS devices) through eBay, and I do not know how

The GPS, which "talks you" through an unfamiliar network of roads, is a remarkable travel advance—don't leave home without one.

much they paid for it. On the Internet, the Garmin sells (in its most modest version) for slightly more than $219. Earlier this year, they took it with them on a trip to Scotland, where they also rented a car and drove to a number of locations. The Garmin worked perfectly even in that foreign country.

I assume that most readers have already used some version of a GPS system for a number of years now. But if you haven't used it, ask a friend who has one to demonstrate the device, and I'm willing to bet you'll rush to acquire a GPS for your own car.

SOME GPS DEVICES CAN ALSO BE USED FOR WALKING THE COMPLEX STREETS OF AN UNFAMILIAR CITY

According to one reader, GPS devices are not only "great on the road, but also wonderful for walking in cities. We brought it to NYC, changed the 'mode' from driving route to walking route, and had no trouble finding the sites we wanted to see easily and also fairly discreetly."

RECREATIONAL VEHICLES (RVS)

EVER THOUGHT OF RENTING A RECREATIONAL VEHICLE FOR YOUR NEXT VACATION?

It's the opposite of chic, somewhat rustic and rough. Yet the fastest-growing means for vacationing in America is the recreational vehicle. And though I'll be drummed from high society for saying so, the people using them are among the most thoughtful travelers our country has.

How do you get started on the RV life? Buying a recreational vehicle is a major investment that can exceed $40,000 and $50,000. Is it worth the outlay? Will you enjoy the lifestyle of the semi-nomad? Will you get restless and claustrophobic, or will you have the travel experience of a lifetime?

Many first-time RVers begin by renting a motor home—and thus determine whether the use of one is compatible with their own temperament and needs.

The first step is to look in your local telephone directory under the category "Recreation Vehicles—Renting and Leasing." Or you can call one of the three major national companies: Cruise America (☎ 800/327-7799; www.cruiseamerica.com); Bates International Motor Home Rental Network (☎ 800/732-2283; www.batesintl.com); and El Monte RV Center (☎ 888/337-2214; www.elmonterv.com). For renting in California, Altman's Winnebago (☎ 877/258-6267; www.altmans.com) may be worth a call. It's also useful to visit the website of the Recreational Vehicles Rental Association at www.rvra.org, which contains a list of companies that rent RVs, including prices and addresses, in almost all the 50 states.

Rental costs vary considerably, depending on type of vehicle, when and for how long you want it, season, and other variables. One way of getting a good price is by regularly checking the websites of the major rental outfits, which periodically post specials. A rather large motor home—either a 26-foot Alumalite by Holiday Rambler or a 27-foot Southwester by Fleetwood—will average $800 a week, plus a mileage fee after an initial number of free miles. That's for a vehicle that can sleep five people and is fully self-contained, with such added features as a microwave oven, roof air conditioning, a generator and propane tank (so that a hookup is not necessary), power steering, and almost everything else you can name.

An autumn oddity: cheap RV rentals for persons who will drive them from place to place

Each fall, RV rental companies need to move vehicles from "summer" pickup locations to "winter" rental spots. Rather than incurring the cost of shipping the vehicles around the country, the companies rent them to customers willing to do the driving—and offer remarkably good prices for their cooperative efforts.

Not long ago, El Monte RV (☎ **888/337-2214;** www.elmonterv.com) was renting RVs at half price for the first 7 days on certain itineraries, including trips from Vancouver to Los Angeles; from San Francisco to Las Vegas; and from Salt Lake City to Los Angeles, San Francisco, Las Vegas, or Dallas. The company threw in some free miles, and of course the usual one-way drop-off charge—normally $300 and up—was waived. Rates vary depending on RV model, but customers can expect to pay around the same as for an SUV rental.

Last fall, Cruise America (☎ **800/371-8042;** www.cruiseamerica.com), another RV renter, arguably offered an even better relocation promotion: RV rentals at $24 per day for drivers picking up vehicles at various spots throughout the country and dropping them off in the Phoenix area. Later

The people who use RVs on their vacations are among our finest—and happiest—travelers.

in the fall, Cruise America offered discounts to drivers who agreed to drive refurbished vehicles from Arizona, Denver, Orlando, Salt Lake City, the San Francisco Bay area, and still other places. Drivers were given 9 days and 3,000 miles from Phoenix to Orlando, for example. Be warned that taxes and fees are extra, and you can expect hefty charges for going above the allotted miles and time frame.

RENT AN RV, LIKE IT, THEN APPLY $2,000 OF THE RENTAL PRICE TOWARD BUYING IT

It sounds like one of those Depression-era offers that desperate merchants made to their customers. And it comes from a company, El Monte RV, that, as best I can tell, is number three in size among the big RV-rental companies. It's a homey, old-fashioned sort of company, responding perhaps to the high cost of gas, which must be decimating RV sales. However the offer came about, it's something you might want to consider. But it's subject to the following conditions:

◆ The RV must have accumulated a minimum of 10,000 miles;

◆ You can deduct only $2,000 of the amount you've paid for the rental;

◆ You must buy the RV no later than 30 days after you've concluded the rental.

You'll learn more by clicking on www.elmonterv.com, or by phoning ☎ 800/478-5040. El Monte RV can also be reached at ☎ 800/EMRENTS (367-3687).

Chapter Five

IN THE FOOTSTEPS OF INDIANA JONES

ADVENTURE TOURS, SAFARIS, CAMPING, TREKKING & YOGA

Adventure travel used to involve the occasional risk of life or limb. You went hang gliding or rock climbing, white-water rafting or cave exploring; you tested your vigor or your nerve in the mountains or deserts by clambering over rocks or rappelling yourself down a cliff. And only a very special person took on these daring challenges.

In the travel industry, that has changed. While adventure tours are occasionally acts of courage, they are more often designed today for you and me, people who simply want to travel to remote or exotic destinations (such as Romania, Nicaragua, Borneo, or the Falklands); to enjoy vacations spent primarily outdoors, camping or on safari; to hike from place to place on our own two feet; to assist a poor community to dig a well or build a school; to join a yoga, Pilates, or tai chi class. That broad range of activities is "adventure travel" today, and it's a big part of the travel industry.

ADVENTURE TRAVEL

THE SMALL-GROUP ADVENTURE TOUR IS BOOMING AS A MEANS OF VISITING EXOTIC OR LIGHTLY TRAFFICKED DESTINATIONS

I'm talking a different kind of "adventure" here, and not about hang gliding, rock climbing, white-water rafting, or otherwise aping Indiana Jones. Plenty of tour companies are still willing to help you risk your life, but they are now outnumbered by the firms that define adventure as simply meaning visits to an exotic or lightly visited nation that hasn't yet been affected by mass-volume tourism—a kind of travel that appeals, I'm sure, to a great many of us.

But though a great many travelers want to visit those unusual destinations (Cambodia and Laos, Honduras and El Salvador, Morocco and Tunisia, Romania and Mongolia), they don't want to be complete pioneers or adventurers—they would still like to travel accompanied by a guide and in the security of a small, even a tiny, group. (But they would rather die than travel with 45 others in a giant motorcoach.) For that intensely independent but cautious individual, a new category of travel known as "small-group adventure tours" is gaining popularity.

Four tour companies, all of them foreign owned, are leaders in the field: Adventure Center of Emeryville, California (www.adventurecenter.com), G.A.P Adventures of Toronto (www.gapadventures.com), Intrepid Travel of Australia (www.intrepidtravel.com), and Djoser Tours of the Netherlands

Previous page: It was once confined to acts of derring-do; today, "adventure travel" more often means outdoor vacations or going to remote or exotic places.

(www.djoserusa.com). All maintain offices in the United States, and attract a great many Americans to their tours.

They limit their groups in all but a few instances to no more than 12 persons, and usually average around 10. And they never make use of large motorcoaches for transporting their clients from place to place, but rather use small vans or, more often, simply public transportation. After participants gather at breakfast to discuss the day's activities, the small group usually boards a streetcar or a public bus to reach the attraction they wish to view, enjoying an encounter with the authentic life of the community.

Usually, too, the four small-group companies do not provide air transportation to the location of the tour; they expect you to make these arrangements on your own, and simply to congregate in the kick-off city on the first day of the tour.

For lodgings, these small-group operators almost always make use of locally owned facilities (inns, guesthouses, and private homes); they eschew hotels, even of the rather basic variety. And because they are dealing with foreign suppliers, they often ask you to bring an additional $200 to $400 in cash, to be paid on the spot to local businesses unused to issuing invoices.

In other words, the four specialists seek to provide contact with the realistic life of the destination. And in so doing, they offer prices that radically differ from the usual. Adventure Center charges $990 (not including airfare) for an 8-day tour of Morocco starting in Casablanca and ending in Marrakech. It charges $1,118 (not including airfare) for a 15-day tour of the Inca Highlands of Peru, starting and ending in Lima. G.A.P Adventures charges $595 (not including airfare or a $200 local cash payment) for a 15-day "El Salvador & Guatemala Loop." It charges $1,095 (not including airfare or $400 in local cash payments) for a 32-day "Central American Journey" from Mexico City to Costa Rica. Intrepid Travel charges $1,865 (not including airfare) for a 21-day tour of China and Hong Kong. Djoser Travel charges $2,205 (this time including airfare from New York and other cities) for a 14-night tour of Costa Rica.

I think the small-group adventure tour is the perfect solution for spirited, intellectually curious travelers who want to visit unusual destinations, but feel the cautious need for a guide. Each of the four companies has enjoyed heavy bookings and enhanced reputations in recent years. Though G.A.P Adventures suffered a setback when it moved outside its normal activities (flush with cash, it bought the MS *Explorer* several years ago and operated cruises of Antarctica until November 2007, when the ship hit an iceberg and sank; it has since acquired a substitute ship for operation in 2009), its other programs have proceeded with no unusual mishaps.

Go to the websites of the four small-group adventure companies, and I think you'll be impressed.

ADVENTURE ON THE HIGH SEAS: IN EVERY PORT FROM WHICH SAILING SHIPS DEPART, IT'S POSSIBLE TO SIGN ON AS CREW

Were you aware that you could hitch a ride on a sailboat or yacht at just about any port around the world without paying a dime? You merely need to be willing to use a little elbow grease during the cruise. You may be cooking meals, swabbing the decks, and/or helping with the sailing itself. You don't even need to have ever set foot on a boat (though, obviously, some experience helps opens up more options).

Many boat owners habitually take on even unseasoned crew in port before setting sail, whether to fill out the boat's necessary complement of hands, provide for a more relaxing trip by having others do the heavy lifting (or cooking), or simply for companionship, or a combination of all three. Of course, since you aren't the captain you'll have little say over the itinerary or destination, but for a free-spirited traveler who relishes making friends and learning new skills while sailing the world's most idyllic coastlines, island chains, and seas, this can be a dream come true.

There are three main categories of crew. First are true hired hands—either for sailing trips or yacht deliveries/repositionings—who will be expected to put in a day's work cooking, cleaning, and hauling on "sheets" (if you don't know that this means pulling on the ropes

You can volunteer to serve as crew on someone else's sailboat; simply head for the major marinas.

attached to the sails, you probably should stick to cooking and cleaning at first). Sometimes these are paid positions—especially if you have a particular skill (gourmet chef?) or previous sailing experience. Other times you simply work in exchange for free passage.

The second category consists of those who are acting as a kind of hired companion for someone who wants company on the trip, though you would, of course, do your bit to help run the boat. These positions might involve a token stipend, but are usually in return for free passage (though you may be asked to pay for your share of the food).

Finally, you may be offered a trip in return for sharing expenses (groceries, port fees, fuel, and so forth). You become a true equal on board—though unless it's a fully crewed yacht to begin with, you'll do your fair share of the work.

You can just head down to any port and ask the harbormaster if he knows of any captains in search of crew, or you can use the online messaging boards of the following sites: www.floatplan.com, www.findacrew.net, www.crewfile.com, www.partnersandcrews.com, and www.crewsearcher.com.

COOPERATIVE CAMPING IS AN OFTEN-OVERLOOKED METHOD OF ENJOYING A MEMORABLE & VERY INEXPENSIVE ADVENTURE TRIP THROUGH THE UNITED STATES OR ABROAD

Cooperative camping is a cheap and sensible means of travel for people who haven't the energy, funds, or commitment to buy and then transport their own camping equipment and/or camping vehicle to regions out of town or overseas. Operators of cooperative camping tours, such as TrekAmerica (☎ 800/221-0596; www.trekamerica.com), schedule departures and then round up as many as 12 or 13 scattered persons for each trip.

The group arrives at the jumping-off point, meets one another, and then boards a van furnished by the tour operator and driven by a professional guide—the only paid employee on the trip. The vehicle is supplied with state-of-the-art tents, elaborate cooking utensils, and (sometimes) sleeping bags—though most companies require that you provide your own. The group rotates shopping for groceries and the preparation of meals. Since they carry their own accommodations (the tents), they don't need to be anywhere at any particular time and are thus able to deviate from the itinerary and travel through areas where standard hotels aren't found.

The entire trip is unstructured and fun, close to nature and informal, adventurous, instructive—and cheap. The average cooperative camping tour operated by TrekAmerica costs around $40 a day, plus airfare—and about $6 per person per day for food.

"FOOTLOOSE" IS, IN EFFECT, THE ADULT DIVISION OF TREKAMERICA, CATERING TO PERSONS MOSTLY OVER THE AGE OF 35

TrekAmerica (see immediately above) has been around for more than 35 years. About a decade ago, complaints from older people that they were being excluded from these outdoor adventures led to the formation of Footloose (☎ 800/221-0596) for travelers mostly on the far side of 38. Footloose trips continue to rely on camping accommodations (though a few are beginning to use actual lodgings); many of them involve lengthy walking tours; most are within North and South America, some in Australia and New Zealand; and most cost between $150 and $200 a day, plus airfare.

With pricing like that, Footloose attracts hardly any young adults but mainly persons 35 to 55 (although participants can be much older). If you're in that age range, you may want to consider this dynamic vacation program.

EVER HEARD OF THE GREEN TORTOISE? ON IT, YOU STRETCH OUT & SLEEP ABOARD THE BUS.

Continuously operated for more than 30 years, and the only survivor of what used to be several such counterculture bus companies, the Green Tortoise has not only remained in business, but grown to fairly large size. It now offers not simply its classic transcontinental tours (14 days coast to coast, Boston to San Francisco and vice versa, during several months of the year) and its famous Los Angeles–to–San Francisco rides, but goes as far afield as Costa Rica and the Baja California peninsula of Mexico, and to numerous other destinations in North America. As you might expect, its low prices and convivial atmosphere attract some of the most congenial and dynamic people (of all ages) in America. And it also operates a fascinating website that you can access at www.greentortoise.com. Or phone ☎ **800/TORTOISE** (867-8647).

Green Tortoise is famous for removing seats from its buses and replacing them with platforms on which passengers place sleeping bags. Buses

On a Green Tortoise trip, everyone pitches in to buy the groceries or prepare the meals.

(the company has many of them, in continual operation) travel only at night, while passengers sleep ("stretch-out-and-sleep-while-we-drive" is the organization's slogan); daytimes they park near sightseeing attractions, and passengers can tour at their discretion. Passengers also share the task of shopping for groceries and cooking, which cuts costs and encourages a lot of social interaction.

$860 to $930, including food, is currently the all-inclusive price of the 14-day, transcontinental trip covering the country's major sights between Boston and San Francisco. A 3-day trip between Los Angeles and San Francisco is $240. All other prices are carefully displayed on the organization's website.

There's now a website for counterculture bus tours in Europe, North Africa & Australia

A number of bus companies in England, Scotland, Ireland, western Europe, North Africa, and Australia offer cheap, "counterculture" bus tours designed for youthful types and using modest guesthouses for accommodations. Some of the trips follow fixed itineraries, while others let you "hop on and off" at your own pace, stopping to inspect sites that most interest you before reboarding the next day's bus.

The most popular services in the British Isles, Europe, and North Africa are now all gathered together in one site at Radical Travel (www.radical travel.com), which represents the well-known Shamrocker Adventures (www.shamrockeradventures.com) of Ireland and Haggis Adventures (www.haggisadventures.com) covering Scotland, England, and Wales. Radical Travel also links directly to the Europe-wide service Busabout (www.busabout.com), which offers "Busabout Adventures" of set itineraries in Spain, Italy, Greece, Croatia, Morocco, and Egypt, and "Busabout Explorer" hop-on/hop-off service. The on-and-off pass is valid for the entire operating season (May–Oct) on your choice of loops through Spain, France, Italy, Switzerland, Germany, the Netherlands, Belgium, the Czech Republic, and Austria.

The hop-on/hop-off bus model has spread to many other countries popular among backpackers. In Australia it's called the Oz Experience (www.ozexperience.com). In New Zealand you're looking for the Kiwi Experience (www.kiwiexperience.com); and in South Africa it's the Baz Bus (www.bazbus.com). All are exceptional opportunities for the right kind of traveler.

"Busabout" travel, available on several continents, has attracted an audience of dynamic young people.

ADVENTURES FROM REI ADVENTURES

Typical of REI adventures are week-long trips kayaking the San Juan Islands or hiking Death Valley for $1,099 to $1,299 (not including airfare). These minivacations are run by REI, America's largest co-op chain of outdoors gear stores. Though REI tends to be pricier than most outfitters, it has trips on every continent and is ideal for those for whom being active is as important as the destination. Contact by phone at ☎ **800/622-2236**, or look them up online at www.reiadventures.com.

AFRICAN SAFARIS

THOSE 1-WEEK SAFARIS ARE PERFECTLY SUFFICIENT TO INTRODUCE THIS KIND OF VACATION TO THE AVERAGE AMERICAN

I've been writing for some time now about the short, week-long African safaris operated by Lion World Travel of Toronto, for under $2,500 per person, including round-trip air to Nairobi from New York City (via London). The reason this remarkable Canadian company can charge so little is that the trips are so relatively brief.

If you've ever been on an African safari, you'll agree with me, I think, that 5 days of lengthy games drives in Kenya are perfectly sufficient for most first-time safarigoers, surrounded as they are by large herds of wildebeest, giraffes, elephants, cheetahs, monkeys, rhino (in the rivers) and—most important—prides of lions.

Unlike safaris in South Africa, Botswana, and elsewhere, safaris in Kenya and neighboring Tanzania never fail to immerse the visitor in the natural world on the grandest scale. In the other countries, whole days can go by with only the hoofprints of a single animal to keep your anticipation alive. In Kenya and Tanzania, Africa comes close to guaranteeing an endless array of wildlife on nearly every day of the trip.

The experience of viewing wildlife in such quantities, seeing the eternal battle between predator and prey, experiencing what the world was like before human beings inhabited it, driving for hours on end through open countryside unmarred by roads or power lines, becomes something mystical, an important part of your life experience. Along with trips to Alaska or to more accessible wildlife areas such as Yellowstone National Park, a safari comes close to being an indispensable trip that every human being should enjoy at some point in their lives.

You contact Lion World Travel at www.lionworldtravel.com or ☎ 800/387-2706. Though it's a Canadian tour operator, its clientele is primarily from the United States.

CAMPING

WOULD YOU BELIEVE THERE'S A WEBSITE THAT LETS YOU PACK A TENT & SLEEP FOR FREE ACROSS THE COUNTRY?

FreeCampgrounds.com is a community-based bulletin board listing more than 1,700 places where you can camp for free across the country (though it is definitely strongest out West). Now obviously, unless you're an avid outdoors person or driving an RV, this may not be your cup of coffee/hot chocolate. But staying in a tent or RV can be an excellent way to save money on a long road trip.

Since the website is designed with an RV crowd in mind, many of its entries are for truck stops, such as Flying J, or in parking lots of such stores as Walmart seeking customers. But it also has a healthy listing of state parks, Bureau of Land Management parks, and other outdoorsy camping spots, making it an excellent tool for anyone looking for a free night's sleep.

Any member can post a listing of free places to spend the night, with details on whether the spot is offered or merely tolerated, the nearest town, the level of noise, a rating of how scenic it is (the parking lots fare poorly on this one), a list of amenities (mostly restrooms and RV hookups for water, electricity, and dumping stations), as well as helpful comments by other users.

CAMPGROUNDS ON THE OUTSKIRTS OF MOST EUROPEAN CITIES SUPPLY AN INTERESTING, INEXPENSIVE MEANS OF LODGING

In our increasingly frantic search for ways to visit Europe inexpensively, campgrounds and camping should not be overlooked.

Almost completely unknown to most American travelers, campgrounds are found on the outskirts of nearly every major European city; indeed, some European cities have as many as a dozen such camping sites in their outlying areas. And although they are usually in fairly remote neighborhoods, nearly all are on a bus or subway line that can whisk you downtown. Search hard for them, and you can also find a few prime camping spots near the historic centers of cities and towns.

Did you know you could camp in Paris along the banks of the Seine in the Bois de Boulogne park (www.campingparis.fr)? How about a campsite with a view overlooking the domes and bell towers of Florence from a hillside terrace in the Oltrarno district (www.ecvacanze.it/ing/michelangelo_home.asp)? Venice even has a campground by the beach on the island next to the Lido, just a short ferry ride from St. Mark's Square (www.camping-miramare.it). Some campgrounds are operated only in warm weather (roughly Easter through Oct or early Nov), but many stay open year-round.

The bill at a European campground can be a bit confusing, since you are usually charged an array of small fees—one for the site, another for each person, yet another for your vehicle—but the total usually ends up around $17 to $26 for a couple in a tent, up to $40 in the most popular campgrounds in the summer high season. Forgot your tent? You can usually rent one for $10 to $20.

If tents aren't your style, most European campgrounds also rent inexpensive bungalows sleeping two to six people and starting around $45 plus $10 to $14 per person—far less than the cost of even a cheap hotel. What's more, the bungalow's access to the campground facilities means you get amenities virtually no inexpensive hotel can offer: a swimming pool, an on-site grocery store, picnic tables, bars, and often a restaurant, grill, or pizzeria—to say nothing of the chance to make friends with vacationing Europeans. Campers tend to be a friendly lot, often insisting their temporary neighbors join them by the campfire or barbecue pit to share dinner and a bottle of wine. This type of invitation rarely comes from the couple staying in the hotel room next door.

National and local tourist offices always have lists of campgrounds (the better ones include them in the searchable accommodations databases on their websites; find them at www.worldtourismdirectory.com). You can also find listings for more than 8,500 European campgrounds at the site www.eurocampings.net, and some 1,500 more on the Polish site www.eurocamps.net (never fear; click on the little Union Jack flag at the top for an English version).

HIKING

FOOTSCAPE (OF BRITAIN) IS FOR THE HEALTHY & FOOTLOOSE

As more and more travelers look for active holidays on which to enjoy healthy exercise, more and more tour operators are looking for ways to cut the cost of that kind of vacation. The solution found by a British company called Footscape (www.footscape.co.uk) is to offer so-called self-guided walking tours. Although you receive prereserved accommodations for every night, and your luggage is transported from place to place, you are otherwise on your own. There is no guide, and you walk only with the people you've chosen, on itineraries for which you receive careful walking instructions. The area of Footscape's concentration is Dorset, on the Channel coast of England, and the price is almost always below $1,000 for a week-long holiday.

HITCHHIKING

FOR YOUNG—OR YOUNG IN SPIRIT—ADVENTURERS, TWO WEBSITES MAY GET YOU A RIDE TO WHERE YOU WANT TO GO

Now that the cost of transportation is rising so greatly, our more adventure-some readers may want to acquaint themselves with two specialist message boards for picking up free rides. These are Hitchhikers.org for travel throughout Europe and Digihitch (http://rideboard.digihitch.com) for the United States and Canada. Note that neither site requires that you stand by the side of a highway waving your thumb; both list available rides that people have offered, departing on certain dates, either for no charge at all other than your companionship on the ride, or else for a nominal fee that offsets some of the driver's expenses.

VOLUNTEER VACATIONS

VOLUNTEER VACATIONS ARE THE CURRENT CRAZE

For reasons hard to explain, but easy to speculate about, the volunteer vacation is currently surging, and people are flocking to places where they can work at a socially beneficial cause; we moderns apparently feel guilty about many things. The three leading organizations to arrange such vacations are, of course, the American Hiking Society (restoring trails and other facilities in national and state parks), the Sierra Club (every sort of environmental improvement), and Habitat for Humanity (construction of low-income housing). But perhaps the broadest program is that of Earthwatch, accessed at www.earthwatch.org, with which you volunteer to accompany a university-level scientist on various research expeditions. Though you pay heavily for such a privilege (but your fee is undoubtedly tax deductible, because it is largely a contribution to nonprofit research), the modest net cost seems well justified by the thrill of the effort and the sense of accomplishment.

OUT OF DOZENS OF SO-CALLED "VOLUNTEER VACATIONS," ONLY A FEW ARE TRULY LOW COST OR FREE

The "volunteer vacation" is a widely misunderstood travel concept. It's a program on which you travel to another community either at home or

Habitat for Humanity, the best-known working vacation, enlists volunteers to erect housing for low-income families.

abroad for the purpose of performing socially beneficial labor for others. You assist various groups in the building of low-cost housing, or teach English, or dig wells, or maintain hiking trails, or perform any number of other useful tasks.

But though you work hard at these arduous services, you don't usually receive free room and board in return, especially if the service you render is a short term effort of only 1, 2, or 3 weeks. The considerable planning, preparation and administration of such programs costs money, for which the sponsoring organization requires payment of a fee from the volunteer. And though such charges are usually much smaller that those of a commercial tour, they can be substantial, nonetheless, and almost never include transportation to the site, which you—the volunteer—must cover.

That having been said, some "volunteer" programs charge only reasonable and sometimes nominal sums, and a small handful do pick up your basic room and board. Here are two affordable, and soul-satisfying, examples of the volunteer vacation for adults of all ages.

Willing Workers on Organic Farms ("WWOOF"; www.wwoof.org) offers to its volunteers from all over the world (all ages, although most are young and earthy types) an opportunity to learn farming techniques while helping to run a network of mostly family-run organic farms in Australia, New Zealand, Canada, Europe, and Korea. You join a small team on each farm, pitch in with daily chores, and acquire first-hand organic horticulture techniques, such as pesticide-free planting and compost fertilizing. You can almost always count on some sheep herding, sowing, harvesting, milking of cows, and making of cheese and yogurt. Time commitment: usually a few days, but up to a few months, depending on your host farm. Cost: a $30 membership fee, and then your half-day's work pays for a full-day's room and meals. Airfare and other costs are the participants' responsibility. Requirements: a willing heart and a strong back, without a minimum or maximum age limit.

Wilderness Volunteers (☎ 928/556-0038; www.wildernessvolunteers. org) works with public land agencies to promote outdoor volunteering in America's wild lands. Each trip is a week long, has 12 or fewer participants who camp in tents or in a dorm, and includes such tasks as restoring streams, planting trees, repairing trails, or taking inventory of species on National Park, Forest Service, and other public lands. Guides do the cooking with the help of participants, and there's ample time to explore the wilderness you are helping to preserve. Groups vary in age, but the program tends to attract people from 20 to 40 who are active. Locations include Hawaii, California, Utah, Wyoming, Washington, Oregon, and Puerto Rico. Time commitment: 1 week. Cost: $239 per week (not including transportation to and from a park, and your own camping gear). Requirements: 16 years old and up, and physically fit.

Eureka! I've just found three more "volunteer vacations" that actually cost less than the commercial, nonvoluntary vacation.

Though everyone claims that "volunteer vacations" are currently the hot travel item, the majority of them are scarcely distinguishable from the commercial variety. (There's lots of blue-sky bombast in the travel world—and people who take advantage of the idealism of young Americans.) Here are three more that actually produce substantial improvements for low-income communities or vital repairs in the national and state parks—and also involve partially free lodgings and meals in exchange for your services:

Sierra Club Outings (☎ 415/977-5522; www.sierraclub.org/outings) in the United States and Canada are short stints at clearing trails in Nevada, maintaining beaches in Puerto Rico, preserving historic sites in Utah, tracking dolphin patterns on Midway Island, removing invasive plants in California, and performing a hundred other useful tasks in the outdoors. Groups of 10 to 18 people (including a leader and cook) stay in accommodations ranging from tents to lodges. Many participants are in their mid-40s to early 50s, and include retired folk. Some trips can be strenuous, but most are accessible to everyone. Time commitment: Most trips are 1 week, some are 10 days. Cost: Almost all are around $500 for a full week, some $100 more. Requirements: age 18 and up. In studying the website, be sure to winnow out the service trips from a larger number of sightseeing trips that Sierra now offers. Be sure to click on "service" wherever that term appears on the site.

La Sabranenque (☎ 716/836-8698; www.sabranenque.com) works to preserve and restore the unique ancient architecture of the Provence region of France and in far northern regions of Italy. Work includes construction and restoration of medieval stone buildings, castles, and ramparts. From March to October, volunteers labor at sites with experienced technicians, acquiring traditional Mediterranean techniques of stone cutting, roof tiling, flooring, arch and vault construction, and masonry. Costs cover double occupancy in restored stone houses and home-cooked, family-style meals with your co-volunteers (groups are limited to 35 people). Volunteers are of all ages, not just the young. Time commitment: 2 to 3 weeks. Cost: around $600 for 1 week, but only $745 for 2 weeks, not including airfare. Requirement: ages 18 and up, and physically fit. (No construction skills or knowledge of French or Italian is necessary.)

El Porvenir (☎ 608/544-2086; www.elporvenir.org) builds village water projects in now-peaceful Nicaragua. Volunteers in 6- to 10-person "brigades" join with local residents and bilingual guides to construct wells, latrines, and community washing facilities. Apart from work, there's time to visit and converse with Nicaraguan organizations and groups. Lodgings are in private homes, village schools, or modest hotels, and there's a recreational weekend at a beach thrown in as well. Participants' ages vary; church and family groups are common. Time commitment: 2 weeks. Cost: $800, including food, lodging, and land transportation (but not airfare). Requirements: physically fit. No Spanish language or construction experience is needed.

OPERATING ARDUOUS VOLUNTEER VACATIONS, AN ORGANIZATION CALLED GLOBAL CITIZENS NETWORK MAKES NO CONCESSION TO DILETTANTES

Some—not all, but some—of the so-called "volunteer vacations" are obvious fakes conceived to satisfy the ego needs of the organizer, and conferring no real benefit upon the communities to which the volunteers go. Nor do the volunteers really participate in the life of the communities they visit.

The Global Citizens Network of St. Paul, Minnesota (☎ 800/644-9292 or 651/644-0960), is, by contrast, the real thing. It sends groups of Americans to indigenous communities of underdeveloped areas (including our own Navajo reservations), where they share the lives of the people they visit and labor at much-needed community projects. In its write-up of a trip to Kenya, the organization bluntly warns: "There may not be running water or electricity. Participants will likely use latrines and bathe using bucket baths." On a trip to remote Mexico, it writes: "Meals will be simple, traditional fare—rice, beans, tortillas and vegetables." At the Navajo Nation in Arizona, "Team members stay in the Chapter House, sleeping on the floor in their community room. Many bring air mattresses if desired."

Trips vary considerably in length and price: as, for example, 8 days to the Navajo reservation, for $800 per person (plus airfare to Arizona); 10 days to a remote Mexican village for $1,400 (plus airfare to Mexico); 2¹/₂ weeks to Kenya, in the Maasai Mara, for $2,100 plus airfare. Payments are apparently tax deductible because of the charitable nature of the work.

You'll get the full flavor of an unusual program suitable for only the most dedicated travelers, by going to www.globalcitizens.org.

GOT AGRICULTURAL SKILLS? IF SO, YOU CAN LIVE FOR FREE ON A VOLUNTEER VACATION RUN BY THE HEIFER PROJECT.

Teaching unskilled villagers in Third World countries about animal husbandry (cattle and poultry), enabling them to produce their own milk, cheese, eggs, butter, and meat, has been the goal for many successful years of a "volunteer vacation" activity called the Heifer Project International, which is sponsored by various Protestant denominations. Volunteers are sent to developing countries at the organization's expense, and live there for free for periods of 3 weeks to several months. Though, theoretically, volunteers can themselves be unskilled at various agricultural tasks (such persons are accepted occasionally for a particular project), most volunteers undergo a screening process, and only those able to contribute substantial knowledge and skills to the villagers are accepted on particular trips. To learn more about Heifer Project International, phone one of its offices in Little Rock, Arkansas, at ☎ 800/422-1311, and ask to speak with either Ray White or Jennifer Pierce.

YOGA

A "YOGA VACATION" AT KRIPALU IN THE BERKSHIRES IS NONTHREATENING, MODERATELY PRICED & JUST WHAT YOU NEED

In this enlightened era, you no longer have to be an aging hippie or a New Age-er to appreciate the relaxing, healthy, and economical vacation opportunities offered by the ever-growing number of centers and resorts devoted to yoga. A lifestyle rather than a religion, these once-exotic exercises have become part of the mainstream culture, popular with every kind of American from bearded rabbis to high-powered businesswomen seeking a break from stress. And the most mainstream of all the centers is Kripalu in the Berkshires.

Kripalu Center for Yoga and Health (☎ 866/200-5203; www.kripalu. org) in Lenox, Massachusetts, is America's largest year-round yoga facility and one of its best known; it houses 300 guests at a time (about 15,000 per year). The beautiful 30-acre spread in the rolling Berkshire Mountains has forests, meadows, trails, gardens, and a lake. Its single most popular (and economical) program is "Retreat and Renewal," with classes in yoga or "DansKinetics," meditation, and workshops. There's plenty of free time for walks, dips in the lake, or (in season) a concert at nearby Tanglewood, summer home of the Boston Symphony Orchestra. Vegetarian meals are good, and lodgings aren't fancy but are clean and comfortable.

Although prices at Kripalu vary according to the theme and activities of its changing programs, nevertheless most of its 2-night stays currently cost $417 per person in dormitory accommodations, $447 to $499 in shared rooms, including all meals each day and full participation in program activities (lectures, classes, group yoga). Numerous 5-night programs cost $700 in dorms, $765 to $890 in shared rooms, including the very same features.

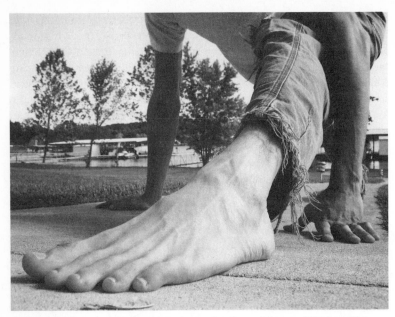

At the Kripalu Institute in the Berkshires of Massachusetts, yoga is regarded as benefiting mind and body.

FROM THOSE FRIENDLY FOLKS AT THE SIVANANDA VISHNU MOVEMENT: ANOTHER KIND OF YOGA VACATION (FOR A MUCH CHEAPER $84 A DAY)

Kripalu Institute at Lenox, Massachusetts, with its largely American staff of instructors, presents only a few practitioners of yoga and related disciplines from India. Readers anxious to take a more serious plunge into all the aspects of yoga, including the spiritual ones, can choose among a half-dozen or so U.S. and North American ashrams of the Sivananda Vishnu movement founded by the late Swami Vishnu-devananda. Their centers, open all year, charge as little as $84 per person per night, including accommodations, meals, yoga exercises, and lectures, at locations scattered around the United States and even in the Bahamas. You'll find these Sivananda Vedanta Yoga Centers described at www.sivananda.org.

The outstanding branch of the Sivananda movement, as you'd expect, is on a picturesque stretch of white-sand beach right across the bay from Nassau, on Paradise Island, the Bahamas, where it offers a sensational vacation opportunity. Here, meditation and chanting begin at 6am, followed by a 2-hour "hatha yoga" (physical yoga) class and veggie brunch (food varies, I've been told, from very good to adequate). Exercise and meditation are required of you, but postbrunch hours are totally free for swimming, snorkeling, or maybe a boat ride into town. There's no lunch (it's a two-meal-a-day, light-on-calories environment), but dinner is served, and afterwards there's more meditation and chanting, perhaps followed by a lecture or concert. Lights are out by 10:30pm, and falling asleep after such a busy schedule is usually no problem.

Drawbacks? I've been told that the small staff is sometimes overwhelmed when the usual 100 to 200 guests increase to nearly 300 during holiday weeks. Some rooms have no closets or bedside lamps, and there are, as you'd expect, no private baths, radios, or TVs. But private rooms (including meals and instruction) are under $100 per person double, and prices are even cheaper for dorm accommodations and tent sites. Call ☎ 800/263-9642 for more information, or access the website listed above.

Chapter Six

"This Land Is Your Land, This Land Is My Land . . ."

AFFORDABLE TRAVEL & VACATIONS IN THE UNITED STATES

The U.S. dollar is currently a weak shadow of its former self, exchanged at such a poor rate against the euro, the British pound, and the Japanese yen that travel has become rather expensive for Americans wanting to visit western Europe, Great Britain, or Japan (the dollar is still strong in Central and South America, Australia, India, Indonesia, and in most Asian countries other than Japan). Travel within the United States has therefore taken on greater importance, and this chapter seeks to explore some of the better opportunities: to the great national parks, to theater cities, to New England, and to some of the lesser-known wine districts where lodgings and tastings are refreshing in price.

ALASKA

FERRY TALE: SAIL THE ALASKAN FERRIES FOR LOW PRICES & LOCAL EXPOSURE

The bulk of Americans taking cruises off the coast of Alaska are passengers on big-name, 14-story-high ships carrying at least 2,000 passengers and sometimes more. Every morning, they flood into the various port cities of Alaska, cameras in hand, wallets at the ready, buses awaiting them, and then—late afternoon—they escape back into the ship's world of food, Las Vegas–style acts, and general luxury. As dusk descends, some determined nature lovers squint at the humpbacks and glaciers through the small portholes of pricey outside cabins.

You might want to consider a more adventurous approach to the 49th state: the Alaska Marine Highway System. Since almost all of Alaska's southeastern cities are blocked from each other by impassable terrain and an absence of roads, ferries are often the only mode of travel. Several times a week, the ferries transport several hundred passengers (and quite a few cars) between various cities: Ketchikan, Wrangell, Petersburg, Juneau, Haines, Skagway, and sometimes Sitka.

The advantage of the Marine Highway over the big-name cruises? Authenticity, flexibility, and low price. You, not the execs at Holland America, decide where to go and what to see. The digs aren't exactly glamorous, but that's also the point of preference for many travelers. There are no discos or casinos, just some lounges, bars, a cafeteria area, and a million-dollar view. There are also cabins for those who require walls, a private bath, and a bed for overnight trips.

Previous page: An Alaskan cruise passes awesome, even mystical scenery, places where no human has ever set foot or is ever likely to.

For everyone else, there's simply a deck and the open sky. Many choose to sleep in chairs or set up tents affixed to the deck by duct tape. This is the allure of the ferries—the adventure, the possibility of meeting local people, the hands-on approach to travel.

For ferry fees and schedules, call the Alaska Marine Highway System at ☎ **800/642-0066,** or log on to www.ferryalaska.com.

AMERICA ON A BUDGET

NAPA VALLEY ISN'T THE ONLY AREA OF AMERICA WITH CLUSTERS OF FINE WINERIES

Visiting the wineries of America has become a major tourist activity, one that used to be focused almost exclusively on the Napa Valley of Northern California. Today, a number of almost-equally compelling and far less expensive alternatives have emerged.

In upstate New York, the 19 original wineries of the Finger Lakes region have now become 239 wineries. (Here, along with wine tasting, many tourists also choose to visit the Corning Museum of Glass.) In Virginia, a "trail" of 21 top wineries has developed near Thomas Jefferson's Monticello. In southern Oregon, the area around Ashland has become popular not simply for its Shakespeare Festival but for the pinot noir of its many wineries. And in central California, the area around Santa Barbara has become famous as

The wineries of Oregon compare well with any other and are far less crowded than their more famous counterparts in California.

a result of the wine movie *Sideways* but remains cheaper to visit than the Napa Valley.

STAYING IN AN UNFAMILIAR U.S. CITY? DON'T OVERLOOK THE FREE OR NOMINALLY PRICED SERVICES OF THE PUBLIC LIBRARY.

Among the services presently offered by almost all U.S. public libraries are not simply Internet access and use of computers, but faxing and photocopying, for which you'd pay big bucks to a Kinko's or a hotel business center. You should keep that in mind when you travel. Internet and computer use is usually free at a public library. Laser copies can cost as little as 10¢, and photocopies only 5¢. And thus, the institution that plays such a big part in the lives of many of us is handier still when you find yourself away from home.

CHEAPEST GOLF VACATION IN AMERICA? IT'S IN FLORIDA, IN SEPTEMBER (OF COURSE).

The Plantation Inn and Golf Resort (9301 W. Fort Island Trail, Crystal River, FL 34429) is centered around a spiffy manor house with 126 rooms on the Gulf Coast of Florida near Tampa, with a stunningly beautiful par-72, 18-hole championship course, and a 9-hole executive course specifically designed for training and practice. The resort offers every amenity imaginable, and yet during the month of September it has a special of $99 per person single and $72 per person double per night (for accommodations in a comfortable room) *and* unlimited golf. The reason, as you might expect, is weather. And yet the Tampa area isn't nearly as hot as in southern Florida, and if you'll simply avoid golfing during the peak of the midday heat, you should do fine. Go to www.plantationinn.com or phone ☎ 800/632-6262.

THE RIGHT KIND OF WORLD-MINDED PERSON WILL ENJOY A SUMMER VACATION WITH LIKE-MINDED PEOPLE AT AN UNPRETENTIOUS RESORT CENTER IN NEW HAMPSHIRE

The World Fellowship Center of New Hampshire is a nonprofit summer vacation camp that deserves publicity. Nearly 60 years old, it is inexpensive and serious, devoted to seminars and classes on important issues in world affairs and personal growth. Weekly programs take place from late June to mid-September, in a stunning setting on a mile-long pond, with 453 acres of forested trails, ideal for afternoon recreation following a morning of discussion. The charge for lodging and all meals can run as low as $309 per adult per week in June or $330 per week in August, with a high of $424 to $452 per person in better rooms, including all three meals. If you'd care to enjoy the company of vital people seeking to better understand the big issues, you'd be well advised to register soon. You can get further information from www.worldfellowship.org.

NATIONAL PARKS

STILL UNDECIDED ABOUT SUMMER? PICK A NATIONAL PARK!

Don't just stand there; get in your car and drive to a U.S. national park!

They offer accommodations for every purse, and for as low as $60 a night per family of four for a tent cabin with comfortable beds, platform deck, and heater. Space for your own tent and sleeping bag, or for your RV, is cheaper still, almost nominal in cost. Cafeterias in every park sell bountiful, tasty meals for as little as $10. In some of the larger parks, free-of-charge shuttle buses take you from one major area to another.

And the atmosphere within is one of near-pure, small-d democracy. Although every major park has one very upscale lodge (the Ahwahnee in Yosemite, El Tovar in Grand Canyon), the overwhelming bulk of lodgings are in rustic inexpensive cabins, tent cabins, and tents. People wear rough sports clothing, generally park their cars in lots that are out of sight, and engage in nature hikes as their chief activity.

Most tourists in Yosemite, Yellowstone, and Grand Canyon appear, visibly, to walk about in a state of near enchantment. (We are so surrounded in our daily lives with highways, pavements, and vehicles that we seem dumbstruck by vast areas of conservation and ecological purity.) Stand for a moment on a trail and view the faces of your fellow visitors and you will find smiles of relaxation and contentment on almost all of them. In their impact on your sense of well-being, the great U.S. national parks are like a giant Jacuzzi, a massive massage table, a steam room. Wealthy patrons of elegant spas spend upwards of $600 a day for such contentment, and even then often fail to achieve the relief from stress that any one of these wonders of nature provide.

At Yosemite, the great activity is to walk on level paths through the famous valley or along mountain trails described in turn as "easy," "moderate," and "strenuous" in helpful free literature. Except for evening films and lectures (again free) on natural science and environmental subjects; except for visiting on-site museums of forestry and Native American history; except for boarding one of the very rare motorcoach tours of outlying and remote places, you simply walk, at your own pace, periodically stopping to enjoy the emotion of viewing some of the most beautiful vistas on Earth. The Alps and the Himalayas have their admirers, but the great natural sights of the U.S. parks, especially those in the West, compare respectably to them.

If you have never seen the geologic formations and awesome waterfalls of Yosemite, if you have never gasped at the extraordinary vista of the Grand Canyon, if you have never marveled at the steam spouting from the earth of Yellowstone, you should make an immediate resolution to go to one of them. And once there, you will resolve to return as often as you can, and to visit others in their turn.

A trip to Yellowstone National Park is one of the blessings of living in or visiting America

---

It is, of course, a bit of a trip. You approach it from Bozeman or Billings, Montana, or from Jackson, Wyoming, and few of us live anywhere near those towns. But after a long drive through the American West, your exertions are repaid by what is, arguably, the top attraction of America.

Yellowstone! Its wildlife—including majestic buffalo and elk—are more diverse and numerous than in any other park. It is, according to experts, the last remaining fully intact ecosystem in the lower 48 states—all in an area larger than Rhode Island and Delaware combined.

Its geysers, steam emissions, hot springs, and mudpots are sobering evidence that our thin crust of earth lies on top of molten rock ("magma"). Yellowstone itself is the largest volcano on earth, a vast caldera 50 miles in each direction that was pushed upward to an average elevation of 8,000 feet by an epic eruption occurring as recently as 640,000 years ago. When you walk through the park on boardwalks that protect you from the steam and boiling waters emerging from cracks in the land's surface, you are made to consider the transitory nature of humankind and of our civilization. At some point in the future, Yellowstone—with perhaps the thinnest earth crust anywhere in the world, and more geysers than Iceland or New Zealand—will erupt again.

Generally, if you are to enjoy the magic of Yellowstone, you must schedule your visit for between May and the end of September. My own visit took place in September, and although one particular road—the mountainous Bear's Tooth Highway—was already closed by snow, almost everything else within Yellowstone was functioning normally, nearly all the lodges were open and thriving, and thousands of lightly clad visitors (wearing "layers" and removing outside jackets and sweaters as the day warmed up) were reveling in the park's extraordinary sights and phenomena.

Obviously, you will need a car. Though numerous national motorcoach tours go whizzing through in a day or two (what sacrilege!) and travel agents in the entrance town of Gardiner will even escort you on visits of 5 hours and less, it is ludicrous to schedule less than 3 days for a thorough experience. Each of a number of widely separated areas—Mammoth Hot Springs, the Canyon Area, the Lake Area, Old Faithful and its surroundings—can consume a full day of intensive and rewarding sightseeing. I'm still recalling the sight of giant herds of bison crossing the road in front of my car; the thrill of Old Faithful casting its plume of water and steam high in the air; and the awesome vision of "the Grand Canyon of the Yellowstone," a respectable runner-up to Arizona's.

THE DECISION TO REQUEST A YELLOWSTONE ASSOCIATION GUIDE IS PARTICULARLY SMART

She didn't wear the Stetson hat and distinctive green-and-brown uniform of a park ranger. Her only ID was a metal name tag pinned to her jacket. But the guide from the Yellowstone Association (www.yellowstone association.org) who met us for breakfast at the Lake Yellowstone Hotel, and then spent the entire day escorting us by van and on foot through a vast swath of the Yellowstone wilderness, was as highly motivated, well informed, and delightful as any member of the National Parks Service.

Nearly every major U.S. national park has a nonprofit "association" which assists in the education of park visitors. Yosemite, for instance, has one, and Yellowstone has a particularly impressive one offering a wide range of "Lodging and Learning" programs—"Trails through Yellowstone," "Yellowstone for Families," "Springtime in Wonderland," "Autumn in Wonderland," and several more—that combine 3 or 4 nights of lodging and meals; in-park transportation by van; and expert instruction by naturalists, biologists, and geologists, who can teach you all you want to know about the complex wildlife, geysers, and hot springs in America's oldest national park.

Their full-time services, and the room and board you also receive in park cabins with private bath, can run as low as $150 a day per adult and $90 a day per child.

On our recent trip to Yellowstone, my wife, Roberta, and I opted for one of the Yellowstone Association's 1-day "Ed-Ventures"—an intense 8 hours spent wildlife-watching and hiking/walking among the thermal geology and unique scenery of this American wonderland in Wyoming. The Ed-Venture charge is around $400 for up to seven people, so if you are lucky enough to have several others scheduled for the day of your Ed-Venture, the entire experience—including transportation and the constant services and lecture-commentary of a Yellowstone Association guide—can amount to less than $75 a person.

There are, of course, numerous free-of-charge walking tours of 45 minutes or so that park rangers also offer at different sites in Yellowstone, and we greatly enjoyed these quick interludes operated by idealistic park service employees. And there are some ranger-led tours of up to 6 hours, for a modest fee. But the ability of the rangers to conduct longer tours using transport has been severely reduced in recent years by cutbacks in appropriations mandated by Congress. And what once was free, no longer is. Fortunately, the Yellowstone Association, staffed in part by former rangers, has taken up the challenge. Call ☎ 307/344-5566 to register for "Lodging and Learning"; call ☎ 307/344-2294 to register for a personal Ed-Venture. And for more elaborate group programs, operated by the association, call ☎ 307/344-2591.

IN CONSIDERING AN INEXPENSIVE U.S. VACATION IN THE DEAD OF WINTER, KEEP IN MIND OUR NATIONAL PARKS

Is it possible to visit any of the great Western national parks in winter? The answer is definitely yes. Joshua Tree National Park and Death Valley National Park are in Southern California, desert parks whose temperatures

Death Valley National Park in California is the lowest spot in North America and often encounters temperatures of 120°F (49°C) in summer; go in winter.

are ideal in winter. You'll find miles of well-marked hiking trails, horseback riding, jeep tours of abandoned mining camps, and swimming in pools fed by hot springs.

In Northern California, Yosemite National Park stays open in winter (despite frosty temperatures), offering downhill and cross-country skiing and even a major outdoor skating rink. The views are just as enthralling in winter as in summer, and a great many nearby residents choose this time to visit.

Yellowstone? Though one or two winter lodges are open, the winter weather here can be so very severe and forbidding that only the hardiest of adventurers chooses to go at that time, mainly for up-close views of the wildlife that remains in the park at those times. Still, it's possible to come, and the toughest of outdoor types comes to visit and to stay next to great fireplaces all ablaze in the big "snow lodge" located next to Old Faithful.

INDULGE IN A WINTER WONDERLAND OF FREE ACTIVITIES AT THE GREATEST NATIONAL PARK EAST OF THE MISSISSIPPI

Pigeon Forge, Tennessee, in the Great Smoky Mountains, goes all-out to entice wintertime visitors with a week's worth of amazing free events, workshops, and guided hikes.

Pigeon Forge's annual Wilderness Week (it was scheduled for Jan 10–17 in 2009) brings some 100 experts to town (or out of the local woodwork) to offer free lectures on subjects from local Civil War sites to regional biodiversity, workshops on everything from birding to nature photography, and lessons as disparate as fly fishing and mandolin or dulcimer playing. There are also 6 to 10 daily guided hikes offered in the park, ranging from 11-mile mountain treks to in-the-field photography workshops to evening "Owl Prowls." And to repeat: The best part is that all of it is free.

For more information and precise schedules, phone ☎ 800/ WINTERFEST (946-8373) or log on to www.mypigeonforge.com/winterfest.asp.

AUTUMN IN MONTANA BRINGS OUTDOOR VACATIONS AT BARGAIN RATES, ESPECIALLY AT THE GREAT NATIONAL PARKS

By mid-October there's snow; but September in Montana's Glacier National Park is usually quite fantastic in terms of climate and foliage. In the fall, lakes and hiking trails are far less crowded than in summer, and visitors are far more likely to spot moose, bighorn sheep, and even bear. Special nightly rates of $100 or so for lodging are available for select dates during September at historic, upscale hotels such as Glacier Park Lodge & Resort and Many Glacier Hotel. In summer, guests seldom find a room at either of these hotels for under $150. By far the best value, however, is just over the Canadian border, in the adjoining Waterton Lakes National Park. Rooms at the gorgeous Prince of Wales Hotel—one of the most photographed hotels in the world—generally start under $300 in August, but several dates in September are available for around $100. Phone ☎ 406/892-2525, or go to www.glacierparkinc.com for reservations.

OUR NATIONAL PARKS ARE UNDER ATTACK

At the famous thermal hot springs known as the Morning Glory Pool, in Yellowstone National Park, the color of the liquid periodically turns from turquoise to dull green because heedless visitors throw coins, stones, and other debris into the water, and there is insufficient staff to clean up after them. In all the great park, only two geologists are on staff.

Elsewhere in other parks, roads, bridges, and historic buildings are in obvious need of repair and are visibly deteriorating. The conditions in which park rangers and other employees are required to live can be unbearably primitive.

Throughout the National Park Service, experienced rangers and administrators have resigned or retired in protest. Under the last administration, their ire was especially directed at a policy statement by the Department of Interior's deputy assistant secretary, opening all national parks to snowmobiling and permitting personal watercraft and noisy helicopters to roam unimpeded over such national jewels as the Great Smoky Mountains and Glacier national parks. We can only hope that other attitudes will prevail in future years, and public concern needs to be expressed.

YOU CAN FIGHT BACK AGAINST THOSE BENIGHTED TYPES THAT STARVE OUR NATIONAL PARKS

You may be receiving in the mail various fundraising appeals from the National Parks Conservation Association (www.npca.org). This venerable nonprofit group has over 85 years of advocacy under its belt, defending a parks system that is one of America's foremost treasures—for environmentalists as much as vacationers. The NPCA rightly warns that much of the remarkable legacy of our national parks has been under attack by drastic, insistent underfunding as well as by campaigns to open more and more of this precious resource to polluting, terrain-destroying vehicles, oil and gas drilling, excessive logging, and road building. We should all heed this organization's urgent message, and contribute to the cost of its work.

Of the Grand Canyon, Theodore Roosevelt said, "Leave it as it is. You can not improve on it. The ages have been at work on it, and man can only mar it."

IF YOU'VE NEVER BEEN TO THE GRAND CANYON, LATE FALL & WINTER ARE FINE TIMES TO GO

Indispensable and thrilling, it's one of the great natural wonders of the world, and its South Rim is open to the public all year round. You obviously must see it at some point in your life, and the best time to do so is in late fall and winter, when the crowds have fled and the entire overwhelming sight is viewable in peace and quiet. That's also when prices plunge. From around November 25 until early March (except for Christmas and President's Week exclusions), all the great lodges of the South Rim reduce their basic price to under $100 per room (Maswik South, Yavapai West, Maswik North, and Yavapai East). Go to www.grandcanyonlodges.com and don't delay your decision too long.

THEATER

WHAT'S THE TOP TOURIST ATTRACTION IN AMERICA?

A caller to my Sunday radio program put this question to me. My answer? Those provocative small playhouses operated in such dynamic theater cities as New York, Minneapolis, and Seattle; they alone can justify almost any trip. The tiny off-Broadway and off-off-Broadway stages—where little-known playwrights present their works—have been the major means by which controversial new ideas and concerns have broken out of academia and into the popular consciousness: apartheid in South Africa (the plays of Athol Fugard); civil rights in the United States (James Baldwin's *Blues for Mr. Charlie*, LeRoi *Jones' Dutchman*); feminism in western nations (plays by Caryl Churchill, *The Vagina Monologues* by Eve Ensler); the AIDS crisis and acceptance of homosexuals (Larry Kramer's *The Normal Heart*); the plight of the young black woman (Ntozake Shange's *For Colored Girls . . .*); and many others. They have changed America. It is disappointing to find tourists flocking to the too-often mindless musicals and neglecting to patronize the smaller theaters where profound new issues are being raised.

THEATER TICKETS

THE SMART TRAVELER USES THE INTERNET TO BUY REDUCED-PRICE TICKETS TO SHOWS & EVENTS PRIOR TO ARRIVING AT THE DESTINATION

It's hard to imagine that any savvy traveler isn't already aware of the recent explosion in online "secondary market" ticket sites—which is just a fancy term for virtual ticket scalpers. The difference is, this kind of scalping is increasingly tolerated, even encouraged, by the industry. At the very least, you won't get into any trouble using the tickets bought on these sites (though some sports teams still penalize season ticket holders discovered reselling their seats).

The biggest players are StubHub (www.stubhub.com), bought by eBay in 2007, and TicketsNow (www.ticketsnow.com), purchased by Ticketmaster, though you should always check competitors, such as TheaterMania.com, RazorGator (www.razorgator.com), and EZTicketSearch.com. Most of these sites limit the bulk of their offerings to venues in the United States, though shows on London's West End do crop up sometimes at TheaterMania.com (as well as at the TKTS outlet in London).

These players excel at providing three categories of tickets: discounts on shows, concerts, plays, and other regularly scheduled events; regular-price tickets for sold-out events; and impossible-to-obtain tickets at a premium price (so, yes, you can get Super Bowl tickets—if you have an extra $3,000 lying around). So if attending a show, concert, or game is part of your upcoming travel plans, you owe it to yourself to check out these sites.

BUT FOR SOME THEATER TICKETS, IT'S BEST TO WAIT UNTIL YOU GET THERE

People write to me that they are planning to represent their company at a convention in Las Vegas but then would like to stay on for a few more days on their own, and where can they get good prices at hotels and evening performances? I respond not simply with the key Las Vegas websites for discounts at hotels, but with the advice that they wait to buy their show tickets until they arrive in Vegas and can go to the two half-price ticket booths that now operate on the Strip. Those kiosks are a real money saver, and depending on the time of year they will even sell reduced-price seats to the popular Cirque du Soleil show that is normally sky high in price. All over the nation, theaters with unsold seats sell them at sacrificial rates on the day of performance, at special central kiosks or ticket booths maintained for that purpose.

Chapter Seven

A New Way to Visit the Old World

OFFSETTING THAT DRAMATIC DECLINE IN THE U.S. DOLLAR

Among all the destinations favored by Americans, Europe has been hit the hardest by a combination of increased airfares and harsh exchange rates. This chapter lays out the basic choices and tactics that a cost-conscious tourist will use to overcome those problems. It deals with the lower costs found in most countries of Eastern Europe, with the seasonal differences in the cost of European travel, and with the many new approaches toward transportation, accommodations, and meals that can greatly lower the cost of a European vacation.

By adapting your travel habits to the new conditions of Europe, by making a deliberate choice of less costly categories of lodgings (which turn out, in many cases, to be far more pleasant than standard ones), by emphasizing free attractions and public transportation, and by taking a number of other steps outlined in the chapter, you can continue to travel in Europe affordably.

EASTERN EUROPE

AS SOON AS YOU CROSS THE OLD BOUNDARY OF THE IRON CURTAIN, PRICES (& CROWD LEVELS) DROP DRAMATICALLY IN EVERY MAJOR CITY OTHER THAN ONE (I'LL GET TO THAT)

While three-star hotels in major western European cities these days start around $120 to $150 (and quickly rise to $250 or more), the same quality of hotel can be had for half as much in such places as Krakow, Ljubljana, Budapest, and Sofia.

In Eastern Europe, and despite the drop of the dollar against the euro (which isn't used in the east), beer is usually priced at less than $1, rental rooms sleeping two can go for under $30, and full meals can ring in at $10 to $15. It is a slice of the Old World as it was 20 years ago—affordable, accessible, and just waiting to be explored.

Plus, compared to the millions who descend upon London, Paris, and Rome each year, a mere fraction makes it to the glorious and well-preserved capitals, villages, and countryside of Eastern Europe, leaving it wide open for you to discover. Go castle hopping in Romania rather than along the Rhine, tour the vineyards of Hungary instead of Tuscany or Provence, and you'll not only save money, you'll discover a whole side to Europe ignored by most tour companies.

Previous page: The costs of a European vacation are far less in Eastern Europe, making a tourist mecca of Croatia and its standout attraction, Dubrovnik.

You can explore 1,240 miles of Croatian coastline peppered by timeless fishing villages and dotted with 1,185 islands. Its Dalmatian Coast is anchored on one end by the medieval city of Dubrovnik and on the other by Split, its historic center actually carved from the remains of the ancient Roman Emperor Diocletian's palace.

In Kraków, Poland, you can bargain for amber jewelry and hand-carved chess sets in the ancient covered market on the main square. In Ljubljana, you can sit under a willow at a riverside cafe in the heart of town and enjoy a sandwich of garlicky salami while gazing beyond the baroque building facades to the city's miniature castle perched stop its hill. In Bulgaria you can wander the cobblestone streets of Plovdiv, sip plum brandy at a Black Sea resort, or pay just $15 to stay at the famous Rila Monastery, a grandiose medieval construction packed with painted icons amidst green mountains.

I did mention one exception to this rule that Eastern Europe is cheaper, and that exception is Prague, which is still riding a 15-year wave of "must-see" status as a gorgeous and bohemian Eastern European capital. This unrelenting popularity has honestly made Prague pricier than Paris these days (not to mention more crowded). Prague is still a lovely and worthwhile city, but don't expect to find it a bargain by any stretch (also, know that the taverns are no longer filled with penniless intellectuals reading Kafka over an 80¢ beer; they're filled with crowds of tourists, fresh off the bus, paying $10 for their beer and looking around curiously for the penniless intellectuals reading Kafka).

EUROPE ON A BUDGET

THE DECLINE IN VALUE OF THE U.S. DOLLAR IS QUITE SEVERE & NEEDS TO BE SERIOUSLY DEALT WITH BY EUROPE-BOUND TRAVELERS

The full impact of the decline of the dollar against the euro and the British pound isn't felt when you're actually in Europe, but several weeks later, when you begin receiving your credit card statements for all the purchases you made, you will realize how puny the American dollar has become.

The dollar (when I last visited Europe) had sunk to a level of nearly $1.60 for 1 euro. But when commissions and a credit card fee were added, the actual rate on my statement came closer to $1.70 per euro. At the time we went to press, the dollar had risen to about $1.40 per euro. Recently, the dollar settled at a level of $1.45 per pound. But with credit card fees, the actual calculation will be more than $1.60 per pound.

Because of these exchange rates, costs for U.S. travelers in Britain have become outlandish. Costs on the continent of Europe have remained more reasonable for Americans, but they are still substantial. It is more important than ever that when you travel in Europe, you lower your expectations and requirements by at least one category: You no longer stay in first-class hotels but in tourist class-hotels; you eat modestly at restaurants where the locals eat, and you split courses with your travel companion. You use public transportation. Arriving at an airport, you pass up taxis and board a bus. You shop for nothing—because nothing is cheaper than what you'd pay at home. And by adopting those frugal attitudes, you continue to enjoy one of the greatest of all travel experiences: Europe.

A big secret of European rail travel: The regional networks offer whopping discounts on their own websites

Ever heard of Thalys? It's the network of high-speed trains that link Paris to numerous cities in Belgium, the Netherlands, and northern Germany (mainly Aachen and Cologne). A little-known fact is that the website of Thalys is constantly offering 50%, 60%, and even greater last-minute discounts on its trains operating between Paris, Belgium, the Netherlands, and northern Germany. If you'll go to www.thalys.com, you'll find sales of that sort currently being offered, and available nowhere else.

Another way to overcome the low value of the U.S. dollar against the euro is to avoid the central tourist areas

Pick any popular area, where tour buses prowl and hotels and restaurants charge a premium. Now shift your gaze slightly north, south, east, or west and you'll find an area that is undoubtedly just as attractive yet far less trammeled and, hence, less expensive. It almost goes without saying that, as with any strategy that takes you off the beaten path, this also offers you a chance to have a more unique and rewarding travel experience away from the madding crowds that infest the most popular areas.

Here are a few illustrations to prove the point. Millions of visitors descend each year upon the beaches and towns of Provence, yet relatively few venture further east along the Mediterranean coast to France's Languedoc region, also full of sunny beaches, Roman ruins, mighty castles, fine wines, and pastel-washed medieval towns.

For every hundred tourists who drive the Ring of Kerry and kiss the Blarney Stone in western Ireland, maybe 10 head just north up the coast into County Clare, famed for its traditional music and dramatic landscapes—and perhaps only one or two of those visitors might continue up into County Sligo, where postcard towns surround roofless abbeys and forlorn Celtic tombs atop windswept hills.

Most visitors to Andalusia stick to the popular western half of the region along the Costa del Sol of the Mediterranean coast and the inland cities of Seville, Cordoba, and Granada; few discover the charms of the eastern, Atlantic Ocean half of the region: the *pueblos blancos* string of whitewashed hill towns, the ancient border town Jerez de la Frontera whence comes the world's sherry supply, pilgrim routes through stunning national parks, and the ancient city of Cadiz—at more than 3,100 years old, the longest-settled city in Europe.

In Germany, consider the castles of the Neckar River rather than those of the Rhine River, the towns of Franconia rather than those of Bavaria. In Switzerland, explore the eastern Appenzell region rather than following the crowds to Interlaken and the Berner Oberland to get your taste of the Alps.

This strategy of setting your sights just off kilter from the tour bus routes can also work by degrees. Central Italy is a perfect example. Take Tuscany, a justifiably popular region, but a place where most tourism focuses on northern Tuscany (Florence, Pisa, and Lucca) and the Chianti/ Siena region of central Tuscany. That leaves the Maremma in southern Tuscany relatively unspoiled, discovered mainly by German bicycling groups.

But perhaps you're an old Italy hand who feels all of Tuscany is overcrowded and overpriced. Move one degree further out and to the east and cross the border from Tuscany into Umbria, a region that features many of the same attractions (medieval hill towns, Renaissance art, Etruscan ruins, picturesque vineyards) but is not nearly as popular and, hence, not nearly as expensive.

To those who say that even Umbria has already been discovered and is on a par with Tuscany, I say: Continue out yet another degree, looking east into the regions of the Marches and, a bit to the south, Abbruzo. The hill towns and wineries continue, but the majority of tourists have turned back to seek out Rome or the Cinque Terre. The areas of central Italy are still almost entirely yours to discover—and at prices far below those of the Chianti country of Tuscany.

You can continue to enjoy Europe cheaply by extending your city stays to 1 week, spending that time in apartments obtained from VRBO

Reeling and disheartened from the continued drop in the value of the dollar against the euro, a great many Americans have overlooked a highly effective way to reduce the cost of a European stay to what it used to be, by staying in an apartment, not a hotel, for a week at a time. If you will go to Vacation Rentals by Owner (www.vrbo.com) and click on various European cities, you will find dozens of fully furnished, often spacious, kitchen-equipped apartments in the center of European capitals, that rent for as little as $800 a week. Even when you pay slightly more than that, you enjoy the added economy of being able to cook an occasional meal in that apartment.

Because www.vrbo.com is used so often for obtaining vacation homes in the United States, we sometimes overlook that it contains plentiful foreign listings (it also lists mouth-watering opportunities in Buenos Aires, among dozens of other Central and South American cities). And it is especially useful for Europe. VRBO is being successfully used by many thousands of smart travelers.

What I've learned about European travel, in the course of my most recent stay there

It wasn't a really substantial trip, my 7 days on a Rhine riverboat (stopping in six cities and four countries), followed by 3 nights in Lucerne, Switzerland. But in any overseas setting, you are reminded by actual fresh experience about the basic principles of smart travel, as follows:

1. **The various European rail passes are more valuable than ever.** From checking the railroad ticket offices, it became obvious to me that the increase in the cost of point-to-point rail tickets in Europe has not been matched by an increase in the cost of the various European rail passes. It's as if the people who market these promotional devices in the United States have deliberately slowed their rise in price to keep the trip attractive; people I met were able to hop-scotch all over Switzerland with a Swiss rail pass for just a little bit more than we paid for two tickets at a Swiss railroad station. In advance of leaving for Europe, look into the various rail pass possibilities at **www.raileurope.com**.

2. **The ATM is your very best bet for obtaining cash.** Over and over, I discovered that I could get a decent rate, and pay no big fee, by using my ATM card at the various ATMs in European cities. By contrast, I

Trains are cost effective for touring Europe, especially with the various rail passes allowing unlimited travel for one lump sum.

was shocked by the fees and poor exchange rates of the various money-changing kiosks—and especially by those kiosks and counters at airports and train stations. The latter, paying high rents to be near the tourist crowds, give you a lousy number of euros for your dollars, and then charge an additional 5% (at least) as a fee. Even banks, I discovered, now charge big commissions for changing your money. Don't use them. Go to an ATM, and you'll receive an honest exchange.

3. **The European equivalent of the American TSA (Transportation Security Administration) will confiscate the same items that TSA does.** In European shopping, you have got to stay sensitive to the security check you will later encounter at the airport. We had friends who deliberately passed up the chance to buy reasonably priced Swiss Army knives (as gifts for their friends) at shops in Lucerne in the thought that they could buy them for much less at an airport tax-free shop. Passing through security in the airport for the flight home, and rushing to the area of the tax-free shops, they of course discovered that none of these shops were able to sell Swiss Army knives (since those knives could no longer be placed in luggage checked aboard). You have got to keep mentally agile on your trips to Europe, you have got to think logically and have eyes in the back of your head.

4. **You can enjoy big savings by crossing the Atlantic on a flight making stops en route to your destination.** I met person after person who

had flown to cities in Europe using frequent-flier mileage not on the carrier whose program they had joined, but on the planes of an "alliance partner" flying out of their way to another European city—and only then to their desired destination. Thus, people flying to Amsterdam on frequent-flier mileage earned through Continental, would go there at very low cost via Dusseldorf on Lufthansa, a "partner" of Continental; this involved a bit of a hassle, but saved big sums. Bear in mind that all the major U.S. airlines—American, Continental, Delta, Northwest, United—belong to global airline alliances whose members will honor your frequent-flier miles (but you are not always told that by the U.S. carrier; you have to raise the subject and insist).

Europe never loses its appeal. As disappointing as the weak U.S. dollar is, a trip to Europe is still memorable beyond measure.

In seeking to keep costs low on your next trip to Europe, you'll want to scout out free performances & attractions

A reader recently admonished me for failing to point out that many activities and sights in Europe are free of charge. Because it's an important point, I'm repeating his statement here:

> In all your writings about keeping travel expenses in Europe down, you have forgotten to mention *free* things. There are a lot of free things besides people-watching out there. Use your favorite search engine to look for "free things to do in *blank*" (whatever city you're traveling to). London has a great number of options. For example, we signed up at a website which offers free tickets to concerts, plays, and so forth, and snagged two tickets to a top concert with top seats. This event turned out to be the highlight of our trip. Museums usually have at least one day a week that's free. . . . You just need to do a little research before you go, and then ask once you're there.

The writers of those sad regrets about the "end of inexpensive international vacations" are overlooking several methods of self-help

My mail is filled with messages bemoaning "the end of the era of inexpensive international travel." They cite the decline of the dollar and the sky-rocketing price of oil. One particularly elegant, elegiac message reads:

The all too brief age of inexpensive, casual travel Mr. Frommer helped to usher in with *Europe on $5 a Day* may be now at an end. It certainly wasn't sustainable, and we may regrettably have entered a new era in which most of us will regard international travel as a rare and extremely precious privilege to be anticipated and savored only a few times in a lifetime, if that.

I vehemently disagree. The persons who have concluded that international vacations are no longer affordable are referring mainly to the use of standard hotels and restaurants.

But the era of low-cost international travel wasn't based on standard lodgings and meals. When I published my first guidebooks, I didn't write about hotels. My advice was to stay in guesthouses, B&Bs, *pensiones,* monasteries and convents, canal-house hotels, private homes, hostels, student hotels, guest-accepting farms, and houseboats. And I still recommend that kind of lodging, not simply to save money but to have a richer travel experience, to interact with actual foreign residents, and also to meet a more interesting, less pretentious, fellow traveler at the lodgings you chose.

Recently, I spoke by phone with friend and travel writer Reid Bramblett, who was calling in from Verona, Italy. On his last trip to Europe, he had stayed in a monastery in the centrally located Trastevere section of Rome for 40€ ($60) a night. At the time of the call, he was in an agriturism lodging near Verona, for under $100 a night. Elsewhere, he had paid $70 (for a single room) in numerous other modest lodgings in nonhotels (namely, *pensiones* and guesthouses) in other cities.

The tourist, and the tourist couple, who make the firm decision to seek out those alternative lodgings are able to continue exploring western Europe at reasonable cost.

Now, obviously it will be a different kind of vacation. It will require a mental adjustment for those who have usually chosen standard hotels for their lodgings. But the Americans who make that leap are invariably delighted with the transformation of the travel experience that results.

And those adventuresome sorts include people of all ages and income

The "gites" of France are low-cost homes or apartments found in unassuming properties of great charm.

classes. They find that by seeking out the "other" life of Europe, they improve the quality of their travels and yet spend less.

Recently, one of the websites devoted to hostel accommodations in Europe published statistics about the increasing use of hostels by middle-aged and even elderly people. The latter have discovered that these former "youth centers" are now fully open and welcoming to people of all ages, and that a growing percentage of them have private rooms available for occupancy by one and two persons.

If you are at all concerned about the high cost of a standard European vacation, then make the decision (and convince your spouse or companion) to use monastery lodgings in Italian cities, the canal house hotels of Holland, the guest-accepting private homes of Britain and Ireland, the *gites* of France, the hostels of Switzerland and Germany, the *hostales* of Spain. You'll be glad you did.

WINTER PACKAGES TO EUROPE

IN WINTER, VACATION PACKAGES HELP TO COUNTERACT THE HIGH PRICE OF THE EURO, WITH RATES AS LOW AS $799 FOR A WEEK IN PARIS & ELSEWHERE, AIRFARE & 6 NIGHTS' HOTEL INCLUDED

How bad is it in Europe? Plenty bad. Even modest, budget-class, two-star hotels in Europe's major cities now average between 80€ and 130€ for a double room without bath—which doesn't sound that bad, until you do the math using the current punishing cash exchange rate of $1.50 to the euro. Then you realize that each night's lodging will cost you between $122 and $198. Take the average of that and over a 1-week trip, lodging alone will add up to a shocking $1,120 for the most cost conscious of travelers.

Enter the packagers, companies that purchase airfares in bulk and make arrangements with hotels (and, in some cases, car-rental agencies) across Europe to obtain plane tickets and rooms at cut-rates, then bundle them together to sell to the public at far less than an individual traveler would pay for the same travel a la carte. Vacation packages are not tours. While a few throw in airport transfers and occasionally a half-day bus tour of the city as part of the package, your time is otherwise your own. You are not part of a group, nor do you have a guide leading you around.

The current titan of the package business is go-today.com (☎ 800/227-3235), which currently offers (for stays in Jan and Feb) such deals as $799 for 6 nights in Paris, $749 for a week in London, and $1,129 to spend

9 nights in Italy split between Rome, Florence, and Venice and including the rail travel between the cities.

(These prices are all per person based on double occupancy and cover at least airfare from New York or Boston and lodging for the number of nights specified. Departures from other cities add anywhere from $50 to $200; air taxes and fees typically add between $40 and $160.)

Other time-tested generalist vacation packagers offering deals to many European countries include Virgin Vacations (www.virgin-vacations.com) and Gate 1 Travel (☎ 800/682-3333; www.gate1travel.com). Two companies offer packages to many European countries but are particularly strong on Italy: Central Holidays (☎ 800/539-7098; www.centralholidays.com) and TourCrafters (☎ 800/621-2259; www.tourcrafters.com).

Then there are the regional or country-specific specialists. They are competitive with go-today.com and its ilk on straight air-hotel packages to the major cities, but where they really shine is in packages that include not only airfare and lodging but also a rental car for exploring the countries in which they specialize. Sceptre Tours (☎ 800/221-0924; www.sceptretours.com) covers Ireland and Scotland but is most famous for its "Ireland Coast to Coast" package: airfare, 6 hotel nights in three Irish cities, and a rental car, for $799 from several gateways.

A few more regional specialists to add to your shopping list: Sophisticated Traveler (☎ 815/301-3482; www.s-traveler.com) does Eastern Europe, especially Poland, the Czech Republic, Hungary, and Austria. Pacha Tours (☎ 800/722-4288; www.pachatours.com) is a Turkey specialist. Eastern Tours (☎ 800/339-6967; www.traveltorussia.com) does Russia; a winter week split between Moscow and St. Petersburg, with sightseeing tours, costs from $999, but you'll have to factor in large departure taxes and visa fees.

Chapter Eight

TRIPS THAT CATER TO YOUR MIND

LEARNING VACATIONS, BRAINY TOURS, CEREBRAL CRUISES

Long ago I concluded that if travel simply consisted of looking at inert physical sights, the kind you could find in picture books or travelogues, it was not worth the effort and expense. I realized that the only kind of travel I enjoyed was travel associated with people and ideas, learning, and personal growth. And this chapter, one of the lengthiest in this book, describes those trips that cater to your mind.

These are the "brainy" tours and vacations that are not always advertised in public media. They can be immensely exciting and rewarding, and can even change some aspects of your life. And once you engage in them, enjoying travel for the sake of learning, you will not easily return to a less dynamic form of travel.

Brainy Tours & Cruises

Talk about brainy vacations! Martin Randall is just about the only source of affordable mental adventures.

If you're like me, you get endless brochures from alumni organizations (even those from schools you never attended) advertising tours or cruises led by a famous and eager-to-talk professor who's a specialist in the destination. They make your mouth water—until you spot the price. These university fundraisers (another of their functions) routinely cost $900 and even $1,000 per person per day.

So you'll want to know about Martin Randall, the source of intensely intellectual tours for well-read people, costing as little as $400 a day (and sometimes less) per person for totally all-inclusive arrangements—still high but at least sensible. London-based Martin Randall Travel (☎ 020/8742-3355; www.martinrandall.com) survives as virtually the sole source of moderately priced tours that can be characterized as genuinely intellectual. Each of his programs departs with a notable expert on board who delivers daily lectures and commentary based on hard-won expertise.

Martin Randall is a real person, not a figurehead invented by marketers, and he takes an active role in designing and shaping each of dozens of educational itineraries, going as far as to help select writers, academics, curators, and lecturers based not only on their smarts in arts, architecture, and history, but also their abilities to engage a group. Experts range from college educators to authors to members of the British Parliament, and themes span history, the arts, and even horticulture.

Previous page: A handful of tour operators and cruise lines offer serious learning vacations for intellectually curious persons; we should all treasure these companies.

Randall, who came to travel by way of an education at London's ultra-prestigious Courtauld Institute for Art History, is nothing if not timely in his selection of experts—the guest lecturer for the company's Crimean War–themed excursion through Ukraine, was Patrick Mercer, an Oxford-educated historian and British MP who made headlines and lost his post in Parliament for speaking about racism in the British military. Randall's "Wellington in the Peninsula" tour of Spain is conducted by the author of a three-volume work about the British military genius. His "Stained Glass" tour of French churches is hosted by a woman who obtained her doctorate in the Gothic architecture of northern Burgundy.

Randall's informational website sets the tone for his briskly intelligent, upmarket tours: "Our clients are grown ups," it states with British pride. "We structure our arrangements to allow you to retain some responsibility for yourselves and avoid excessive mollycoddling."

Most of Martin Randall's European and North African tours depart from London, and airfare from London and back to London is always included in the price of his programs. If you're paying in pounds, the rates are not bare-bones but certainly do-able—£200 to £300 a day is the norm, and each day, including the first and last, is programmed with activities. Of course, the unfavorable exchange rate from the pound to the dollar currently means that you'll be paying nearly $300 to $450 a day. But that fee gets you most meals, four-star hotels, many flights (except the ones from America), ground transportation, tips, tickets, and unparalleled access to experts and art.

No other company currently provides such an erudite service for such a reasonable daily price. Try to snare one of his lower-priced tours, and you'll have purchased a top value in vacations.

A CAUSE FOR REJOICING: THREE HIGH-BROW, SMALL-SHIP CRUISES IN THE TRADITION OF SWAN HELLENIC

Three unique British cruise lines are operating small, 300- to 600-passenger ships, and yet charging moderate rates for what is normally an expensive way to sail. The three companies are also alike in the intellectual focus of their cruises; none of them operates a casino or offers popular evening entertainment, and each instead sponsors weighty lectures by experts in the destinations about to be visited. They attract a thoughtful clientele, and their charges are low enough to enable most international travelers to participate.

1. **Swan Hellenic Cruises** (☎ 444-462-180; www.swanhellenic.com), revived by the former chairman of Britain's P&O Cruises, Lord Jeffrey

Sterling, operates a single ship, the 350-passenger *Minerva II* (furnished in country-club style), on cruises that normally last for 2 weeks and sail in summer through all interesting parts of the Baltic, Adriatic, and Mediterranean, always accompanied by a top-category group of academic lecturers—professors, authors, and scholars of major repute. Like all the small-ship British lines, its cruise prices includes round-trip air from London to the embarkation port, all daily shore excursions, all tipping to staff—and are thus as fully all-inclusive as a cruise can get. And yet prices start (for minimum-rate cabins) at about $350 a day per person. You couldn't pick a more memorable vacation, enjoyed in the company of the best sort of intellectually curious British traveler.

2. **Martin Randall Cruises** (☎ 020/8742-3355; www.martinrandall.com) is a new venture for the highly esteemed, long-established British tour company discussed above. It makes no concession to popular tastes, and calls for real involvement and commitment by its passengers.

Martin Randall's cruise program to classic sights of the Mediterranean, on the chartered, 236-passenger *MV Columbus*, sailed on only three occasions in 2008, but will be greatly expanded in 2009. Prices in 2008 included round-trip air from London to the embarkation port, and ran as low as $300 a day, for a classical adventure led by famous scholars and lecturers, a very impressive bunch. Martin Randall has set himself a high standard, and issued a cocky challenge, saying that his cruises "are designed for people with intellectual curiosity and an interest in history, archaeology and the arts. We make no apology for the academic emphasis of these cruises. They return unashamedly to the century-old tradition of high-brow cruises: this is a dumbing-down-free zone."

3. And for the third, moderately priced British cruise program aboard small ships, consider Gerry Herrod's Voyages of Discovery (☎ 866/623-2689; www.voyagesofdiscovery.com). The two ships—the *MV Discovery* and the *MV Ocean Majesty*—carry about 500 and 600 passengers respectively, in slightly older vessels a tiny bit less comfortable than the quite-lovely *Minerva II* of Swan Hellenic and the German vessel chartered by Martin Randall. It's likely that rates will start at $300 a day in 2009 (they haven't yet been announced as we prepare this book in late 2008).

From the claims of Herrod's brochure, it's probable that lecturers aboard the Voyages of Discovery will be an impressive lot, but without the top academic cachet of the noted professors and others who sail with Swan Hellenic and Martin Randall.

The ship used for Swan Hellenic cruises is a comfortable vessel with an outsize library and no casino or nightclub.

A COMPANY CALLED THE TRAVELLER IS STILL ANOTHER SOURCE OF ULTRABRAINY TOURS

To the small list of companies operating brainy tours at a reasonable price, you can now add the programs (easily available to Americans) of the Traveller (☎ 020/7436-9343; www.the-traveller.co.uk), which used to run the worldwide tour program of the British Museum. Stung by 9/11, that august institution got out of the travel biz, leaving the Traveller as an independent tour operator but with the same list of outstanding guest experts.

The Traveller's destinations tend toward the rare and the arcane—just the sort of places where a curator from the British Museum might pick up another rare artifact. The company is the first British tour operator to undertake tours to Algeria, the troubled North African country, in 15 years. It even goes to Timbuktu, in the African country of Mali.

You might think that given the pedigree of the guides and the exotic destinations of the trips, that the Traveller would be priced for the upper crust. Not so: A 16-day tour cost the equivalent of about $360 to $500 a day in late 2008, which is uncommonly affordable considering (a) that the price includes round-trip air from London, as well as all-inclusive arrangements, and (b) so few outfits arrange such exotic tours without charging playboy prices.

Tours, which average 18 people, span the world. Its "Splendors of Angkor Wat," an intensive 10-day study of the famous Cambodian temple complex, was recently led by an art historian who has written a book on the subject (he also discovered and excavated the Sanctuary of St. Lot on the Dead Sea in 1991). While he may not be the lecturer in 2009, a scholar of equal eminence will undoubtedly be substituted.

HERE'S A FINAL BRITISH SOURCE OF ULTRABRAINY TOURS AT A REASONABLE PRICE

To the tours offered by Martin Randall and the Traveller, let's add those of Andante Travels (☎ 1722-713800; www.andantetravels.co.uk), whose focus since 1985 has been archaeology and the ancient world. In practical terms, that means its subject matter also includes classic literature and history.

Typical tours: "Ravenna and Acquileia" seeking out decorative arts from the Roman period that are still found around the Po Valley of Italy, and "Great Abbeys of Central Italy" tracing the early days of Christianity by way of the country's gorgeous old monasteries. Another trip spends a week exploring the famous cave art of the Pyrenees in France, led by a specialist in prehistoric art. Guides usually consist of professors at English universities, where study of the classics is still held in esteem.

On the tours operated by Martin Randall, well-preserved ancient Greek temples are the object of intense study.

Prices, while not dirt cheap because of the exchange rate, are still reasonable considering the status of the expert guides and the small size (averaging 19) of the group—and the fact that nowadays you're unlikely to find many brainy tours for much less. Travel with Andante usually costs around £200 a day, including all meals (with wine), hotels, and transportation from London, which works out to about $300 in American currency.

There's also a budget alternative, for which Andante deserves special praise. Ten of its tours are classified as "'Bare Bones" trips, which don't include lunch or dinner, and use only moderate-level hotels. These, such as the exploration of the Croatian seaport of Split led by a woman who wrote her doctoral thesis on Croatia, cost around £1,000 for 8 days, which brings the cost down to around $187 a day, before flights. Other "Bare Bones" destinations include Jordan's Petra (supervised by an archaeologist specializing in the Bronze Age), Pompeii (led by a professor in classics and a field archaeologist), and a 2-day exploration of Stonehenge outside London.

DURING AT LEAST ONE SUMMER OF YOUR LIFE, YOU'VE GOT TO ATTEND CHAUTAUQUA

Chautauqua in upstate New York is a summer vacation destination so popular that it always sells out long before its opening date—you'll need to book as soon as you can. Essentially, Chautauqua invented the "learning vacation" more than a century and a quarter ago. The core of its program is a body of some 400 classes in every conceivable subject ranging over a 9-week period. For as long as you wish to stay, at extremely moderate rates ($16 a day in 2008 for daytime admission, not including room and meals), you enjoy a verdant campus with golf, boating, and swimming, as well as lectures delivered by nationally recognized names ranging from Nobel laureates to Supreme Court justices. You also have access to reasonably priced concerts, films, and plays, at an extra charge for evening events. If you'd like to know more about Chautauqua, log on to www.ciweb.org.

LANGUAGE INSTRUCTION

WOULD YOU BELIEVE IT? THE INTERNET IS NOW FULL OF WEBSITES OFFERING TO TEACH YOU A FOREIGN LANGUAGE FREE OF CHARGE.

Sooner or later, it seems, the Internet responds to nearly every human need, and one subject matter of importance to travelers is the learning of foreign languages. A typical language-instruction site is operated by the British

Broadcasting Corporation, www.bbc.co.uk/languages, which uses every high-tech, computer-related device (recorded sound, iPods, animation) to make its courses effective and interesting to pursue. Most important, the service is entirely free of charge, requiring only that you register to receive weekly e-mailed lessons. While the focus is on teaching French, German, Spanish, and Italian, Chinese and Greek have recently been added and more languages are coming.

I suggest that you look right away at www.bbc.co.uk/languages and at the various options for picking up at least a smattering of commonly used phrases. Knowing a bit of the language can make all the difference in your travels to foreign countries. *À bientôt, mes amis.*

LEARNING VACATIONS

HERE'S AN ODD SUGGESTION FOR YOUR UPCOMING SUMMER VACATION: SPEND IT AT HARVARD!

Attracted by an advertisement of the Harvard Summer School, in which programs were described as being for "high school and college students, and adults," I phoned Harvard's public relations department and learned, to my surprise, that the entire summer program is available to adults of any age (although overwhelmingly attended by younger persons). Provided you are willing to spend a minimum of 4 weeks on a program, you can sign up for any summer school course, and take it without subjecting yourself to grades or exams (but, of course, you'll get no college credit). What's more, the authorities will attempt to find you accommodations in a Harvard dorm, or in the many private residences scattered throughout the Cambridge, Massachusetts, area, in which Harvard students are housed.

So here's an alternative to Oxford or University College Dublin this summer. I've written a great deal about the residential summer programs offered in the universities of the British Isles and strongly recommended them as a supreme vacation activity. To check into an Oxford "quad," take instruction from a celebrated Oxford "don," and then enjoy meals in the same cavernous Gothic dining room pictured in the Harry Potter movies, is a once-in-a-lifetime thrill. But now, at lesser cost, you can have a similar experience in one of America's leading universities.

When my daughter was a teenager in high school, she attended Harvard's Summer School, and it was a top moment of her life. The faculty is Harvard's faculty, the level of instruction is high, and the Harvard campus is full of cultural opportunities. Although the Harvard Summer School website itself makes no reference to "adults," I'm told that every program in it can be taken by an adult (as the advertising for the program states), provided only—once again—that you are willing to sign up for a 4-week session (the minimum duration of programs). Go to www.summer.harvard.edu for all the details.

SEVERAL OTHER EMINENT UNIVERSITIES OFFER SUMMER LEARNING VACATIONS TO ADULTS OF ALL AGES

A more serious summer learning opportunity is the "Summer Classics" program of St. John's College in Santa Fe, New Mexico. Here, for 1 week at a time, you sign up to read and discuss one book—such as Dante's *Inferno,* or Thuycidides' *History of the Peloponnesian War*—for a full week, while residing in student quarters on the scenic, mountainside campus of St. John's. Your seminar leaders are from the noted faculty ("tutors") of St. John's, who lead a 4-hour daily discussion by each small seminar group. Expect to pay $1,250 per person for 1 week's tuition, plus $510 for 1 week's room and board.

My own two summers at St. John's, where (together with my wife) I studied the Great Books series on these 1-week programs, was a memorable intellectual adventure, a highlight of my vacation life. Go to www.stjohnscollege.edu/outreach/SF/SC/classics.shtml for all the details.

A compromise between Harvard, on the one hand, and St. John's, on the other, is Cornell's Adult University (www.sce.cornell.edu/cau) in Ithaca, New York, usually scheduled for the month of July. This is for adults (whose children, if they come, pursue a separate program) in a wide variety of subjects in the liberal arts, all presented by eminent members of the Cornell faculty and discussed with serious intent by the intellectually curious people who sign up for this kind of "vacation." The cost ranges around $1,400 for a week—and that includes not only your tuition, but housing in a Cornell dorm, all three meals a day, various social programs, access to the gym, and many other extras.

The popularity and acceptance of Cornell's Adult University is proven by its 30-year-long history and by many enthusiastic recommendations. If a trip to England's Oxford (for its famed summer school) seems too costly this year, and St. John's Great Books discussion seems too heavy, you might settle instead on Cornell.

PREPARE NOW TO ATTEND OXFORD SUMMER SCHOOL NEXT YEAR

Because all the most interesting courses are usually sold out by the end of March, you may be too late to apply for the finest learning vacation in all travel, a program known as the Oxford Experience, a week spent on the campus of Britain's famous university an hour and a half from London. But make a note to send in your request soon for the summer session.

Here's an adventure of the mind for adults from all over the world, who attend Oxford without tests, examinations, or grades, living in the ancient Christ Church College and taking meals in a 15th-century Gothic dining hall, while they pursue such courses as "The Public and Private Lives of British Prime Ministers" or the "Tyranny of Henry VIII," to name just two.

The 2009 program takes places from June 29 to August 2. A choice of some 50 subjects is offered during the 5-week period. And there are optional daytime excursions to stately homes (such as Blenheim Palace and Melmscott Manor) or the Bodleian Library. Evening events include pub walks, whisky tastings, Morris Dancers, croquet and wine in the Masters Garden, special lectures, and evensong in the college chapel, which is also the Oxford Cathedral.

The price of a 1-week course in 2009—tuition, accommodations, and meals (except those on excursions) is £980, approximately $1,425. There are additional charges for excursions and rooms with private bath. If you're at all interested, go to Google and type in the words "the Oxford Experience."

I should point out that Oxford operates a separate program called the Oxford University Summer School for Adults (OUSSA), primarily for British residents but also open to Americans (Roberta and I enrolled several summers ago, and pursued a course called "Ancient Egyptian Civilization," the only class still open when we applied late, just 2 weeks prior to the start). OUSSA is a great deal more serious than the Oxford Experience; it requires preparatory readings, a 1,500-word essay before classes begin, and a 1,000-word essay at the end of the week, in addition to dealing with far more serious subjects of philosophy, science, and history. The cost is about £1,000 ($1,500) for a fully inclusive week.

MUSEUMS

ALONG WITH MONUMENTS TO ACHIEVEMENTS, WE SHOULD ALSO GO TO SOBERING EXHIBITS OF HUMANKIND'S FAILURES

Most travelers have a vague desire to visit the world's most famous museums of art: the Louvre in Paris, the National Gallery in London, the Kunsthistorisches in Vienna, the Rijksmuseum in Amsterdam, the Prado in Madrid, the Hermitage in St. Petersburg, the Uffizi in Florence, the Metropolitan Museum of Art in New York City, the various components of the Smithsonian Institution in Washington, D.C.

To these should now be added museums of conscience, places that commemorate acts of inhumanity, that tell of our failures over the centuries to create a better world. It is only recently that the travel industry has awakened to these unsettling exhibits that should figure prominently in an individual's development and growth.

The museums of conscience include the following:

◆ Goree Island in Senegal, site of "Slave House," where as many as 25 million African slaves were shackled and herded into boats and sent to continents far away. Millions of them died in the course of the voyage.

◆ Manzanar National Historic Site in California, where 110,000 Japanese Americans, all of them full citizens, were interned from 1942 to 1945.

◆ The Leper Colony on the Kalaupapa Peninsula on the island of Molokai, Hawaii. To an almost impenetrable area flanked by steep cliffs of rock, thousands of persons suffering leprosy were forcibly sent and simply abandoned in conditions of famine, exposure, and other hardships. Because leprosy (Hansen's Disease) is now under control, the colony can today be toured, led by the few remaining residents who once suffered from that disease and have opted to stay on.

◆ The Workhouse in Southwell, Notts, Great Britain, constructed in 1842 as a model for many other such institutions, in which unfortunate people were imprisoned in circumstances of great hardship, simply because they were poor. The operation of such "poorhouses" reached a peak in Victorian times, when Britain was colonizing the world.

◆ The Holocaust Museum in Washington, D.C., our American equivalent of Yad Vashem in Jerusalem, describing the extermination of millions of Jews by Nazi Germany in World War II.

◆ The Tenement Museum in downtown Manhattan (the Lower East Side), re-creating the horrendous conditions to which immigrants to the United States were often subjected from 1863 to 1932.

Usually on our trips abroad, we visit monuments (museums) to the rich and famous. Visits to museums of conscience (including such places as Auschwitz and Dachau) are a healthy counterbalance.

POLITICAL TRAVEL

ALL YOU DENNIS KUCINICH FANS, HAVE I GOT A TOUR OPERATOR FOR YOU!

The San Francisco tour operator Global Exchange (2017 Mission St., San Francisco, CA 94110; ☎ 800/497-1994; www.realitytours.org or www.globalexchange.org) wears its heart on its sleeve. It is a self-professed

Political tours immerse their participants in the authentic life of India, Asia, Africa, and Latin America.

political tour operator, openly radical and left wing, a fierce advocate of viewpoints that, over the years, have been wildly at odds with majority viewpoints in the United States. It operates 60 departures a year of 8-to 17-day tours taking you to politically controversial nations, to support the dissident forces, poverty communities, anti-American movements, and revolutionary policies found therein.

Though you may not agree with many of its viewpoints—and I, for one, disagree with several, but not all—you will have to admit that a Global Exchange tour shakes you up, makes you think, compels you to re-examine your most cherished assumptions. A Global Exchange tour produces the kind of mental convulsion that the First Amendment was enacted to provoke.

The tours of Global Exchange are quite different from the somewhat shy and tentative political excursions of the Wisconsin nuns who operate the program known as GATE (Global Awareness Through Experience), discussed below. The good sisters of Wisconsin simply take you to converse with political activists and dissidents in various Latin American nations— and then allow you to reach your own conclusions. Global Exchange knows what it believes, and shapes its tours to teach a desired lesson, as clearly seen in the subtitles it appends to its tours going to Ecuador ("Environmental and Social Justice," 10 and 13 days), Mexico ("Chiapas: Tierra & Libertad," 8 days), Palestine and Israel ("Prospects for Peace & Justice," 10 days), Vietnam ("Legacies of War & the New Vietnam," 13 days), Nicaragua ("Fair Trade and Alternatives," 9 days), Iran ("Citizen Diplomacy," 13 days), India

("Kerala—A Third World Model," 14 days), Afghanistan ("Women Making Change," 9 days), and many more. Inclusive prices range from $1,000 to $2,500, but airfare is extra.

WAIT 'TIL YOU READ THE TRAVEL PAMPHLET OF THE FRANCISCAN SISTERS OF PERPETUAL ADORATION!

It's like no tour brochure you've ever seen. In place of "today we go to the Tower of London," it hits you with shockers, such as in this trip to El Salvador:

> [We visit the site] where Oscar Romero, the six Jesuits and their co-workers, and the four North American church women were killed. We take part in spirited dialogue with people in grassroots movements . . . and [others] who experience this democracy facing global challenges. We learn how trade agreements affect immigration and the poor.

Now in its 28th year, the program known as GATE (Global Awareness Through Experience), designed and escorted by members of the Franciscan Sisters of Perpetual Adoration (of La Crosse, Wisconsin), offers numerous departures to nations ranging from Guatemala to El Salvador and Mexico, and the countries of Eastern Europe.

Among the obstacles the sisters have had to overcome are those thrown up by their superiors. Compelled to drop the words "liberation theology" from their literature, and other highly charged language about the wealthy elites that dominate certain Latin American and other countries, they seemed for a time (I've been following them for years) to be growing cautious.

But as far as I can see, the basic themes of these tours—the emphasis upon contact with low-income people in foreign countries—remain unchanged. Thus, in the spring and summer of 2009, GATE will escort groups of Americans to meet "the indigenous peoples of Guatemala." Participants will "explore human rights issues and an active resistance that stretches across centuries as well as the implications of a more recent development, CAFTA." On escorted tours of Oaxaca, Mexico, "a poor state," members of the traveling group "will learn something of the problems [Oaxaca] faces in education and agriculture, especially as they touch the lives of indigenous women."

Costs are remarkably low, an average of $1,175 per person plus airfare and $150 registration fee, for stays of 9 and 10 nights' duration, including lodging and most meals. Additional information is had by writing to GATE,

912 Market St., La Crosse, Wisconsin 54601-8800 (☎ **608/791-5283;** fax 608/782-6301; www.gate-travel.org). The tours are open to people of all ages and of all faiths.

RETREATS (SECULAR & RELIGIOUS)

SUMMERTIME—& THE LIVIN' IS EASY

With gas prices high and the economy slow, many moderately priced resorts and travel programs are showing vacancies for a great many dates. This may be a sensible time to visit America's foremost New Age resort, the unusual Omega Institute (www.eomega.org) near Rhinebeck, New York (2 hours by car north of New York City), which has served as a model for similar "personal growth centers" all over the world.

At Omega, a wide range of thoughtful, open-minded people of all backgrounds and age groups discuss personal relationships, spiritual cravings, psychological hang-ups, better friendships, and preventative holistic health (I've been there and can attest to the fact that these are tolerant, supportive participants, even to a skeptic like me). You have only to phone ☎ **800/944-1001** and reserve a week at the pleasant country resort (a former adult summer camp), receiving dorm accommodations (or higher-priced private facilities) and three vegetarian meals a day, for under $90 per person per day. That includes free yoga and tai chi in the morning, and use of all lakeside facilities, but not the various extra-charge seminars held each day.

Chapter Nine

SPECIAL INTERESTS & SPECIAL PEOPLE

FROM STUDENTS TO SENIORS TO SINGLES, FROM NUDISTS TO VEGANS, THERE'S TRAVEL FOR EVERYONE

A large part of the travel industry caters to special interests. They—the so-called "specialty operators"—group their participants by age, marital status, or interest; offer courses in such subjects as arts, crafts, cooking, or country dancing; send them to inexpensive hospitals and clinics overseas; or take care of any number of other subject matters or concerns. In so doing, they almost guarantee enjoyment of the trip, for people who go with others sharing the same interests are invariably the happiest of travelers.

ARTS & CRAFTS

WORKING WITH YOUR HANDS, IN ANY NUMBER OF SPECIALTIES, IS THE VACATION ACTIVITY OF A POPULAR NORTH CAROLINA SCHOOL/RESORT

Arts and crafts instruction at North Carolina's renowned Penland School is a classic vacation activity, so popular that space is generally spoken for by mid-May; make your own reservation long in advance. Under $1,000, including tuition, three solid meals a day, and dorm-style accommodations, brings you a full week at this famed school in western North Carolina. The 83-year-old institution is currently teaching courses covering the likes of glass blowing, drawing, weaving, jewelry making, photography, and manuscript illumination. Tuition alone for 1 week in summer (through Aug, after which only 8-week courses are available) is around $425. Send your inquiries to www.penland.org or call ☎ 828/765-2359.

COUNTRY DANCING

A CLASSIC RECREATION, PURSUED FOR A FULL WEEK, IS A POPULAR SUMMER VACATION AT A CAMP IN MASSACHUSETTS

A handful of summer vacations deserve to be called "classics"—and that's the case with a week of ethnic or country dancing in Pinewoods, Massachusetts. But be warned: This reasonably priced program is so popular that it often sells out by early May.

Country dancing at Pinewoods costs as little as $795 per person for an all-inclusive (accommodations, meals, instruction) week. Every year from mid-July until September 1, the 93-year-old Country Dance and Song

---

Previous page: Where there's a special interest, there's a tour program—or at least a specialized travel agency to adapt the trip to your needs.

Society operates its main summer camp in the Eastern United States at the 25-acre Pinewoods near Plymouth. There you can wallow in traditional (mostly American and British) music and moves, past and present—from the ancient lute to the Delta banjo, and from medieval English minuets to the Virginia reel. Accommodations are in rustic but well-maintained cabins. (There's tennis and swimming, too.) Get details at ☎ 413/268-7426 or www.cdss.org.

EATING

THE TRAVELING GOURMET: EATING CHEAPLY BUT WELL

Napoleon told us that "an army marches on its stomach"; so do tourists. People enjoy their trips if the food is tasty and cheap; they feel vaguely dissatisfied if the meals are dull and expensive. It's often as simple as that. And the country that can't provide decent dining at a reasonable price is doomed to lose its vitality as a tourist destination. Russia is a current example.

Often, however, visitors themselves can lower the cost and increase the enjoyment of eating by wise decisions. From pondering different approaches to meals in foreign countries, I've developed just short of a dozen rules for my own conduct:

1. **Eat what they're eating.** Concentrate on the local specialties: pasta in Italy, steak-and-kidney pie in Britain, herring in Scandinavia, moo goo gai pan and similar dishes in Taiwan. Local favorites are any nation's best dishes, well prepared and also cheap. Try ordering your own familiar favorites instead—a hamburger, a martini, apple pie—and you'll pay far too much for items poorly prepared.

2. **Drink what they're drinking.** In a wine-drinking country (France, Italy), order wine, not beer. The wine is marvelous and cheap; the beer execrable and no bargain. Contrary-wise, in a beer-drinking country (Germany, Scandinavia), drink beer, not wine—the former is cheap and top-notch.

3. **Eat what they're eating at the time when they're eating it.** Follow the food patterns of the country in question. If their habit is to have a tiny breakfast and a giant lunch (Spain, France, Italy, Greece), you have the same. If, instead, you order a big breakfast in those countries, you'll pay through the nose for an inadequate meal. By contrast, if the tradition in a particular nation is to have a giant breakfast and a tiny lunch (Britain, Israel, Australia), do the same: You'll find that the mammoth breakfast is the best-prepared meal of the day, and relatively cheap.

4. **Eat less than you think you want.** We all eat far more while traveling than we are normally accustomed to at home. We feel intimidated, among other things, by foreign waiters. Will they think us an "ugly American" if we don't order a soup-to-nuts meal? At home, none of us would dream of having four courses for lunch; yet overseas, we think it obligatory to order the table d'hôte meal, and stuff ourselves into a state of torpor, at considerable expense, while the local resident at the next table has a refreshing, inexpensive single plate.

5. **Split, share, and divide.** Order one plate for both of you, or an appetizer for one and a main course for the other, and then split what arrives. You'll still send uneaten food back to the kitchen, and save money at the same time. The servings in most foreign restaurants are enough for a family (I exclude, of course, the haughty, haute cuisine places with their tiny portions). How many times, in a touristic setting, have you ordered a meat course for yourself, only to find it overflowing the plate, gargantuan, and impossible to finish? By ordering, say, one prime rib for the two of you, you end up with still more than enough, and save $17 or so at the same time.

6. **Eat picnic-style once a day.** Instead of going to restaurants three times a day, and devouring one after another of those overly rich, overly sauced hot meals, alternate the routine; make one of those meals a cold, light snack, such as a sandwich lunch at home. Go to the local equivalent of a delicatessen or to the food section of a department store. Order a slab of pâté, some cheese, rolls, tomatoes, pickles, and wine, and then take the lot to a park bench or a river bank, and eat healthily, cheerfully—and for pennies. Oh, happy days!

7. **Look before leaping.** Never order any dish without first knowing its cost. Never patronize a restaurant that does not openly display its menu outside. Order nothing listed at "today's market price" or "s.g." (*selon grosseur,* according to weight). Give that latitude to a restaurant, and you'll pay a hideous price.

8. **Beware of waiters bearing gifts.** Eat nothing that's been placed on the table in advance of your arrival (such as a jar of pâté); it's priced at princely levels. Refuse anything (other than bread, butter, radishes, and the like) brought to your table unbidden in the midst of the meal unless it's explicitly described as free.

9. **Avoid the "household words."** If the name of a restaurant immediately springs to mind in an unfamiliar city, it's because you've subliminally heard of it for decades. And that means you're 20 years too late. The "household words" are too often riding on their reputations, careless and blasé, and hideously overpriced. They can afford to be.

Foodies of the world support a large and growing corps of food tour operators who take you to try the world's tastiest dishes.

10. **Never eat at airports.** Bring sandwiches from home, either in a bag or carry-on. Stick pastries in your purse. Do anything, but don't place yourself in the position of ever having to eat at an airport. Need I explain why?

11. **Patronize the marketplaces.** And finally, when in doubt over where to eat in a foreign city, head for the big marketplace, the stalls under canvas, or in a warehouselike building where all the ingredients of meals are sold. Wherever there's a marketplace, there's a nearby restaurant with especially good prices for fresh food; that's because those marketplace eateries buy the makings for their meals from people they deal with throughout the day, at the very best rates.

SEVEN MORE RULES FOR SMART EATING

After much reflection (and suggestions from readers and friends), I've concluded that an additional seven approaches are needed to fully cover the topic:

12. **Call up for takeout.** You can order pizza delivery in Italy just as you do at home, or stop by a grocery store to pick up the ingredients of a home-cooked meal (it helps if you have a kitchenette, though it's also

easy to cobble together a more picnic-style meal that doesn't require cooking). Many restaurants in Europe let you order to go, so you can enjoy your meal in the comfort of your hotel room without paying cover charges, service fees, or tips (plus, takeout makes it much easier to order fewer dishes per person and then share them).

13. **Skip the main course.** Frankly, cooked meat tastes pretty much the same everywhere—so you don't get much of a cultural experience from ordering it—yet main courses are the priciest items on any menu. I'd advise you to skip the main meat plates and concentrate on a medley of appetizers, first courses, and desserts. Not only will this save you the cost of the entrees, but by ordering a kaleidoscope of first courses you get to sample far more of the dishes that make the local cuisine special.

14. **Stick with the house wine or local beer.** Don't bother paying $40 for a labeled bottle when a liter carafe of the house red or white will almost invariably be just as tasty and just as genuine, yet cost less than $15. In beer countries (Germany-speaking nations, the Low Countries, much of Eastern Europe), just order whatever's on tap—at home you'd pay through the nose for such an "import."

15. **Drink tap water.** The water in western Europe is generally safe to drink. While many Europeans order mineral water with their meals to the tune of $3 to $5 a bottle, a carafe of tap water is free. You do the math.

16. **Patronize pricey restaurants only at lunch.** If you want to splash out on a fine restaurant in Paris, by all means do so—but go at lunch, when the prices are frequently and mysteriously much lower than at dinner, or when a set lunch menu may be available, allowing you to sample the haute cuisine without paying the haute price.

17. **Order the tourist menu or fixed-price menu.** Most restaurants in Europe offer set-priced meals that cost a good 10% to 25% less than a la carte. Some deals are better than others (the best include wine, water, dessert, and coffee), and for some reason a "fixed-price menu" usually offers more options (but slightly higher prices) than a "tourist menu," where your choice is usually pasta with tomato sauce followed by roast chicken or veal and fruit or dessert.

18. **Always ask, "Is service included?"** This might be printed at the bottom of the menu, but even if it is not, always ask (and call it "service," a word more widely understood than "tip"). It's usually 10% to 15%, which is standard in Europe. Whatever you do, don't double-tip. If service is included, you needn't pay anything beyond the total on the bill. However, if the waitstaff were particularly good, feel free to leave behind an extra euro per person to show your appreciation.

FOR THE TRAVELER WHO HAS DONE EVERYTHING, SEEN EVERYTHING, GONE EVERYWHERE: A 5-DAY COOKING VACATION IN THE COLORADO ROCKIES

Would it be worth a week of your time to learn how to prepare *soupe au pistou,* spice-rubbed roasted chicken with a pan reduction sauce; bananas Foster; a traditional niçoise salad; bitter greens, toasted pecan, and bacon salad with honey buttermilk dressing; braised pork roast with dried fruit sauce; and crème caramel with fresh ginger? You bet it would!

For 15 years, the Culinary School of the Rockies in Boulder, Colorado (☎ 877/249-0305; www.culinaryschoolrockies.com), has been offering weeklong vacation stays for travelers that consist of an intensive 5-day, 5-hours-a-day, hands-on course in basic cooking techniques costing roughly $645 per person—and guaranteed to teach the dishes described above. Lodging in low-cost Boulder is your own responsibility, not included in the fee, but easy to find via recommendations offered by the school.

ANY VEGETARIANS AMONG OUR READERS? VEGANS? HERE'S A TRAVEL WEBSITE JUST FOR YOU.

A friend was recently regaling me with tales of a business trip to South America, during which eight members of his group were taken to "an excellent Argentine restaurant." Anyone who knows Argentina knows that it is one of the world's most red meat–obsessed countries, a mecca for anyone who enjoys a good, hearty steak. The problem was, two members of my friend's group were vegetarians, and a third was a vegan, and spent a morose evening picking at plates of overcooked spaghetti in what turned out to be, indeed, a typical Argentine steakhouse.

If you are a vegetarian or vegan who has become resigned to vacations of endless salads and pasta bowls, take heart. There's a Web travel guide called Happy Cow (www.happycow.net) that describes more than 7,700 meatless restaurants, health-food stores, and vegetarian B&Bs in more than 55 countries, complete with user reviews. There's also a smattering of everything from organic cooking schools in Tuscany to a vegetarian hot springs resort in Guadalajara, Mexico.

In one of many thoughtful touches, the site for each country includes a list of topical phrases in that country's language (how to say "Do you have a vegetarian dish?" or "I don't eat butter, cheese, eggs, or honey.") The site also has a primer on air travel for vegetarians, links to vegetarian guidebooks, ratings of the top 10 vegetarian-friendly cities, and tips for staying healthy on the road.

Other, less well-organized and less complete resources include www.
vegetariansabroad.com, www.vegtravel.com, www.vrg.org/travel, www.vegeats.
com, and www.vegetarianusa.com (lots of good resources, but only for
domestic travel).

HONEYMOONS

A LOW-COST CRUISE OF THE EASTERN MEDITERRANEAN IS AN EXCELLENT HONEYMOON TRIP FOR COUPLES GETTING MARRIED IN THE NEXT SEVERAL MONTHS

When one of my step-daughters got married a few years back, she and her
husband chose a cruise off the waters of Greece, Turkey, and Croatia for
their honeymoon. It was an excellent choice; all three countries are among
the least expensive of European nations, and shore excursions (including
restaurant meals) were far less costly than if they had cruised in the western
Mediterranean.

I mention that choice because the newest ship of MSC Cruises (www.
msccruisesusa.com), the MSC *Poesia,* is making 7-day cruises of Greece,
Turkey, and Croatia departing from Venice on most Saturdays from spring
through autumn in 2009, and inside cabins aboard those cruises will be
available for as little as $1,149 per person. Here's a remarkable honeymoon
trip at an affordable price, even adding round-trip airfare to Venice. Go to
www.vacationstogo.com to book.

These honeymooners swimming off the coast of Turkey are part of a giant audience for
postnuptial travel.

MEDICAL TOURISM

LET'S SPEND A MOMENT ON MEDICAL TOURISM

I've learned from my weekly radio call-in show that the surest way to set off a barrage of hate mail is to suggest that Americans travel overseas for low-cost medical or dental treatment. Instantly, dozens of doctors and dentists accuse you of putting peoples' lives at risk.

If the United States had universal health insurance, I would not be disposed to argue the matter. But more than 40 million Americans are uninsured for medical care, and a great many more have no dental coverage. For purely elective treatments, what else are they to do than to consider medical or dental tourism?

In a recent book called *Patients Beyond Borders,* Josef Woodman argues the case for that kind of travel. He claims that in Thailand, Hungary, Singapore, South Korea, South Africa, Brazil, Antigua, and Barbados are dozens of accredited hospitals and clinics providing high-quality medical and dental care for a fraction of what's charged here at home. And though U.S. doctors and dentists will obviously challenge him, the mere publication of a heavily buttressed, book-length defense of medical and dental tourism shows that the controversy is very much alive and that globalization has expanded beyond manufacturing and commerce to include medical and dental treatment overseas. Give a thought to *Patients Beyond Borders.*

SINGAPORE HAS SUDDENLY SURGED AS A DESTINATION FOR "MEDICAL TOURISM"—& I WANTED TO KNOW WHY

When Woodman published a sequel, a special "Singapore edition" of the best-selling *Patients Beyond Borders,* I was curious to know why. So I dialed his cellphone number, reached him in South Korea, and asked that he send me an e-mail explaining why the sudden emphasis on Singapore. He responded as follows:

> The reason I decided to write a special Singapore Edition of *Patients Beyond Borders* was to inform readers who are becoming priced out of the U.S. healthcare market about the breadth and depth of procedures offered by Singapore hospitals and clinics. In brief, Singapore had become the gold standard of global healthcare, and the list of excellent medical travel opportunities was too large to cover in the pages of our general edition; to name a few:

1. Singapore has 13 JCI-accredited hospitals, more than any other Asian country, giving Americans comfort that the largest American hospital accreditation agency has certified so many treatment centers there;

2. Thirty-five hospitals in Singapore serve more than 400,000 international patients each year, covering nearly every imaginable medical diagnosis and procedure;

3. Johns Hopkins has its own hospital there.

4. A full-blown women's specialty center (KK Women's and Children's Hospital) offers pediatric and reproductive diagnoses and treatments;

5. Asia's largest hospital network (Parkway Health) is headquartered there, with three of Asia's finest hospitals a stone's throw from each other;

6. Biopolis, a new $600-million life sciences and medical research institute, hosts medical leaders from all over the world, and is at the forefront of several important areas of research, including stem cell and other regenerative therapies.

To top it all off, Singapore (as a former British colony) is English-speaking throughout, and the city is so squeaky clean you can eat off the sidewalks. Not to mention a host of 3-, 4-, and 5-star hotels, and some of Asia's best food.

So, in cooperation with Singapore Medicine, we released the 356-page *Patients Beyond Borders, Singapore Edition,* last July, to an enthusiastic international audience. The book covers 35 hospitals in depth, featuring their specialties and subspecialties.

Over the phone, Woodman emphasized that medical treatment in Singapore is often priced at 60% less than in the United States. Whatever you may think of "globalization" in other economic contexts, you might want to study the increasing "globalization" of medical care. It's a subject of special interest to those 40-some-odd million Americans who don't possess health insurance capable of paying U.S. medical bills.

SPAIN & PORTUGAL ARE THE LATEST LOCATIONS TO ADVERTISE THE BENEFITS—& LOW COST—OF THEIR HOSPITALS FOR FOREIGN TOURISTS

A few years ago, when various commentators began discussing the benefits of medical and dental tourism, they were usually talking about travel to hospitals in far-off Thailand, South Korea, or Singapore, or occasionally about inexpensive dental treatment from the many highly skilled dentists of relatively far-off Hungary. Other possibilities included cosmetic surgery in Rio de Janeiro and other remote locations. But recently, a new medical/dental tour company (they make the travel and the hospital arrangements) called Fly2Doc (www.fly2doc.com) began advertising the professional, scientific, and cost advantages of medical treatments in Spain and Portugal, both of them relatively easy to reach. According to Fly2Doc, the fully accredited hospitals of Spain and Portugal offer dentistry, eye surgery, cosmetic surgery, weight-loss programs, and orthopedic treatment and surgery at a fraction of the cost you'd incur in the United States Anybody who has recently been in modern Spain will treat seriously the claim by Spanish hospitals that they are up to world-class standards.

It's Juarez, Mexico, for cheap, reputedly well-qualified dentists

Against all the advice of U.S. dentists, Americans who don't have dental insurance are flocking to Mexican border towns, and especially to Juárez, Mexico, for all sorts of dental treatments that are too expensive for them in the States. Juárez is the sister city to El Paso, Texas, and all the big dental clinics in Juárez will send a van to pick you up at your hotel in El Paso and quickly deliver you to a dentist in Juárez. They'll later drive you back to El

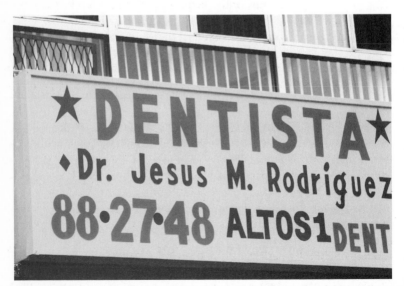

Medical and dental tourism are among the fastest-growing segments of travel, especially to low-cost Mexico.

Paso. Interestingly enough, although a prominent late member of Congress (a former dentist) once loudly claimed that using Mexican dentists is dangerous, the U.S. consulate in Juárez actually lists three recommended Mexican dentists on its website, at http://ciudadjuarez.usconsulate.gov. And each of the dentists recommended has an impressive set of qualifications. It's your decision, of course; but what else can you do if you don't have dental insurance and need an expensive course of treatment?

NUDITY

A GROWING TRAVEL ACTIVITY, STRIPPED BARE

At a travel show in Long Beach, California, at which I spoke, there was always a crowd in front of the booth of the American Association for Nude Recreation. Staffed by well-spoken, dignified, and fully clothed representatives, the booth carried listings for scores and scores of nude resorts in the United States, in what I counted as 42 states. States with the largest number of nude resorts? California, Florida, Texas. Yet even Mississippi has one of them—and more amazingly, Utah has three (Family Skinnydippers in Sandy; Utah All-Natural Recreation in South Jordan; and Utah Naturists in Salt Lake City). The American Association for Nude Recreation (AANR) claims its membership is now at a historic peak of 50,000 members and their families. If you'd like to join, or obtain their literature, visit www.aanr.com or phone ☎ 800/TRY-NUDE (879-6833).

SENIORS

IF YOU'RE 50 OR OLDER, THERE'S ONLY ONE U.S. HOTEL CHAIN TO USE

I've been reminded by several aging readers that I should occasionally seek out the travel tactics that will assist the middle-aged or older American to travel. At a time when nearly all the airlines and even some hotels have dropped their senior-citizen discounts, there remains one travel company—Choice Hotels—that heavily promotes its price cuts for mature travelers and makes sure that those cuts are substantial. Choice Hotels is a travel giant, with tens of thousands of properties operating as Comfort Inns, Quality Inns, Rodeway Inns, Econo Lodges, Clarion Inns, Sleep Inns, Comfort Suites, Cambria Suites, and MainStay Suites, and every one of them provides a 10% discount to people 50 and older (the "Mature Travelers Rate"), and a 20% to 30% discount to people 60 and older (the "Sixty Plus

Rate"). The latter requires an advance reservation made to ☎ **800/4CHOICE** (424-6423). Choice also offers a 15% discount to members of AARP, who can be as young as 50.

Because all the above brands have good rates to begin with, an additional discount of 10% to 30% brings them into bargain territory. Readers seeking the cut should first have their reservations confirmed at the rate quoted to them, and then advise the telephone reservationist that they are eligible for either the Mature Travelers Rate or (better yet) the Sixty Plus Rate.

IF YOU'VE GOT RELATIVES OR FRIENDS OF MIDDLE AGE OR OLDER, ALERT THEM TO GRAND CIRCLE

Nothing could be more dramatic than the recent sharp growth of Grand Circle Travel (www.gct.com), the leading operator of tours for middle-aged and elderly Americans. And nothing could be more unusual than the manner in which Grand Circle has achieved that increase. It does not deal with travel agents (and most travel agents get livid when they hear the name) and it does not accept bookings over the Internet. It markets vacations in the old-fashioned way, by mailing massive quantities of its catalogs to literally millions of potential customers and then accepting inquiry phone calls from them. And it apparently operates its programs with such aplomb that a large army of mature Americans sign up for one trip after another. If you'd like a Grand Circle catalog (and you should at least look it over), call ☎ 800/959-0405.

A WEBSITE CALLED SENIORS HOME EXCHANGE SERVES A DIFFERENT SET OF TRAVEL NEEDS

When I first heard about Seniors Home Exchange (www.seniorshome exchange.com), I was frankly puzzled. What could such a site accomplish that wasn't better done by larger and longer-established home-exchange websites for persons of any age?

The language and organization of Seniors Home Exchange made the explanation obvious—but one that doesn't normally occur to most of us. Since many (if not most) seniors over the age of 50 are retired, they are able to take longer vacations than younger persons tethered to a job and restricted to short, 2-week vacations. To satisfy this need, many of the home exchanges featured on Seniors Home Exchange are for several weeks or longer. And because many seniors go on several trips a year and need to make frequent use of the Seniors Home Exchange service, there is a fairly stiff $79 charge for a 3-year membership.

The site, which has been in existence since 2001, currently lists over 30,000 properties. It offers not only home and apartment exchanges (you stay in theirs while they stay in yours), but also the opportunity to stay free of charge as a guest in the home of a member while they remain in residence.

I have now received multiple recommendations for Seniors Home Exchange from readers of my blog, and its bona fides seem more than established. If you're over 50, or know someone who is, you might want to take a look.

SO FEW DISCOUNTS REMAIN FOR SENIOR TRAVELERS THAT I CAN COVER THEM IN TWO SHORT PARAGRAPHS

People over the ages of 62 or 65 used to receive substantial discounts from the airlines and other travel suppliers. Today, the pickings are slimmer, but there do remain a handful of advantages for the mature American.

The National Park Service's Golden Age Passport, costing only $10 and allowing unlimited lifetime admission to the national parks, is the preeminent perk. It can be obtained in person at one of the parks or over the Internet. Runner-up is Amtrak's discount of 15% for persons 62 and older, available on every train other than the weekday Acela, the Auto Train, and sleeper cars. Greyhound gives 10% off for seniors, Avis gives them 5% to 20% off, and Club Med claims to have senior reductions as great as 30%.

With more and more of the nation's population entering the category of "seniors," other travel suppliers are surely missing a good bet by not publicizing an attractive discount program that will lure these dynamic vacationers to their products.

THERE'S IMPRESSIVE, CHANGE-YOUR-LIFE ADVICE FOR TRAVELERS OVER THE AGE OF 50 IN A WEBSITE AWKWARDLY ENTITLED OVER50ANDOVERSEAS.COM

Joining the Peace Corps, or volunteering for a dozen other arduous volunteer programs overseas, is normally regarded as a young folks' choice. John Dwyer, who is well over 50 in age, doesn't agree. He has created a fact-filled website called Over50andOverseas.com which describes a whole host of idealistic overseas programs that most mature Americans are fully capable of joining.

His own biography supplies the best example of how a person in the midcourse of his life, so to speak, can change his life through travel overseas:

In 1991 (when he was over 50), John joined the Peace Corps, a decision that led to international service in 14 countries and travel to 38 countries. After Peace Corps service in Guatemala, he served as a United Nations volunteer in the first elections in Bosnia after the Bosnian War and subsequently has worked elections in Serbia, Croatia, Kosovo, Macedonia, Albania, Montenegro, Russia, Ukraine, and Bangladesh. He managed camps for internally displaced persons (IDPs) in Herat, Afghanistan, and did development work in Kandahar, Afghanistan. He continues to work internationally.

If you're of retirement age, you may want to study John's website, which lists opportunities for rewarding volunteer service overseas.

Shopping

Take a look at the duty-free price guide & you'll never again go shopping in any airport's duty-free stores

Because it would be so difficult to compare prices on the vast array of goods sold in so-called "duty-free" airport shops, a website called the Duty Free Price Guide (www.thedutyfreepriceguide.com) devotes most of its attention to cigarettes, perfume, and liquor. But the huge price variations for those products are obviously representative of similar variations for electronic products and clothing. They show that certain airport shops and airlines mark up the cost of goods to such an extent as to cast doubt on whether the public receives any financial benefits at all.

Although shopping remains among the key activities of travel, I'm dubious about the values offered in tax-free airport shops.

Take the product identified as "Marlboro 200 packs Cigarettes." From various exotic airlines or remote airports (Ethiopian Airlines, Middle East Airlines, Qatar Airport), you can buy a 200-cigarette carton of Marlboros for $10 to $12, according to the website. Yet the very same carton is being sold for $24 to $26 by Northwest Airlines, American Airlines, and United Airlines; for $27 at the Los Angeles Airport; and for $41 by British Midland Airways and at Vienna Airport.

The same discrepancies are reported for perfume and liquor. A 50mL bottle of Dior Perfume ranges in price from $26 to $77, depending on the airline or airport selling it.

It's a crazy world out there. On several recent trips, I didn't see a single product selling for much less than I would pay at Best Buy or Circuit City in New York, or at the perfume wholesalers on lower Broadway. And I haven't any present plans to fly to Qatar or Dubai to pick up a cigarette bargain.

GO TO THE WEB & YOU'LL GET DISCOUNTS OF UP TO 70% ON TRAVEL GEAR & CLOTHING

Next time you're in the market for travel gear or specialty travel clothing, don't buy retail. Whether it's an Eagle Creek backpack or Swiss Army rolling bag, travel pants with zip-off legs and hidden pockets, or a performance button-down shirt that offers SPF 50 sun protection and built-in bug repellant, you can get it at big savings from a travel specialty discounter.

The king of the discount catalogs is Sierra Trading Post (www.sierratradingpost.com), which sells outdoor gear and travel apparel from major labels such as Ex Officio and Columbia Sportswear for anywhere from 35% to 70% off the retail price. Sometimes the product may be last year's model, or be available in a limited range of colors, but these savings more than make up for it.

Other travel specialty catalogs? In the "outlet" section of REI (www.rei.com/outlet), the popular camping and travel cooperative, all items are at least 60% below list; there's also a nifty display of items under $20 (the virtual version of the "impulse buy" rack at a checkout counter).

And finally, the website of Travel Smith (www.travelsmith.com), known for its own brand of high-quality travel clothing, offers up to 75% off items in the "Clearance" and "Weekly Specials" sections. Or you can get discounts (usually of 20%–50%) on a range of gadgets and clothes among the "Web Specials" at Magellan's (www.magellans.com)—select "Sale," then "Final Clearance" for the deepest cuts, up to 75%.

CARE TO BUY A VOLVO? BUY ONE FOR DELIVERY IN EUROPE & SAVE UP TO $4,000.

Most Volvo dealers will deliver a car to you in Europe that comes equipped with all U.S. specifications. And they will then ship it free to your own home city, after you have used the car for your touring needs in Europe. Since the car then comes in as an already-used, "second-hand" vehicle, it's

Fly to ancient Gothenburg, Sweden, and you can pick up a largely tax-free Volvo at an advantageous price.

taxed at lower-than-usual rates. You save up to $4,000, considering also that you have had the "free" use of the car for your touring.

You'll also receive, thrown into the deal free, two round-trip tickets to Europe with Scandinavian Airlines (SAS); a night at the Radisson Hotel in Gothenburg, Sweden; 15 days of European car insurance to drive and explore Europe; and, of course, shipment of the car home from your choice of 15 European cities.

Information about Volvo's overseas delivery program, including trip add-ons and pricing for all available models, is available on its website: www.volvocars.us/salesandservices/overseasdelivery.

DESIGNER SALT, ANYONE? AT $3 A PACKAGE WHEN BOUGHT IN EUROPE, IT HAS BECOME THE PERFECT GIFT PURCHASE BY INDIGENT AMERICAN TRAVELERS.

Now that the dollar's weakness has put an end to normal shopping (by Americans) in Europe, you may want to know about an item that you can buy affordably and in quantity overseas, and that will positively enthrall your relatives and friends when presented to them back home: designer salt! According to shopping maven Suzy Gershman, author of *Born to Shop* travel guides, designer salt sells for $30 and up in the United States (or on Amazon.com), but for only $3 a package at numerous groceries and supermarkets in Paris, Frankfurt, Rome, and the like.

And what is "designer salt"? It's salt with a special flavor, such as raspberry salt. There's semicoarse Hawaiian red Alea salt, small-flake Fleur de Sel, Jurassic salt, Peruvian pink and Sicilian white salt, kosher salt, lavender salts, ginger salts, French sea salt, Australian sea salt, Maldon salt, Murray River salt, La Baleine, Danish Viking smoked salt, and (most expensive of all) Japanese Jewel of the Ocean salt, among many others. They come in coarse, plain, or chunky grains, and are "saltier" than usual salt. True gourmet chefs, I'm assured, would never dream of using just plain salt (sodium chloride).

Look at the lengths to which we've been driven by currency changes.

SINGLES

THE SINGLE TRAVELER DOES BEST ON A VACATION DEVOTED TO A SPECIAL INTEREST OR A CAUSE

What sort of vacation is best for a single person traveling alone? The answer is an obvious one: volunteer vacations, study vacations, themed vacations—activities where no one cares whether you are part of a couple or are single, where everyone is absorbed in a vital cause or special interest outside of themselves, and where the cost of housing is the same for everyone.

If you must sign up for an escorted motorcoach tour (and have an unquenchable yen to roam across large swaths of the world), at least sign up for those programs that are specifically designed for adventuresome people. On the small group tours operated by G.A.P Adventures of Toronto (www.gapadventures.com), in which cultural sensitivity is cherished and accommodations are often in local guesthouses and private homes, no one cares whether you are single or a couple, and a great many singles are usually found. On the daring overland safaris or trekking expeditions operated by the many companies represented by Adventure Center of Emeryville, California (www.adventurecenter.com), singles of every age are a heavy component of every departure. The same applies to the scientific trips sponsored by the great Earthwatch organization (www.earthwatch.org) that sends you to aid university researchers and often accommodates you—singles and couples alike—in improvised bedding in a local house rented for the occasion.

Each of these opportunities is available to singles of all ages. And if any of them seem overly daunting, then repeat to yourself the famous admonition of Mark Twain: "Twenty years from now, you will be more disappointed by the things you didn't do than by the ones you did. So throw off the bowlines! Sail away from the safe harbor. Catch the trade winds in your sails. Explore. Dream. Discover."

A LONG-ESTABLISHED BRITISH TOUR OPERATOR HAS COME TO THE AID OF SINGLE PERSONS TRAVELING ALONE

Among the most frequent questions on my weekly Travel Show (Sun from noon–2pm; otherwise heard by podcast at www.wor710.com) has to do with the vacation woes of single persons traveling alone. How can they avoid a single-room supplement and other discriminations?

That problem has plagued the travel industry almost since the world began. Since hotel rooms are typically designed to hold couples, those who wish to travel alone will often have to pay two times as much per person—once for themselves and once for the person who isn't accompanying them—for the privilege of going anywhere.

The major cruise lines once made special arrangements for single travelers, and if a solo tourist needed a roommate, many of the major companies would often help matchmake them with other solo travelers. No more. Now, the onus is on the traveler to supply a body for the other bed.

I have recently found a company based in Britain, SpeedBreaks (www.speedbreaks.co.uk), that specializes in singles' travel. It began simply as a tour operator for singles' weekend trips from London and has grown to include vacations of many lengths and to a variety of European locations. In all cases, it aims to supply single people with trips at a reasonable rate.

Those prices, it must be said, are most reasonable to British tourists, who pay in pounds. Americans, who must pay about $1.45 per British pound, will find them slightly less reasonable, but considering how rare it is to find an outstanding singles' travel company with plenty of departures from which to choose, even the exchange rate–hobbled prices of SpeedBreak are worth considering, and there's no denying that many of its trips will qualify as unusual and interesting to most American tourists.

Prices are usually around £250 to £300 ($363–$435) for 3- and 4-night trips, which isn't a spectacular savings, but isn't bad for singles' travel. One of its walking tours of the Cinque Terre goes for £400 ($580) for 5 nights. A 6-night cycling tour of Catalonia is £429 ($622). Neither of those includes airfare, leaving you to get there on your own, but they do include meals and hotel. For the best prices, you must share a room with another participant (so SpeedBreaks doesn't actually solve the problem of sleeping single in a double room—it merely introduces participants to other singles).

Trips, which are described on the company website, also include sailing in the Mediterranean, beach vacations in Egypt, and interestingly, single-day meet-and-greet activity days throughout London.

Don't expect a beer-soaked romp in Ibiza from the company, though. "Our events are great fun but aimed at adults," explains the SpeedBreak website. "If you're expecting an 18 to 30 atmosphere you've probably come to the wrong place."

Frequently, the Specialty Travel Index will list tours unusually suitable for single persons traveling alone

The best-matched married couple I know (other than my wife and myself) are a university professor (he teaches political science) and a psychological therapist (she maintains an active practice). In their late 40s, and recently divorced, they met at an Appalachian music camp where they had each gone on vacation to pursue an interest in regional folksongs.

I am not suggesting travel as a means for meeting your spouse. But for those many single persons in search of a vital vacation trip, I frequently suggest that they book aboard a tour that focuses on a special interest, a theme, a cause. On that sort of trip, it hardly matters whether you are married or single; everyone maintains a high level of involvement, and they mix and mingle with enthusiasm. The single person is rarely alone.

But where do you discover such travel opportunities? For starters, there's the long-established Specialty Travel Index, which began as a magazine and is now also a free website (www.specialtytravel.com) listing the special-interest tours offered by some 500 specialty tour operators. For every conceivable interest—from African heritage to zoology, from agriculture to astronomy, church tours, fashion, horse breeding, jazz, music and dance, psychiatry, and social transformation—there's a company operating tours that cater to persons with that preoccupation. Whether you're interested in doctors' and nurses' tours, jazz or kosher tours, tours for people over 50, tours for collectors of antiques or horse breeders, and so on, you can join a group of like-minded people, in which the fact that you are single and traveling alone has no importance whatsoever. And the experience is bound to be fascinating.

Several special-interest magazines carry advertisements & listings of tours especially suitable for single persons traveling alone

Special-interest magazines also provide a way to find tours in which participants are focused on an interest outside of themselves, and therefore travel pleasurably regardless of whether they have a travel companion. Virtually all such magazines carry classified listings of tours for readers of similar interests.

Interested in natural history (archaeology, the wilderness, the world's wildlife and inland waterways)? Go to a newsstand or a public library, pick up a copy of *Natural History* published by the American Museum of Natural History, and turn to the "Explorer Guide" section of small colorful ads at the back. There you'll see a broad assortment of trips to the Amazon and Galapagos Islands, to the Himalayas and Papua New Guinea, to fossil beds in Nebraska and Crow Canyon in southwestern Colorado, all attracting people with interests like yours. From the same library racks, pick up a copy of *Sierra* magazine for lower-priced volunteer vacations to wilderness areas of the United States. On such journeys, you'll never feel alone.

Interested in yoga and holistic healing, in physical development using Eastern therapies? Buy a copy of *Yoga Journal* at any college bookstore or other intellectual newsstand, and you'll find a large array of residential yoga retreats and schools. Interested in traveling with fellow progressives? Buy a copy of *Utne* (formerly known as *Utne Reader*), turn to "Classifieds" and then to "Travel/Adventure" and you'll find options ranging from Quaker-led visits to New York, to homestays offered by political "greens," to "Goddess Tours of Greece" led by a "feminist theologian." Interested in cooking and cuisine, or arts and crafts, folk dancing and folk music, fine art and sculpture? Pick up the relevant special-interest magazine and in a small, back-of-the-book ad section will be notices for special-interest tours for that discipline.

One of the most powerful travel opportunities for the single person traveling alone is a special-interest tour.

SEVERAL WEBSITES TRY HARD TO FIND BENEFITS FOR THE SINGLE PERSON TRAVELING ALONE

In an ongoing effort to be of assistance to the solo traveler, I've resolved to pass on every new website on travel for singles that comes to my attention. None of my recent discoveries is earthshaking, but they may contain some nuggets of advice that will prove valuable.

Start first with:

SoloTravel.org is loaded with tips on travel, safety, dining alone, hostel etiquette, and making friends, along with plenty of first-hand accounts of traveling solo. Its advice can be a bit generic and thin (and the site is designed so that its Google ads blend a bit too well into its own content, making it difficult to tell which is which), but it does link to many other resources for the single traveler out there, from tour companies to information sites.

And then there's freelance travel writer Ellen Perlman, who has recently begun blogging about the joys, perils, and pitfalls of traveling alone at Boldly Go Solo (http://boldlygosolo.typepad.com), with recommendations on everything from tour operators and tips to accounts of her own adventures (skiing, hiking, rafting, and more) and musing about the relative benefits and costs of traveling alone versus with companions.

Women in particular will want to consult the sites of Journeywoman (www.journeywoman.com) and Women Travel Tips (www.womentravel tips.com), both of which pay special attention to the issues of women traveling solo.

I'll keep them coming as soon as I uncover more.

Skiing

For addicts of the sport looking for a way to ski without charge, there's a strong probability that Crested Butte will repeat its traditional freebie offer this coming winter

Here's a cheapskate's delight, found in central Colorado during the earliest part of the winter ski season. For several years now, Crested Butte Mountain Resort (☎ 800/810-7669; www.skicb.com) has offered free skiing (that is, a free ski lift ticket every day) from around November 26 to December 17 to persons who booked an accommodation through the resort's website. While it's too early to predict whether the resort will repeat that offer for late November to mid-December of 2009, I find the probability to be so strong as to warrant this mention. Call them later in 2009, and you may be able to snare a top bargain.

The development of modern, high-speed, detachable lifts has greatly improved the ski experience.

From mid-November until December 20, many of the great ski resorts offer package stays in which the cost of lift tickets is, in effect, totally free

Early in the season (from mid-Nov until mid-Dec), many other great ski resorts offer lodging packages in which the cost of lift tickets is virtually free. That's good news because the cost of lift tickets has skyrocketed and many top U.S. resorts charge in the neighborhood of $90 a day for lifts alone.

These packages are often available at the end of the season, too, though the early season seems to draw more attention. Vermont's Killington, the biggest ski resort on the East Coast, for example, offers early-season (until Dec 20) rates starting at under $100 per person per day, which includes lift tickets and lodging. Phone ☎ 800/621-6867, or log on to www.killington.com, for details.

Snowbird, the Utah resort which averages 500 inches of snow annually, also has an early-season deal, supplying lift tickets and lodging in a studio condo starting at around $100 per person based on double occupancy and a 3-night minimum stay (☎ 800/232-9542; www.snowbird.com).

Seventh Mountain Resort, the property closest to Oregon's Mount Bachelor ski area, offers one-bedroom standard condos for two adults starting at $129 per night in early season, but not including lifts (☎ 800/452-6810; www.seventhmountain.com). Maine's popular Sugarloaf Mountain sells seasonal packages beginning at under $100 per person based on two adults staying in a ski-in, ski-out hotel room or condo (☎ 800/843-5623; www.sugarloaf.com).

In costlier Colorado, among Breckenridge's best early season deals in 2008 was a 4-night, lift ticket–and-lodging package for $323 per person, based on four people sharing a two-bedroom condo (☎ 877/620-0942; www.breckenridge.snow.com). Never again, as the season proceeds, will you find deals quite as cheap. Can you and your friends wait until next December?

Spring Break

We are about to enter the season of collegiate spring breaks & I have various stuffy comments to make about traveling at that time

The month of March, for many college students, is the month of their spring break, and thousands of them plunge into drunken revelry in such places as Daytona Beach, Florida, or South Padre Island, Texas.

Now the great majority of students don't do that, of course, but a small minority behaves like fugitives from *Animal House* and sours the atmosphere for everybody else. At spring break in the Tropics, they not only drink to excess, but perform all sorts of stunts from hotel balconies, creating a threat to people strolling below; and they often line up to make boorish comments about young women passing by. I think parents have a positive obligation not to finance these trips to Florida, Texas, and Mexico, and I can't think of a better substitute than a spring-break trip to a European capital.

Nearly all the great cities of Europe enjoy low-season airfares in the month of March that aren't much more expensive than a domestic trip. And although European hotel and meal costs are high, they are surely a better investment for parents to make than a rock-bottom motel in Daytona Beach. In Europe, spring break can become a profound experience for your college-age children rather than simply a waste of time. Can anyone even pronounce the words South Padre Island and Paris, France, in the same breath?

STUDENTS

STA TRAVEL HAS EMERGED AS A POWERHOUSE OF TRAVEL FOR YOUNG VACATIONERS

STA (Student Travel Association) is the purchaser of and successor to the now-defunct Council Travel (the former U.S. student travel agency), and has achieved a size and influence within the travel industry that Council Travel never had. If you're of student age and you haven't recently studied the STA website (www.statravel.com), you really should. It offers travel opportunities at prices of which the older traveler can only dream.

The student is, and should be, a privileged traveler, benefiting from every sort of discount and preference. By constantly consulting the STA site, a student can engage affordably in far-ranging travels.

A PROGRAM KNOWN AS "AIRTRAN U" PERMITS YOUNG PEOPLE AGES 18 TO 22 TO FLY FOR $69 TO $89 ANYWHERE IN THE UNITED STATES

Young people ages 18 to 22 should know that AirTran permits them to stand by for $69 to $89 per flight, depending on the length of the trip. The program is known as AirTran U (www.airtranu.com), and all the traveler needs to do is show up at the ticket counter with a carry-on bag 2 hours before a flight. If there's still a seat available a half-hour or less before departure, the seat is theirs for the cut rate. Naturally, there's some risk involved—if a flight is full, the traveler will have to wait and hope for space on the next one. To improve your odds, trying this on lower traffic days such as Tuesday, Wednesday, and Saturday is a good idea. And don't try standing by twice in a row (as for a connecting flight), which involves just too much luck; you may get on one flight but be turned back on the second, stranded in an intermediate town. Finally, keep in mind that there are black-out dates during holidays.

Chapter Ten

THE PREPARATIONS YOU MAKE, THE PRODUCTS YOU BUY

FROM PASSPORTS TO PET CARE TO PACKING

What you do before departing on a trip can often be just as important as the choices you make en route. And people who fail to take important predeparture steps will often find that their travels have been badly affected by that lack of preparation. From renting a cellphone to choosing the right luggage, from buying travel insurance to arranging care for your pets, this chapter is my attempt to anticipate all the right pretravel choices.

CELLPHONES

NEED A CELLPHONE FOR YOUR NEXT OVERSEAS TRIP? RENT IT!

A large number of us have cellphones that don't work overseas. So on the eve of a trip, we frantically search for a new cellphone from AT&T or T-Mobile (which do work in some—not all—countries), or we pay $75 for a chip that can be inserted into some (not all) phones to render them capable of making and receiving calls abroad. And if we find a phone that will work in the country to which we're traveling, we then have to worry about whether our recharger will plug into foreign sockets.

One sensible alternative is to rent a globally enabled phone from a company, such as the 12-year-old TravelCell (www.travelcell.com), bearing in mind that a dozen other firms are undoubtedly just as effective (a trip to Google will reveal that many and more). Using TravelCell simply as an example, a call to its toll-free number (☎ 877/CELLPHONE [235-5746]) connects you with a specialist who is well versed with what phones work in what countries and under what conditions. By hearing the countries to which you plan to travel, they are able to recommend a rental phone that will work in every place to which you will be going. And after agreeing on the price, the phone is mailed to you overnight, along with a recharger that will also work in the sockets of those destinations.

Most of these companies—such as Cellomobile (www.cellomobileusa.com) or Phonerental (www.phonerentalusa.com), to broaden the list—will charge around $30 per week for rental of the international phone, plus $1.40 a minute for most outgoing calls from most countries. Significantly, most of them also allow you to receive unlimited, free incoming calls.

Previous page: Often, preparations for the trip (shopping for a travel hat, packing, scheduling) can be just as important as the steps you take once there.

ANOTHER SMART TACTIC IS TO TRAVEL ABROAD WITH SKYPE

I find it surprising that so many travelers fail to download Skype onto their laptops before departing on an overseas trip. Because, many times, their cellphones don't allow international calls, they end up paying exorbitant sums when the need arises to make constant calls home. They could have phoned for free or almost for free by simply using Skype.

Your first step: Go to any Radio Shack or Best Buy and purchase a small headset (for about $10) that plugs into your computer's USB port.

Then go to www.skype.com, and download the software onto your laptop. From that moment on, you're able to make calls for about 2¢ a minute to normal numbers in the United States, and for nothing at all to persons who already have Skype.

Once overseas, of course, you'll want to stay at a hotel with high-speed Internet access. A little research will turn up all sorts of moderately priced chains that provide such access free of charge.

Skype's not perfect. Sometimes calls are dropped and depending on how fast your connection is, you may experience a short lag time in your conversation. But much of the time, it's far clearer than a traditional telephone call, and the person you talk to sounds like they're in the room with you. Besides, when something goes wrong, you just hang up and try again—the connection/download is either free or nominal in cost.

A NEW TELEPHONE DEVICE FOR TRAVEL MAY POSSIBLY BE MORE USEFUL (GULP!) THAN SKYPE

Skype (www.skype.com), as I've said, is an excellent piece of software that allows for either free (to other Skype users) or nominally priced (to normal phones) calls made through your computer. And the system itself is free to download into your computer.

But now there's a new gadget called magicJack. Basically, magicJack (www.magicjack.com), which is smaller than a deck of playing cards, turns your computer or laptop into a phone jack. It's a small unit that you insert into one of your USB ports. You can then plug a regular phone into that and start dialing. For a $40 fee (thereafter $20 for each additional year that you wish to subscribe), you get this phone jack and the right to make free calls in the United States and Canada, plus free international calls back to the United States and Canada. It doesn't use your standard phone line; you just have to be connected to high-speed Internet for it to work. magicJack also comes with voicemail and an American phone number through which you can receive free phone calls (Skype makes you pay extra for those things).

A few other companies have introduced similar products (Vonage's V-Phone is one of them), but those require that you not only purchase the device but also pay a monthly subscription fee starting around $15. That makes magicJack, with its initial fee of $40 then an annual fee of $20, period, the better deal. It also comes with a 30-day money-back guarantee, which few new electronic inventions do, so you can send it back if it doesn't work.

I haven't used magicJack myself yet, so I can't vouch for it. It seems to me that not all foreign hotel phones have jacks that are the same size as the phones in use in the United States, so a user of magicJack might need to also pack a lightweight phone handset or earpiece for use on the road. Also, all new electronics gadgets go through a period during which their kinks are worked out. Still, $40 for a device that provides unlimited calls on the road as well as back at home seems a very good deal to me.

How you can obtain free-of-charge directory assistance from any telephone

In this age of the Internet, you can find pretty much any answer with Google. But what if you're on the road without a computer and need to find a phone number—say, to find that great restaurant your friend recommended, or the nearest Motel 6?

Once upon a time you could call directory assistance to get the number of any business for free. Then, in the 1990s, 411 started charging a modest fee of around 35¢. Now the charge for calling 411 has jumped to a ludicrous $1.25 to $3.50.

Dial ☎ 800/FREE-411 (373-3411; www.free411.com), a "free" directory assistance number. I call it "free" although there is a kind of cost: about 30 to 40 seconds of your time spent listening to brief ads, one before you ask for the listing, and another before you get the number.

The system is not perfect. For one thing, the automated voice recognition software has a few bugs. I tested it by asking for the number of a favorite pizza parlor called Caserta Vecchia. The automated system thought I had asked for "conservative party." A live operator came on to sort things out and I did get the proper number in the end. A test to find a residential number worked much better.

CLOTHING

Hidden pockets are a fine addition to clothing specifically designed for travel

Sometimes the best travel devices are so obvious that no one thinks of actually producing them for sale. Such a product is the "hidden pocket" manufactured by a one-woman entrepreneur, Frieda Newton, from a home-based plant in Connecticut. She recently mailed me a "hidden pocket," and I actually tried it out, leaving my wallet at home and filling the "pocket" with cash (a few bills) and several credit cards. I probably could also have stuffed in my ultranarrow cellphone.

The device is simply a little nylon pouch, Velcro-fastened, that's large enough for cash, credit cards, and driver's license. It is attached to a broad elastic strap, also Velcro-fastened, which you can wrap around your arm, wrist, or ankle, always concealed by your clothing. And thus you can walk the streets of Moscow or Naples completely protected from pickpockets or purse snatchers who will never know where you're carrying your valuables.

You can order a hidden pocket by phoning ☎ **888/300-4161,** by e-mailing sales@thehiddenpocket.com, or by consulting www.thehidden pocket.com.

FESTIVALS

A BUNCH OF LONDONERS HAVE NOW CREATED THE WORLD'S FINEST ONGOING CALENDAR OF FESTIVALS

One of the joys of travel is to arrive in a destination and encounter a harvest festival where the food and locally brewed beer flow freely, a concert series held in parks or ancient ruins, or a spectacular celebration of the local saint's day. There once was a time when, aside from such major festivals as Carnival in Rio or Venice, you either had to contact the local tourist office to learn of such events or rely on sheer dumb luck to land you in town on the right day.

Now you can just log on to Whatsonwhen (www.whatsonwhen.com) to learn about every sort of special event, from festivals to concerts, trade shows to art exhibits. The site covers annual events and once-in-a-lifetime experiences, offering one-stop shopping, whether you want to find out the dates for the New York marathon, get directions to the Buffalo Wallow Chili Cookoff in South Dakota's Custer State Park, or learn more about the Water Festival along the Mekong River in Cambodia.

You can browse by country, region, or city, getting a full annual calendar or just focusing on the dates you'll be traveling. Each destination guide cover some sightseeing and basic info, but the true treasure trove lies under the "Events" menu. These are divided into event categories: Festivals & Heritage, Music & Nightlife, Arts, Sports & Outdoors, Classical Music, Lifestyle, Kids & Family, Science & Knowledge, Gay & Lesbian, and Weird & Wonderful (including such oddities as Italy's Duck Festival, donkey racing in Croatia, or the annual Arizona Cowboy Poets Gathering).

The site can help you fine-tune your itinerary in two ways. You can alter your schedule to make sure you'll be in town for the annual uncorking of

Planning to arrive during the time of a festival may add an important dimension to your trip.

the new wine . . . or shuffle your plans to avoid a city during some huge convention that will keep prices high and hotel rooms booked.

Note: You can also find all these events at http://events.frommers.com, as Whatsonwhen is a sister site to Frommers.com and also part of Wiley Publishing (my publisher).

INSURANCE

A NEW COMPARISON SITE FOR TRAVEL INSURANCE POLICIES IS AN UNUSUALLY HELPFUL SERVICE

Vacations cost so much money, and so many things can go wrong, that it's only wise to ensure that should accidents happen, you'll be able to recoup your losses or, at worst, be flown back home with a doctor at your side.

But there's no need to waste hours of time researching policies. One of the easier ways to find the right insurance policy is to turn to the Internet, where you now have, for the first time, two different comparison sites. Squaremouth (☎ 800/240-0369; www.squaremouth.com), like the better-known and longer-established InsureMyTrip.com, canvasses a multitude of travel insurers based on criteria selected by the user, including the length of the trip and how much was spent booking it.

Interestingly, Squaremouth offers the following refreshing "zero complaint policy": "If any one of our clients has a complaint against an insurance carrier that cannot be resolved to our satisfaction, we will remove the carrier from our site and no longer sell its products." The generosity of this promise may have something to do with the fact that many of the companies listed on its site are partners—the site is technically an insurance agent for these other companies—so it's easier to police them than it would be if there were no professional association.

The site also allows users to compare policies side by side in a grid format. Whenever I have tried its comparison chart, policies from as many as eight different insurance companies have been offered for my inspection. Although I can't proclaim it the best insurance site out there (InsureMyTrip. com should also be consulted), I can say Squaremouth is another resource worth including in your list of browser bookmarks.

LUGGAGE

YOU NOW NEED A COMPLEX CHART TO TELL YOU WHAT CAN & CANNOT BE CHECKED ON, OR CARRIED ABOARD, YOUR FLIGHT, WITHIN THE UNITED STATES & ABROAD

Would you believe that the United States Tour Operators Association is now displaying (on its website) a multipage chart showing you the numbers and sizes of suitcases you can check on, or carry aboard, the plane? It's at www. ustoa.com and reveals such stunning details as the fact that the weight allowance for domestic U.S. flights is totally different from the weight allowance on intra-European flights. There's even a different standard for flights within South America, and you can be hit in the purse if you're not aware of it.

To make things worse, a slightly different chart is published by the travel-clothing house known as TravelSmith at www.travelsmith.com, setting forth—to my eye—slightly different dimensions and weights. Luggage is getting loonier all the time.

YOUR CARRY-ON LUGGAGE WILL BE ACCEPTED ON FLIGHTS OVERSEAS ONLY IF IT'S SMALL ENOUGH & UNDER 22 POUNDS

We are starting to hear horror stories of Americans showing up for a Lufthansa flight in Frankfurt or a Ryanair flight in London and being prevented from taking a carry-on bag onto the plane because it is too large (or heavy). This doesn't happen that often at American airports, and thus we become complacent.

It's extremely difficult to learn the exact outer specifications for carry-on luggage imposed by the overseas carriers. From a number of unofficial sources, I've compiled these dimensions: 21.7×15.7×7.9 inches. And bear in mind that checked luggage on such an airline as Ryanair is accepted only on payment of a stiff fee, and of unusually harsh charges if the checked luggage is in excess of 33 pounds. An American flying within Europe on Ryanair, and checking a suitcase that weighs 50 pounds (the usual limit on transatlantic carriers), can incur a penalty charge—without exaggeration—of more than $150. Beware.

A TOP TRAVEL SECRET: LUGGAGE PURCHASED ON THE INTERNET USUALLY COSTS LESS

We need luggage to travel, and too often we pay too much for it. The high cost of high-quality luggage has sparked the emergence of luggage stores on the Internet, which often undercut the normal prices because they don't have the expense of a brick-and-mortar business.

These e-luggage stores have grown immensely popular. They overcome the reluctance of some people to buy luggage without inspecting the product by offering free shipping (on returns, too) and radically reduced prices.

The leader in online luggage retailers is a Colorado-based company called eBags (www.ebags.com), whose website sells thousands of bags (far more models than even the largest store would carry) from dozens of popular manufacturers, including Samsonite, Eagle Creek, the North Face, Liz Claiborne, and Pierre Cardin. Shipping is free for most orders over $35; returns are free of hassles and costs; unused bags are refundable within 60 days; and the company includes a prepaid UPS label with every shipment.

eBags offers many options to help the shopper find exactly the right bag (or the right price). You can search by brand, style, price, bag material (canvas, suede, polyester, nylon, cotton, leather), bestsellers, closeouts, and other categories. Each bag is rated by customers who own it on a scale of 1 to 10, and unlike many hotel-review websites, which often only have a handful of ratings on which to base your decision, many pieces of luggage on eBags have hundreds of reviews to guide you.

The closeouts section of eBags is where to find the very best deals. Recently, a JanSport expandable carry-on in a discontinued color with a retail price of $160 was selling on eBags for just $50. Even items that aren't closeouts are usually priced far below retail.

Two online luggage retailers based in New Jersey are also worth searching for bargains: Luggage Online (www.luggageonline.com) and LuggagePoint. com. A recent sale at the former offered a six-piece luggage set from American Tourister, originally priced at $450, for only $170. A closeout special at LuggagePoint.com was a 31-inch four-wheel Samsonite bag, originally priced at $260, for $117, or $143 off.

All the Internet luggage companies allow for free returns and cover the cost of return shipping, though their policies differ sometimes. Luggage Online only has a 30-day money-back guarantee, while LuggagePoint.com is more generous, giving the customer 90 days.

Another difference is the price-matching guarantee. All three companies have one, but while Luggage Online promises to match any competitor's prices, LuggagePoint.com and eBags take it a step further with a 110% price guarantee.

Even with the presence of helpful product reviews and easy return policies at these websites, however, some consumers may still be concerned about purchasing such a large item without inspecting it first-hand. For them, the solution is to go in person to a store that has the item in question. If the product proves satisfactory, ask the store to match the price you found earlier online. If it won't, head to a computer and make the purchase.

UNITED AIRLINES' DECISION TO CHARGE $25 FOR THE SECOND SUITCASE CHECKED PER FLIGHT IS THE BEST THING THAT'S HAPPENED TO TRAVELERS IN YEARS

We all take too much clothing and other paraphernalia when we travel. We pack every conceivable outfit for every possible occasion and end up devoting half our time to laboriously packing and unpacking multiple suitcases. We become beasts of burden, sweating that luggage into a taxicab, dragging it up stairs and down, paying for porters to carry it. And we discover at the end of the trip that we haven't used 80% of the items we've packed. We have dragged around two heavy cases of unworn, useless apparel.

They travel best who travel light. There is no better travel sensation than the joy of moving from place to place in carefree fashion, with one small suitcase lightly packed. That's why I think—contrary to others—that the decision by United Airlines to charge $25 for a second checked suitcase every time you fly (and $50 if you lug that second suitcase round-trip) is a good thing. It will create happier travelers.

The new policy, now adopted by nearly all other airlines, will bring them a considerable amount of additional income. If what it also does is persuade the smart traveler to travel light, to limit his or her luggage to one small suitcase, then it will set off a spasm of delight. People will learn they are happier when they travel light, that they become light-hearted and carefree, that they avoid porters and taxicabs, that they are able to shop around when it comes to choosing a hotel; that they need not collapse from exhaustion at the first lodging they see.

So to all you greedy, fee-charging, profit-hungry execs at United Airlines: thank you.

Don't leave home without a few tiny, packaged items

Let's talk today about a few trivial travel purchases, or items for packing, that can often reduce the price of a trip.

Film (or memory cards for digital cameras), batteries for electrical devices, and such over-the-counter medicines as aspirin and Tylenol are almost always far more expensive overseas and should be brought along.

Peanut butter and Nutella are helpful items to carry with you. They're life saving and money saving; take up only the smallest space in your suitcase; need no refrigeration; are high in protein and energy; and when spread on bread or crackers can save the day—inexpensively—when hunger pangs hit, or when you're fearful of eating local foods. Peanut butter, you know; Nutella (a semisweet chocolate hazelnut spread) is available at most good U.S. supermarkets and in every grocery store of France, Italy, Switzerland, and Spain.

For some travelers, peanut butter is an always-satisfying snack on the road: It needs no refrigeration, and it allays hunger.

Another essential item for any long trip is a tiny spool of dental floss. A friend is the source of this puzzling advice. She claims that you can do many things with dental floss. You can stitch with dental floss and a needle. You can make dental floss into a fishing line. You can tie things with it. You can secure the locks on your luggage with dental floss, since it can't easily be broken or untied. Dental floss, she claims, is the secret weapon of smart travelers!

PowerBars join peanut butter as essential, "don't leave home without them" items to be stuffed into your checked-on luggage

I'm staring, as I write, at a chocolate-covered PowerBar which I just bought for $1.50 at a corner drugstore. I made that purchase out of curiosity

Some trendy young people swear by PowerBars as an essential item to bring along, forestalling hunger and producing energy.

provoked by advice from a number of Frommer's readers. They all claim that you should buy several PowerBars on the eve of an international trip, and scatter them through your suitcase, just as you should also carry a plastic jar of peanut butter (and hard crackers) to ease you through those travel moments when you're hungry and can't find anything suitable to eat.

They also suggest that I travel with Zone Bars, Jaybars, Quaker Oats Granola Bars, Slim Fast Granola Bars, Banana Balance Bars, and Clif Bars purchased at Trader Joe's. One reader insisted that a bagel thrown into his carry-on is only slightly larger than a bar and serves the same purpose for only 65¢. Like the tobacco chewers in baseball, granola crunchers are apparently dominating the world of travel.

FOR $4.95 AT WALMART: A "BUCKY" THAT KEEPS YOUR HEAD FROM FALLING FORWARD ON AN OVERNIGHT FLIGHT

Some travelers swear by them; others think them absurd. For $4.95 at Walmart, you can buy a "bucky" that you deflate and inflate at your convenience (and is thus easy to carry). A "bucky" is a wrap-around-the-neck head pillow that prevents your head from slumping forwards (and waking you up) when you fall asleep in the seat of an airplane. It comes in a stuffed version that changes shape to accommodate the size and shape of your head, or a less expensive, inflatable version. The Walmart version is a far more sensible purchase than the $25 stuffed variety of the bucky sold in some department stores.

Ever heard of a "Tilley Endurable"? It's a travel hat that people swear by.

The Canadian company called "Tilley" has become something of a legend in travel clothing, with its handsome cloth hats for men and women, guaranteed against any deterioration or mishap. And if you think I'm balmy for mentioning it, you'll want to look at the website, www.tilley.com, which goes into some details about why the hat is so helpful for the male and female traveler (catch that Velcro fastener for sticking your sunglasses against the side of the hat, and the fact that the brim buttons up on the side if you should care to wear it Australian-style). At $60, it's not the most economical purchase, but after looking at the various photos, you may succumb.

You can double the room in your luggage by carrying your clothes in space-saving compression bags

I have friends who swear by these compression bags, which are essentially like giant Ziploc baggies fitted with one-way pressure valves along one edge. Once you fill the bag with all your clothes and seal the top, you squeeze all the air out of the bag by rolling it up, then unfurling it again. This compresses your kit into literally half its original size.

These bags were originally hawked as a way of shrinking sweaters, bed comforters, and other bulky seasonal items to maximum household storage space, but they also make an excellent space-saving tool for travelers. As a bonus, they help organize the mess in your bag—at least this way all your clothes are compartmentalized into one place. One warning: They can wreak havoc on wrinkle-prone materials, but savvy travelers know to avoid packing wrinkly clothing in the first place.

There are two main brands. Compression Sacs from Eagle Creek (www.eaglecreek.com), sold at luggage stores and in travel gear catalogs such as Travel Smith (www.travelsmith.com) and Magellan's (www.magellans.com), are the heavier-duty option and sized for travelers, but are also more expensive: $8 to $12 a piece, depending on size.

Less expensive, but also less sturdy, is the Space Bag (www.spacebag.com), which you may recognize from its infomercials. These are widely available at such places as Target (www.target.com) and Walmart (www.walmart.com), the latter selling a set of eight travel-size bags for around $20. If you choose the Space Bags, be sure you pick up the smaller sizes and not the Extra Large bag (or the kind that needs to be sealed by a vacuum cleaner hose) intended for household uses.

Also, pay little heed to the user reviews on some retail sites that complain about the bags' inability to stay vacuum sealed. It's true that, if not sealed properly, the bags can slowly lose their compression over time (and, after several years of use, will start springing slow leaks even when sealed properly). However, this is only an issue if you're trying to keep a brace of sweaters compressed for 6 months at a stretch in your basement. The bags have no problem holding a tight, compressed vacuum seal for the brief period they'll spend in your luggage, and besides, you'll be opening and resealing it every time you switch hotels.

PASSPORTS

WHEN YOU NEED TO HAVE A PASSPORT ISSUED IN A DAY, ALL IS NOT LOST—MEET THE EXPEDITER

Whaddya do if you suddenly must make an overseas trip and discover that your passport has expired? Or if you've lost your passport and need a replacement right away? Or if you need to show picture I.D. and a certified birth certificate, and you don't have such a birth certificate and need to get one in a day?

Expediters. Though their services don't come cheap, they are highly effective. In some mysterious fashion, they have an allotment of daily passports, and are often able to get you a passport or birth certificate within a day. One of them boasts that if you'll give him notice late at night, he'll have a representative at the passport office at 7am the next morning—and you'll have your passport in time for an evening flight that day. The cost? $100 to $200, depending on the difficulty of the request.

There are several such services, and I'm not recommending any particular one. But the company called It's Easy (www.itseasy.com) has set up a 24-hour/7-day-a-week desk at Terminal 4 of JFK Airport in New York, and I find that impressive. It's headed by David J. Alwadish, who claims that if someone needs a new passport and discovers that at the airport, he can arrange for a photo to be taken and an application downloaded at the airport. Depending on the timing, he will then get the new passport back to the airport, often on the same day.

It's Easy also claims that it has been expediting passports and visas for movie stars and such for 30 years, and has now decided to make its miracles available to us hoi polloi. It's Easy can also be reached at ☎ 866/ITS-EASY (487-3279).

BELIEVE IT OR NOT, THERE'S ALSO A COMPANY THAT ASSISTS YOU IN OBTAINING CERTIFIED COPIES OF YOUR BIRTH CERTIFICATE (FOR PASSPORT PURPOSES)

If the passport you need is the first one you've ever had, you will also have to obtain a certified copy of your birth certificate to accompany your application. Although It's Easy does that for persons who were born in New York State, another company called VitalChek (www.vitalchek.com) can assist Americans who were born elsewhere in the United States.

Domestic birth certificate offices are usually quite forthcoming in obtaining and mailing to you a copy of your birth certificate. But VitalChek can perhaps do the job a bit better than you could yourself.

IT'S OFFICIAL: JUNE 1, 2009, IS NOW THE FINAL DATE FOR HAVING A PASSPORT OR PASSPORT CARD TO ENTER THE UNITED STATES BY LAND OR SEA

After much hemming and hawing, after announcements of the dreaded deadline followed by frantic withdrawal of such announcements, after contradictions between two agencies—the State Department and the Department of Homeland Security—after all that, the two government departments have finally collaborated on a joint announcement of the absolutely final, cross-my-heart, definitive date for needing a passport or passport card to enter the United States by any means—cruise ship, car, train, or airplane—from abroad. The date is June 1, 2009.

Let me set forth the verbatim report of the Cruise Line Industry Association (which obviously has been fighting to put off the requirement for cruise passengers). Their release reads as follows:

> Final U.S. Passport Requirements
>
> The U.S. Department of Homeland Security and Department of State have announced that as of June 1, 2009, travelers will be required to present a passport, passport card or other approved secure document denoting citizenship and identity for all land and sea travel into the United States. This includes U.S., Canadian and Bermuda citizens. Special provisions will be made for organized groups of children under 18 to enter with only proof of citizenship.
>
> C.L.I.A. urges all consumers to obtain a passport. The expense and minimal effort required (applications can be submitted at post offices throughout the country as well as at passport offices) are well worth the result: an official document proving identity and citizenship that will facilitate easy travel throughout the world.

If you are to have any sort of future travel life, you must now proceed to obtain a passport (or a less expensive passport card, discussed below).

Steps have finally been taken to substitute less-expensive passport cards for land & sea crossings of the U.S. border

Heeding widespread complaints about the high cost of passports incurred by every member of a large family, the U.S. State Department has provided partial relief. When you apply for a U.S. passport, you can now specify that you are willing to accept a cheaper ($45) passport card, which will be valid for crossing U.S. borders by land (car, bus, or train) or sea (on a cruise)—but not on a flight.

Standard passports, however, will still cost $97. And there are no discounts for families needing multiple passports. Doesn't the high charge—almost $400 for a family of four—prevent or discourage a great many Americans from traveling internationally by plane?

By the State Department's own admission, it does not cost anywhere near $97 to issue a passport. Indeed, it's argued by some that the State Department makes a considerable profit from the issuance of passports.

New rules require a U.S. passport for any border crossing, including those by car; expect lines when you drive back from Mexico.

NEED A PASSPORT? FAST? WITHOUT USING AN EXPENSIVE EXPEDITER? GO TO A CITY WITH A SMALLER BACKLOG.

The backlog in processing applications for U.S. passports differs from city to city. In New York and Boston, the lag may be as long as a month, while in Philadelphia, the lag may be less than a week to people who pay an expediting fee. By being willing to travel to a city whose regional passport office has a shorter backlog, you can often obtain your passport in just a few days.

That was the recent experience of a relative of mine. Her company needed her to fly to Toronto in 2 weeks. Yet her U.S. passport had expired (and passports are now required of people flying to and from Canada). She called the passport offices in New York and Boston, but with no luck—they would need 3 weeks. She then called the passport office in Philadelphia and was told that if she went there on a Tuesday morning, they would have her passport later that afternoon. Though it was a hardship to make the trip, she had no choice.

So if you can't obtain a timely passport, phone around. The central passport information office (known as the National Passport Information Center), reached at ☎ 877/4USA-PPT (487-2778), may know of a nearby passport office able to quickly issue your passport. And if you're willing to go to that other city, you can often shorten the necessary time—and shorten it dramatically.

(A final hint: People without a touchtone phone are eventually able to speak with a human being at the National Passport Information Center. And these humans often have good information to impart.)

PETS

NEW SOLUTIONS TO TAKE CARE OF FIDO & FLUFFY DURING YOUR VACATION

In speaking with friends about how their recent holidays went, I was surprised by how many mentioned that they had to alter, curtail, or sometimes even abandon their vacation plans simply to accommodate the schedule of their pet sitter.

Some people are lucky enough to have a nearby family member who can temporarily adopt the dog, or a neighbor who can stop by the house to care for the cats (and, as a bonus, pick up the mail and water the plants). But what happens if you don't have a trusted pet sitter or if your usual helper is unavailable, as is often the case around popular holidays?

Many people would rather ditch their travel plans than board their beloved pets in a kennel, where animals typically spend 20 hours or more per day in a small cage (for cats, 24 hours a day) and may be exposed to

Arranging care for a pet left at home is simply one example of the planning needed for any trip.

diseases (including the common and dreaded "kennel cough"). What's more, kennels frequently book up early for popular travel times.

When your choice is between the kennel and canceling your plans, consider using the Internet to find a pet sitter. The options range from using the unvetted virtual classifieds of your local Craigslist (www.craigslist.org) to signing up with one of the new, specialized services that have popped up.

Fetch! Pet Care (www.fetchpetcare.com), founded in 2002, has 120 franchisees offering pet sitting, dog walking, private boarding (a kind of "free-range" kenneling), and related services in some 32 states. Care.com, founded in 2006, maintains lists of independent pet sitters, babysitters/nannies, care givers, and tutors across the United States.

Care.com lets you view in-depth profiles of caregivers for free, but you must pay to become a "premium" member if you want to get the contact information and run background checks (at Fetch!, all employees are subjected to a background search). Fees are $15 for registration plus $25 for 1 month, $45 for 3 months, or $120 for a year.

Preparations

Going on vacation? Remember to cancel the services that will otherwise be unused & wasted.

It's fairly easy to suspend many of your paid subscriptions while you travel. Depending on how long your trip is, you might save money that you would otherwise have thrown away on unused services.

For example, there's no sense in paying a full month's fee to your gym if you're only going to be using it for half that period. Cable television, too—or just the pay channels, such as HBO or Showtime—can be halted with the flip of a switch. Some companies require payment of a small fee to activate such temporary stoppages, but ask what they are and do the math—in many cases, even with the fee, you might save money by suspending services during your vacation.

Granted, now that DVRs and TiVos are popular, many people will prefer for their televisions to be operational and recording in their absences. But newspapers? They are of no use to someone who's away.

Go though your regular expenses and determine what you can save money on during your vacation. Why throw the money away?

Never go to an airport without first phoning the airline to learn whether your flight is scheduled to depart on time

On our recent trip to Panama, Roberta and I were scheduled to fly back at 9am from Panama City. We placed a wake-up call at the hotel for 6am, were downstairs with our luggage at 7am, and reached the airport at 7:30am, only to learn that the flight had been postponed until 2:15pm, nearly 6 hours later. We had made the classic mistake of greenhorn travelers: We had failed to phone the airport in advance to learn of our flight's departure time. Instead of a morning at the pool, or shopping in downtown Panama City, we cooled our heels for several hours in a very uninteresting airport—and were groggy from a 6am awakening for the rest of the day. Never, never leave for an airport without first phoning the airline to learn whether the departure is on time.

REGISTERED TRAVELERS

Are these "registered traveler" programs just a lot of pretentious status seeking?

Would you pay $100 for the right not to take off your shoes when passing through a security check at airports? Essentially, that seems the advantage offered by the various "registered traveler" programs approved by the Transportation Security Agency. For a fee of $100 (which includes $28 paid to the T.S.A.), affluent travelers who undergo a security check will receive an I.D. card carrying a computer chip that incorporates their fingerprints and their eyes' iris patterns. And these I.D.-equipped passengers will then breeze through a special "clear lane" at designated airports without having to take off their shoes or pull out their laptops from the briefcases or luggage they carry aboard (the second great advantage of the registered traveler plan), thus saving a few seconds of time and a bit of indignity. It all seems to me like the kind of empty privilege and social status on which affluent people waste money, as well as a procedure which terrorists will easily be able to tap into. Am I missing something?

SCHEDULING TRAVEL

A QUICK NOTE ABOUT VACATION SCHEDULING

The last 2 weeks of August are increasingly recognized as a "slump" period in travel, when bookings fall off sharply for flights, cruises, and resort stays. The main reason: The increasing tendency of schools to begin classes at that time or to require that students make initial preparations for the start of school; many parents start gearing up for the academic year at that time, and do not travel. The lesson: If you're looking for an available cabin on a cruise, a transatlantic flight, or a Caribbean resort stay, August 15 to 31 is an easy "high-season" period to find one.

THINK NOVEMBER: THAT'S WHEN PRICES PLUMMET TO & WITHIN EVERY EUROPEAN NATION

November 1 is the start of the European off-season. Not earlier, but November 1, and continuing until mid-December (when prices spike for the Christmas season) and resuming again from January 8 until the end of February. If you can possibly delay your departure to fall within those dates, you'll experience marvels of pricing for your airfare and air-and-land packages.

Since the weather in Europe is rarely bitter (it is almost never as cold as in Chicago or Minneapolis), the time is perfect for a stay focusing almost entirely on the indoor attractions—museums, galleries, shops—of the major European capitals.

Think November.

THANKSGIVING TRAVEL

THE TRICK TO HAVING TURKEY WITH YOUR FAMILY AT THANKSGIVING IS TO FLY THERE ON THANKSGIVING MORNING, WHEN THE NATION'S PLANES & AIRPORTS ARE EMPTY

Right after Labor Day, Thanksgiving is always "around the corner." And people looking to buy plane tickets for that long weekend are repeatedly

London's monumental new sites, as pictured here, are viewed as well in off season as in summer.

finding that annual sky-high prices have kicked in. Flights that should cost about $300 are now being quoted at over a grand.

But if you simply have to get away then, there is one last trick for you to try: Fly on Thanksgiving itself. Few people want to, so whereas the airports are a nightmarish zoo on Wednesday the day before, by the holiday itself they're virtual ghost towns, and airfare prices reflect it. If you fly in the morning, chances are you'll be around the banquet table in the afternoon.

As for flying home, Sunday and Monday are fiendishly busy, so look toward Tuesday, when rates simmer back down to more reasonable levels.

Yes, you can have turkey with your family this year!

GATE 1 TRAVEL HAS BECOME THE OVERSEAS "THANKSGIVING KING," WITH AIRFARE & 4-NIGHT STAYS IN SIX CITIES FOR $599 TO $699 PER PERSON

From the amount of attention tour packagers are giving to short Thanksgiving stays in Europe, it appears that the eat-turkey-with-the-family tradition is fast dissolving. That's the only explanation for Gate 1's surprisingly broad array of yearly Thanksgiving offerings: air and land to six European cities, leaving the United States 2 or 3 days before Thanksgiving and spending 4 hotel nights there (with breakfast included) for the following prices back in 2008, which should be about 5% higher in 2009: London for $699, Paris

$669, Rome or Florence $799, Madrid $799, and Budapest $739. Prices are from New York, but Gate 1 will quote only slightly higher rates from dozens of other U.S. cities. Access them at www.gate1travel.com or by phoning ☎ 800/682-3333.

IF YOU'RE FLYING AROUND THANKSGIVING, PRINT YOUR BOARDING PASS AT HOME BEFORE GOING TO THE AIRPORT TO AVOID BEING OVERBOOKED & BUMPED

I can't absolutely guarantee you'll avoid those consequences if you print out your boarding pass on your personal computer, as many airlines now permit you to do, but it will help your odds. The airlines have a strange tendency of bumping those passengers who have paid the lowest price for their tickets, regardless of whether they arrive at the airport with a boarding pass and assigned seat. But expert after expert has told me that in a period when airports will be jammed, and overbooking widespread, it's smart to do as I've suggested (within 24 hr. of your flight). And how can it hurt?

Other tips for the airport around holidays: Key in the toll-free number of your airline into your mobile phone so that you can quickly phone reservations and get another seat if your flight is canceled. Reserve a parking space at the airport through www.airportparking.com—those places will also be jammed. Ascertain the average waiting time to clear security at your airport, and then add another half-hour in planning your arrival at the airport—go to http://waittime.tsa.dhs.gov for that information.

WEBSITES (FOR TRAVEL MISCELLANY)

11 LITTLE-KNOWN WEBSITES CAN BE USEFUL TO YOUR TRAVEL PLANNING

Nearly every user of Frommers.com is aware of the big airfare and hotel booking engines on the Internet. But nearly a dozen websites of much lesser renown can be just as important to your travel planning.

Viator (www.viator.com) lists thousands of sights, tours, and attractions in important cities and islands all over the world, and then lets you book them prior to leaving home, avoiding long lines at the destination or being shut out during busy holiday periods. The service appears to include everything, from London's giant Ferris wheel (the London Eye) to golf courses in Hawaii, always at the same price as you'd pay on the spot.

Theme Park Insider (www.themeparkinsider.com) provides impartial theme park advice on when to go, what rides to take, safety issues, and hotel reviews—it's well worth visiting. Click on "Park Reviews" for outspoken comments on more than 60 theme parks, from Universal Studios to Tokyo DisneySea. In addition to staff reviews, readers rate attractions and parks.

Roadfood (www.roadfood.com) steers you to that sumptuous diner where waitresses call you "Honey" and the apple pie tastes like Grandma's. Though fast-food joints have taken over the interstates, Roadfood helps you find affordable, nonfranchise restaurants with tasty, home-cooked food. About 1,000 restaurants are listed for the United States (also see www.dinercity.com for photos and addresses of classic diners).

LateRooms (www.laterooms.com) is a British service for obtaining last-minute discounts on hotels located primarily in the U.K. and Europe (its section on London hotels is especially comprehensive). But it also offers some deals in Australia, New Zealand, and a handful of other countries. Its major competitor is an Australian site called Wotif.com that also primarily lists discounted hotel rates for England, Europe, Australia and New Zealand. Both sites can bring about remarkable savings on your next overseas trip.

Travelaxe (www.travelaxe.com) is a U.S. service that claims to compare the specially discounted hotel rates found on nearly 20 other Internet booking engines covering more than 30 countries (including the United States). Its one-stop shopping saves you the trouble of scanning multiple websites to find the best-priced room for your next trip.

TravelWorm (www.travelworm.com), the king of the search engines for casino resorts, primarily surveys the rates of hotels in Las Vegas, Reno, Biloxi, Atlantic City, Laughlin, and other gaming locations. Recently, it got me a sharply discounted price for a popular hotel in Las Vegas.

BootsnAll Travel (www.bootsnall.com) connects would-be travelers with resident experts on destinations all over the world, and particularly on the subject of their accommodations. Need advice on Bali, London, Kathmandu, San Francisco? They claim to get you answers free of charge from a volunteer corps of generous advisors.

GORP (http://gorp.away.com) is the unchallenged expert on all varieties of adventure travel—mountain climbing, white-water rafting, trekking the Himalayas, going on safari, and the like. You'll find comprehensive information for would-be Indiana Joneses, including the lodgings that house them.

TheMouseForLess.com, MouseSavers.com, and AllEars.Net are all sites privately owned by Disney enthusiasts who constantly search out the discounts at resort hotels in and around the theme parks, and similar reductions at restaurants and from tour operators in Orlando and Anaheim. If anyone is discounting in the big theme park cities, their offers quickly appear on these sites.

Chapter Eleven

THE PEOPLE WHO ASSIST YOU

TO SEPARATE THE TALENTED FROM THE NOT SO, GET REFERENCES

Some people claim—with a fair degree of support—that travel is the world's single largest industry, employing more persons than the automotive industry, the food processing industry, and many others. When you travel, you will find yourself surrounded by persons willing to aid you. This chapter describes what some of them do and discusses whether you should take advantage of their services.

AGENTS

CAN YOU REALLY BE A TRAVEL AGENT FROM YOUR HOME? HERE'S AN INTRODUCTION TO TRAVEL JOBS.

"Sell travel and travel for free!" "Travel as a travel agent does—for free!" Never in years has the pitch for "part-time travel agents" been more strident and pervasive, a veritable blizzard of ads in a whole variety of publications. From their frequency, it's probable that thousands of Americans are paying out $495 to $975 for correspondence-course "instruction" in becoming a part-time travel agent working at home.

So how about it? Can you operate as a travel agent from your own living room? Actually, you can. But can you earn a living from it, or at least a reasonable sum? Ah, there's the problem. Next time you pass a travel agency, look through the window at the agents sitting there with phones glued to their ears, taking one call after another, uninterruptedly, for hours—and still earning what most travel people concede is a modest weekly sum. Unless you have a large number of potential clients who can generate a lot of bookings, you can't hope to enjoy more than a nominal income, especially since you will need to pay out at least half your commission revenue to the traditional travel agency for which you work. Two or three clients a week—if that's all you can generate—will earn you perhaps $100, no more, for a lot of time and effort.

If you are the kind of gregarious, dream-spinning, fast-talking, sales-oriented type with a large circle of friends and acquaintances who will buy their travel from you in big numbers, you needn't take a course or pay a fee to become a part-time travel agent. You simply visit the nearest local travel agency, and ask whether you can use them to issue your tickets; since they take on no salary obligation, and pay you only when you bring them business, they almost always say yes—and they don't ask for an upfront fee!

As for the free or heavily discounted travel arrangements that some people think they can obtain by going through the motions of becoming travel agents, those privileges are no longer easy to get. The travel trade press is full of alarms and warnings about imposters, and most hotels, car-rental companies, cruise lines, and the like extend discounts only upon solid proof that you are a full-time travel agent. Unless you're deeply committed to the sale of travel, don't waste your time.

DON'T FALL FOR ONE OF THOSE PHONY TRAVEL AGENCY ID CARDS

Tricksters all over the nation make a good living by selling phony ID cards identifying the bearer as a travel agent. With one of those cards, goes the claim, you'll be able to obtain discounts on car rentals, hotels, cruises, and tours.

Don't you believe it. Increasingly, travel suppliers are requiring that an alleged travel agent display an IATAN card with picture ID, issued by the international association of airlines. To get one, you must go through an elaborate process of proving (1) that you earn at least $5,000 a year selling travel, (2) that you spend at least 20 hours a week selling travel, and (3) that you are affiliated with an authorized travel agency belonging to various industry associations. And beyond that requirement, you must pay $30 a year.

My warning remains. Travel suppliers (cruise lines, airlines, hotel chains, auto-rental firms, tour operators) aren't fools. They are able to identify those people who are genuine travel agents and those who have simply purchased an ID. Much more than the card is now required to qualify you for travel discounts. And companies that simply take $400 or $500 from you for an I.D., without operating a genuine, disciplined course of instruction or chain of retail agencies, are scam artists. Dealing with them, you are simply exchanging $400 or $500 for a worthless piece of cardboard.

MEET THE PURE TRAVEL CONSULTANT, A NEW SOURCE OF TRAVEL ASSISTANCE

Although most travel agents refer to themselves as "travel consultants," a tiny band of 40-or-so enthusiasts from all over the country are offering to provide just that—travel counseling—and nothing more. Specialists in a particular area or country suggest itineraries, recommend unusual lodgings, and map out hourly schedules, but often leave the reservations and the ticketing to a standard travel agent. Their compensation is an hourly fee, not a commission. I recently steered a friend to the services of one such independent travel consultant—Marjorie Shaw's "Insider's Italy" (☎ 914/470-1612; www.insidersitaly.com)—and was highly impressed by the

A great many travel consultants specialize in particular areas of the world, such as the popular Tuscan region of Italy.

brilliantly conceived, well-priced trip that resulted, involving the use of convent hotels and aristocratic mansions, authentic restaurants off-the-beaten-track, and precise hourly schedules for driving from one Tuscan town to another.

Other examples of this new breed of travel advisor: Holly Chase Travel, designing custom tours of Turkey primarily, but also Greece, Syria, and Jordan (☎ 941/330-8738; holly@hollychase.com); Off the Beaten Path, for the Rockies, the Southwest, and Alaska (☎ 800/445-2995; www.offthe beatenpath.com); Our Personal Guest, for India (☎ 212/319-1354; www. ourpersonalguest.com); and Pacific Northwest Journeys for Oregon, Washington, and southern British Columbia (☎ 800/935-9730; www. pnwjourneys.com). While their advice doesn't always come cheap—expect to pay from $300 to $600 for all the planning—most clients regard that cost as offset by hotel savings and rewarding travel experiences.

IT PAYS TO USE A TRAVEL AGENT IF THAT PERSON IS TALENTED & KNOWLEDGEABLE

Retail travel agents have launched a major campaign to promote their services. It's claimed that travel agents provide valuable assistance, especially in emergencies. They have contacts with the airlines, cruise lines, hotel chains, and so forth, and can get you out of all sorts of scrapes.

I have this to say about the benefit of using a travel agent: If that person has been to the destination you are considering, or is exceptionally well traveled in general, or has a substantial record of successful contacts with travel suppliers; if the travel agent strikes you as knowledgeable about all the tactics for obtaining advantageous rates; if, in short, the agent shows the same aptitudes you look for in a dentist, accountant, or other professional, then by all means make use of his or her services.

But always be aware that your travel agent, in most instances today, will need to bill you a fee over and above the amount charged by the airline, hotel, or tour. And that's because more and more suppliers are now charging your agent the same price that they would charge to you. For the travel agent to earn income representing you, he or she must add an amount of money to the price billed by the travel supplier.

Once upon a time, this was not the case. A dozen or so years ago, almost every supplier paid a commission to travel agents, and the agents made a living from these commissions, not from you. It cost you no more to use a travel agent than to make a booking yourself. In such cases, it wasn't really necessary to seek out a really exceptional agent. You had nothing to lose by using one. If the cost of a ticket from New York to Los Angeles was $400, you paid $400 whether or not you used a travel agent. Today, now that commissions have been eliminated by the airlines and a large number of other suppliers, it will cost you $400 plus a fee (sometimes as much as $60) to buy that ticket from a travel agent.

I'm an enthusiastic supporter of the use of talented, knowledgeable travel agents who earn their fees. I am not an enthusiast about using some of the newly coined, totally inexperienced, home-based "travel agents" who pay $500 or so for a mass-produced identification card which falsely states they are travel professionals. The smart consumer adopts the same precautions in choosing a travel agent that they would use in choosing any professional: They seek references.

GUIDES (LIVE ONES)

ALONG COMES A WEBSITE FOR THE SELECTION OF LIVE GUIDES TO SHOW YOU AROUND A FOREIGN CITY

The Web is clogged with travel sites that purport to introduce travelers with like-minded individuals willing and ready to host (and guide) them on their vacations. One of them, called Viamigo (www.viamigo.com), lists about 1,500 such people. Probably because the website has no method for vetting the quality or experience of the guides, who post themselves on the site, it advertises itself, rather murkily, more as a place to meet locals than as a way to connect with guaranteed top-notch guides. In fact, its rubric is "Be local."

Still, one might assume that anyone who goes through the effort of creating and posting a guiding profile online will be serious about providing a quality experience to anyone who contacts them. There is also a rating system by which those who have used a guide can come back to the site and review and rate them, although at this early point, the system is little used.

Some of the guides require payment, and some simply want to meet interesting foreigners and show them what's so great about their hometowns.

TOURIST OFFICES

FINALLY, AN ONLINE TREASURE TROVE OF LOCAL TOURISM RESOURCES AROUND THE WORLD

There are two primary resources for planning a trip anywhere. The first, naturally, is a good guidebook for independent, expert opinions and reviews. The second is the local tourist office—especially in the age when everything is online—which provides up-to-the-minute information on everything a visitor might need, from directories of hotels, restaurants, museums, sights, and nightlife options to the latest calendars showcasing local events, special exhibits, festivals, and art shows. The best tourist offices will give you leads on where to rent bicycles, hire a guide, take a free walking tour, and even help you book such things as hotel rooms and theater tickets.

The problem was, until recently, that there existed no single, intelligent database to help you find the official websites of local tourist offices and tourism authorities around the world. Guidebooks list them, of course, but Googling rarely works, as you end up with hundreds of hits from hotel-booking engines and other commercial interests. The actual tourist office is often hidden somewhere on page 3 or 4 of your Google search. There have been a few attempts to compile a master list of official tourism authorities, but all have been woefully incomplete, often out of date, and nearly always designed so poorly as to be nothing but confusing.

That's why I'm delighted with the launch of www.worldtourism directory.com, a true database of official online tourism resources: a staggering 120,000 addresses in 330 nations, countries, and territories. It links not only to the sites of those local tourist offices but also to tourism associations, hotel chains, consulates, chambers of commerce, national parks, foreign-language media, tour operators, tourism news, sports, reservations agencies . . . I could go on listing, but there are more than 100 categories.

TOUR OPERATORS

A LONG-DESERVED TRIBUTE TO A SMALL-TOUR OPERATOR

A travel organization called Escapes Unlimited operates as much for the love of travel as for profit, pricing its packages so low that one is sometimes concerned for them. It was founded a quarter-century ago by a California social worker named Roe Gruber to introduce travelers to the cultures of the world's most exotic destinations at prices well below what everyone else was asking. Imagine enjoying a 5-night stay in Bali or Vietnam, including breakfast, sightseeing, and round-trip air from Los Angeles or San Francisco, for around $900 per person. Or 5 nights in Ecuador or Panama, including round-trip air from Miami, for $600 to $749. Or 5 nights in Buenos Aires, on the same basis, for $859. Roe Gruber's goal is to create an enhanced sense of social consciousness through travel. If you'd like to join her trips, go to www.escapesltd.com.

Laos is the specialty of a small but dynamic tour company called Escapes Unlimited, operated with great success by a former social worker.

THE CANADIANS ARE COMING!

Ever gone on a Canadian-led tour? Indications are growing that three Canadian tour operators—G.A.P Adventures, Eldertreks, and Lion World Travel—are attracting so much business from the United States that a clear majority of their clients are now Americans attracted to their reasonable prices, relatively serious tone, and authentic lodgings.

G.A.P Adventures (☎ 800/708-7761; www.gapadventures.com) is the largest of the three, servicing some 40,000 travelers each year with small-group "adventures," so-called not because groups engage in daring physical feats, but because they go to more exotic destinations. G.A.P began almost 2 decades ago with small-group tours to Central America. They still specialize in that area, but presently operate trips for persons of all ages to every continent, including Antarctica (where it owns its own expedition ship, replacing one that sank 2 years ago). Participants are sometimes required to pay mom-and-pop lodgings in cash at the time of the visit, as these locally owned properties do not normally deal with the world of organized travel. Most tours are limited to 12 persons, some to 16 or 22 (only the Antarctic cruises take more).

Eldertreks (☎ 800/741-7956; www.eldertreks.com), in business for more than 20 years, operates small-group tours for persons over the age of 50 to more than 40 destinations primarily in Latin America, Europe, and Asia, at prices averaging (except for higher-priced tours within North America) $300 per person per day, not including airfare, for totally all-inclusive arrangements: Everything down to the last dessert is included. Guides with extensive experience are named and described in the promotional literature. Destinations are, for the most part, the unusual ones, "from Easter Island to the South Pacific to the Gobi Desert in Mongolia, from the Arctic to the Antarctic, from Baja California to the Galapagos, from the Amazon to Alaska." Participants must be capable of walking for as many as 3 or 4 hours.

Lion World Travel (☎ 800/387-2706; www.lionworldtravel.com), 40 years in business, has pioneered in the creation of affordable African safaris. Its popular "Best of Kenya" flies you there on British Airways, via London, puts you up on arrival at a Nairobi hotel, and then speeds you to the remarkable, wildlife-filled games parks of Kenya (Lake Nakuru, Shaba, the Maasai Mara) for 5 full days of a classic safari (twice-daily games drives in seven-seat minibuses; lodging and all meals included) from as little as $2,199.

THOUGH THEY THEORETICALLY OPERATE FOR PROFIT, A NUMBER OF LOW-COST TRAVEL FIRMS ARE OBVIOUSLY IN BUSINESS FOR THE LOVE OF IT

Three travel organizations provide such important services to cost-conscious vacationers, at such low prices, that they deserve recognition:

Adventure Center (☎ **800/228-8747** or 510/654-1879; www.adventure center.com) is a 28-year-old California firm that acts as the U.S. representative for a dozen major budget-priced operators of exotic and/or adventurous trips throughout the world (such companies as Britain's Guerba Expeditions or Explore Worldwide). You travel in groups limited to between 8 and 24 persons. By keeping its own markups at exceedingly low levels, Adventure Center enables cost-conscious Americans to enjoy the world's lowest-priced adventure travels (truck safaris, walking tours in underdeveloped countries, Antarctic expedition cruises, and so forth) operated by highly skilled specialists with a long record of safe and successful touring. Scan its literature or website and you'll be struck by how affordable these once-in-a-lifetime expeditions can be.

The Evergreen Club (☎ **800/962-2392;** www.evergreenclub.com) has, for almost 3 decades, arranged comfortable but rock-bottom-priced homestays for persons over the age of 50 traveling to nearly 2,000 cities in North America and a growing number of locations abroad. Members offer rooms in their homes to other members at the nominal charge (they call it a "gratuity") of $10 per single, $15 per double, per night, including a big breakfast. Yearly membership fee is $30 single, $38 double. Participation is by persons who do frequent traveling in the United States, who enjoy the camaraderie and friendship of private homes, and who are themselves willing to act as hosts on occasion in exchange for receiving such nominally priced hospitality.

Intervac International Home Exchange (☎ **800/756-4663;** www. intervacus.com), founded more than a half-century ago and operated today in the United States by Paula Jaffe, is typical of the several vacation-exchange clubs that enable Americans to swap their homes or apartments with those of persons in other cities, in the United States or abroad, during their respective vacations. By permitting individuals to make use of a valuable asset—their own home or apartment—to live free elsewhere, it enables tens of thousands to travel in the best possible manner. And as you learn the modest charges for participation in Intervac ($65 for United States membership, $95 international, for a yearly Web-only membership), you immediately see that its managers are not involved in this business to get rich.

Let's give a cheer for the selfless, budget-minded operators of low-cost travel programs!

THOSE PURCHASE DEADLINES IN TOUR LITERATURE ARE OFTEN A MARKETING DEVICE & NOT A TRUE CUT-OFF DATE

A number of travelers find themselves intimidated by those scary conditions that often appear at the bottom of tour literature, either in print or on the Internet: "Book by October 10," or "Available only until June 16." While I'm not saying that some of these warnings aren't legitimate, many are intended simply to pressure the customer to book early, to the tour operator's advantage. Funny thing is, many of these are "rolling" deadlines that invariably get extended when the date is reached. Having been told that you must book by April 8, you reach April 8 and discover that the date has been changed to April 22. And later, the date becomes May 5.

Travel decisions should not be made under pressure. In most cases, you can book a package up to 1 or 2 months before departure. If you're intrigued by a budget-friendly trip that departs in April, you can usually book it as late as February or March. I can't guarantee this, but it's often true.

IT'S THEIR FAILURE TO INCLUDE A SUBSTANTIAL FUEL SURCHARGE THAT PERMITS SOME TOUR OPERATORS TO OFFER WHAT APPEAR TO BE COMPETITIVE PRICES

You should always determine whether "fuel surcharge" is included in the price of an air-and-land package anywhere in the world. Some tour operators include it, some don't. The some that don't thereby succeed in publicizing a product that looks competitive but isn't.

An example is a package to Paris offered by a leading tour company, which consisted of round-trip air from New York or Boston and 4 nights at a Left Bank hotel, for $545 per person, double occupancy. It is only when I went deep into the language of the offer that I, for one, learned that the $545 price didn't include a fuel surcharge of $210 per person, bringing the total charge to $755 plus taxes.

When I looked at the Paris packages of another tour operator, I found that they offered a 6-night deal (2 nights more than the other), staying at exactly the same hotel (Comfort Inn Mouffetard), with round-trip air, for $699 per person including—repeat—including the fuel surcharge, but plus taxes.

Always take pains to determine whether the tour price you've been quoted includes the all-important fuel surcharge and taxes. Otherwise you may end up paying hundreds more than you need to.

FOR SOME OF THE CHEAPEST HOTEL STAYS IN AMERICA TODAY, GO TO THE TOP PICKS SECTION OF THE SPIRIT AIRWAYS WEBSITE, A VERITABLE TOUR OPERATOR

As if it were a charitable organization with no thought for its own commercial interest, Spirit Airways (www.spiritair.com) devotes a portion of its website to listing hotel bargains that aren't associated with a Spirit Air flight—you can use them without going near a Spirit Airways plane.

And what bargains they are! This budget champion among airlines has apparently made itself a magnet for attracting the lowest-priced deals, or is regarded as such by various hungry hotels. I found a suite sleeping six persons in Kissimmee, Florida, near Walt Disney World, for $45. All I had to do was call the hotel directly and ask for the "Top Picks" special. Around $70 would have gotten me a weekend double, including continental breakfast, at the Comfort Inn of Dulles International Airport, Washington, D.C. (they normally sell for $189).

Other sample prices: $25 a night for a winter room in Myrtle Beach, South Carolina; $36 per room at the Rodeway Inn International Drive in Orlando, Florida; $49 per room at the Xanadu Beach Resort & Marina in Freeport, Grand Bahama; 50% off the rate of a room at a resort hotel in Roatan, Bay Islands, Honduras.

With Spirit currently challenging Southwest Airlines as the patron saint of cost-conscious Americans, its website seems to contain unbeatable bargains in the areas (especially Florida) to which Spirit flies.

PAUL LAIFER HAS RETIRED & CLOSED HIS COMPANY, LEAVING A BIG GAP IN THE OPERATION OF AFFORDABLE PACKAGES TO CENTRAL & EASTERN EUROPE

For years, whenever a reader sought help for a trip to Prague or Budapest, I immediately referred them to Paul Laifer Tours of Parsippany, New Jersey. Specializing in central Europe and pricing his services at breathtaking low levels ($599 for air and land to Prague was a recent offer), Paul Laifer was the model for a sensitive, well-motivated tour operator. He loved his work, he enjoyed sending cost-conscious people to cities he loved, and tens of thousands of Americans have enjoyed well-organized, low-cost trips to Prague, Budapest, and Vienna because of him.

Paul has now retired. For a replacement, look up the offerings of Tatra Travel of Brooklyn, New York (www.tatratravel.com), whose owner is from the Czech Republic. His specialty is all things Czech, but he also offers combined tours of Prague and Budapest; Prague, Budapest, and Vienna; and numerous other cities in the region, at competitive prices. I've had good vibes about Tatra from several of its customers.

Chapter Twelve

These Are a Few of My Favorite Places

THE CITIES, ISLANDS & NATIONS TO CONSIDER FOR YOUR NEXT TRIP

AMSTERDAM

A SEAMY SIGHTSEEING ATTRACTION, IN AMSTERDAM, MAY BE ON THE VERGE OF EXTINCTION

It might seem odd to write about European sex workers in a travel book, but a story that ran in the U.K.'s *Guardian*—about Amsterdam closing down a third of its brothels—is truly tourism news.

For better or worse, Amsterdam's red-light district is one of the most famous tourist attractions in Europe, as firmly on the list of Amsterdam's top sights as the Rembrandts in the Rijksmuseum, the canal boat tours, or the Anne Frank House. It's a standard stop for any bus tour, and it is not unusual to see these seedy streets teeming with families from around the world.

Many have argued that Amsterdam's red-light district draws as many if not more tourist gawkers (and their tourism euros) than actual customers who visit with an eye to purchasing services. This is what makes travel news out of the fact that the mayor's office is closing dozens of the infamous "windows" in which lingerie-clad women advertise themselves.

The official line on the crackdown is that the neighborhood draws an unhealthy share of crime, from pickpocketing to money laundering. The local prostitutes—who, under the Dutch system, are licensed, pay taxes, and receive free health services—claim the officials are going after the easiest target, and that the real problems are the unlicensed brothels and street pimps that attract and abet the associated acts of lawlessness.

I'm not taking sides.

ANDALUCÍA

I'M TALKING ABOUT SEVILLE, GRANADA, CORDOBA, MALAGA & THE "COSTA DEL SOL"

You know the creaky old stereotyped images of Spain—the bullfighters and the castanet-clacking flamenco dancers, *olé!* Well, the southern region of Andalusia (in Spanish, Andalucía) is whence they originally hail, and you'll still spot them in action.

But there's far, far more to this arid area around the size of Maine. Maybe not the pebbly beaches, if you're used to the Caribbean—though many Europeans do flock to its sunny (and increasingly overdeveloped)

The 14th-century Alhambra, in Granada, is surely among the most exquisite, romantic palaces on earth, a highlight of Spain.

Mediterranean shores in such places as Málaga, Marbella, Torremolinos, and Benidorm. Instead, go for the astonishing mix of Christian and Moorish (Islamic) culture and architecture that defines Andalusia.

The majestic city of Seville (Sevilla) with its quaint old town and vibrant dining, music, and nightlife. Regal Granada, whose highlights include a pair of breathtaking Moorish palace-garden complexes called the Alhambra and Generalife (the tales of Scheherazade come to life) and the ancient Sacromonte hill, riddled with caves where gypsies still mesmerize with flamenco. Intensely atmospheric Córdoba, which will literally stagger you not just with its medieval old town's byways but especially its Mezquita, a mammoth mosque whose interior is a mysterious forest of columns and arches. Ronda, perched spectacularly on the edge of a 90m (300-ft.) gorge. The Rock of Gibraltar, still a British colony but accessible from Spain, where English, Spaniards, and North Africans mingle in a time-capsule-like minicity clinging to the gargantuan cliff.

You can of course fly here independently, directly into Málaga or Almería or via Madrid and other European cities; getting around is easy, whether via train, bus, or rental car, and good-quality lodging and dining abound in all price ranges. If you prefer an escorted tour, contact area specialists, such as Abreu Tours (☎ 800/223-1580; www.abreu-tours.com) and Club ABC (☎ 888/TOURS-ABC; www.clubabc.com). And for more information, go to www.andalucia.com.

ANTIGUA

TOGETHER WITH ITS NEIGHBOR, BARBUDA, THIS VEDDY-VEDDY BRITISH ISLAND OFFERS AN ARRAY OF VACATION LURES

So why choose Antigua, of all the many islands in the Caribbean? Sure, the beaches here are top quality—a different one for every day of the year, so they claim—even if the island's not the prettiest around or the people the friendliest. The sailing's swell—a boffo Sailing Week and numerous other regattas are held here each year. And there's a strong sense of local Anglo-Caribbean culture—cricket is king, for example, and the island's something of a world power in the sport.

Still, plenty of other islands offer most or all of the above. Perhaps Antigua's ace in the hole is the impressive breadth of its historic sights. An area on the south end called English Harbour, with its 18th-century centerpiece Nelson's Dockyard, is certainly a case in point. Named after the legendary Lord Horatio Nelson, it was once Britain's premier Caribbean naval base, and today offers loads of museums and forts to visit; antique inns to stay in; and of course myriad ways to spend money in shops, bars, and eateries. Other draws: Betty's Hope, a partly restored 17th-century sugar plantation and mill; the fort (and sweeping views) at Shirley Heights, site of a restaurant where some major weekly partying goes down with the sun; and the atmospheric capital, St. John's, whose sights include its cathedral, museum, covered market, and restored historic wharf, Redcliffe Quay. In contrast, a ferry ride away on Barbuda, the appeal is nature and an extremely laid-back vibe—nothing much here except a bird sanctuary, a tiny village, and a handful of very exclusive resorts.

A clutch of Caribbean specialists offer packages here, including Funjet (☎ 800/558-3050; www.funjet.com), GOGO Worldwide Vacations (☎ 800/229-4999; www.gogowwv.com), and Travel Impressions (☎ 800/284-0044; www.travelimpressions.com), and several major carriers provide direct flights from North America. For more information, phone ☎ 888/268-4227, or go to www.antigua-barbuda.org.

ARGENTINA

THOUGH IT HAS RECOVERED A BIT FROM ITS DIRE ECONOMIC CRISIS, ARGENTINA HAS REMAINED A TOURIST BARGAIN

Birthplace of the tango, home to great theaters of opera and concerts, Buenos Aires is a sophisticated, Europe-themed capital of South America.

It's been more than 5 years since the Argentine peso crashed against most other currencies, making a tourist mecca out of the city of Buenos Aires. Drawn by tales of $4 steaks and $1 tango lessons, visitors from all over the world poured into the elegant Argentine capital and bought up everything in sight. During that period, the peso sold as low as 3.18 to the U.S. dollar, as compared with a rate of one to one that prevailed prior to the financial crisis.

From all reports, the Argentine economy has recovered greatly from its low, though when we went to press the peso was still selling at almost exactly three to one U.S. dollar. To what extent does the tourist continue to enjoy advantages there? A friend of mine provided this recent report:

We had dinner at the most high-end, exclusive *parrilla* (steak restaurant) in town for about $25 a person, a meal at another very elegant modern-style nouvelle Argentine restaurant for $15, and several very good meals at more run-of-the-mill places for less than $10. A room at a tango-themed boutique hotel went for $74; bottles of fine wines for as little as $3; high-quality leather wallets for $4 to $6; great suede shoes for $20; and a drop-dead gorgeous, butter-soft leather jacket for $110, probably a quarter or less of what such a thing would cost here in the United States. Cab rides, antiques, and many other things were also amazingly cheap. . . . We also took a side trip to a gorgeous UNESCO World Heritage colonial city in Uruguay called La Colonia, where the cheap prices were even more impressive in many ways.

Though most Americans confine their stays to Buenos Aires, I'm hoping you'll venture out to the pampas & Patagonia

One of South America's biggest and most influential countries, this huge swath of the continent's southern tip—it's almost a third the size of the United States—is also one of its most diverse. You'll likely enter via big, bustling Buenos Aires with its superb menu of culture (the tango was of course invented here), museums (and don't forget one of the world's most famous and elaborate cemeteries, La Recoleta), nightlife (get ready to stay up late), dining (especially if you like beef and Italian cuisine), and shopping (bodacious bargains and selections in leather and lots of other buys).

But try to make time for the vast expanse of Argentina beyond B.A.—there's a lot of something for any taste and budget. You'll experience nature at its most spectacular at Iguazú Falls up north (they're the world's largest) and down south in Patagonia, with its towering mountains, glaciers, penguins, and whale-watching. In the Mendoza, San Rafael, and San Juan areas, producing some of the world's best wine, you can visit vineyards and attend festivals galore. And don't miss out on the classic cowboy/rancher culture of the pampas by overnighting on a working *estancia* (ranch).

More? Lovely colonial architecture in Salta and Córdoba; Quechua Indian villages in the Quebrada de Humahuaca; beaches in Mar del Plata; skiing in Bariloche and Las Leñas. You get the picture: For the visitor, Argentina's truly a happy hunting ground (and, maybe apart from the airfare, a major bargain).

Traveling independently, you can fly direct from the United States on such carriers as Aerolíneas Argentinas (☎ 800/333-0276; www.aerolineas. com.ar), Air Canada (☎ 888/247-2262; www.aircanada.com), American (☎ 800/433-7300; www.aa.com), and LAN (☎ 866/435-9256; www.lan. com/index-en-us.html). But if you're interested in an escorted tour, try Ladatco (☎ 800/327-6162; www.ladatco.com), G.A.P Adventures (☎ 800/708-7761; www.gapadventures.com), and Marnella Tours (☎ 866/993-0033; www.marnellatours.com). For more information, call ☎ 305/442-7029 or 212/603-0443 (www.turismo.gov.ar and www.argentinaturistica.com).

ARUBA

Why do so many Americans choose the island of Aruba for their Caribbean vacations?

Though it's full of casino addicts (the types who remain at the gaming tables until 4am, then sleep until 2pm before reentering the casinos) and is therefore a favorite of people whom you wouldn't want to be with (one of the reasons I no longer go there), this island in the Netherlands Antilles has one countervailing advantage: some of the world's greatest beaches. The two main beaches of Aruba—Palm Beach and Eagle Beach—are a deep expanse of fine white sand stretching for miles and lined with modern hotels (each one with a giant casino). Detractors call it "Las Vegas in the Caribbean," but Vegas could only wish for such a beach.

Tourism is supported here by elaborate resorts; more modest hotels and inns; happening nightspots; plenty of dining, plain and fancy; those flashy casinos; and fab duty-free shopping.

As for those beaches: Gorgeous, powdery Palm Beach north of Oranjestad is where all the bigger resorts are located, while equally attractive Eagle Beach tends to sport more of the lower-key, lower-rise properties.

It's true (I've got to be fair) that there's plenty of good sightseeing, cultural and natural. Of the former, check out Oranjestad's Fort Zoutman, or the archaeological museum. Nature, though, is where Aruba especially shines, and you can roam the cactus-lined byways of the desertlike interior, including 54-square-mile Arikok Park, an aloe farm/museum/factory, caves, and even an ostrich farm. But the problem remains: too many mindless sorts attracted to Aruba by casino gambling.

You can arrange it all yourself—flying down on a number of major U.S. and Canadian airlines—or look for package deals from such outfits as Funjet (☎ 800/558-3050; www.funjet.com), Inter-Island Tours (☎ 800/245-3434; www.interislandtours.com), Liberty Travel/GOGO Worldwide Vacations (☎ 800/271-1584; www.libertytravel.com), and Travel Impressions (☎ 800/284-0044; www.travimp.com).

AUSTRALIA

THE AUSSIE AIRPASS BRINGS TRAVEL TO—& AROUND— AUSTRALIA DOWN TO $1,199

From the sail-like contours of the Sydney Opera House and the wines of South Australia to the underwater life of the Great Barrier Reef and the crocs and kangaroos of the outback, Australia is a once-in-a-lifetime trip.

But the problem with traveling in Australia is that the place is so enormous. This is, after all, not just a country but a continent. Don't expect to be able to drive quickly from one part to another. You really have to fly. That's what makes the Aussie Air Pass from Qantas (☎ 800/227-4603; www.qantas usa.com) an important tool and, starting at $1,199, one of the best deals in transpacific travel.

The pass includes the round-trip transpacific airfare from Los Angeles, San Francisco, or Honolulu (15 other major U.S. gateways are available for add-on fees of $100–$400) into Sydney, Melbourne, or Brisbane. The big bonus is that you also get three additional flight segments within Australia at no extra charge.

The pass divides Australia into three zones. The first, southeast Australia, includes the three arrival cities as well as the Gold Coast, Tasmania, and Adelaide. Zone 2 covers the rest of eastern Australia—and, frankly, everything else most visitors want to see. This includes Cairns, gateway to that wonder of the natural world, the Great Barrier Reef; Darwin in the tropical Top End, the land of didgeridoos, crocodiles, and the massive Kakadu National Park; Alice Springs, the unofficial capital of the outback in the deserts of Australia's Red Center; and Ayers Rock/Uluru, that iconic mound of red sandstone rising out of sandy plains in the geographic center of the continent. (Zone 3 covers western Australia, an unlikely destination for first-time visitors to the land down under.)

Backpackers of America, rejoice! You can stay up to a year (& work) in Australia.

Because backpackers don't have the fat wallets of business travelers or luxury vacationers, the big glossy travel magazines don't pay much attention to them. However, Australia has gotten wise to the value of the backpackers' market. It has calculated that more than half a million visited their country in a recent year, and that during that period, they spent some $2.8 billion of their dollars.

Some 48,000 of those backpackers were Americans. Cleverly, Australia's enlightened immigration authorities have decided, based mostly on these impressive figures, to give American backpackers a better opportunity to explore down under. Australia has now introduced a visa that allows Americans aged 18 to 30 to legally spend up to a year in the country, working, and traveling. The previous cut-off for American visitors was 3 months, after which they had to leave the country, and working was out of the question.

To my mind, these new rules are a positive development not just for American youth who'd like to spend some time exploring a sister nation, but also for Australian industry, which now has access to a temporary workforce that's willing to do jobs (picking fruit, waiting tables) that locals may not be keen to do themselves.

One of the directors of the Australian Tourism Export Council described a fringe benefit this way: "We will have a whole new generation of Americans who will have a first-hand love for and understanding of

Australia, who will have friends and roots here, and who will hopefully return to visit again and again throughout their lives."

And, by the way, under the past U.S. administration, what did our immigration authorities do to ensure that a whole new generation came to know and love America, and what did they do to encourage peaceful cross-cultural exchanges? The gloomy answer: virtually nothing, which is why our international visitor figures and our reputation abroad have been taking dramatic plunges over the past few years.

HIP HOSTELS ARE OPENING ALL OVER AUSTRALIA & RESEMBLING BOUTIQUE-STYLE HOTELS, BUT AT BACKPACKER PRICES

Hostels were once the almost-exclusive domain of penny-pinching back-packers in their late teens willing to put up with rough sheets, noisy cot springs, crowded dorms, inadequate shared bathrooms, and an avalanche of rules in exchange for a cheap bed. But over the past 15 years or so, hostels have been giving themselves a makeover and appealing more to young families, seniors, and budget-minded 30-somethings looking for a bargain.

When you're down under, the name to look for is Base Backpackers (www.basebackpackers.com), a chain of funky hostels—bars, rooftop BBQs, satellite TV lounges with pool tables—aimed at the adventurous backpacker. It currently has eight locations in New Zealand and three in Australia (Sydney, Melbourne, and on the beach of Magnetic Island). Each one offers something a bit different. The Auckland location has a spa and sauna (NZ$5/$4 per hour each). One in Rotorua has a rock-climbing wall, while the other sports thermal mineral pools. Per-person prices recently ranged from NZ$25 to NZ$30 ($17–$21) in New Zealand, and from A$26 to A$32 ($21–$26) in Australia.

TRAVEL TO AUSTRALIA IS ABOUT TO BOOM; KEEP CHECKING THE WEBSITES OF QANTAS, AIR NEW ZEALAND—& ESPECIALLY V AUSTRALIA

In a historic, recent "Open Skies" treaty signed by the United States and Australia, air traffic between the two countries has been totally deregulated. Any airline can now fly between the two countries, using any airports in either country, and operating as many flights as they wish. As you'd expect, the flamboyant British tycoon Richard Branson was the first to take advantage of those opportunities with a new airline called V Australia (www.vaustralia.com), for which he has bought six Boeing 777s. Service between the United States and Australia on V Australia will begin early 2009, when an unholy price war will undoubtedly break out.

BAHAMAS

THEY'RE IN THE ATLANTIC, NOT THE CARIBBEAN, BUT THEY ARE KNOWN FOR THEIR CARIBBEAN-LIKE QUALITIES

This 700-island archipelago that practically touches Florida (Bimini's a piddling 45 miles offshore) and sprawls southeast for some 500 miles, is technically in the Atlantic, not the Caribbean. But whatever—the Bahamas delivers the same kind of subtropical experience in all its sun-splashed variety, from glitzy casinos and world-class duty-free shopping to colonial architecture and remote castaway beaches and cays—you just need to know how to choose your island.

The two big boys are Grand Bahama (whose resort area is Freeport/Lucaya) and New Providence, which hosts a generally better class of resorts, as well as the country's quaint colonial-era capital, Nassau (just a hop over a bridge from Nassau is Paradise Island, whose megafancy resorts include the mammoth, over-the-top Atlantis. The latter, with its elaborate waterparks, casinos, and aquarium, is a major tourist attraction).

The many beaches of the Bahamas are its chief touristic lure, along with its British flavor, its casinos, and its extensive shopping opportunities.

All the rest are referred to as the Out Islands, and are accessible by puddle-jumper or ferry from Nassau or Freeport. The main Out Islands are flyspeck Bimini (especially popular with anglers), the Abacos (charming pastel-painted clapboards), the Exumas (a mostly uninhabited yachting/fishing paradise), Andros (the largest island, largely unpeopled, a divers' dream), and Eleuthera/Harbour Island (pineapple plantations and colonial villages, including the historic first settlement).

For air-hotel packages, check with Funjet (☎ 800/558-3050; www.funjet.com), GOGO Worldwide Vacations (☎ 800/229-4999; www.gogowwv.com), Travel Impressions (☎ 800/284-0044; www.travelimpressions.com), Air Canada (☎ 800/247-2262; www.aircanada.com), and Bahamasair (☎ 800/222-4262; www.bahamasair.com). Most U.S. airlines also run direct flights, mostly to Nassau and Freeport. For more information, websites include www.bahamas.com, www.nassauparadiseisland.com, and www.myoutislands.com. You can also call ☎ 800/224-2627 in the United States, 800/667-3777 in Canada, and 800/327-9019 for questions about Nassau/Paradise Island.

BALI

WHERE'S THE WORLD'S BEST SHOPPING? IT'S ON THE ENCHANTING ISLAND OF BALI.

When shopaholics ask me to suggest the best possible destination for a holiday devoted almost entirely to shopping (and there are such people), I answer "Bali" without a moment's hesitation. And I give them the following directions:

From the airport of its capital city, Denpasar, take a taxi (less than $30) to the town of Ubud in the central uplands far from the commercial atmosphere of the beach resorts. And once there, seek out low-cost accommodations from the dozens of choices to which a city tourist office on the main street will direct you.

Then, most days, simply negotiate with a taxi driver to bring you back and forth to the various crafts villages—they specialize in oil paintings, furniture, batik cloth and clothing, wooden sculptures, or stonework—that surround Ubud. Prices are a fraction of what you'd pay for similar items elsewhere, and what you buy will usually be reliably and cheaply shipped home to you by the various crafts manufacturers and shops.

As Bali recovers from the tourist drop-off caused by two terrorist attacks on beachfront nightclubs several years ago, prices for every purchase and other elements of your stay will be lower then ever before. My own living room is graced by a large and quite stunning Balinese oil painting acquired several years ago for less than $70, including the equally stunning frame.

Bali is one of those places—such as Yellowstone, Egypt, the safari games parks of Kenya—to which every human being at some point in their lives must go. For remarkably low-cost air/land packages, I highly recommend that you contact Roe Gruber's Escapes Unlimited (www.escapesltd.com). I have never understood how she maintains her prices to Bali, but she does so year after year. And I have never heard a critical word about her tour arrangements from the many people I have known who booked Escapes Unlimited to Bali. Phone ☎ 800/243-7227, or access www.escapesltd.com.

BALTICS

A QUICK LOOK AT ESTONIA, LATVIA & LITHUANIA

Swallowed up in the drabness of the Soviet Union till breaking free in 1991, Estonia, Latvia, and Lithuania have burgeoned into prospering free-market democracies, European Union members, even groundbreakers (some dub Estonia the planet's most Internet-wired country).

Relative flyspecks wedged between Russia, Belarus, and Poland, a short hop across the Baltic Sea from Scandinavia, they manage to pack in plenty of gorgeous scenery as well as architecture and sights dating from the 12th

It used to be called "the Paris of the Baltics," and Riga, Latvia, still offers a lively nightlife scene and countless cultural attractions.

century. Since '91 they've also evolved a great menu of cool dining, night-life, and lodging options—a good number still very attractively priced. You could easily tour most of the highlights by car or train in a week.

Estonia's trendy capital, Tallinn, boasts a Brothers' Grimm fairy tale of an Old Town, with red roofs, cobblestone lanes, and Gothic gables, spires, and towers (it's a UNESCO World Heritage Site). Outside Tallinn, check out the wonderful open-air museum, the czarist palaces of Kadriorg, nice beaches in Pärnu and elsewhere, plenty of nature preserves and castles (including one on an island), and a window into the grim Soviet past in Narva.

In Latvia you'll find a fun and elegant capital, Riga (once called "the Paris of the Baltics"), with another fetching old quarter that mixes medieval with neoclassical and especially Art Nouveau; the Belle Époque beach/spa city of Jurmala; and the castles of the Sigulda lakes district.

Lithuania's capital, Vilnius, offers a handsome Gothic-Baroque-neoclassical mélange (plus a monument to Frank Zappa, go figure), while other pretty cities and towns include culturally rich Kaunas, seaside Klaipeda, and medieval Trakai. All three local languages are fairly impene-trable (Estonian's related to Finnish; Latvian and Lithuanian to—believe it or not—Sanskrit), but even if you don't speak the lingua franca, which is still Russian, many locals have learned English.

All flights are via other European cities, and tour operators offering Baltic packages include Escapes Unlimited (☎ 800/339-6967; www.escapesltd.com) and Djoser (☎ 877/356-7376; www.djoserusa.com). For more information, go to www.balticsww.com, www.visitestonia.com, www.latviatourism.lv, or www.tourism.lt.

BARBADOS

HERE'S BARBADOS "IN A NUTSHELL"

Considered possibly the most buttoned down and British of Her Majesty's former Caribbean colonies, Barbados is one of the more southerly islands of the West Indies, 166 square miles of gorgeous tropical landscapes (and beaches, of course) dotted with genteel estate mansions, gardens, and vari-ous other attractions, man-made and natural, for you to visit; several great golf courses; and some of the Caribbean's finest restaurants and resorts (the shopping's pretty darn good, too, duty-free and in terms of local art and crafts).

Barbadians (aka Bajans) also have a distinctive Afro-Caribbean culture, but while they know how to have a good time—the January jazz festival is one of the Caribbean's premier parties, and there's something or other shakin' most nights of the week in the capital, Bridgetown, and other areas such as Holetown and St. Lawrence Gap—this island's probably not your best bet if you're here to party all the time.

Tonier (and pricier) resorts tend to be the norm up the west coast in the parishes of St. Michael, St. Peter, and especially St. James, whereas the east and southeast coasts are more rugged and draw more surfers than swimmers (the Soup Bowl surf break is world famous); this is also where you'll land more bargains.

Several major airlines fly direct from North America and the U.K., and a number of companies offer air-hotel packages, including Funjet (☎ 888/558-6654; www.funjet.com), GOGO/Liberty Travel (☎ 888/271-1584; www.libertytravel.com), Inter-Island Tours (☎ 800/245-3434; www.inter islandtours.com), and Travel Impressions (☎ 800/284-0044; www.travel impressions.com). For more information of the touristic variety: in the U.S. phone ☎ 800/221-9831, in Canada, 800/268-9122; and on the Web go to www.barbados.org.

BARCELONA

IT'S LIKE A "NEW YORK" OF SPAIN, COMBINING ART & ARCHITECTURE, LIVE THEATER & MUSIC & A STUNNING CUISINE

Many of Spain's cities are exciting places these days, but few offer the pizzazz and variety of this once somewhat dingy port that's now one of the Mediterranean's greatest metropolitan areas. The Gothic Quarter is a picturesque, medieval-feeling warren of residences, restaurants, and hip/elegant shops, and its city museum preserves fascinating artifacts including parts of the original Roman foundations. And the Ramblas! The Ramblas is one of the world's great strolling boulevards, jammed day and night with animal vendors, buskers, and visitors from across the planet rubbing shoulders with locals.

The 19th and 20th centuries made their own major contributions, particularly in cutting-edge architecture recent and historic (Art Nouveau modernista buildings are all over, most famously the towering, melted-wax-like, and still unfinished Sagrada Família church designed by the movement's "patron saint," Antoni Gaudí). The art museums and galleries in Pablo Picasso's former stomping grounds are outstanding, as is the music and performance scene.

You'll notice that locals proudly keep their Catalan language and culture alive (if you know some Spanish you'll catch a bit of it, particularly in reading). You'll also find that the Catalonia (Catalunya) region is rich with

The architecture of Gaudi, found throughout Barcelona, is only one of the many reasons to visit this sophisticated and prosperous city.

day and overnight trip possibilities: Tarragona with its expansive Roman amphitheater; Sitges, Cadaquès, and other fetching beach towns; the wine country of Penedès and Priorat; haunting medieval cities, such as Girona and Vic; monasteries, such as Poblet (a Gothic masterpiece) and still active Montserrat (spectacularly perched amid conical hills and home to a venerated Black Virgin); and ancient ruins, such as the Greek colony at Empúries.

You can of course fly here independently, directly or via Madrid and other European cities, and though bargains aren't as easy to find these days, you can still save a fair amount by sticking to *pensiones* and prix-fixe restaurant menus. If you'd rather have everything set up for you, check into tours with area specialists, such as Abreu Tours (☎ 800/223-1580; www. abreu-tours.com) and Club ABC (☎ 888/TOURS-ABC; www.clubabc. com). And for more information, phone ☎ 212/529-8484, or access www. barcelonaturisme.com or www.spain.info.

AS A VISITOR TO CATALONIA, YOU'LL ALSO WANT TO TOUR THE SEASIDE CITIES LOCATED JUST OUTSIDE BARCELONA

You'll find so many wonderful little towns and cities in Catalonia, within an easy car, train, or bus trip outside of Barcelona, that your choice will need to depend on your own particular (and often eccentric) tastes (do you need lots of good local dining and/or shopping, for example?). An almost bewildering number of seaside resort towns are less than an hour away, of which the most prominent, attractive, and amenities-laden is Sitges (a 40-min. straight shot by RENFE train; www.sitgestour.com). Alternative towns nearby on the same train line include Castelldefels and Vilanova.

If you're wine lovers, consider a pair of towns in the marvelous Penedès wine country, which produces excellent *cavas* (champagnes). Just under an hour away by train are, first, Vilafranca del Penedès, larger of the two (pop. 28,000), with a bit more to see and do, and the smaller town of Sant Sadurni d'Anoia (a 45-min. ride and also closer to some of the main vineyards, such as Freixenet and Cordoniu).

Other inland towns to consider include Martorell (36 min.), with its outstanding Gothic bridge, and Sant Celoni (50–60 min.), near the UNESCO biosphere Montseny Park.

BELIZE

A QUICK COMMENT ABOUT AN INCREASINGLY POPULAR CENTRAL AMERICAN DESTINATION

Belize (☎ 800/624-0686; www.travelbelize.org) is the region's only English-speaking country. Its earliest attractions were the beaches of some

An English-speaking nation of Central America, Belize is primarily visited for the endless varieties of its sea life and beaches.

30-or-so offshore islands (such as Ambergris Caye or Caye Caulker) and the barefoot charms of coastal Placencia. It is increasingly renowned for its awesome diving (especially at the legendary Blue Hole, 60 miles east of Belize City and visited daily by dive boats) and for such Mayan sites as Altun Ha. And most recently, Belize has become popular for second homes and timeshares. Although developers have rushed to erect new high-end resorts, such as Placencia's $300-a-night per room Chabil Mar (☎ 800/819-9088; www.chabilmarvillas.com), the tourist board continues to stress such budget-worthy attractions as the Toucan Trail (www.toucantrail.com), dotted with more than 160 lodgings costing $60 a night and less.

BORNEO

AROUND $1,400 (PLUS AIRFARE) FOR MORE THAN 2 WEEKS OF SHEER ENCHANTMENT, IN A UNIQUE WORLD OF BIODIVERSITY, INCLUDING AN ORANGUTANG SANCTUARY

For just about $2,800 per person total (once you include the transpacific airfare), you have 17 days of jungles, orangutans, caverns, and river trips in Borneo, including all internal flights, guides, and lodging from hotels to rainforest lodges and a longhouse stay with native inhabitants. The tour operator is the long-established Adventure Center, which maintains low prices on all seven continents by contracting with expert local outfitters and specialist operators. Most trips are priced without airfare, though they can arrange it.

For information or to book, phone ☎ 800/228-8747, or access www.adventurecenter.com.

BOSTON

WINTER BRINGS SUBSTANTIAL HOTEL DISCOUNTS IN SUCH COLD-WEATHER CITIES AS BOSTON—A GOOD TIME TO VISIT THEIR RESTAURANTS & MUSEUMS

As soon as the temperature drops, so do hotel prices in chilly U.S. cities, such as Boston. Urged on by its convention and visitors bureau, hotels in and around Bean City offer really impressive discounts, as well as packages padded with extras at no additional charge.

For winter hotel deals in Boston, and all over Massachusetts for that matter, go to www.massvacation.com and click on "Warm Winter Specials."

Rates start as low as under $100 a night for brand-name lodgings, such as Holiday Inn and Best Western. And several hotels in the greater Boston area are available for about half what travelers pay in the peak of summer. The Best Western Terrace Inn, for example, is on Commonwealth Avenue, within walking distance of a T stop, and costs around $100 per night. These, and other winter hotel specials, are available through the end of March and always include complimentary breakfast.

BUDAPEST

THERE'S NO DOUBT THAT BUDAPEST REMAINS LESS COSTLY THAN NEARLY EVERY OTHER GREAT CAPITAL OF EUROPE

Smart travelers have learned that the large, central European city of Budapest offers many of the pleasures of the more heavily visited European capitals but at a fraction of the cost. Several four-star Budapest hotels charge less than a hundred dollars in winter for a double room. Restaurants in downtown Budapest will serve you pork cutlets with a paprika cream sauce, together with the excellent beer of the country, for less than $30 for two

Budapest is stately, regal, and imposing; it's also famed for its spas, where visitors work off the ravages of a luscious, sauce-drenched cuisine.

persons. And the Király Baths in Buda bring you an hour-long soak in a 97°F (36°C) communal pool for only $6. For a 1-week air-and-land package to Budapest costing under $1,000 in November, early December, and in January through March, contact Tatra Travel at www.tatratravel.com, or phone ☎ 800/321-2999 or 212/486-0533.

CANADA

LOOKING FOR A MEMORABLE SUMMER VACATION AT A REASONABLE COST? GIVE SOME THOUGHT TO VISITING THE TOP CANADIAN NATIONAL PARKS.

Capital of the Canadian Rockies, the national park of Banff, in Alberta, is a dream of mountains and natural wonders.

Though we're all aware of the low-cost vacation opportunities at Yosemite and Yellowstone, too many American travelers fail to think about visiting the two major Canadian national parks: Jasper and Banff, in the province of Alberta. Despite the recent rise in value of the Canadian dollar (it's now selling almost at par to the U.S. dollar), their admission charges are modest (a family group pays about $20 a day to enter the parks, individuals around $10), and there are lodgings and campsites in every price range, in Banff National Park (soaring scenery) and the more-northerly Jasper (remarkable varieties of wildlife).

CARIBBEAN

A CANVAS HUT FOR YOUR NEXT HOLIDAY IN THE TROPICS

A recent Caribbean vacation was spent at probably the most unusual resort in all the Tropics called Maho Bay Camps, on the little island of St. John in the U.S. Virgin Islands. Its rooms are small, canvas-sided bungalows on wooden platforms perched along a steep hill sloping down to a ravishing white-sand beach, and with a view that is the full equivalent of anything you'd find in the most luxurious locales. You pay a maximum winter price of $130 a night for two people ($80 in off season), you have $17 dinners on an open-air pavilion, and you hobnob with some of the most intellectually curious and down-to-earth people in all the nation. If you're interested, go to www.maho.org or phone ☎ **800/392-9004.**

FOR THE SAKE OF YOUR SANITY, AVOID THOSE OVERLY POPULAR PORTS IN THE CARIBBEAN

I returned from my trip to the U.S. Virgin Islands, stunned as always by their awesome beauty but astonished by the impact that the cruise industry is now having on these tiny islets. With dozens of giant 2,000- and 3,000-passenger cruise ships now sailing each week in winter, there are days when a little town, such as Charlotte Amalie in St. Thomas, receives as many as five ships in port at the same time, spilling 10,000 to 12,000 passengers (and sometimes more) onto a delicate infrastructure. Nowadays, in my view, the smart seagoing American simply has to select those smaller, more exotic, lesser known islands that do not receive multiple visitations each day from the humongous vessels known as "ships."

LOOKING FOR A CHEAP VACATION THIS SUMMER? TRY THE CARIBBEAN.

Would you ever have believed that the Caribbean would be relatively cheap compared to Europe?

When I last checked, the packager known as CheapCaribbean.com was charging under $800 in summer and fall for 5 nights at the four-star Sun Village Resort & Spa in the Puerto Plata beach area of the Dominican Republic, including round-trip air from New York (and about the same from most other cities), all three meals daily, unlimited drinks, sports, and entertainment. The same figure was still under $1,000 at the peak of the winter season, and an extra 2 nights (with meals and all else) adds only about $140. To the five-star Ocean Blue Resort in the Dominican Republic's Punta Cana area, it charged the same.

When you consider that such rates cover literally every feature of your vacation stay, you discover that such destinations as the Dominican Republic, the Mexican Caribbean coast, and Jamaica are picking up the fallen budget standard of the currently expensive Europe. If all you're seeking is a total rest without pocketbook concerns, but also without cultural distractions or mental exercise, these three budget-priced areas of the Caribbean will do the job.

The Punta Cana region of the Dominican Republic currently offers more than 40,000 hotel rooms—but in well-spaced properties along a superb beach.

I've been spending some time looking at the various air-&-land packages to Mexico & the Caribbean in July & August—& they are dramatic in price

The cheapest high-quality destinations for Americans today are in the Tropics just south of Florida. If you haven't yet made your plans, you might now want to scan the offerings of Vacation Travel Mart of Miami (www.vacmart.com) and the similar site of CheapCaribbean.com. You might also want to go to Apple Vacations (www.applevacations.com) for more examples.

Now it's true that increases in the cost of fuel were late in being fully incorporated into the price of summer packages to the Caribbean. Until recently, they weren't prominently featured in the headlined rates, but suddenly cropped up in the form of independent fuel surcharges when you booked the package. Now they're in the basic price, which has therefore gone up by about $150 per person.

But even with those increases, the cost of a Caribbean vacation this summer remains one of the great bargains. Using Vacation Travel Mart, a 7-night stay at La Romana on the south coast of the Dominican Republic, at the attractive beachfront Oasis Canoa Beach Hotel, including round-trip air from Miami, lodgings, all three meals a day (supplemented by a late-night snack for a total of four meals daily), unlimited drinks and beverages, sea sports, and entertainment, comes to around $1,000 per person, with children staying and eating for free. Add about $100 for flights from most other cities.

That $1,000 is less than what you'd pay for round-trip airfare alone to most of Europe in the months of July and August this year. Bear in mind that most of the packages described in such websites as Vacation Travel Mart or CheapCaribbean.com are all-inclusive, covering every one of your basic expenses.

It isn't too early to rent a Caribbean (or Hawaiian) villa for Christmas/New Year's

Among the great bargains of travel are the large and rambling beachside villas accommodating up to three couples in dreamlike locations of the Caribbean. If you can gather six persons to partner in the rental of such a villa for the Christmas/New Year's period, you can enjoy an idyllic winter vacation for not much more than you would have spent at a hotel. Many of the villas come staffed with a cook and maid, enabling you to enjoy the most sybaritic 10 days or so of your life, but at modest cost.

For more than 15 years, a Richmond, Virginia, company called Unusual Villa & Island Rentals has maintained an unusually large inventory of rental villas in the Caribbean and Central and South America. They make a specialty of Christmas and holiday villa rentals. And their rates can go as low as $1,000 per person for an entire week, when six persons are combining to rent a multibedroom villa. Try www.unusualvillarentals.com or phone ☎ 800/846-7280 or 804/288-2823.

In the peak of the tropical hurricane season, you can allay your fears by choosing islands with a very low probability of storms

There is no such thing as a Caribbean island which is absolutely, positively, cross-my-heart outside the hurricane belt. Even the allegedly storm-free Curaçao has had a couple of hurricanes in the past 100 years, and Aruba and Bonaire were brushed by the fringes of Hurricane Felix (though not seriously damaged by it).

But there are islands whose extremely low probability of a hurricane makes them almost totally safe for autumn vacationing. And thus, vacationers who want safety from storms will go the ABC Islands (Aruba, Bonaire, Curaçao), to Venezuela's Margarita, to Trinidad and Tobago, and to St. Vincent and the Grenadines. Or they will fly to that easternmost island of the Caribbean, Barbados (which last had a hurricane 30 years ago). All these places tout themselves as being "outside the hurricane belt."

But how real is the fear that an island which is clearly within the hurricane belt will suffer one at the time of your stay? The odds are very low, surely less than one in a hundred. But because that fear exists among many, September and October are two of the cheapest months for traveling to the Tropics. To enjoy excellent weather, a lack of crowds, and low airfares and hotel rates, the fall is the time to go.

▷ ## YOU WON'T HAVE TO WORRY ABOUT THE PLUNGE IN THE VALUE OF THE U.S. DOLLAR IF YOU VACATION ON ISLANDS WHOSE CURRENCY IS TIED TO THE GREENBACK

As the dollar continues its plunge against the euro and the British pound, it's wise to choose destinations where the currency is the U.S. dollar itself— or tied to the dollar.

That list of places where the U.S. dollar remains in use includes, of course, Puerto Rico, the U.S. Virgin Islands, and Panama, and a number of islands where the local currency is effectively tied to the greenback: the Dominican Republic, Jamaica, Mexico, the Bahamas, Barbados, the Cayman Islands, Trinidad and Tobago, and the Netherlands Antilles (Curaçao, Aruba, Bonaire).

However, the entire Caribbean does not present such a rosy exchange rate. Remember that many islands have currencies tied to the euro (currently trading at around $1.50), which means sticker shock still applies on such islands as Martinique, Guadeloupe, St. Barts, and, in an odd case, the French half of St. Martin (as a member of the Netherlands Antilles, the other half uses a currency tied to the U.S. dollar).

I'M RECOMMENDING VACATION TRAVEL MART OF MIAMI AS A SOURCE OF ULTRACHEAP WEEKLONG VACATIONS AT A TROPICAL HOTEL

Though I'm not a fan of all-inclusive resorts (and actively avoid them on my own trips), I can nevertheless understand the desire of many workaholics to choose resorts that let them turn off from the world, which is what all-inclusives do (by eliminating the daily search for meals, by confining you psychologically to the grounds of your hotel). I've already mentioned all-inclusives in the Dominican Republic offered by CheapCaribbean.com. But you should also check out a few other popularly priced tour operators to find the best values. One of the major competitors in this field is a Miami company called Vacation Travel Mart, headed by Jacques Abitan.

His website, www.vacmart.com, is full of superspecials for most of the key all-inclusive resorts of the Dominican Republic. Though the lead price is always for a 3-night package including air from Miami or Fort Lauderdale, he also quotes prices for 7-night stays from New York; Chicago; Washington, D.C.; and elsewhere.

When the post–Labor Day rates appear on the site, you may be gratified to discover that you can enjoy a September or October week—a full 7-night stay—at a first-class hotel of the Dominican Republic for as little as $500 to $600 from Fort Lauderdale and $600 to $700 from New York.

ANOTHER CURRENT CHAMP IN BARGAIN-PRICED AIR-&-LAND PACKAGES TO THE CARIBBEAN IS ATLAS VACATIONS OF BROOKLYN

I base this claim on numerous offerings, such as a price of about $575 per person, including round-trip air from New York, for a stay in April or May of 7 nights at the White Sands Beach Hotel in Negril, Jamaica, offered by

All the classic attractions of the Caribbean—weather, seasports, cuisine, music, a gracious people—are found alongside the beaches of Jamaica's Negril.

the aggressive Atlas (other firms would probably charge that amount for round-trip airfare alone) of Brooklyn (which is not to be confused with a generally higher-priced Atlas Tours & Cruises). This one (with the bargains) is reached at ☎ **800/634-1057** or 888/285-3390, or at www.atlas vacations.net.

FINALLY, IN PLANNING A CARIBBEAN VACATION THIS SUMMER, BE SURE TO CHECK THE OFFERINGS OF LIBERTY TRAVEL

There was a time when Liberty Travel (☎ **800/897-9999;** www.liberty travel.com) was always the cheapest to the Tropics. During my own years as a tour operator, I used to rub my eyes when I saw the rates that this competitor offered for a weeklong stay at various Caribbean resorts. On one occasion I even called the president of Liberty Travel to suggest that a price in his ad might be a typographical error. He burst into laughter. I subsequently learned that Liberty's power with the public enabled them to get unbeatable airfares from American Airlines and rock-bottom rates from the hotels they used. No one else could come close.

In more recent years, Liberty seemed to relinquish its role, and you would often find lower rates from much smaller firms. But that seems to be changing. Acquired by a rich Australian conglomerate, Liberty's current prices are again quite impressive, and though they don't always undercut those of Vacation Travel Mart (www.vacmart.com), Apple Vacations (www. applevacations.com), or CheapCaribbean.com, they frequently give battle to those firms. The Aussies are apparently intent on reestablishing Liberty's cost-cutting reputation.

Though their offices are mainly along the eastern seaboard, they quote prices from every major U.S. city as far west as Los Angeles.

CHICAGO

WINTER BRINGS SUBSTANTIAL HOTEL DISCOUNTS IN SUCH COLD-WEATHER CITIES AS CHICAGO—A GOOD TIME TO VISIT THEIR RESTAURANTS & MUSEUMS

As soon as the temperature drops, so do hotel prices in chilly U.S. cities, such as Chicago. Urged on by its convention and visitors bureau, hotels in and around the Windy City offer really impressive discounts, as well as packages padded with extras at no additional charge.

For discounts in Chicago, go to www.choosechicago.com.

CHINA

IF YOU'LL CHART THE DAILY EXCHANGE RATES APPEARING ON XE, YOU'LL WITNESS THE STEADY UPWARD RISE OF THE CHINESE YUAN. TO CHINA—GET THERE QUICK.

The most popular website for currency exchange rates—XE (www.xe.com)—carries a daily value for the Chinese yuan (CNY). I've been following it, with a sinking heart, for many months now.

When I first traveled to China several years ago, a traveler received about 8.30 yuan for US$1, a joyous, exhilarating rate. Then strong international pressure was exerted on the Chinese to revalue its obviously undervalued currency. Though the Chinese denied they were giving in to these demands (and thus saved face), they proceeded to do just that. Every single week or so, the value of the Chinese yuan went up a tiny bit. By the middle of 2008, you received only 7 yuan for US$1. When we went to press, you received only 6.88 yuan for US$1. By early spring of 2009, the rate will undoubtedly be down to around 6.75 to the dollar, and to 6 to the dollar by the end of the year.

Historic Suzhou, on the Yangtze River, is a great tourist attraction of China, studded with pagodas, bridges, and gardens.

All this is by way of suggesting that if you have any interest in visiting China, you should get there quick. Though China remains an inexpensive destination, it will get costlier and costlier with every passing month.

STILL, AS LONG AS THE CHINESE YUAN STAYS REASONABLY LOW IN PRICE, A TRIP TO CHINA—IN ANY PRICE CATEGORY—IS ONE OF THE GREAT BARGAINS OF TRAVEL

Jim and Mary Patterson (those aren't their real names) paid an astonishing $1,299 per person for their escorted low-cost tour to five Chinese cities in 10 days, including round-trip air from the States. Too frightened to sign up for a bargain, William and Ellen Cartwright paid some $4,000 per person for round-trip air and 14 nights in six Chinese cities.

The costs varied wildly. Yet once in China, both couples walked the same stretch of the Great Wall, attended the same show of Chinese acrobats in Shanghai, walked on the same ancient brick floors of the Forbidden City and the Summer Palace, strolled around Tiananmen Square, beamed at similar Chinese kindergarten children in an elementary school in Suzhou, even ate in the same mammoth restaurant with singers and orchestra, to which nearly every tour group is brought in Beijing.

To the extent that their tours differed, it was in the number of passengers (30 for the cheap tour, 15 or so for the expensive ones), and the hotels in which they were housed. But since most hotels in China are modern and less than 15 years old, the difference between them was not in the comfort of the rooms but in the elegance of the public areas—and thus utterly unimportant.

How little can you pay?

That's $1,049 per person, plus taxes and fees of $415, from San Francisco; add $200 from New York. The unchallenged price leader to China is the remarkable China Focus of San Francisco (☎ 800/868-7244; www.china focustravel.com), whose 12-day, meals-included trip to five cities (spending a total of 9 nights in Beijing, Shanghai, Ji'nan, Tai Shan, QuFu, and Suzhou) is a great value for the $1,049 plus $415 price—it also includes round-trip air on Air China. The only condition is that you pay by personal check or money order, not via credit card (plastic requires an extra $200 charge). The firm's Chinese-American management is so reliable that I've never received a complaint about them, only compliments. How to book? Go to www.chinafocustravel.com, or phone ☎ 800/868-7244 or 415/788-8660.

The East Coast runner-up to China Focus, charging slightly more, is New York's Champion Holidays (☎ 800/868-7658; www.china-discovery.

com), offering departures from Los Angeles (and from New York for an additional $100–$120). You receive round-trip air (Air China or Japan Airlines), and 7 nights in China (Beijing, Suzhou, Wuxi, and Shanghai) at good first-class hotels.

CHINASPREE.COM IS A NEW & WORTHY CONTENDER IN THE WORLD OF INEXPENSIVE TRIPS TO ASIA

All the recognized names in tour operation to China—ChinaFocus, Champion Holidays, Pacific Delight Tours, Ritz Tours, and a couple of others—are currently doing tons of business, and it sometimes happens that you encounter harassed telephone reservationists or endless busy signals when you call them to book. I don't mean this as a negative criticism; no one anticipated the skyrocketing rise in the number of Americans seeking to visit China.

But because the best-known agencies are so busy, you may want to know about ChinaSpree.com of Blaine, Washington (☎ 866/652-5656 or 360/332-7970). It matches the promotional lures offered by ChinaFocus and Champion Holidays, at least for one or two departures, and matches their higher fares during many months of the year. Its tour program is just as comprehensive, just as varied, with numerous options; and because it's a licensed tour operator in Washington and California, your payments are deposited in a trust account monitored by a bank and not released to the tour operator until the tour is successfully concluded.

I've had favorable comments about ChinaSpree.com from readers of Frommers.com, and I'm impressed with its well-designed website. If you're considering a trip to China, you might give them a call.

ADD RIM-PAC INTERNATIONAL TO YOUR LIST OF SOURCES FOR LOW-COST TOURS OF CHINA, BUT USE THEM FAST—BEFORE THE CHINESE CURRENCY APPRECIATES FURTHER

Travelers who live in the eastern half of the United States should also consider using the services of Rim-Pac International (☎ 800/701-8687; www.rim-pac.com), which has matched the prices of several of the West Coast operators.

For its departures from New York, Rim-Pac will take you to China on a 13-night trip, spending 11 nights in Chinese cities (Beijing, Ji-an, Qufu, Suzhou, and Shanghai), for around $1,600 plus a fuel surcharge. Meals, hotels, and airfare are included.

At last! A Chinese website enabling you to obtain low-cost air tickets to & within China—directly from the Chinese.

For several years now, Ctrip.com has been China's leading source of travel news, accessed by Chinese-speaking readers. It maintained a barely usable version in English, but it was the Chinese-language website on which most attention was lavished. Lots o' luck.

Ctrip.com has now given its English website a big face-lift and a crystal-clear address, www.english.ctrip.com. And it has also created a phone number (☎ 86-21-34064888, ext. 6) for inquiries or to make a booking (you'll hear a Chinese-language announcement until you press extension 6). Today, you won't find cheaper tickets to China, or within China, than on Ctrip's English-language site.

Prices are set forth in Chinese yuan (CNY), which you convert into dollars by dividing by approximately 7. Thus, 2,100 yuan equals $300. Here are some examples of offerings (all round-trips):

Vancouver and Shanghai on Air Canada: 3,670 yuan ($524)

Chicago and Shanghai on American Airlines: 3,150 yuan ($450)

London and Shanghai on China Eastern Airlines: 4,080 yuan ($582)

Saigon and Guangzhou on Vietnam Airlines: 1,610 yuan ($230)

Shanghai and Xian on China Eastern Airlines: 1,000 yuan ($142)

Although you can book intra-China flights directly on the website, you cannot yet book international flights in that manner—you simply learn about them and then phone a toll-free number staffed by English-speaking representatives (☎ 800/820-6666) to make the booking. Even if you don't find a deal between the United States and China, you might nevertheless phone Ctrip.com to inquire about the current rates for round-trip flights between the United States and China. You might be pleasantly surprised.

You can also e-mail Ctrip.com at e_service@ctrip.com. And you can book beach vacations in China (you've been dying to do so) at sharply discounted rates. See you on the sands at Qingdao!

IN CHINA, TAKE A CAB—THEY RARELY COST MORE THAN $1.50 FOR 10 OR 15 MINUTES—& INDEPENDENT TRAVEL THUS BECOMES EASY & INEXPENSIVE

Although you'll need to ask your hotel desk clerk to write out the Chinese name for the museum or sight you're hoping to visit (as well as the name and address of your hotel), that simple act will win you freedom from the tour guides and the group-jammed motorcoaches. And the sights themselves charge a pittance to enter (usually, the yuan equivalent of a dollar). By either taking a cab or walking to nearby places, you can enjoy independent travel in any Chinese city, which is infinitely preferable to joining a chattering crowd of fellow tourists. As for meals, nearly every Chinese restaurant of size has either an English-language menu or English translations under Chinese menu items—or even more frequently, photographs of the dishes they serve.

Tourism is so highly developed in China today that the lone tourist or tourist couple can enjoy their stays solely on their own, without surrendering to the rigidities and cultural barriers of escorted group travel. As for visiting out-of-town places (such as the Great Wall or the Summer Palace), stop by a Chinese travel agency or at the tourist desk of your hotel, and they will book you aboard either half-day or full-day tours to such heavily visited attractions.

A READER HAS DRAMATICALLY CONFIRMED MY ADVICE THAT A PRIVATE TAXICAB TOUR ($1.50 OR SO PER RIDE) IS THE BEST WAY TO SIGHTSEE IN CHINESE CITIES

Sharing my disdain for sightseeing in a big motorcoach with 40 other tourists, a reader who has twice been to China has described her own preference for moving about independently in big Chinese cities—even to the extent of taking meals in restaurants frequented only by locals. She writes:

> Three years ago I travelled to Beijing and Shanghai through www.friendlyplanet.com. My friend and I took a guidebook that had Chinese characters for most of the major tourist attractions that we wanted to see (and a hotel card with the name of the hotel we wanted to return to). We would flag down a cab, show them the Chinese characters and wait for a nod before getting into the cab. We always got to our destination and the cost was cheap.

In one area where we were walking, we got lost and wanted lunch. We walked into a place (Muslim Hot Pot) that was way off the tourist track. They had one menu translated into English. The staff probably hadn't seen many non-Chinese in their restaurant, but they were so patient and helpful. They pointed to suggestions and brought out samples. It was a memorable lunch—for us and them; the whole kitchen staff checked us out as we ate.

Friendly Planet offered à la carte tours that we passed on, choosing the cab method. We saw almost twice as much as the people who took the tours. Occasionally, we would hire a guide at the entrance gates. Even doing this, we saved a huge amount of money over the organized tours and we could control the amount of time we spent in various places. We even saw a few places that the tours didn't get to.

Increasingly, tourism to China is resembling tourism to Europe. With preparation and ingenuity, it becomes easily possible to sightsee on your own.

WITH VERY LITTLE PUBLICITY, GO-TODAY.COM IS CURRENTLY OFFERING AWESOMELY CHEAP PRICING FOR QUICK TRIPS TO CHINA

Who would have dreamed that a quick trip to China was available from go-today.com? Fresh from its triumphs as a package operator to Europe (where it consistently leads the field in low-cost weeklong air-and-land packages to London and Paris), and regarded by most travelers as simply a source for cheap package deals to Europe, go-today.com has suddenly blossomed as a source of short air-and-land trips to Shanghai and Beijing.

Interestingly enough, lunch and dinner are not included in their prices—you are actually expected to strike out on your own to any of numerous Chinese restaurants, and act like an intelligent human being, exactly as you would have done on an independent tour of Europe. China has finally shaken off the group-travel straitjacket.

The cities from which these prices are valid include Los Angeles, San Francisco, San Diego, Phoenix, Tucson, Portland, and Fresno.

COLOMBIA

A WEAKENED INSURGENCY AGAINST THE GOVERNMENT OF COLOMBIA MAY PERMIT THE RESTORATION OF TOURISM

What a difference a few days make! In one week, Venezuela and Ecuador threatened war against Colombia for crossing the Ecuadorean border to kill an anti-Colombia insurgent. The next week, at a summit conference in the Dominican Republic, all three South American nations shook hands, declared the crisis over, reestablished diplomatic relations, and toasted each other in the warmest terms. As a side consequence, it now appears that the insurgency against the Colombian government has been seriously weakened.

That's a totally different situation from the one that prevailed until recently. Just a few years ago, the Colombian insurgents (FARC) were a few miles from Bogota. Now, they have been greatly reduced in numbers and in their ability to function.

And as a consequence of that, Colombia may possibly reenter the world of tourism.

Recently, 50 major tour operators from countries all over the world completed an extensive, government-sponsored tour of Colombian cities (especially the historic capital city of Bogota) in which they were asked to believe that the major urban areas are not only especially attractive but entirely safe.

I spoke several weeks ago with one of them—Martha Tavera, sales director of the distinguished South American specialist, Marnella Tours (☎ 866/993-0033; www.marnellatours.com).

Though I continuously peppered Mrs. Tavera with skeptical doubts and strong negative comments, she held to her position and proudly announced that Marnella Tours is about to add several programs to Colombia to the many tours and packages it already offers to Argentina (especially Patagonia), Peru, Chile, and Brazil ("We'll do it within the next 30 days", she said). Although she admitted that the drug lord–led groups are still in the field, she maintained that their strength has declined so greatly that they are now no threat to tourism. And though she admitted that nearly 100 people are still held as hostages by the insurgent groups, she maintained that these were all Colombian political figures and that no one on any side is targeting the tourist.

She waxed rhapsodic about the attractions of Bogota, in the interior of the country, about its superb hotels and restaurants, its historic neighborhoods and architecture, its sophisticated people. She was equally positive about numerous historic and cultural attractions in the countryside of Colombia. And she constantly returned to the point that no element in Colombia has any intention of bringing harm to any tourist.

The same views, she maintained, are held by nearly every one of the major tour companies that have recently visited Colombia.

Marnella Tours is so busy sending a greatly increased number of Americans to South America (a substitute destination for costly Europe) that it remains prosperous without the added lure of Colombia. She has no need, she maintained, for additional business. And yet she is so enthusiastic about this large country (twice the size of France) that she is taking determined steps to add it to her roster of travel programs.

Cautioning you that the travel "advisories" of almost every western nation continue to warn against going to cities in Colombia other than Cartagena ("While security in Colombia has improved significantly in recent years, violence by narco-terrorist groups continues to affect some rural areas and cities," says our State Department), I pass along the enthusiastic opinions of this well-reputed tour company, Marnella.

COSTA RICA

FOR A TRULY AUTHENTIC EXPERIENCE OF COSTA RICA, TURN TO BELLS' HOME HOSPITALITY

If you honestly want to learn about the nontouristic life of a vibrant Central American nation, you will dispense with all the standard tours and itineraries. For you there will be no zip-lines over trees of a rainforest, no mule rides up the Arenal volcano, no resort all-inclusives on the Guanacaste coast. Instead, you'll stay in the heart of a residential suburb of San Jose, Costa Rica, interacting with the hosts of the private home in which you'll be staying and with other Costa Ricans who live in the vicinity. You'll use public transportation to reach the downtown sights, and on those occasions when you wish to visit other towns, beaches, and natural wonders of Costa Rica, you'll again simply board a public bus.

Bells' Home Hospitality (☎ 506/225-4752; www.homestay.thebells. org) was founded in 1990 by Marcela and Vernon Bell, two outstanding pioneers in Costa Rican tourism. They give close personal attention to the needs of their clients, and answer a phone number which you'll be given for inquiring about any and all aspects of Costa Rican life.

In turn, the hosts of your homestays are carefully chosen for their willingness to share the life of their households with their guests, exactly as if you were a member of the family. You'll participate in family activities, meet relatives and friends, involve yourself to the extent you choose, and get a native's view of *Costaricana*. From your phone calls to the Bells, you'll get tips on places to go and things to see, on shopping and transportation, and as a result you'll experience Costa Rica as you never would in any other way.

The rates are breathtaking: for a single room (occupied by one person): $30 a night. For a double or twin room shared by two people: $45 a night. Breakfast is always included.

For a room with private bath, add $5. To be picked up at the airport on arrival, add $15 for the first person, $5 for each additional person. And you can arrange to have dinner with the family for an extra $7 a meal, paid directly to your hosts.

The Bells are among those occasional treasures you find in travel, whose services are priceless. They have marvelously transformed the nature of the Costa Rica travel experience for thousands of Americans.

A STRONG CASE CAN BE MADE FOR TOURING COSTA RICA INDEPENDENTLY & NOT IN A GROUP

Why travel Costa Rica in a motorcoach group? Some of the best reactions I've heard to that popular Central America nation have been from people who rented a car on arrival and then simply went on their own to Guanacaste (the beaches), Monteverde (cloud forest), Manuel Antonio (national park along the sea), Arenal (the active volcano), Tortuguero, Puerto Viejo (the Caribbean coast), and elsewhere.

If you'll go to www.gapadventures.com, and click on "Central America," "Costa Rica," and "Independent," you'll find a large assortment of self-drive tours that cost about $525 per person for a week, $765 for 11 days (all plus airfare), including a self-drive car and hotels with breakfast. You fly into San Jose, pick up your car, and thereafter follow the indicated route, arriving at each hotel on the prescribed day. Here's an appealing way to absorb all the sights and atmosphere of Central America without the burden of having 40 other people dog your every step.

And for persons who themselves don't want to drive, the tour company offers a similarly priced alternative, a hotel shuttle bus that will pick you up at the end of your stay in one hotel and drive you and your luggage to the next hotel. It's called an "adventure bus" in G.A.P's literature, but it is more like a shuttle van and certainly not (in most instances) a large bus.

Although you'll find complete descriptions of these independent pro-grams on G.A.P Adventure's website, the people handling reservations are an independent unit of G.A.P reached by a separate phone number ☎ **800/ 667-1221.** (The normal G.A.P number is ☎ 800/708-7761.)

TOUR OPERATORS ARE SCRAMBLING TO CREATE THEIR OWN "AFFORDABLE" COSTA RICA

A few years ago, when the Chicago-based Caravan Tours created a 10-day, $995 tour of Costa Rica (not including airfare), it attracted so many book-ings that it is today the largest single source of tourists to that Central American nation. Caravan (☎ **800/CARAVAN** [227-2826]; www.caravan tours.com), which has always been known for its somewhat pricey tours of Europe, was suddenly launched as an operator of no fewer than 10 quite frugal, 8- to 10-day tours of Central America, Mexico, and parts of the American Southwest, each one of them selling for $995—never a dollar less or more.

It's clear that other big tour operators are frantically scrambling to match Caravan's success in Costa Rica. In its 7-day "Affordable Costa Rica" trip from April through October of 2009, Gate 1 Travel (www.gate1travel. com) will be charging exactly $899 including round-trip airfare from Miami to San Jose, Costa Rica, and fully escorted motorcoach arrangements for 2 nights in San Jose, 2 nights in Arenal, and 2 nights in Monteverde, with breakfast daily as well. *En garde,* Caravan!

G.A.P Adventures of Toronto (www.gapadventures.com) will be offer-ing a 16-day escorted tour of Costa Rica for $950 per person, plus $250 "extras," and round-trip airfare to San Jose. In typical G.A.P Adventures fashion, transportation will be by "public bus, tractor, van, boat or horse-back," lodging will be mostly in simple hotels or inns, and each group will consist of no more than 15 persons. Whichever trip you choose, prices are low and you now have no excuse for failing to go.

CROATIA

CROATIA IS EUROPE'S HOTTEST DESTINATION THIS YEAR & TRAVEL TIME OFFERS WELL-PRICED FALL/WINTER INTRODUCTIONS TO IT

Its Adriatic Coast (Dalmatia) is—according to many observers, including myself—the most scenically awesome in all the world. Its stately capital, Zagreb, and its timeless fishing villages are a delight. Its Dubrovnik is a

The stunning coast of Croatia, with its ancient port towns, has become an immensely popular tourist area of Europe.

perfectly preserved medieval knockout. And its prices are among the lowest on the Continent.

Though the best travel deals can come from any source, there's something to be said for tour companies run by expats who specialize in their home region and enjoy close relations with the local suppliers they use. One such company is Travel Time (☎ 800/354-8728 or 718/721-1132; www.traveltimeny.com), founded more than 30 years ago by a Croat now living in Queens, New York.

What makes Travel Time an even more useful resource is that independent packages to Croatia—bundling airfare and hotels—are hard to come by; most companies only sell fully escorted tours. Travel Time, however, offers a whole slew of packaged deals that take in the best of Croatia. If you have 2 weeks (that's 14 full nights in Croatia) and some $2,000 to spare, you can explore the entire Dalmatian Coast, the country's stunning southern Adriatic coastline strung with island chains, lined by secluded pebble beaches, and peppered with gorgeous historic cities.

This area was once part of the Roman Empire, and the entire historic center of Split is actually converted from the ruins of Emperor Diocletian's royal palace. The ancient palace's rooms are now houses and shops, its roofless corridors and open spaces now serve as city streets, and the emperor's mausoleum has been converted into the cathedral. Split has become a glamorous, club-dotted hangout for various jet-setters. And as for the island of Korcula, it's renowned as the probable birthplace of Marco Polo (Venice conquered much of this coast in its glory years, and among the spoils of war were captured sailors, including young Polo). Dubrovnik, anchoring the coast's southern end, is a postcard medieval town of red rooftops curling into the sea along a spit of land.

DOMINICAN REPUBLIC

SUCH TYPICAL RATES AS $549 FOR 5 ALL-INCLUSIVE NIGHTS HAVE MADE A POPULAR FAVORITE OF THE DOMINICAN REPUBLIC. WHAT'S THE DRAWBACK?

The wholesale rush to vacation in the Dominican Republic is one of the great current trends in travel, and proof positive that low prices attract vacationers. On this cheapest of all Caribbean islands, thousands of hotel rooms are currently in construction at resorts offering all-inclusive stays. To get a glimpse of what's being offered for the immediate months ahead, go to www.vacmart.com and read about Vacation Travel Mart's packages to the Grand Oasis Punta Cana in the D.R. for $649 per person, including round-trip airfare from Miami, 5 nights at the Grand Oasis (four restaurants, seven bars, children's pool, fitness room, Jacuzzi, and kayaks) directly on the island's most popular beach, three meals a day, unlimited snacks and beverages, nightly entertainment, and hotel taxes and gratuities (extra nights cost only $66). And there is no cut-off date to book.

So what's the catch? These new resorts of the Dominican Republic offer all-inclusive stays that confine their guests, in essence, to the grounds of their hotel (where they receive all meals, drinks, and sports, enticing them never to leave). I'm dismayed by the artificial nature of the vacation that then ensues, which involves no contact at all with the culture of the island, and effectively separates the visitor from the resident. Most of these hotels give meringue dance lessons each afternoon, in which scores of vacationers couple off with each other under the tutelage of an American dance instructor. Some foreign experience!

DUBAI

IF YOU'VE BEEN INTRIGUED BY ALL THE HYPE ABOUT DUBAI & ARE THINKING OF A TRIP THERE, THINK AGAIN . . .

Turns out that the social policies of Dubai, that fun-loving ministate of the Middle East, leave a bit to be desired. Last month, according to the *Times* of

Dubai, benefiting from massive investment of oil-based riches, is fast becoming the most modern resort city of the Middle East (and possibly the world).

London, two young Brits, aged 22 and 27, were each sentenced to 4 years of imprisonment for carrying into Dubai, for their own use, .04 ounces of marijuana (barely enough to make one joint) in one case, and 1.18 grams in the other. Another young British tourist, 25 years of age, was sentenced to the same 4 years for carrying in his pocket two-thousandths of an ounce—a bare trace or particle of marijuana, a hardly noticed speck. "I mistakenly forgot it in my pocket," said the evil-doer as he was led away to begin his 4 years of punishment.

A few years ago, according to the Associated Press, a number of homosexuals meeting peacefully in a home of Dubai were arrested and sentenced to jail terms for their sexual orientation, and made to undergo forcibly administered shots of testosterone.

No matter how luxurious its hotels; its theme parks of enclosed, artificially refrigerated ski slopes; its eventual display of the *QE2* as a maritime museum (the grand old ship was purchased by the emir of Dubai)—who can enjoy themselves in a place whose morals are those of the 15th century, where freedom of speech and advocacy have never been allowed, where young tourists can be hauled before a Sharia court for carrying a few specks of a recreational drug?

I am constantly hearing of Americans joining group tours to Dubai. Can anyone tell me why? What is there to do there? Though Dubai may possess the world's most luxurious hotels with service and physical amenities beyond imagining, does anyone go to a destination primarily to stay at a hotel? Dubai has an indoor ski slope, but what else does it offer in the way of vacation pleasures other than hot weather?

Can anyone enjoy themselves in a country whose government is headed by a single, all-powerful ruler? Or relax and feel pleasure in a country with obvious restrictions on the free dissemination of opinions and no tolerance for individual lifestyles? Here's a relevant comment in Wikipedia: "Internet content is regulated in Dubai. Etisalat uses a proxy server to filter internet content that is deemed to be inconsistent with the values of the country, that provides information on bypassing the proxy, dating, gay and lesbian networks, sites pertaining to the Baha'i faith, and sites originating from Israel."

DUBLIN

IT'S EASY TO ADD DUBLIN TO A LONDON TRIP

Though more and more travelers are simply flying to Dublin (from London) on the ultracheap airline known as Ryanair (you'll need to book your seat on the Internet, via www.ryanair.com), many more simply continue to take a ferry from Holyhead in Northwest Wales (which you reach by train from London) to an Irish port called Dun Laoghaire (pronounced "Dunn Leer-y"), a 15-minute commuter train ride from Dublin. The 4-hour crossing costs around £20 ($40). Traveling in the opposite direction I once boarded the ferry at Dun Laoghaire at breakfast time and made it to London for dinner.

EDINBURGH, SCOTLAND

TOO MANY AMERICAN TRAVELERS OVERLOOK EDINBURGH, UNAWARE THAT MOST OF ITS MAJOR MUSEUMS ARE TOTALLY FREE OF CHARGE

Just as in London, most of the major museums of Edinburgh charge no admission. You can create a fascinating Edinburgh stay around visits to these amazing attractions, and enjoy the entire experience for a moderate sum.

Free of charge, first, is the National Museum of Scotland, filled with the great achievements of great Scots (such as Alexander Graham Bell). You'll also find Dolly here, the world's first cloned sheep. Free of charge, too, is the Museum of Edinburgh, run by the city and located in a prime position on the famous Royal Mile. It tells the complicated tale of the city's history (most of which centers on the Scots' ongoing feud with the English). Free of charge, as well, are the Scottish National Portrait Gallery which displays the face of Sean Connery among its celebrity portraits; the Modern Art

Galleries with Warhols, Bacons, Hirsts, and lots of Dada and surrealism; and the National Gallery of Scotland on busy Princes Street, honoring European art with an emphasis on Scottish works. Expect high-quality paintings collected by some of Scotland's richest titans of industry, including Rembrandts, Botticellis, and Monets. The museum is conjoined with the Royal Scottish Academy Building (free of charge), which is stocked with much of the same.

And finally, there's the City Art Center in a towering building overlooking Waverley train station, displaying some 3,500 works of Scottish art. As the main center for Scotland's visual art treasures, it's always changing its exhibits, so you never know what you're going to find. It charges no admission.

There isn't a cheesy tourist trap in the bunch. Just from this list, it should be evident that in Edinburgh, as in London, you can craft a rich multiday vacation out of exclusively free things to see and do.

Then, when you've exhausted the list, you can (if you choose) move on to the city's collection of excellent paid historical attractions, such as the castle; the queen's official Scottish residence, Holyroodhouse; *Britannia,* the queen's famous royal yacht; and Rosslyn Chapel, the romantic and wildly carved sanctuary located in the countryside just south of town. Important sights all, but by no means required for a memorable Edinburgh experience.

FLORENCE

A SMALL CITY BUT A GIANT IN TOURISM, SO HEAVILY VISITED THAT YOU MUST EMPLOY SPECIAL TACTICS TO SEE ITS MAJOR ATTRACTIONS

A visit to Florence is a crash course in Renaissance art, thanks to such homegrown talents as Leonardo da Vinci, Michelangelo, Giotto, Botticelli, Brunelleschi, and Donatello. The city is crammed with more great works of painting, fresco, sculpture, and architecture per square foot than anywhere else in the world.

The one problem with this gaggle of world-class museums and frescoed churches is the amount of tourism that the city receives. Although a mere fraction of the size of Rome, Paris, or London, it sometimes seems crammed with just as many tour buses. In summer especially, admission lines can last hours, so it is vital to book in advance (☎ **39-055-294-883;** www.polo museale.firenze.it/english) for entry to the two most popular collections—the Uffizi Galleries (home to da Vinci's *Annunciation* and Botticelli's *Birth of Venus*) and the Accademia (housing Michelangelo's *David*).

Other collections not to miss include the sculptures in the Bargello, the Fra' Angelico frescoes in the monastery of San Marco, and the many small museums of the Pitti Palace in the Oltrarno, an artisans' quarter just across the Arno River via the Ponte Vecchio, a medieval bridge scenically lined by (overpriced) jewelers.

The churches of Santa Maria Novella and Santa Trìnita are slathered in courtly Renaissance frescoes, while the tombs in Santa Croce are a who's who of Tuscan luminaries (Michelangelo, Galileo, Rossini, Machiavelli; that of Dante is empty, as the great Florentine poet of the *Inferno* died in exile). Santa Croce also contains wonderful Giotto frescoes and a famous leather school—though prices are better (if quality spottier) at the outdoor market stalls around San Lorenzo.

Across from the baptistery, with its glided bronze *Gates of Paradise,* rises the mighty Duomo (cathedral). Leave enough time for a climb to the top, which takes you in between the layers of Brunelleschi's ingenious dome, affording a peek inside this greatest architectural achievement of the Renaissance—not to mention outstanding views from the top. Cap off your visit with a hearty dinner of Florentine steak and beefy Chianti wine.

Italy is a destination you can easily tour independently, especially since competition from the new carrier Eurofly (☎ 800/459-0581; www.eurofly usa.com) has begun to lower airfares. As in the rest of western Europe, hotels have gotten quite expensive (around $100–$150 for even lower-end tourist-class hotels), so the two wisest strategies are (1) to look beyond hotels to bed-and-breakfasts, apartments, and rental rooms (and, in the countryside, *agriturismo* farmstays); or (2) to purchase a vacation package from go-today.com (☎ 800/227-3235; www.go-today.com), Gate 1 Travel (☎ 800/682-3333; www.gate1travel.com), or such Italy specialists as Central Holidays (☎ 800/539-7098; www.centralholidays.com) and TourCrafters (☎ 800/621-2259; www.tourcrafters.com). For more on Florence, visit www.firenzeturismo.it.

TRAVELERS TO ITALY SHOULD BE AWARE OF THE FLORENCE INTERNATIONAL THEATRE COMPANY

Important historic cities aren't noted for their nightlife. And the multitudes of young travelers descending on such places as Florence, Italy, usually congregate in bars at night for want of anywhere else to go. The result is public drunkenness, litter, noise that keeps whole neighborhoods awake, and an increasing demand by residents of Florence, Rome, Prague, and the like to crack down on the boorish behavior of young tourists.

Which is why it's important to alert your Italy-bound friends or relatives to the Florence International Theatre Company that presents provocative new plays, in English, on most nights in high season. At www.florence theatre.com, you'll see a listing of productions planned for 2009 (previous years witnessed Harold Pinter's *Betrayal,* Sam Shepard's *True West,* Yasmina Reza's much-produced play *Art, Memories of the [Florence] Flood, Sewers of L/vov, Agnes of God*) and much other useful information for enjoying a rewarding and entertaining evening during a stay in Florence.

FLORIDA KEYS

THEY ARE AN EASY DRIVE FROM MIAMI, BUT ONCE THERE YOU'RE IN A DIFFERENT WORLD

A string of coral isles stretching from the bottommost tip of Florida 150 miles south and west to Key West, the Keys have been a marine wonderland for generations, their mangrove-lined shores usually more given to fishing, boating, and snorkeling than to beach lolling and swimming (that's not to say there are no decent beaches).

In spite of the commercial, strip-mallish feel along Overseas Hwy. 1 (U.S. 1), which runs for the entire north-to-south length, the Keys—once you get off the beaten path—are more like some laid-back Caribbean backwater. Resorts range from insanely pricey (Little Palm Island, reachable only by shuttle boat) to funky mom-and-pop motels around $100 a night. Attractions center on nature, from the SeaWorld-ish Theater of the Sea to John Pennekamp and Bahia Honda state parks—and you haven't lived till you've spotted itty-bitty Keys deer skittering along the side of the road.

Key Largo, Islamorada, Tavernier, Marathon—all have their charms, but the Big Kahuna hereabouts is of course Key West, the biggest and southernmost island. Stuffed with Victorian gingerbread cottages and mansions, the old town has interesting (if a tad touristy) attractions such as an aquarium and pirate museum, but you can also tour Ernest Hemingway's house and Harry Truman's quarters on the naval base; visit old forts (including one, on the Dry Tortugas, you have to sail to); and choose between sailing boats and catamarans offering offshore, snorkeling, and booze cruises. Dining is superlative, but the nightlife is kinda particular, tending toward noisy bars and gay hangouts, and if a cruise ship's in, it can get crowded on Duval Street. Guesthouses are the main type of lodging, but you'll also find big resorts and small motels—even a hostel. Scoring anything under $100 a night, though, is practically impossible.

Direct flights are available from Miami, Fort Lauderdale, Atlanta, Tampa, and Orlando; you'll also find bus service from Miami and ferries from Miami, Fort Myers, and Marco Island. Get info from Keys tourism at
☎ 800/352-5397 or www.fla-keys.com.

FRANCE

GUESS WHICH NATION IS THE WORLD'S MOST POPULAR TOURIST ATTRACTION?

According to the U.N.'s World Tourism Organization, la belle France was the world's most heavily visited tourist destination in 2008, receiving 78 million visitors from abroad (more than its own population). In second place was Spain and in third place was the United States.

But here's the unexpected news: Foreign tourism to China is increasing so rapidly that China in 2009 will pass up the United States for third position, and by 2010 will become the world's second-most-popular tourist destination. Ten or so later years from now, it will be number one, replacing France as the champion of all vacation countries.

THOUGH THEY'RE STARTING WITH THE LESSER MUSEUMS, THE FRENCH HAVE EMBARKED ON AN EXPERIMENT THAT EVENTUALLY MAY ELIMINATE CHARGES FOR ALL THEIR MUSEUMS

Ooh la la! It's one of the few occasions when the French have brazenly imitated the British. Starting in 2009, many French museums and monuments will test a new admission policy: They'll be free.

The courtyard of the Louvre, with I.M. Pei's iconic glass pyramid, fronts the world's most famous museum, a must-see attraction of Paris.

But don't expect to waltz up to the Louvre with an empty wallet—at least not initially; most of the eligible attractions are small (and yet it's a start). In Paris, the free museums include the Cluny (a rich mansion displaying medieval arts and crafts) and Guimet's Asian art, where admission is usually $10 a pop. Those aren't normally on the first-time visitor's wish list, but they will please true fans of antiquities. And in a lesser gesture to tourists and residents, the esteemed Musée d'Orsay, stuffed with Impressionist wonders, and the Centre Pompidou, famous for modern art, will now be open free of charge for one evening a week to visitors aged 18 to 25.

The ultimate goal, of course, is to spread culture to the general public. Eventually, the French government will decide whether to continue or expand the plan.

London long ago made free admission a priority, and the gift continues to reward the public. It's estimated that some 30 million additional visits were made after the government eliminated admission fees starting in 2001 at major attractions, such as the British Museum, National Gallery, Tate Modern, National Portrait Gallery, Victoria and Albert Museum, and a great many more.

CRAVE AN AFFORDABLE VILLA-RENTAL IN FRANCE'S PROVENCE? GO TO COLORADO!

For many years, one of the best sources of villa vacations in Provence was a company called Provence West, Ltd., located in the unlikely city of Evergreen, Colorado. It was run by Linda Posson, who made a point of actually seeing each of the 80-odd French villas that she rented for 2 to 4 weeks at a time to adventurous American vacationers. Posson has now transferred ownership of Provence West, to a Coloradan couple with equally impressive knowledge of the French rental market. Provided only that you request dates after the month of August, they can provide delightful villa rentals for under $2,000 a week for villas capable of housing from two to six (sometimes even eight) persons. You contact Provence West by phoning ☎ 303/674-3726 or by logging on to www.provencewest.com.

FRANCE'S PROGRAM OF MUNICIPAL BIKE RENTALS IS SPREADING THROUGH THE CONTINENT & DESERVES ATTENTION FROM YOUR OWN CITY OFFICIALS

Though no U.S. mayor has yet suggested the same for downtown areas in America (Washington, D.C., is possibly an exception), the system of short-term municipal bike rentals launched in Paris a few years ago has now spread to multiple cities in Europe. In Seville, Spain, I recently came upon a cluster of bike stations into which you inserted a credit card and thereupon obtained a bike to use for 1 or more hours. When you are finished with the bike, you take it to another cluster of bike stations, lock it to a modern-day hitching post, and your credit card is wiped clean of a $200 deposit needed to ensure return of the bike.

Several other cities in Europe have now followed Paris's lead.

Mayor Mike Bloomberg of New York City, inspecting one such cluster of bikes for hire in Paris, indicated that New York officials were looking into the possibility—still fairly remote—of emulating this program in Gotham. Much more is required than simply installing metal stands for each bike; clearly, a city needs traffic lanes reserved for bikers, of the sort that I saw in Seville.

If your city would benefit from a similar system, enabling people easily and conveniently to make their way about the central area, you really should suggest that municipal officials contact Paris's city hall for information about the outcome of this interesting experiment.

Incidentally, the Paris system is now available to tourists visiting the city, as a result of a recent agreement honoring standard American Express credit cards. Prior to that agreement, only a credit card containing a chip in widespread use in Europe would work. Today, tourists in Paris are making a good use of the bike-rental facility.

GERMANY

HERE'S A SITE DEVOTED TO GERMAN AMERICANS TO HELP THEM RESEARCH THEIR ROOTS & PLAN A HERITAGE-THEMED TRIP TO GERMANY

Just in time for Octoberfest (it's over now), the German National Tourism Office inaugurated a new website—www.germanoriginality.com—aimed at the largest (but rarely singled-out) ethnic group in America, the some 42.8 million Americans who are of German descent. The first German Americans were among the settlers of the Jamestown colony 400 years ago, and today some 15% of Americans have some German in them. As so-called "roots tourism" grows, sites such as this can prove invaluable to travelers wishing to discover "the Olde Country" whence their parents or grandparents came.

The site covers a variety of heritage sites in Germany (museums, moments, and memorials), tells the story of German emigration, contains briefs on more than 50 German destinations, most with a focus on emigration, lists famous German Americans from Dr. Seuss to Hugo Boss, provides links to genealogical research tools, and is interlinked with the general tourism site to help you plan a trip to Germany.

If nothing else, it is a fantastic cultural resource from which you can learn as much about America as you can about Germany. For example, did you know the Easter bunny is German? The story first showed up in German literature in the 16th century; edible Easter bunnies and baskets of colorful eggs followed in the 1800s.

The site also contains entertaining essays on many other aspects of German culture that have been incorporated into the American experience, from basic vocabulary (pretzel, kindergarten, poltergeist) to Christmas traditions (Christmas trees, of course, but also gingerbread houses, nutcrackers, Advent calendars, and most of the best carols: "Away in a Manger," "O Christmas Tree," "Silent Night," and others).

GREECE

HERE'S A DIFFERENT WAY TO ENJOY THE GREEK ISLANDS NEXT SUMMER & FALL

After several seasons of sailing the French and Italian rivieras, easyCruise.com is going to Greece. That's the unpretentious, budget-priced cruise ship for young people that mainly stays in ports at night, and sails in the morning, enabling its party-happy clientele to enjoy the disco life of the famous Mediterranean locales to which it goes. EasyCruise.com is sailing not only to the famous Greek islands—Mykonos, Paros, and Naxos—but to several virtually unknown ones (such as Spetses, Milos, Amorgos, Folegandros, Serifos, and Sifnos).

These islands are strung together in three different loops, each starting in the Athens port of Piraeus, on itineraries scheduled for 3, 4, or 7 nights.

Essentially, easyCruise.com offers the opportunity to go island hopping without the discomfort of milk-run ferries—but almost as inexpensively. Rates for a two-person interior cabin start around $160 per person for the 3-night or midweek cruise, or $460 for the 7-night itinerary.

You can get more information or make a booking at www.easycruise.com. Cruises run from early spring through mid-November.

GREETERS

ON YOUR NEXT VISIT TO NEW YORK CITY OR CHICAGO, DON'T FAIL TO SIGN UP FOR A FREE-OF-CHARGE "GREETERS PROGRAM"

On a visit to any big city, your most valuable asset is a resident cousin or friend who can show you around. If you don't have access to such a treasure, and you are visiting New York or Chicago, your next best asset is a city-run "greeter program."

New York's Big Apple Greeter program (www.bigapplegreeter.org) was started by New Yorker Lynn Brooks in 1992. It has since grown into an army of 300 volunteers who can serve as that "friend of a friend" in town and help orient new visitors to the city and their choice of neighborhood—and it doesn't cost a dime.

It's important to stress that this isn't a tour guide service, and these greeters aren't paid. They are simply New Yorkers willing to volunteer their time—typically 2 to 4 hours—to help newcomers settle in. Depending on your needs and interests, this may take the form of lessons in how to untangle the subway system maps and master the cross-town bus transfers, or a stroll together around the East Village or Upper West Side or any other neighborhood you've longed to explore, your greeter pointing out favorite shops, cafes, bars, and restaurants and sharing the kind of local history and knowledge that there's little room for in a guidebook.

You must submit a request for a greeter at least 3 to 4 weeks in advance of your visit, and you must be staying in New York for at least 2 nights. You only get one greeter per visit and, especially during the busiest times of year, you should be prepared for the program to run out of volunteers for your dates.

The program has been such a success it has spawned a sister program in the Windy City: Chicago Greeter (www.chicagogreeter.com), for which advance notice can be as little as 7 business days.

Shouldn't other U.S. cities create their own greeter programs?

FROM PARIS TO BUENOS AIRES TO TORONTO & ELSEWHERE, VOLUNTEER "GREETERS" ARE AVAILABLE TO SHOW TOURISTS THE ROPES

Happily enough, "greeters" networks are found around the world, from France to Australia. Each works a bit differently, but the basic premise is the same. The greeters act as unofficial ambassadors of their hometowns, and the network offers to link tourists up with these local residents who will show them the ropes, teach them about the city, and perhaps even take them on a neighborhood walking tour. Best of all, each and every program is completely free of charge.

Here's an initial list of "greeters" networks:

In Argentina: Buenos Aires (www.cicerones.org.ar)

In Australia: Melbourne (www.thatsmelbourne.com.au), Adelaide (www.adelaidegreeters.asn.au)

In Canada: Toronto (www.toronto.ca/tapto)

In France: Paris (www.parisgreeter.org) and Nantes (www.greeters-nantes.com)

In the U.K.: Thanet, Kent (www.thanet-greeters.org.uk)

In the U.S.: Fairbanks (www.explorefairbanks.com) and Houston (www.houstongreeters.org), in addition to New York City and Chicago, already discussed.

There are bound to be other programs out there. If you know of one, please drop me an e-mail (afrommer17@gmail.com) and I'll add it to the growing list.

HAWAII

THE POSSIBILITY THAT MAUI WILL OUTLAW B&Bs & VACATION-HOME RENTALS COULD TURN THAT BEAUTIFUL ISLAND INTO A PLACE FOR HIGH-PRICED HARRYS

There's trouble in paradise. Hard as it is to believe, the mayor of the popular Hawaiian island of Maui has launched a serious campaign to outlaw the operation of B&Bs and the short-term rental of vacation homes (although rental of condominium apartments to tourists will continue to be allowed).

And why? Several reasons (which may not be the real ones) are advanced. According to the mayor, residents are complaining about the infestation of their residential communities by tourists occupying low-cost rooms. A second reason: The growing market for the short-term rental of vacation homes has greatly increased the value of homes generally, making them unaffordable for residents, especially native Hawaiians.

(Condominiums, on the other hand, are already found mainly in areas inhabited by tourists, and thus life in these areas isn't affected by rental of apartments to short-stay tourists, according to the mayor.)

That's the news reported to me by my daughter, Pauline, upon her return from 3 weeks of researching and revising the Maui chapter of *Pauline Frommer's Hawaii*. She was unable to determine whether those alleged justifications are really a smokescreen for a campaign initiated by the hotel industry, which has an obvious self-interest in wiping out B&Bs and vacation-home rentals. Her gut reaction, however, is that the Maui mayor is sincere in claiming that B&Bs and vacation-home rentals are harmful to the quality of life on her island.

Regulations prohibiting such rentals are supposed to have taken effect on January 1, 2009. The island will then assess fines of $1,000-a-day on persons violating the ban. Lawsuits have already been commenced by B&B and vacation-home associations to block the new rules, and it's anyone's guess as to what will occur.

Meantime, an effort to adopt the same prohibition on the Island of Kauai was beaten back when opponents pointed out that thousands of jobs on that island are created by B&Bs and vacation-home rentals. The drive to ban the B&Bs was instantly dropped when its effect on island incomes was noted.

Because hotel rates on Maui are already so high (many modest properties charge $300 a night per room), the ban on B&Bs and vacation-home rentals will have a devastating impact on the middle-income and low-income tourist. Maui is likely to become an elite island, and ordinary Americans will be relegated to overcrowded Oahu.

A visitor to Maui writes me:

> I read with disappointment today the mayor of Maui's stance on rental homes. For several years my family and friends have come to Maui to vacation. We rent homes, bring our children and their friends, and enjoy the great Island. We spend tons of money on rental equipment, food, entertainment and local arts, etc. We would never stay in the hotels due to the price of a room and the price of food.
>
> This is a huge mistake and will drastically reduce the travel dollars spent on the Island. I will now take my money to Mexico and so will many of my friends. We will miss you, Maui.

I should add that the mayor of Maui also has jurisdiction over Molokai and Lanai, where the only hotels are expensive four-star and five-star properties. Eliminating B&Bs and vacation homes there will also restrict these islands to the rich.

IF YOU'RE FEARFUL OF CARIBBEAN STORMS THIS AUTUMN, FLY TO HAWAII INSTEAD

Still worried about autumn hurricanes in the Caribbean? Then fly to Hawaii. Though the weather there is perfectly fine in October and November, the

Hawaiian autumn season is nevertheless the slowest time of the year for tourist arrivals, and most of its hotels and airlines offer all sorts of sales.

For a different holiday (to put it mildly), consider a visit to the Kalani Oceanside Retreat Center on the Big Island of Hawaii

If you bring your own tent, you'll be given a campsite, three meals daily, two full-body massages, daily yoga classes, and the right to engage in all resort activities (hula, ecstatic dance, meditation, weaving, pool, hot tub, and sauna) for around $800 per person per week, single or double. If you're one of two persons traveling together, you'll pay under $1,000 each per week for a room with shared bath, slightly more for a private bath. I'm talking about a dreamy, laid-back, unpretentious Hawaiian resort named Kalani (☎ 800/800-6886; www.kalani.com), on the "Big Island" of Hawaii, that's designed for the same people who patronize yoga centers and meditation camps on the mainland.

It's been around for some 31 years, and is still following the gentle precepts of its founder: a mainly vegetarian cuisine (but lots of fresh fish); yoga and tai chi everywhere you look; supportive and nonaggressive fellow guests who follow their bliss; plain but adequate accommodations; and none of the conspicuous consumption or boisterous behavior that you might find at a standard resort. A typical dinner ("prepared with aloha") starts with coconut squash soup, goes on to seared ahi with pineapple salsa, baked tempeh, quinoa with sunflower seeds, broccoli stir-fry, and cucumber salad, and ends with lemon-ginger cake.

It's the kind of Hawaiian vacation where you'll never complain about the islands having changed their character or gotten overcrowded. It's like the Hawaii of a century ago. A final touch: Volunteers willing to work 30 hours a week for a month pay $1,000 for an all-inclusive 1-month stay at Kalani, attending all classes and activities, receiving accommodations and all meals.

Call up a small Los Angeles travel agent when you're in the market for round-trip airfare or air-&-land packages to Hawaii

Planning a trip to Hawaii? The tiny travel agencies of the Los Angeles area are in tight competition for Hawaii-bound clients. And because they are small and inconspicuous, airlines and hotels will occasionally funnel unbeatable discount rates to them.

I'm not saying that the smaller agencies will always have the best prices to Hawaii. But it pays to call them when you're planning a trip, to see whether they are able to undercut the larger Hawaiian operators. Examples:

World Class Vacations (☎ 800/755-2417) often has low-season round-trip fares of $499 between Los Angeles and Oahu. So do Travel Services (☎ 800/675-4050) and Hawaii Vacation Specialists (☎ 714/841-4540). Another firm to try is Paradise Unlimited (☎ 800/634-5568). All these companies will offer economical air-and-land packages to Oahu for rates under $700, and all should be consulted before you sign on for one of those nationally advertised packages to Hawaii from the big-name firms.

AIRFARES TO HAWAII HAVE TAKEN A BIG HIT FROM (A) THE BANKRUPTCY OF ATA & ALOHA AIRLINES & (B) THE INCREASED COST OF FUEL; HERE'S HOW TO COPE

The probability that the disappearance (through bankruptcy) of ATA and Aloha Airlines would cause airfares to Hawaii to rise sharply has been confirmed. Bookings on Los Angeles–to-Hawaii flights have jumped by $100 and more. To make things worse, such airlines as Delta have announced airfare surcharges of at least $110 round-trip.

It's important to experiment with different dates to find economical off-season fares to Hawaii, keeping in mind that September prices are usually far below those of July and August. Try to postpone your Hawaii vacation, if possible, until September, October, or November.

The other smart alternative is to buy an air-and-land package to Hawaii rather than airfare alone. Pleasant Holidays, the major tour operator to Hawaii from the West Coast, is still occasionally charging only $650 or thereabouts for round-trip airfare from Los Angeles and 5 nights of hotel accommodations in Oahu or Kauai (Maui costs $25 more). But here, too, you'll need to anticipate a $110 fuel surcharge.

The sharp rise in the cost of oil is having a heavily adverse impact on travel. You can minimize the effect of that hit by traveling off season (autumn to Hawaii), being flexible in your schedule (experimenting with different dates as you scan the airfares), or by purchasing package arrangements.

HONDURAS

HONDURAS IS HOT (BUT NOT YET INUNDATED WITH TOURISTS)

Honduras (Tourism Board, ☎ 800/410-9608; www.letsgohonduras.com) is a newcomer to mass tourism and thus lacks the megaresorts that are beginning to sprout elsewhere in the region. And yet an increasing number of culturally sensitive, scuba-loving Americans are flocking to its ancient ruins of Copán ("Athens of the Mayan World") and inexpensive diving facilities on the offshore island of Roatán and other nearby meccas (the Bay Islands) of the underwater world. Roatan is undergoing special development and expanding its appeal beyond divers to honeymooners and sun worshipers by throwing up midsize condos and small boutique properties, such as Turquoise Bay (☎ 786/623-6121; www.turquoisebayresort.com), where doubles rent from $100. Near Copan, a new airport will make the stunning ruins and lovely colonial town more accessible, and sustainable-development plans for eco-sensitive resorts are underway for the Caribbean coast, with its fascinating Garifuna (Afro-Caribbean) communities.

IF YOU'RE AN AVID SCUBA DIVER, THE PLACE IS ROATAN & THE TOUR PACKAGER IS CAPRICORN

Probably the world's cheapest top-quality scuba diving is off the English-speaking Bay Islands of Honduras in Central America, and especially at the island of Roatan, to which Delta Airlines flies nonstop from Atlanta in both directions on Saturday (go from any other city or on any other carrier or day of the week and you've got to fly from the United States to San Pedro Sula in Honduras, and then spend most of the day waiting for a connection to Roatan). And the top, moderately priced scuba diving "hotel" here is Anthony's Key Resort (☎ 800/227-3483; www.anthonyskey.com), whose 1-week package includes all the equipment (air tanks, belt weights) and scuba boat rides you'll need. Anthony's is not really a hotel but a collection of cottages with two grades of rooms: standard (without air-conditioning) and superior (with air-conditioning).

The foremost tour operator to Roatan is the 30-year-old Capricorn Leisure (☎ 800/426-6544; www.capricorn.net).

THE CHEAPEST LOCATION FOR SCUBA IN HONDURAS IS THE ISLAND OF UTILA

And then there's the Honduras location for scuba diving and snorkeling that's been overshadowed to date by the thriving Roatan, in the Bay Islands of that nation. The island of Utila is currently like Roatan used to be, and is frequently recommended by connoisseurs of scuba locations. Go to AboutUtila.com (www.aboututila.com), click on various houses and apartments for rent, and you'll be agreeably surprised by the bargains available to you in this smallest and least developed of the Bay Islands of Honduras.

ICELAND

ICELAND, ANYONE?

Can a trip to Iceland be enjoyed on a budget? It's difficult, unless you buy one of the promotional air-and-land packages offered by Icelandair and designed to put you aboard their planes to Europe. Many people, in fact, break up a trip to Europe by flying on Icelandair and enjoying a several-night stopover in Reykjavík en route to a European capital. You stay at the charming but rather worn old Loftleidir Hotel, the only hotel in Reykjavík with its own mineral water swimming pool. On your first day you tour Reykjavík. Your second day you journey to stunning waterfalls and lava fields. The third day, you stop en route to the airport at Iceland's famous Blue Lagoon for its geothermic hot springs. And to do all this, you access www.icelandairholidays.com.

IF YOU HAVE $650, YOU CAN DANCE THE NIGHT AWAY (FOR 2–3 NIGHTS) IN REYKJAVIK, ICELAND

Various partygoers I know will argue that the world's hottest nighttime dance scene is in Reykjavík, Iceland. From all over the world they come to witness and join in the frenzy; and the prospects of enticing more of them has led Icelandair to create a blockbuster winter air-and-land package for music-mad, dance-hungry travelers. For departures in November, Icelandair will fly you round-trip to Iceland from either New York, Baltimore, or Boston, with 2 to 3 nights in a double room at a hotel in Reykjavik including airport/hotel transfers, for about $650, including fuel surcharge.

Once in Reykjavik, the people I've described show up at the clubs after dinner and dance late into the night. Most of the clubs are at their peak of activity on the weekends, of course, when some stay active till 5am.

Go to www.icelandair.com, or phone ☎ 800/779-2899.

ITALY

A TRAVEL SECRET: IT'S UMBRIA (& ESPECIALLY THE TOWN OF GUBBIO), NOT TUSCANY, WHERE YOU'LL MORE EASILY CAPTURE THE CULTURE OF ITALY

The big and famous tourist towns of Italy's Tuscany have unbeatable attractions and undeniable allure. But their very popularity makes it often difficult to have a unique experience or truly sample the culture. It's in the

Just north of Rome, the graceful city of Perugia, capital of the province of Umbria, is a center of Italian art and ancient architecture.

smaller, less trafficked towns of nearby Umbria, where tourists are more of a welcome novelty, that the visitor can more easily find ways to engage the local culture.

Take the example of ancient Gubbio, set at the edge of the Abruzzi Mountains high in northern Umbria. Like other towns in central Italy, it offers a mix of fine wines, hearty Italian food, ancient Etruscan remains and Roman ruins, and a medieval atmosphere, yet it draws a mere fraction of the crowds that often plague its neighbors. The few intrepid travelers who make the trip here can not only enjoy an Italian hill town charm without the tour-bus crowds (and at the slightly reduced prices that come with staying off the tourist track), but also gain invaluable cultural insight via a whole host of activities.

While most tourists merely admire Italy's hand-painted ceramics and lush Renaissance frescoes, or enjoy pasta dishes decorated with precious shaved truffles, the city of Gubbio offers visitors the chance to sample these aspects of Italian life and culture via a series of inexpensive, single-day classes held in conjunction with the private agency known as In Umbria da Nord Est (☎ 39-075-922-0066; www.inumbria.net/eng_fr_servizi.htm).

Among the courses: the making of the ceramics for which Gubbio is famous (12€–25€), fresco painting (15€), mosaic crafting (20€), cooking (8€ for breads, 55€ for more complex courses), and even truffle hunting (10€). Gubbio's mountainous locale also makes it a minimecca for certain outdoor sports, and this initiative offers sampler days of mountain biking (13€), horseback riding (15€), canyoning (35€), and hang gliding (65€).

JAMAICA

FOR A REAL BARGAIN TO JAMAICA & A MEMORABLE STAY, USE A 21-YEAR-OLD TRAVEL FIRM MADE UP OF JAMAICAN EXPATS

I've been remiss in failing to make more mention of Atlas Vacations (☎ 800/634-1057; www.visitatlasvacations.com), a New York tour operator founded more than 20 years ago by Jamaican expats. They currently book you to places all over the world, but their arrangements in Jamaica are their special pride and best values. I've had numerous favorable comments from people who used them.

A current off-season example is their amazing rate of only $579 for round-trip airfare from New York, Philadelphia, or Baltimore to Jamaica and 6 nights of accommodations in the Fun Holiday Beach Resort in Negril, Jamaica. The same package sells for $476 from Orlando, $500 from Charlotte, $598 from Chicago, and $660 from Los Angeles. And those rates are available all throughout September, October, and November.

Jamaica is the classic Caribbean destination, with all the outstanding pleasures and attractions—beaches and waterfalls, inland waterways and lush mountains, reggae and steel drums, jerk pork and jerk chicken, phenomenal Red Stripe beer, an articulate and dynamic people—for which the Tropics are known. In considering a trip to Jamaica, you can't do better than to use this firm of Jamaicans who have scored such a success in America.

KENYA

IF CALM CONTINUES IN KENYA, A GREAT MANY ADVENTUROUS SORTS WILL BE FLYING TO NAIROBI & PICKING UP, ON THE SPOT, A LAST-MINUTE SAFARI BARGAIN

If there are empty seats on the imminent departure of a van traveling by land, or a DC3 going by air, from Nairobi to the famous games parks of

Kenya, those empty places are usually sold at sacrificial prices to adventurous tourists seeking a bargain; and the seats on the van or plane are always matched by rooms in the safari lodges.

Even during normal conditions in Nairobi, a great many safari-seeking tourists would fly into Nairobi with a hotel reservation for the first night, but with no continuing reservations beyond their arrival day. The moment they passed through airport Customs, they would find numerous representatives of safari operators thronging the airport and offering last-minute places on the next day's safari departures (of which several depart daily) at 50% to 75% discounts off the price normally charged. On a safari leaving the next morning, it behooves the safari operator to get any price it can for an empty seat.

Go to an aggregator, such as Momondo (www.momondo.com); buy a cheap flight to Nairobi; make a reservation for your first night; and then bargain for a last-minute seat on a safari leaving the next day. Do that bargaining either at the airport on arrival (you'll see many representatives of safari operators searching for customers) or simply go into Nairobi and visit any retail travel agency.

Such advice is based, of course, on the assumption that the political truce in Kenya is holding. So far, it seems successful, and calm has returned to Nairobi. It has nearly always been calm within the actual games parks, and most observers would say it is now safe to return to this remarkable African nation.

Keep watching four websites, in particular: those of Lion World Travel (www.lionworldtravel.com) and 2Afrika (www.2afrika.com) for standard low-cost safaris, and those of G.A.P Adventures (www.gapadventures.com) and Adventure Center (www.adventurecenter.com) for safaris conducted from overlanding trucks (camping at night, preparing meals over a campfire). Here's an opportunity to enjoy a travel adventure while helping a people in need.

KRAKÓW

IF YOU'RE LOOKING FOR A QUICK TRIP TO AN INEXPENSIVE BUT HISTORIC & IMPORTANT CITY OF EUROPE, CONSIDER GOING TO KRAKÓW

Eastern Europe hasn't yet adopted the euro as its currency, and still endows the U.S. dollar with considerable value. During this period of dollar weakness, a great many travelers are shifting their gaze to Eastern Europe, where Poland—and especially its touristic standout of Kraków—is attracting more and more Americans. In terms of art, architecture, and attractions, it compares favorably with many of the key cities of western Europe.

Founded in the 9th century, Kraków was the seat of the kingdom of Poland from 1038 to 1596, then capital of a grand duchy from 1846 up to 1918; in many ways it's still considered the country's cultural and religious capital. All that pomp and circumstance has left this city on the Vistula River, $2^1/_2$ hours by train or $4^1/_2$ by road from Warsaw, with some mighty fancy buildings, and its old town is one of the gems of Europe (and a UNESCO World Heritage Site).

The grandest edifices of all are the majestic Renaissance castle and cathedral on Wawel Hill, but you'll see equally impressive architecture by wandering the Old Town, bordered by an impressive fortification wall called the Barbican and with the Rynek Glówny (Main Market Square), the Gothic Cloth Hall, and St. Mary's Church, at its center. Meanwhile, the Kazimierz district with its synagogue, museum, and narrow streets is one of the best preserved Jewish quarters in Europe (*Schindler's List* scenes were shot here).

As for don't-miss day trips, a grim but extremely worthwhile bit of Jewish and European history lies an hour's drive south at the infamous preserved Nazi concentration camp near Oscwiecim (and better known as Auschwitz-Birkenau). A happier (and pretty amazing) attraction lies just 20 minutes away: the ancient Wieliczka salt mine with its underground lakes, statuary, and even an underground "cathedral" (actually a succession of chapels) carved out of salt (all local tour operators run excursions to both).

Kraków boasts a good number of fine hotels and restaurants these days, a decent percentage of them quite affordable (there's also a great clubbing/nightlife scene, fed by a vibrant Jagellonian University student population). Throughout your stay, you'll be pleasantly surprised by the reasonable level of prices not simply for rooms and meals, but for tours, transportation, and nightlife.

All flights from North America connect through Warsaw and other European cities, such as London and Frankfurt. North American specialists that offer escorted or unescorted land-air deals to Kraków include Orbis Tours (☎ 800/867-6526; www.orbistravel.com) and Sophisticated Traveler (www.affordablepoland.com). For more info, contact the Polish National Tourist Office at ☎ 201/420-9910 or www.polandtour.org, or the Kraków City Hall website, www.krakow.pl/en.

Ever heard of Wizz Air? It will fly you from London to Kraków, Poland, for as little as $88 to $140 round-trip!

Most U.S. tourists traveling to Europe make no use of the continent's cut-rate carriers, mainly because they service cities of primary interest to European vacationers (but also because they are often for short hops of the sort that are far more interesting to traverse by train). But the longer flights of the cut-raters bring you to such interesting destinations, and cost so little, that they have to be considered.

London to Kraków, Poland, on Wizz Air is one such route. Go to Cheapflights.co.uk, click on the Union Jack button for flights from London, and you'll quickly find the schedules and prices of Poland's cut-rate carrier, Wizz Air. Your luggage allowance may be as low as 40 pounds, but through much of the year, Wizz Air charges as little as $140 round-trip between London and Kraków, and occasionally has a "special" bringing the round-trip cost down to $88 (such a price stays up for a day or two but is quickly sold out). Another search engine you might try for Wizz Air prices is CheapOair (www.cheapoair.com).

A special tip: After you've scanned the results at Cheapflights, go directly to the website of Wizz Air (www.wizzair.com) itself, and click on its specials. There, identified as flights from London's Luton Airport to "Katowice/Kraków" (Katowice is a sister city of Kraków), you will occasionally find Wizz Air prices far below those of other websites.

KYOTO

At around $1,200 per person, including airfare from the West Coast, a winter trip to uncrowded Kyoto is a top opportunity

Kyoto of the 2,000 temples and shrines, quiet canals, and wooden houses is the most gorgeous of Japanese cities. It is also celebrating winter this year with some tantalizing incentives for visitors through March (see www.kyotowinterspecial.com).

Chief among these, from January 12 to March 18, the city will throw open the doors to 10 heritage site temples that are usually restricted to the monks, an unparalleled opportunity to see some of the gorgeous and glorious Buddhist sites normally not open to the public.

Wintertime visitors will be able to enjoy some of the special events that will take place around Kyoto, including festivals of lights and cherry blossoms, nighttime candle-lit tea ceremonies, and various Buddhist traditions from the New Year's Eve ringing of every temple bell 108 times to the February 2 to 4 Setsubun, acrobatic rites to exorcise demons from shrines and temples.

There are also special rates or room upgrade offers at about a dozen major hotels and traditional *ryokan* inns. However, you might want to consider the "Kyoto at its Best" package from go-today.com (www.go-today.com), which includes round-trip airfare and 5 nights' lodging.

Winter in Kyoto is cool (usual average of 41°F/5°C, and damp), but the chance to participate in wintertime rituals, see the city without hordes of summer tourists, and get into those normally closed sights make it more than worthwhile.

LAS VEGAS

AN INSIDE LOOK AT LIVING CHEAP IN LAS VEGAS, AVAILABLE FOR ONLY $5

I don't usually recommend other people's travel literature. But a newsletter called "Las Vegas Advisor," published by Anthony Curtis, is so very delightful and helpful, that you really ought to request a copy to learn whether you'd like, or benefit from, a subscription.

The "Las Vegas Advisor" is not for the casual visitor to Las Vegas, but for those hooked on that awful city, the gambling-oriented people who go there frequently each year and want to know where the odds are best in your favor, where to get the best coupon (discount) booklet for all your needs, how you can be comped for a free stay, where to get other discounts, where to attend a show for less, how you can occasionally beat the odds. Its text is racy and fun, its knowledge is based on many years as a resident, and it sometimes makes for good reading even if you haven't plans for an early trip there. A 1-year subscription is $50; but a better approach is first to request a sample issue for $5. You do this by going to www.lasvegasadvisor.com, or by contacting Las Vegas Advisor, c/o Huntington Press, 3665 Procyon St., Las Vegas, NV 89103.

And for a guidebook to the accommodations of Las Vegas, the most affordable full-scale meals, the top attractions, and the excursions outside the city, the definitive work is Pauline Frommer's Las Vegas, reflecting a several-month stay there in which she personally sampled (1 night at each) no fewer than 40 hotels.

Believe it or not, there's a decent Las Vegas hotel that still charges as little as $16 a night for rooms in its older wing

It's not in the best area of town and is as far east of the Fremont Street Experience (the giant electronic canopy over the main street of Downtown, north of the Strip), as you'd normally care to go. But 3 "slummy-looking blocks from Fremont," as my daughter, Pauline, writes in her guide to Las Vegas, the 300-room El Cortez hotel (www.elcortezhotelcasino.com) has unusually low prices for decent accommodations and therefore justifies the trek.

Stay in the recently renovated North Tower, and your $33-a-night price tag—a common rate here for much of the year—will buy you a slightly larger than normal room, with clean carpeting, fine beds, ultrasuede green armchairs, and a small but spotless bathroom. If you're willing to accept one of the tiny rooms in the oldest section of the hotel—built in 1941—you'll feel as if you're in an Old Western (the white-painted board walls, tiny loo, old-timey flowered curtains, and bedspreads seem to whisper "yee haw"), but you could pay as little as $16—the lowest rate I know of in Vegas for a private room with bathroom.

Pauline goes on to point out that these are all smoking rooms, with the smallest closets she's ever seen, and you'll have to climb a stairway to get to them. "You'll [also] have to ask specifically for these very old rooms, as they only go to those who request them."

Why do so many Americans opt for zany Las Vegas weddings?

Periodically, I've asked why it is that so many Americans fly to Las Vegas for the explicit purpose of getting married in a happy-go-lucky, comical ceremony conducted by a minister dressed to resemble Elvis Presley or Rodney Dangerfield. Hundreds of such weddings take place each month in Sin City, and I've wondered why anyone in their right minds would seek out such an experience.

While saving money is itself a reason for choosing to marry in Las Vegas (some chapels there charge as little as $75 for the license and ceremony), why the zany part? After receiving many unsatisfying explanations from readers, I received the following, which I print without change:

> My wife and I are in our mid-30s and were married at the Little White Wedding Chapel in the fall of 2003. As we waited in the lobby for the preacher, I noticed a picture of Lorenzo

Lamas on the wall, claiming he was married here, so I knew we were in the right place. We had paid an extra $150 for a tacky Elvis impersonator to host the ceremony.

He showed up in a yellow velour jacket and sang a bad version of "Viva Las Vegas" after the wedding. We then went outside and had our picture taken with the King and that wedding picture is now framed and hangs on our bedroom wall. After the wedding we treated ourselves to the $18 self-service buffet at the Bellagio for our "reception."

Getting married in Las Vegas was the perfect solution for us. My wife had been married and divorced before so she felt no need to go through the stress, hassle, and expense of another wedding. I, being a typical guy and nonreligious, had no need whatever to get married in a church or have an expensive reception. She was thrilled at the idea of a $200, completely stress-free wedding.

We probably saved over $20,000. We took the unspent cash and used it for a down payment on a house. We get much more use out of that house then we would have paying for our friends to get drunk at an open bar and gorging themselves.

My wife is my perfect soul mate and getting married at a tasteless chapel in Las Vegas in no way lessened or cheapened our love for each other. It was a fun-loving, upbeat, humorous experience that is what a wedding should be.

VEGAS WITH HIZZONER THE MAYOR

One of the unexpected dividends of a trip to Las Vegas is the chance to meet the city's mayor, a flamboyant individual named Oscar Goodman. At least once a month, His Honor holds a meet-and-greet at a local restaurant or diner to which there's no admission charge, at which he answers questions that are put to him by constituents or by tourists. He sips from a martini while he responds. He's everything you'd think a mayor of this over-the-top city would be: a brash, controversial, humorous character who makes a point of going to most public ceremonies flanked by a showgirl on one side and an Elvis impersonator on the other. If you'd like to meet the mayor, go to a website called www.lasvegasnevada.gov, which lists the dates and place of his next meet-and-greet.

IF YOU'RE AN INCURABLE FAN OF CASINO-RESORTS & LEISURE DESTINATIONS (SOB!)—THEN TRAVELWORM IS FOR YOU

TravelWorm has been around for more than 15 years, seeking out the most simple-minded of travel bargains: hotel discounts, in Sunbelt cities of the resort variety. Its recent offer of $34 a night per room at the Sahara Hotel in Vegas was a few dollars less than any other offer I had been able to find on the Internet. Its $37 per room offer at Vegas's Stratosphere Hotel was also a few dollars less. If you're planning a trip to a resort, you'd do well to go to www.travelworm.com, which also lists various meal discounts and other bonuses (free spa visits, for instance).

All in all, it's a pretty impressive website that has grown unusually popular and mighty, enabling its managers to pressure big reductions from the hotels they feature. I believe you can book directly on the Web, but you can also phone TravelWorm at ☎ 888/700-8342.

AMONG THE DIVIDENDS OF LASVEGASADVISOR ARE LISTINGS OF THE NONGAMBLING VALUES IN SIN CITY

Among TravelWorm's competitors is LasVegasAdvisor (www.lasvegas advisor.com), which also reveals hotel discounts but is just as well known for its up-to-date descriptions of the city's best nonhotel values. These are utterly factual but tremendously amusing, too, and trying them out is a practice far more entertaining, in my view, than spending time at the gaming tables. Here are 10 champions:

1. $1 for a shrimp cocktail at the Golden Gate casino.
2. $7 for a complete steak dinner at Ellis Island: a 10-oz. sirloin with salad, green beans, choice of potato, and fresh microbrewed beer.
3. A $1.50 breakfast special at the four "Wild" Station casinos (Wild Wild West, Wildfire, Gold Rush, and Magic Star): two eggs with sausages, hash browns, and toast.
4. $100 in "free play" for signing up at the Hoosiers Players Club, including free entrance to the raunchy Bobby Slayton comedy show.
5. $11 for a steak dinner at the Gold Coast casino: a 16-oz. T-bone with five sides and a glass of beer.
6. Reduced-price, $11 admission to the Magic Show at Greek Isles.
7. $14 to $25 for an all-you-can-eat buffet at the Mirage casino in center Strip: the best and highest quality buffet in all the city, says LasVegasAdvisor.

8. Reduced-price, $20 admission to the Comedy Stop at the Tropicana.

9. The entertainment viewable from the Fontana Bar of the Bellagio Hotel, where purchase of a $6 drink entitles you to a seat all evening.

10. $10 for the prime rib special at Mr. Lucky's Coffee Shop in the Hard Rock Hotel, where you can continue to order additional slices of beef as long as you can finish them.

Who said that Las Vegas was just about gambling?

THAT DECLINE IN TOURISM TO LAS VEGAS IS SURELY A POSITIVE DEVELOPMENT

It took them quite a while to say so. But they finally have the message. The mainstream media have at last confirmed that Americans have cut back heavily on their single most destructive habit, gambling at games of choice in the famous Sin City.

One enormous casino company—Tropicana Entertainment—has filed for bankruptcy. Everywhere, would-be casino-hotels are being halted in midconstruction. Other projects are being canceled for failure to obtain the necessary bank financing. Hotel occupancy is down by several percentage points, and hotels are furiously discounting, offering free coupons and vouchers to lure innocents to the tables.

One hopes the trend will continue. The billions spent developing Las Vegas and other casino centers are the most misspent outlays of our economy. Those monies are diverted from urgently needed investments in our infrastructure, in higher education, in health care and low-cost housing. Casino gambling teaches our children that something can be had for nothing, that by sitting mindlessly at a green felt table, you can become fabulously rich. And until now, those useless fantasy clubs have risen to breathtaking levels of prosperity because of the fear of our politicians that the casino moguls will crush them with their political contributions if fair taxes are assessed on casino income. One such right-wing magnate, Sheldon Adelson, is among the highest contributors to a political party in America today.

Other opinion molders in the media are also hopelessly obsessed with gambling and enamored of it. One such commentator, the oh-so-righteous William Bennett, was revealed to have lost hundreds of thousands of dollars at the Vegas gaming tables until forcefully kept from further visits there by his wife. He had earned his fortune, ironically enough, by writing bestsellers about the need to live an ethical life.

But most of the money hopelessly squandered in Vegas is from people who can't really afford the loss. This national sickness has impoverished multitudes of people.

What has this to do with travel? Well, many of our readers are enamored of the Strip and enjoy spending countless hours feeding coins into a slot machine. For their benefit, I need to point out that this is your chance for a great deal. In phoning the Vegas hotels for reservations, bargain. Threaten to hang up unless they cut the rate by 60%. Hang up if they don't. By making enough toll-free calls, you'll eventually snare a bargain, and you can then double your savings by resolving never to gamble once you get there.

LONDON

CUT-RATE MEANS FOR VISITING LONDON

If you're among the pressured types who make frequent trips to London, then you'll want to know about two British websites called www.laterooms.com and www.lastminute.com (the latter not to be confused with an American site called www.lastminutetravel.com). Both sites find hotels that have serious vacancies and are therefore willing to slash their prices for certain imminent dates. The straightforward nature of this service is shown by the fact that occasionally, the sites will report that there are no bargains to be had during busy times in the British capital. But just as frequently, when you insert the dates of your stay and the kind of hotel you're seeking, you'll find remarkable hotel savings.

TOUGH TRAVEL TIMES REQUIRE NEW TRAVEL TACTICS, SUCH AS STAYING IN UNIVERSITY DORMS AROUND EUROPE. HOW ABOUT THE LONDON SCHOOL OF ECONOMICS?

If you're to enjoy an affordable transatlantic trip this summer, you have got to start thinking about alternative accommodations costing far less than hotels or even guesthouses.

Start with the college accommodations. Nearly all the universities in Europe throw open their (temporarily unoccupied) student housing to the general public (of all ages) when school is out, which can vary from late May or early June through late August or early September.

Though you can sometimes get deals as good as $150 for a full week, usually a university room in a major city, such as London, costs between $30 and $60 a night. (The higher the price, the more likely the room will have a private bath rather than a shared one down the hall.) Your neighbors will likely be a mix of other savvy travelers, students sticking around for summer courses, and overseas visitors participating in summer study programs.

The best way to find campus housing open to tourists is to go directly to the tourist authority of a given country or city. For example, at the official tourism site Visit Britain (www.visitbritain.us) you can search the accommodations database under the category "budget and student" and find, alongside a dozen hostels, eight campus housing options in London alone. You can find links to official tourist office sites at www.worldtourismdirectory.com.

How suburban London guesthouses can save you big money

The savings generated by a decision to locate yourself a half-hour away from the center of London, can often save you as much as $900 in a single week. As proof of that, you might want to go to the website of the charming Avalon Cottage (www.avalon-cottage.com) in the Borough of Richmond-upon-Thames, literally 30 minutes by subway from central London.

For other low-cost digs in the very same charming area, consult www.visitrichmond.co.uk, and click on "stay." You'll find some 32 properties whose rates go down to as little as £25 ($36) per person, including breakfast—a price that can no longer be found in central London.

More tactics for overcoming the high prices of London

On the continent of Europe, prices are high but usually manageable. The American tourist will often discover that they are no worse than the rates of America's priciest cities: New York, San Francisco, Washington, D.C.

The tabs in England are a different matter altogether—they're positively depressing. A friend of mine, traveling with his partner and her parents, decided to rent an apartment in London after figuring out that a week in a flat for the four of them would cost about half of what two double rooms would have been at a Premier Inn (a reliably inexpensive, but bland, hotel chain).

He found a high-quality, extremely comfortable, and well-furnished flat (apartment) through VRBO.com (www.vrbo.com), though Rentalo.com (www.rentalo.com) and Coach House London (www.chslondon.com) also provided good leads. What's more, the apartment came with a free laundry room, one-and-a-half baths, a perfect location in the center of London half a block from a Tube station, and a full kitchen. This last feature, he found, was the key to avoiding pricey restaurant bills. They ate about half their dinners at home—either takeout or home-cooked after a relatively inexpensive trip to a nearby grocery store.

The B&Bs of London supply basic but comfortable lodgings to millions of cost-conscious visitors.

In all, the four of them paid a total of £1,276 ($1,850) for a 9-night rental, which worked out to £142 ($205) per night.

If you're a group of three or four traveling together, consider an apartment rental in London.

A READER'S STRATEGY FOR OVERCOMING THE HIGH COSTS OF LONDON

Responding to my comment that prices in the British Isles have become "offensive," a reader named Mary responded:

> This past spring I took a trip to England with two of my 20-something children. All the advice says that England, particularly London, is out of reach of the average traveler. But we did it the budget way and looked on it as an adventure and challenge to make it affordable.
>
> In London we stayed in LSE [London School of Economics] university housing that was available during the spring break. We paid about £34 per person per night, which included a full breakfast and access to laundry facilities. We were in Bloomsbury, close to three tube stops, and the bus stop was a block from the hotel. We ate semi-fast food for lunch, often

Pret a Manger or something from a Tesco [Supermarket]. Sometimes we had a picnic in the park.

We had lovely dinners at little Italian restaurants or pubs. Before the trip I had done lots of research and found discounts available to those who used the trains or had a tube pass. We had several two-for-one entrance coupons to major tourist destinations, such as the Churchill War Rooms and the Globe Theatre tour. We bought theatre tickets at the Half-Price booth. The exchange rate was not pretty, but we managed to buy souvenirs and a suitcase full of books.

I wouldn't trade this trip for anything in the world. I was able to share my love of England with my two kids and we had a terrific time.

ARE TV DINNERS FROM TESCO A WAY TO BEAT THE HIGH COST OF VISITING LONDON?

As you just read, American travelers are cutting their London meal costs by purchasing microwavable dinners at Tesco, and then borrowing a microwave from their guesthouse to heat them up. It's a sign of growing desperation as visitors rebel against the high cost of British suppers.

And what is Tesco? It's the largest supermarket chain in the U.K., always featuring a department with frozen dinners costing around $4 (a tenth of what you'd spend for a restaurant meal). Its various London branches are usually only a few minutes from your hotel, as are branches of its competitor, Sainsbury's. Even Marks & Spencer now operates London supermarkets, and all of them sell frozen dinners.

What else you need is a sympathetic guesthouse proprietor or hotel front desk clerk willing to find you a microwave. And incidentally, what works in London should also do the same in other European cities.

IF YOU CAN AVOID CHANGING PLANES AT LONDON'S HEATHROW AIRPORT, OR AVOID FLYING INTO THERE AT ALL, BY ALL MEANS DO SO

It's sad but necessary to sound an alarm about the virtual breakdown in luggage service at London's Heathrow Airport, largest of the four airfields—the others are Gatwick, Stansted, and Luton—serving the British capital. Baggage handling has so overwhelmed the staff assigned to it, that even a British publication, the *Economist,* candidly admits that "thousands of bags are lost each day." That report is confirmed by numerous persons sounding off in the U.S. press about the nightmares they've encountered at Heathrow.

The notion of scheduling a 1-hour connection to another flight at Heathrow has become ludicrous. The prospect that your luggage will be taken from one flight and placed on another within 1 hour is even less likely. A 2-hour connection is still dicey, and only a longer interval is reasonably safe.

It will come as a surprise to some that Heathrow is not owned by the city of London or the British nation, but by a private Spanish firm, which borrowed money to buy it. Since it is highly unlikely that these entrepreneurs have the funds or the will to make major improvements, the crowds, the lines, and the baggage mishandling are all bound to continue. An airport that was designed for 45 million passengers a year is now handling 67 million passengers a year, and things will undoubtedly get worse before they get better. Try to avoid it.

ON YOUR NEXT VISIT TO LONDON, DON'T MISS SHAKESPEARE AT THE RE-CREATED GLOBE THEATER

I am standing in the pit, my elbows and chin upon the stage. Behind me the other so-called groundlings are shouting lusty comments to the actor playing Lorenzo, who replies in kind. We are watching *Merchant of Venice* as Shakespeare meant it to be presented, in a duplicate of the very setting that he helped construct, and near the very same location; and it is a culmination, for me, of a lifetime of theatergoing, intensely moving, even awesome.

In one of the most compelling sightseeing attractions of London—a full-size, authentically built, wooden replica of the Globe Theatre on the banks of the Thames near the Southwark Bridge—a modern audience can now understand the stagecraft of Shakespeare as they could never know it before: as the intimate interaction between the Bard's characters and his audience, with entrances and exits through curtained doors, the comic relief, the loud asides directed to onlookers packed about a protruding stage, often only inches away from the actors on it.

You take the underground to the Mansion House station near the riverside docks; the Globe is a 10-minute stroll away. On my own last trip, it never occurred to me that on a Tuesday afternoon in late August (the Globe's performances are in daylight only at 2 and 7pm, from May through mid-Sept) I would need advance reservations. But when I showed visible dismay at the ticket seller's statement that the house was full, she quickly advised that I could go in as a groundling (she actually used that word) in the central open pit, for exactly £5 ($7.25). Groundlings are the low-income viewers standing jammed against the stage, who earlier paid only one penny (the cost at that time of a loaf of bread, or two pints of beer) in 1599, when the original Globe opened.

Your time as a groundling will undoubtedly be as enjoyable as mine was. And sunk in reveries, knowing that your consciousness of art and drama has been illuminated, you later ride back aboard the underground to Leicester Square and equip yourself with a £15 ($22) evening balcony seat for a modern nonmusical play of the London stage.

GOING TO LONDON? CONSIDER FLYING TO STANSTED—& SAVE!

London has four major airports (Heathrow, Gatwick, Luton, and Stansted), and all but Luton accept standard coach flights from the United States. Though Heathrow and Gatwick are well known, Heathrow has acquired a dismal reputation, with dreadful rates of luggage loss, and Gatwick is hardly state of the art. It's not surprising, therefore, that shiny new Stansted (www. stanstedairport.com), located in the green countryside north of the city, is gaining traction as a popular landing field. American Airlines (www. aa.com) now has daily flights there from New York–JFK.

The bright side of AA's Stansted flights is that they are often slightly cheaper than flights to Heathrow or Gatwick. But even with all things being equal, including base fares, the flight to Stansted currently comes with lower mandatory fees: £75 versus £81 at Heathrow.

Given that American Airlines will likely, over the coming months, periodically slash fares even further for its Stansted route in order to drum up business, you may be able to score a deal on flights to the United Kingdom.

Stansted is also a much easier airport to navigate than is Heathrow. Lacking the size and import of Heathrow, its security clearances are much quicker. It's not uncommon to go from airplane to front curb (or vice versa) within 30 minutes, whereas Heathrow is plagued with delays, long walks, and interminable lines. All of London's airports have rail links directly to the city, and Stansted's station goes from underneath the terminal to Liverpool Street station. The trip takes about 45 minutes on a commuter train (£15) or about 75 minutes using the discount easyBus (www.easybus. co.uk) service (as little as £2 with prebooking).

When pricing flights to London by Internet search engines, make sure you include Stansted (code: STN) in your searches, or else you may never be shown the prices to that less crowded and potentially less expensive airport.

TRAVEL'S BEST BUY IS LONDON FROM NOVEMBER TO MID-MARCH

I am often asked to name what I regard as the single best bargain in travel, and I answer right away: It's the $749 that go-today.com will probably be charging for a round-trip flight to London and 6 nights with breakfast daily at a modest London hotel, from November to mid-December, and again from early January to late February. That rate, surprisingly, is not simply from New York but from Boston, Baltimore, Washington, D.C., and Philadelphia, as well; and the add-on price is only an equally astonishing $70 from Los Angeles or Seattle. Though you add $175 in taxes, fees, and surcharges, the total for these basic elements of your 1-week trip comes to less than $1,000—and to today's Europe, that's a bargain.

Once you arrive in London, you'll also discover that an extraordinary number of sightseeing attractions are free of charge, even though they display major achievements in history, art, and culture. The British Library is free of charge and displays the actual Magna Carta and musical scores in Mozart's own hand. The National Maritime Museum, free of charge, has the blood-stained uniform in which Admiral Lord Nelson died. The Science Museum, free of charge, displays a computer designed in 1950 by Alan Turing. The Natural History Museum, free of charge, is probably the most beautiful museum facility in the world. The ability to sightsee for free in London, and yet to experience some of the world's outstanding sights, partially offsets the cost of London's meals.

Call me crazy, but I think all of us should try to get to London at least once a year—it does good things for our outlook on life.

THOMAS COOK SWEARS IT WILL FOREGO COMMISSIONS ON CHANGING YOUR DOLLARS INTO POUNDS IF YOU BRING A VOUCHER TO THEIR LONDON OFFICES

Here's an oddity that will save you at least 5% on your next visit to London (hey, every little bit helps!).

If you'll go to Visit London's special offers section (www.visitlondon.com/offers/currency), you'll see a deal from Thomas Cook. If you download the PDF file, print it, and take it with you when you exchange your currency at any Thomas Cook store, you'll receive your British pounds without paying a commission—and that's a saving of at least 5%.

There are 10 Thomas Cook offices in London: at Marble Arch, Great Russell Street, Hammersmith, Wembley, Old Brompton Road, St. James's, Victoria Place, London Wall, Wimbledon, and Islington.

Thomas Cook also claims that when you change your currency with them, you'll receive a special offers booklet offering such savings as two-for-one admission to the Tower of London, which would alone save you at least £15.

MACAO
THERE ISN'T A SINGLE REASON I CAN THINK OF FOR VISITING MACAO

The world's press has been full of wonder about the opening in Macao, the former Portuguese colony on the coast of China, of the largest casino in the world, the Venetian Macao. It has 3,500 slot machines, heaven knows how many roulette wheels, and 16,000 employees. Other new casinos and casino hotels are sprouting up nearby.

Any reason for you to go there, perhaps on your next trip to Hong Kong? I can't think of a single one. Though the Venetian and some of the newer casinos are belatedly scrambling to offer forms of entertainment other than gaming, nothing compelling has yet emerged. The casino industry, catering to a Chinese public in love with gambling, is obviously far

Macau, on the coast of China, is beginning to challenge Las Vegas in the size and number of its casinos; here's a typical street scene.

more intent on cramming more players onto the seats at its tables than into seats in its cultural auditoriums (which are few). And such entertainment as exists will be directed to a Chinese-speaking audience, who make up 99% of the visitors to Macao.

When you consider the pressing needs of people all over the world, spending billions of dollars to erect new casinos comes as close as I can imagine to an unethical crime. Unless you're an addict of this mindless activity, I'd stay away.

MADRID

IN SHARP CONTRAST TO ITS ECONOMIC & CULTURAL TORPOR THROUGHOUT THE FRANCO ERA, MADRID HAS BECOME ONE OF THE MOST PROGRESSIVE CITIES IN EUROPE

Madrid sits on the plains of Castile near the center of Spain, the capital of what was once an enormous empire. It may not be the country's oldest city, but centuries as the seat of the monarchy have left it with a bang-up collection of palaces, churches, museums, grand buildings, monuments, and plazas. And since the 1980s it has also become one of the world's hippest, most progressive cities, at the cutting edge of culture, cuisine, fashion, nightlife, and more. All this is in sharp contrast to the Madrid that reflected the baleful outlook of dictator Francisco Franco and his followers, and that persisted into the early 1980s.

Central Madrid is today one of the world's great downtowns for strolling and hanging out. Enjoy a sangria and a nosh at one of the tapas joints on the massive Plaza Mayor (central square); people watch and rent a rowboat at the lake in splendid Retiro Park; barhop in the Santa Ana and Huertas neighborhoods; feast on suckling pig in a tavern while being serenaded by *tunos* (costumed college students playing traditional songs); sample "molecular cuisine" in the chic, minimalist restaurant of the moment; catch one of the "nontouristy"

Defying all your expectations of how the capital of Spain should appear, Madrid is today modern to a fault.

flamenco shows; wander the enormous Rastro flea market; and rub shoulders with hot young Spaniards in one of Europe's trendiest discos or the outdoor cafes along Paseo de la Castellana.

Besides all that, you'll want to check out the sumptuous Oriente royal palace and museums, such as the famous Prado (Velasquez, Goya, El Greco) and nearby Thyssen Bornemisza (for other old masters), as well as the Reina Sofía (for contemporary art, especially Picasso's monumental *Guernica* mural).

Side-trip possibilities are seemingly unending, including the atmospheric hilltop city of Toledo, dating back 2,000 years; Cuenca, with its "hanging" houses; Segovia, crossed by a huge Roman aqueduct; the medieval walled city of Avila; and the severe and mammoth Escorial monastery.

Iberia (☎ 800/772-4642; www.iberia.com) and various U.S. and Canadian carriers fly direct from North America. For air-hotel packages (escorted or otherwise), check Abreu Tours (☎ 800/223-1580; www.abreutours.com), Petrabax (☎ 800/634-1188; http://petrabax.com), and Club ABC (☎ 888/TOURS-ABC; www.clubabc.com). For additional information, call ☎ 212/529-8484 or go to www.turismomadrid.es or www.spain.info.

A PERSONAL REACTION TO THE DYNAMIC DEVELOPMENT OF MADRID & WHAT IT SAYS ABOUT THE INCREASING PROSPERITY & MODERNITY OF SPAIN

In the museum of Madrid that displays Picasso's unforgettable Guernica, among other masterworks (the Museo Nacional Centro de Arte Reina Sofía; www.museoreinasofia.es), the admission charge is waived for persons under 18, over 65, disabled, or—can you believe it?—unemployed *(desempleado)*. And there, in a single gesture, you find a new Spain of social compassion and innovation. After decades as the pitiable "poor man of Europe," held back by dictator Francisco Franco (who remained in power and alive until 1975), backward in every aspect of its society and fundamentalist in its beliefs, Spain has suddenly emerged as a modern, progressive, and important nation—as I learned on a recent visit.

The streets of Spain's capital city (and everywhere else I went) are filled with well-dressed young people striding with confidence to discos and cultural and social gatherings that would have been unthinkable in the past. The facades of buildings are refurbished and colorful, the plazas marked by gigantic fountains surrounded by fresh flowers and spouting huge plumes of water high into the air, the shop windows filled with modern merchandise and fashions, the movies showing provocative films, the bookstores large and filled with browsers, the new architecture stunning and like none other on earth. Even the bullring, once hemmed in by shabby tenements reaching to its walls, has obtained a new lease on life with the clearing of those structures to create an immense surrounding open plaza. In terms of its modernity and optimism, Madrid is today in the same league as New York, London, or Paris.

On your own visit, as on mine, it's instructive to question the many English-speaking Spaniards you can easily meet. You'll learn that Spain currently enjoys the highest rate of economic growth of any major European nation; that its government has a budgetary surplus, low levels of public debt, and the lowest rate of mortgage delinquencies in the world. Its parliament has enacted a broad social program premised on full legal and social equality for women; and Spanish women—far from being sheltered by *dueñas* and tyrannical fathers—are today prominent in the ranks of doctors, dentists, and managers of every sort. Abortion is legal, the average age for marriage is now in the 30s, and the lesser emphasis on child rearing has resulted in zero degrees of population growth. Spain is also the only European nation to recognize same-sex marriages.

MAYAN RIVIERA

THOUGH EVERYONE GLIBLY REFERS TO THE "MAYAN RIVIERA," WHAT EXACTLY IS IT?

Strictly as a matter of geography, it's Mexico's stretch of Caribbean coastline starting just below Cancun and proceeding southward to Tulum. But in terms of substance, it is one of the world's fastest-growing resort hot spots, ranging from enormous all-inclusives (moderately and exorbitantly priced) to exclusive and secluded boutique properties.

Cheaper digs are found in the main town of this Riviera, which is bustling, nightlife-filled Playa del Carmen. There, options include funky, inexpensive little inns and pricier hipster hotels (there's also Puerto Morelos, a smaller, more laid-back town closer to Cancun).

The beaches along this coast aren't its main draw—if you want to get wet, it'll most likely be in a pool—but there's a full panoply of fun activities, including famous eco-parks such as Aktun Chen, Tres Ríos, and the glitzier Xel-Ha and Xcaret (where you can snorkel, among many other things).

The giant inland area—the Yucatán Peninsula—is culturally more important than that strip of beach. What makes it special are the many ancient, awesome ruins of the sophisticated Mayan civilization. The observatory, ball-playing court, and stepped pyramids of Chichén Itzá are the most famous, but there are numerous other ruins on the coast and inland (Uxmal, Palenque, Cobá, Ek Balam, and Tulum, with its spectacular

The Mayan civilization of Mexico is still present in the well-preserved structures of its ancient cities and religious sites.

seaside setting). You can overnight at lodgings near most of them, but they're also doable in day trips from the Mayan Riviera, Cancun, and the Spanish colonial–flavored capital of the Yucatan, Mérida.

Another very atmospheric lodging option is the network of inns occupying restored haciendas (colonial-era estates) in the interior, such as Xcanatún, Yaxcopoil, and Ketanchel.

Packagers servicing the Yucatan include Pleasant Holidays (☎ 800/742-9244; www.pleasantholidays.com) and TrekAmerica (☎ 800/873-5872; www.trekamerica.com), but you can also get there yourself via Cancún (with the most direct flights from the United States and Canada, on many carriers) or Mérida (via Mexico City); there's regular bus service throughout the peninsula and driving is fairly easy.

A VALUABLE INTRODUCTION TO NUMEROUS, WELL-PRICED, SMALL HOTELS OF THE MAYAN RIVIERA (SOMETIMES CALLED "COSTA MAYA")

Let's say you love Mexico but you hate the overdeveloped Mexican resorts. Let's assume you're yearning for a Mexican beach vacation but without the crowds. Let's suggest that Mexico's island of Cancún is fairly close to your own home city, enjoying a low airfare, but that you're dismayed by the thought of all that commercialism, of those endless ranks of motionless tourists sacked out on canvas chairs.

What do you do? You opt to vacation on the Mayan Riviera south of Cancún (but reached by flying to Cancún) in a charming, small Mexican hotel operated by a Mexican family. Or in an equally tiny Mexican villa perched on its own beach. And you find that low-cost lodging with your name on it by consulting a Mexican website called www.locogringo.com. It's a world's wonder.

LocoGringo offers an indispensable array of low-cost houses, bunga-lows, *casitas,* small hotels, and resorts—more than a hundred of them—located up and down the sugar-soft sands of Mexico's Caribbean coast (the Riviera Maya) just south of Cancún. Most are low cost and on a human scale, and so beautifully illustrated in color photos that you will have a good idea of what you're renting. Spend a few minutes at the site and you'll end up scheduling a trip to a beachside area of Mexico that hasn't yet been ruined by the excesses of tourism.

THE MEXICAN EQUIVALENT TO MAHO BAY IS A SOMEWHAT SIMILAR TENTED COMMUNITY ON THE MAYAN RIVIERA

I'm a sucker for a Caribbean tent. On my very first visit to those Tropics, emerging from the plane into 90-plus degrees, I asked myself: "Why am I staying at a hotel? Why doesn't some entrepreneur place tents, or simply scatter cots, along a beach (and maybe hang a canvas awning over the cots to protect guests from rain)? With heat like this, why do I have to spend big money for a hotel?"

The first person to take advantage of those natural conditions was Stanley Selengut, who proceeded to construct simple, cheap, canvas-sided "huts" alongside a hill overlooking the sea on St. John in the U.S. Virgin Islands. Maho Bay, as it's called, has been a stunning success ever since.

Another such canvas-sided colony is called Cesiak, for Centro Ecologica Sian Ka'an. This time, your lodgings are simple tents placed atop wooden platforms facing the sea, in the midst of a gigantic (1.3 million acres) "bio-sphere reserve" (protected area) of the Mexican Caribbean, alongside the so-called Mayan Riviera near Tulum. A tent accommodating two persons costs $90 a night ($45 a person) during high season (mid-Jan to the end of Apr)—and that's a good price for winter in the Caribbean. As Cesiak describes its tents, "They offer spectacular views from their private patios as well as plenty of shade and cooling breezes. Raised on platforms to allow ecological and hydrological processes to continue, the spacious tents come fully furnished. Shared bathrooms are always clean and also have stunning views over water."

I haven't been there myself (although I have vacationed at Maho Bay), but a look at the illustrations in the organization's website—www.cesiak. org—should give you the confidence to try what may be a promising new discovery off Mexico's Caribbean coast.

MEXICO

IF YOU'RE A "MEXICOPHILE," YOU'LL WANT TO CONSULT A BLOG MEANT JUST FOR YOU

There's a new name in the blogosphere for anyone who loves Mexico, Mexico Premiere (www.mexicopremiere.com). This is not your standard "I love [insert name of destination], don't you?" fan-boy blog. The posts on Mexico Premiere come from a group of professional, award-winning travel journalists who have long specialized in Mexico.

It's only 6 months old, but already packed with a little bit of everything: travel tips, tourism briefs on major cities and regions, articles on upcoming festivals and medical tourism, reports on low-cost airlines and new resort hotels, dissertations on Mexican cuisine, and the latest news on everything from hurricane damage to local politics that might affect your travels. There are also sections aimed at expats (and wannabes) on politics, arts and culture, and real estate.

DISCOURAGED ABOUT THE HIGH COST OF TRAVEL TO EUROPE? WHY NOT SUBSTITUTE MEXICO?

In sharp contrast to the rise of the euro and the British pound against our dollar, the currency of our southern neighbor has narrowly fluctuated between a rate of $10^1/_2$ and 11 pesos to the dollar for the past 2 years. That means our money hasn't sunk in value at all.

The culture of Mexico is remarkably rich and diverse, attracting tourists with powerful lures of art, music, dance, history, archaeology, and community activities. The south and east have secluded beaches, the center has countless colonial towns renowned for their cuisine, and both its coasts are dotted with high-rise resort getaways. It has always amazed me that people are willing to fly halfway around the world to some countries but completely ignore the wonders of tropical Mexico, whose people are friendly, sophisticated, and welcoming to tourism. If you haven't yet been there, you are missing a lot.

For a comfortable, safe & cheap vacation in Mexico, consider a condo in the heart of Puerto Vallarta or Playa del Carmen

If you're still reeling from news of the plummeting value of the U.S. dollar against the euro and the British pound, replenish your high spirits with thoughts of Mexico. The dollar still does quite well south of the border, and every week brings news of remarkable vacations there.

At a recent conference in Panama, I met Sarah Booth, a perky young American woman who regaled me with talk of condo vacations in the big Mexican resort cities. Condos? They rarely existed in Mexico in previous years, and developers seemingly knew nothing except hotels. But that's all changed, and futuristic, balcony-equipped, high-rise apartment houses are springing up immediately alongside the beach in the very center of key Mexican resort cities. And Sarah, an American, has built a thriving business by acting as a rental agent for Americans looking for a short-term (as little as a week, but more often 2–4 weeks) vacation rental.

Her websites are three: www.stayinmexicocondos.com, www.stayinpv. com, and www.stayinpdc.com. There you'll find enticing photos of the condos she represents, all in busy seaside areas dotted with restaurants, shops, and grocery stores (where you can pick up the ingredients for your own home-cooked meals). Her condos are either one or two bedrooms, with full kitchen and living room, plus other features depending on the property, and rates in high season (Jan–Apr) average $700 a week for a one-bedroom condo (that's per condo, not per person) and $1,100 a week for a two-bedroom condo (large enough to house four). You book by sending an e-mail to Sarah.

A condo in Mexico is a new kind of vacation, one that doesn't involve the relative solitude of a vacation home rental; you're in a large, modern apartment house with a lobby staff and numerous neighbors. And you can't beat the rates, which reflect the continued strength of the U.S. dollar against the Mexican peso.

Where can a group vacation cheaply? Try the Yucatan.

People write that they are a group of friends, let's say five couples, all wanting to vacation together for 5 to 7 days in some tropical location that will offer something for everyone—scuba diving, jungle treks, serious culture— and at a cost of no more than $900 per person, including air. Where to go?

Think: Mexico and the Yucatán Peninsula. You can find all sorts of inexpensive home rentals able to accommodate 10, and some of them come with a cook who can reduce the pressure of shopping and preparing meals. The Yucatán also offers a remarkably diverse number of attractions and activities. Remember also to rent a car.

MY OWN MINIGUIDE TO AN UNDERVISITED MEXICAN CITY

Perfectly preserved, its rooftops uniform in style and color, it has the visual impact of a Florence or a Siena, and is infinitely easier to reach. Yet Guanajuato—less than 3 hours by car from Mexico City—is rarely visited by the bulk of American tourists, who flock instead to its trendy neighbor and 18th-century counterpart, San Miguel de Allende. Is it because we have no taste for the truly authentic?

You'll find here a surprisingly large Mexican student population—50,000 of them—steeped in their own culture, and enrolled in a historic university that occupies the most dramatic of neo-Moorish buildings, in the very center of town. Though scattered entrepreneurs here have erected makeshift classrooms for the teaching of Spanish to American teenagers, their number is small and doesn't dominate the scene, as sometimes it does in Mexico's better-known colonial towns.

Here, too, are no clusters of tourist restaurants displaying multilingual menus. Though there are tourists, they are mainly Mexicans. The dining experience is thoroughly Latin, in quiet patio settings of silence and space, where patrons come to relax and unwind as much as to dine, lingering for at least 2 hours.

The city's cultural observances are also designed for the Spanish-speaking world. Each weekend through at least half of the year, it presents evenings of entremeses (fast-moving historical vignettes of 15th-c. life performed by students and faculty of the university) under the stars (they're enjoyable even to a non-Spanish-speaking visitor). And there are two resplendent opera houses of the 19th century, both active, and other well-maintained stages confirming the city's love of concerts, recitals, and musical drama.

The city itself is a daytime drama of Spanish colonial life, its residential streets so narrow that you can sometimes touch buildings on both sides with your outstretched arms. Scattered about the central area are seven tree-shaded and beflowered plazas where people read and converse.

Some isolated attractions of Guanajuato—apart from the city itself, its churches, theaters, and plazas—include its Museum of Diego Rivera, the artist's birthplace home containing, among other things, his initial sketches for a mural commissioned for Rockefeller Center and removed by the

Rockefellers the moment they saw its political content; an imposing central marketplace erected by the dictator Porfirio Diaz, and looking like a giant airplane hangar covering acres of colorful, fresh vegetables priced remarkably cheap; the ghoulish Museum of Mummies, displaying disinterred bodies of ancient people, at which Guanajuantans gaze with utter calm.

Shouldn't you visit Guanajuato? We travelers constantly tell ourselves to pick an "undiscovered destination" for our next vacation. Yet when the time comes, we "blank out" or lose our nerve or, under the pressure of decision, take the easiest route and book the next departure to Cancún. That is the only explanation to date for the relative lack of American tourists in Guanajuato. Get there fast.

IF YOU'RE THINKING OF A VACATION ON THE PACIFIC COAST OF MEXICO, THINK NAYARIT

We are all aware of the household words in travel—Acapulco, Monte Carlo, Taormina, Florence, Venice—and we automatically choose them for our vacations. When we arrive, we find them awash with crowds, inundated by commercial tourism, and thus ruined for the sensitive, intellectually curious traveler.

More and more, it's important to select the places of which no one else is aware. And the Mexican state of Nayarit, between Puerto Vallarta and Mazatlan, is just such a place. It has no airport, so you fly into Puerto Vallarta. But from there, you take a public bus (under $10 from the bus station), a self-drive car, or a taxi (be sure to negotiate a price with the driver) to the seaside town of Rincon de Guayabitos, about an hour north of Puerto Vallarta. And there you find the Mexico that once was.

Or you go even further north to Chacala, Platanitos, or San Blas.

Get there quick. The travel trade press reports that GOGO Worldwide Vacations has signed a contract with the tourist board of Nayarit to bring that long-neglected place into broad-scale commercial tourism. Ay-yay-yay!

LAS BRISAS IS THE PLUPERFECT MEXICAN SITE FOR ROMANCE

I am constantly asked to recommend a very special resort hotel in the Tropics for young couples on their honeymoon—and I immediately cite Las Brisas (☎ 800/228-3000), on a mountainside overlooking the Bay of Acapulco in Mexico. Las Brisas is mainly made up of individual, one-room, beautifully furnished villas, each with floor-to-ceiling windows that open onto a small patio in front of which is a small private swimming pool—kidney shaped with lotus blossoms floating atop the warm water. You awake in the morning and almost roll over into the pool. You also receive use of a pink jeep that can take you to a beach at the bottom of the mountain or to an exquisite restaurant on top that looks out onto the brilliant lights of Acapulco. The resort itself is only moderately expensive, and the best hotel I know for spectacular romance.

MEXICO CITY

TAKING REASONABLE PRECAUTIONS (ALL THAT'S NEEDED), YOU CAN HAVE A FINE TIME IN THE CAPITAL OF MEXICO

The conventional wisdom about Mexico City (also known as the current cliché) is that Mexico's capital is polluted and dangerous. Well, there's no question that one of the planet's biggest metropolises (a whopping 22-million-plus) has traffic, safety, and air-quality issues, but anyone with a reasonably healthy pair of lungs can visit for a few days without any problem.

And security? *No problema,* as long as you take the precautions you would in any big city and board taxis from established stands instead of on the street. And that you not walk around in quiet areas at night. Except for those two intelligent steps, advisable in dozens of other large cities (including those in the United States), you will enjoy Mexico City to the same extent that you would enjoy London or Paris.

For all its problems and poverty, Mexico City delivers a rewarding urban vacation; for starters, its offerings stretch back into the precolonial Aztec/Toltec past with the fascinating Templo Mayor ruins and museum off the Zócalo (the enormous main plaza of the UNESCO World Heritage Site downtown) and the National Anthropology Museum—one of the most fabulous repositories of ancient archaeology on earth.

Throughout the city, there's an abundance of Spanish colonial architecture, from the Zócalo's enormous cathedral to Chapultepec Castle to the cobblestone lanes and villas of the gemlike San Ángel neighborhood.

Modern history and art buffs can visit, among many other sites, a pair of Diego Rivera museums and the homes of Leon Trotsky and Frida Kahlo, and stroll her leafy, artsy old stomping grounds, Coyoacán. Afterward, take a tour through Mexican musical and dance history at the art nouveau Ballet Folklórico and dive into the world-class dining, shopping, performance, and clubbing scene in such neighborhoods as Polanco, the Zona Rosa, and especially hip Condesa.

Wonderful excursions include Xochimilco, another UNESCO spot that was once an Aztec water garden and is now a canal network plied by flower-adorned boats (sounds touristy, but locals like it, too); the breathtaking pyramids at Teotihuacán; and gorgeous colonial cities such as Guanajuato, Guadalajara, Cuernavaca, San Miguel de Allende, and Taxco.

Finally, in a country where the U.S. dollar has retained its strength, quality budget lodging and dining abound, as you'll immediately see by scanning the pages of any Frommer's guide to Mexico.

Aeroméxico (☎ 800/237-6639; www.aeromexico.com), Mexicana (☎ 800/531-7921 in the United States, 800/281-3049 in Canada; www.mexicana.com), and various U.S. and Canadian carriers fly into Mexico City, and for air-hotel packages that include Mexico City, check with Aeroméxico and Mexicana as well as Caravan Tours (☎ 800/CARAVAN [227-2826]; www.caravantours.com), Pleasant Holidays (☎ 800/742-9244; www.pleasantholidays.com), and SunTrips (☎ 800/514-5194; www.suntrips.com). For information, call ☎ 800/446-3942, or check online at www.mexicocity.gob.mx or www.visitmexico.com.

MIAMI

A STAY AT THE CLAY IS AN EXCITING (& CHEAP) WAY TO ENJOY MIAMI BEACH

If I were asked to name the single best hotel bargain in America, I'd probably refer to a charming, Roaring '20s pile once inhabited by the likes of Al Capone and Desi Arnaz in south Miami Beach, Florida. It's called the Clay Hotel; its nicely furnished private rooms have phones, TV, and air-conditioning, and yet they rent in summer for only $60 a night per double room with shared bath and $70 per double room with private bath (high-season rates in 2009 are $75–$90 per room). The hotel also has dormitory-like hostel facilities for young travelers that are among the best of their kind and cost only $20 off season, $27 to $29 per person high season, per night. And yet the Clay is within an easy walk of the beach, and a quick stroll from the Lincoln Road pedestrian mall/restaurant row and all the rest of the sizzling scene in South Beach. Call ☎ 800/379-2529 or log on to www.clayhotel.com.

MINNEAPOLIS/ST. PAUL

A RECENT TRIP TO MINNEAPOLIS/ST. PAUL SERVED TO REMIND ME OF THE TOURISTIC PLEASURES OF THIS UNDERAPPRECIATED U.S. CITY

Together with my guidebook-writing daughter, Pauline, I delivered a speech on travel at the biannual convention of the Public Libraries Association in Minneapolis/St. Paul, attended by some 10,000 well-read, intellectually curious, open-minded librarians. There is no better audience in all the world for preaching the delights of intelligent, sensibly priced travel.

The city added to the pleasures of the occasion. Unappreciated by most Americans, Minneapolis/St. Paul is one of the most culturally alive locations in America; it probably enjoys more theatrical performances each week than any U.S. city other than New York and Chicago—and some would argue that the intellectual content of those presentations is matched only by New York's off-Broadway scene. The city's Ordway Center is one of America's most vibrant opera houses (presenting experimental and avant-garde productions of the sort one rarely sees at New York's Met); its Guthrie Repertory Theater is the best in America; its children's theater is another standout; and its many smaller playhouses are always a delight to attend. Add a number of outstanding art museums, then throw in the Mall of America for shopping fun, and you have the ingredients for a different type of urban weekend that more of us should enjoy.

I'm not sure I would recommend Minneapolis/St. Paul for a winter stay; the weather then is appalling. But April and onward are excellent months, and if you'd like to explore a different kind of American city, you couldn't choose better.

MONTRÉAL

A CASINO VACATION IN A CULTURED CITY? TRY MONTRÉAL.

It's among the best-kept secrets in travel. Supported by only a small advertising budget, and little known to the vast majority of Americans, is the fact that casino gambling is legal in Canada's Québec. The five-story Casino de Montréal is one of the world's largest, and there are other casinos (such as at Charlevoix near Québec City) scattered elsewhere in the province of Québec. If you must indulge an urge to gamble, you might at least do it in a city of theaters, museums, and galleries, as far removed from the atmo-sphere of Las Vegas or Atlantic City as one can get, in a country where the dollars one loses in gambling are worth only 95 or so U.S. cents apiece. For further information, go to www.casino-de-montreal.com.

MUNICH

IN A CONTRAST TO THE MANY SERIOUS, STOLID GERMAN CITIES, MUNICH STRESSES THE PURSUIT OF PURE PLEASURE

And the life of the city is far more varied than is generally assumed. To many, Munich means just one thing: Oktoberfest, those boozy few weeks of late September/early October when 6.5 million party-heartys descend upon the capital of Bavaria to indulge in the kind of massive collective beer bash that even the most depraved college fraternity can barely imagine.

Munich certainly is the undisputed capital of Germany's sausages-and-beer heartland, and nearly every visitor makes a pilgrimage to the Hofbrauhaus, a rambling, neo-Gothic *bierhalle* (one of several around town) where the atmosphere is provided by a brass oompah band and the beer is served in liter-sized mugs accompanied by *brezeln* (soft pretzels) and platters of sausages (try the *Weisswurst* dipped in spicy mustard).

But Munich is also a city of market squares, soaring church spires, and great museums. The Alte Pinakothek contains a who's who of old masters (Giotto, Botticelli, da Vinci, Raphael, Titian, Tintoretto, Rubens, Rembrandt, Van Dyck, Holbein, and Dürer, to name but a few). The Neue Pinakothek is devoted to more modern masters such as Goya, Delacroix, Monet, Degas, Cézanne, van Gogh, and Klimt. Then there are the medieval and Renaissance woodcarvings in the Bayerisches Nationalmuseum, and the brilliant, kid-friendly, see-and-touch displays at the Deutsches Museum of science and technology.

Munich also sports two elaborate and history-steeped palace-cum-museums—the rambling downtown Residenz and the suburban baroque Schloss Nymphenburg—that once belonged to Bavaria's Wittelsbach fam-ily, the longest-ruling dynasty in Europe (in power from 1180–1918). The Neogothic Rathaus (Town Hall) on the main square has a beer hall in the basement and Europe's fourth-largest glockenspiel on its facade; the mechanical figures dance the hours at 11am, noon, and, in summer, 5pm.

Germany is easy to visit on your own—when researching airfares, don't forget to check out alternative German carrier LTU (☎ 866/266-5588;

www.ltu.com) with direct Munich flights from New York, Miami, Los Angeles, and Fort Myers—but it is sometimes hard to beat the savings you can enjoy by traveling on a packaged vacation from German flag-carrier airline Lufthansa (☎ 800/399-5838; www.lufthansa.com) or go-today.com (☎ 800/227-3235; www.go-today.com). For more on Munich, visit www.muenchen-tourist.de.

NAPLES

WHY TRAVELERS TO ITALY MIGHT WANT TO VISIT CHAOTIC BUT FASCINATING NAPLES

Naples is a distillation of Italy's glorious chaos, a city where the sun seems brighter, the food tastier, the traffic crazier, the baroque churches more elaborate, and the people more boisterously friendly. Naples is also a major port, which entails a certain degree of seediness (the central rail station and bus-clogged Piazza Garibaldi out front constitute Italy's epicenter of pick-pocketing) and some dicey neighborhoods (the dingy, narrow alleys of the Quartiere degli Spagnoli overflow with colorful street life by day, but are best to avoid after dark). However, this also means prices are generally lower than in other Italian cities, especially for the fantastic seafood. Spaghetti with clams is a local classic, but don't ignore Naples's single greatest contribution to world cuisine: pizza.

The intensity of Naples's noisy carnival of life means most visitors are happiest spending only a day or two here. That's time enough to hit the major sights—the stupendous Archaeology Museum with its riches from Pompeii, the dramatically moody canvases by Caravaggio and his followers in the Capodimonte Galleries, the cloisters of medieval Santa Chiara, and the fancifully baroque Sansevero chapel—and perhaps attend an opera at the renowned Teatro San Carlo before hurrying on to some of the outstanding (and notably calmer) destinations around Naples Bay.

Looming over Naples to the southeast, the still-active volcano of Vesuvius famously blew its top in A.D. 79, blanketing the cities of Pompeii and Herculaneum in ash and lava. Now excavated, these two ancient Roman ghost towns offer an amazing glimpse into daily life during the empire just 15 to 30 minutes from downtown Naples by commuter train. Just beyond Pompeii lies the resort of Sorrento, gateway to the amazing Amalfi Drive, a thrill ride of a road strung along sea cliffs between fishing towns. Ferries from Naples and Sorrento cross the bay to the famed jet-set holiday island of Capri.

Italy is a destination you can easily tour independently, especially since competition from the new carrier Eurofly (☎ **800/459-0581;** www.eurofly usa.com) has begun to lower airfares—and it flies direct to Naples. As in the rest of western Europe, hotels have gotten quite expensive (around $100–$150 for even lower-end tourist-class hotels), so the two wisest strategies are (1) to look beyond hotels to bed-and-breakfasts, apartments, and rental rooms (and, in the countryside, *agriturismo* farm stays); or (2) to purchase a vacation package from go-today.com (☎ **800/227-3235;** www. go-today.com) or Gate 1 Travel (☎ **800/682-3333;** www.gate1travel.com), or such Italy specialists as Central Holidays (☎ **800/539-7098;** www. centralholidays.com) and TourCrafters (☎ **800/621-2259;** www.tourcrafters. com). For more on Naples, visit www.inaples.it.

NEW ORLEANS

IT CAN NOW BE SAID WITH CERTAINTY & JOY THAT NEW ORLEANS HAS RETURNED TO LIFE: YOU REALLY SHOULD VISIT THIS UNIQUE NATIONAL TREASURE

The history of New Orleans is so very different from that of the rest of America, so exotic, and—to some people—so weird, that it provides a unique travel experience. Its culture is a crazy amalgam of the French, Spanish, Creole, Cajun, African, pagan, and gay; it was, prior to the Civil War, one of the richest cities in America; it developed a cuisine that's a pure joy, a form of music that excites the senses. And it now possesses several outstanding museums, including one—the Museum of World War II—that compares favorably with anything the Smithsonian offers.

And it's back. Nearly 4 years after Hurricane Katrina (late Aug 2005), New Orleans's tourism industry has finally recovered to such an extent that the visitor scarcely notices any decline in the city's ability to entertain. My daughter Pauline was there for several days, and responded as follows to questions I put to her:

Q: What was your overall impression?
Pauline: The recovery of the touristic districts is all but complete. What's notable is how much has finally been restored. Everywhere I went, I heard about businesses finally reopening and people returning in large numbers. Convention business is back. The St. Charles streetcar, a major tourist attraction, is also back.

Because most media coverage of New Orleans continues to focus on its problems, I heard over and over from locals that visitors are often surprised that the floodwaters have receded. In fact, in the main areas where tourists go, the French Quarter and the Garden District, streets are cleaner than they were before the floods, thanks to a new system of garbage collection. And Bourbon Street is just as rowdy as ever. I walked through on a Monday night, typically the slowest time of the week, and it was jumping with live music and people toting drinks.

Q: So what has changed in the tourist's experience of New Orleans?

Pauline: Visiting the outlying, residential areas of the city affected by Hurricane Katrina has become a must-do activity. I took one such tour, and it didn't feel like a voyeuristic experience. The guides were locals who were personally affected by Katrina, who saw this as a way for outsiders to learn what's still going on in the city and help lobby Congress to fund the still-needed restoration. You get the feeling that these people all share the same goals. They wave at the vans, and even come over and talk. It's important to pick the right tour. Some tours visit all the levee break areas, which for many visitors may just be overkill (I took one that lasted over 4 interminable hr.).

The most moving sight is the Ninth Ward, because it's at one and the same time the one with the most promising projects (Habitat for Humanity's Musician's Village, Brad Pitt's project) and the most totally unreconstructed areas, with huge plants growing up the side of battered, half-demolished houses, or simply a set of stairs standing on a lot, the rest of the building swept away by the tidal surge. Probably the best general tours are being run by Gray Line, or, if you want a more intimate experience, Cajun Country.

Q: Beyond the Katrina tour and the French Quarter, what are New Orleans's other lures?

Pauline: Well, New Orleans isn't usually thought of as a top museum city, but it has become just that. Its National World War II Museum has been designated by Congress as the official WW2 museum for the nation, and it's truly one of the most remarkable museums anywhere. I've now spent 7 hours there and I feel like I've just scratched the surface. Through a mix of newsreels, interactive exhibitions, oral histories, and more, you learn about the war from a very personal standpoint and from a strategic perspective. Most moving: Many of the volunteer docents are sprightly but elderly World War II veterans, and they enthusiastically lead you through the exhibits.

Along with this is a terrific art museum and a Cocktail Museum, appropriate for the city that invented the Sazerac and the Hurricane.

Q: Is it an appropriate place for children?

Pauline: Absolutely. Believe it or not, the school-age kids I saw were absolutely entranced by the WWII museum, and by the French Quarter, the zoo, and aquarium. The city also has a wonderful new museum called the Audubon Insectarium. I was dragged to it, and ended up loving it (I stroked a remarkably soft silkworm, learned all about the mosquitoes that spread yellow fever in NOLA in the 19th c., and could have tasted fried grasshoppers if I had the nerve).

Q: And I have to ask, since it is New Orleans: How did you eat?
Pauline: Spectacularly! New Orleans remains one of the top three restaurant cities in the nation (along with NYC and San Francisco) and I think I've probably gained 5 pounds since I last saw you. The nice thing about NOLA is that, for all its fine dining, the tabs aren't as high as they are in the other foodie cities. I went to a restaurant called Couchon, which Frank Bruni, the restaurant critic of the *New York Times,* named one of the top 10 restaurants in the nation, and the top entree was $22, with many in the teens. In New York and San Francisco, that's often where the entree prices start, peaking at $36. But you don't just eat well in the high-end places; I gorged on pralines, and gumbo, and oysters, and fried alligator at little no-name hole in the walls and never had a bad meal. Rumors were swirling when I was there that the next season of *Top Chef* was going to be filmed in NOLA.

The prices plummet & yet the partying picks up during the month of December in New Orleans

---

For reasons hard to explain, travel slumps to New Orleans in December, just as it does in Las Vegas. But the Big Easy fights back by offering a program of hotel discounts known as "Papa Noel Rates" (Papa Noel being the Cajun equivalent of Santa Claus). These deals should be back this winter with rates well under $100 per night at fine hotels in the city's most exciting neighborhoods. Rates must be booked directly with hotels.

New Orleans in December has a much less crowded French Quarter, uncrowded restaurants, uncrowded jazz clubs, and a busy schedule of events. Famous Jackson Square hosts free shows leading up to Christmas, with local choirs performing jazz and gospel.

For more on New Orleans during the winter holidays, contact French Quarter Festivals, Inc., at ☎ 800/673-5725 or www.fqfi.org. The organization lists all sorts of happenings, including free cooking demonstrations by renowned area chefs, assorted concerts, tours, book signings, steamboat rides, and even a day for decorating gingerbread houses. For New Orleans, December is a top month.

Take a day out of your vacation to help rebuild New Orleans

It has been nearly 4 years since hurricanes Katrina and Wilma devastated the Crescent City, and while the tourist areas are mostly up and running again—historic districts such as the French Quarter were built on the highest ground and therefore suffered the least damage—New Orleans is still struggling to rebuild its less visited residential areas and its infrastructure. So many visitors have expressed a desire to lend a hand that the Convention and Visitors Bureau now helps connect them with the organizations that so desperately need the manpower.

Go to www.neworleanscvb.com and click on "Voluntourism" on the left-hand menu bar. You'll get links to Volunteer Louisiana (www.volunteer louisiana.gov), a site created by the governor's office to help affected communities along the Gulf Coast, and to a downloadable PDF listing more than a half-dozen charities that welcome volunteers to help various rebuilding projects in New Orleans, even if it's just for a day.

So long as you don't mind rolling up your sleeves and getting a little sweaty, you can pick up a hammer to help Habitat for Humanity construct the Musician's Village in the upper Ninth Ward, pitch in to restore city parks and playgrounds, or gut ruined houses so the owners can begin to rebuild their homes and their lives. If hard labor isn't your thing, donations are just as much appreciated.

New York

The difficulty of finding affordable accommodations in New York has reached crisis proportions & calls for innovative planning

New York's advertised rack rates can average $300. Innocent visitors on a tight budget are in for the shock of their lives.

To avoid those outlandish charges, you need to use alternative lodgings, such as apartments.

To find one, go online and survey such national apartment-rental organizations as VRBO.com (www.vrbo.com), Rentalo.com (www.rentalo. com), HomeAway (www.homeaway.com), Zonder (www.zonder.com), or Endless Vacation Rentals (www.evrentals.com). Only recently, I went to www.zonder.com and found a two-bedroom apartment in midtown Manhattan renting for under $150 a night.

AN ODE TO THE TOURISTIC PLEASURES OF THE UPPER WEST SIDE OF MANHATTAN

In writing the script for a forthcoming video travel guide to New York City, I suggested the inclusion of a section on the Upper West Side. My proposal was promptly overruled on the grounds that there were far more important attractions to cover, such as the U.N., Statue of Liberty, and Radio City Music Hall. Yet stubbornly, defiantly, I contend that a 1-hour walk along Broadway between 62nd and 95th streets (the heart of the Upper West Side) will expose the visitor to New York at its most unique and dynamic. So what won't appear in my video guide will at least enjoy a fleeting moment here.

I live in the residential west side of New York and periodically take that 1-hour walk, starting at the marquee of the Lincoln Plaza Cinema at Broadway and 63rd Street. Listed here, every week of the year, are six superb foreign movies for viewing that day, and three new ones scheduled for the coming week. North of the celebrated theaters and concert halls of the Lincoln Center for the Performing Arts (across the street) is such an unheralded festival of local life and culture that I feel like shouting out my appreciation of it.

I walk by sidewalk vendors selling hardcover books from folding tables, and more tables stacked with petitions and leaflets for various political causes. I pass other live theaters patronized almost wholly by residents (the Beacon, the Promenade) and additional cinemas (the Walter Reade, the Thalia, still others) showing festivals of international films and revivals of classics. I pause not just at one but two megabookstores and several smaller book specialists (Murder Ink, Westsider Rare Books, others) and wander through markets (Zabar's, Fairway, Citarella) famous for exotic foods and other gourmet delights. Zabar's alone is an immense thrill. I step aside for a parade of young people defending animal rights, and stop at Symphony Space, known for its readings of classic short stories and performances of ethnic music.

It's an eruption of ideas, artistry, and food for the mind as would be found in few other cities. As a tourist to New York, you couldn't do better than to take this untouristed walk up Broadway.

FROM JANUARY 2 & THROUGHOUT THE MONTH, HOTELS IN NEW YORK CITY GO ON SALE

In early December, Gotham is chock-a-bloc with shoppers, and hotels record some of their highest occupancies. Things slump starting around December 20 (people want to stay home for the holidays), and except for

New Year's Eve, they remain slow throughout January. If you'll go to www. quikbook.com, you'll discover that well-known New York hotels offer greatly reduced rates for January stays: $144 per room per night is the lowest I've found for a 3-night stay at the Paramount Hotel, but prices also go down to $170 per room per night for a 3-night stay at the Time Hotel, $127 at the Milford Plaza, $102 at the Hotel Thirty Thirty (on W. 30th St. in Manhattan), $136 at the Eastgate Tower Suite Hotel. If you've been thinking about a bout of theatergoing in New York City, January is the month to do it.

THERE'S AN INEXPENSIVE HOSTEL IN MANHATTAN WITH BEDS AVAILABLE IN DORMS & PRIVATE ROOMS

Because it's not nearly as well known as it eventually will be, and doesn't enjoy the marketing advantages of hostels belonging to the worldwide Hostelling International (to which it doesn't belong), the Central Park Hostel (19 W. 103rd St.; ☎ 212/678-0491; www.centralparkhostel.com) is a top bet for your next New York stay. The location is just alongside Central Park, on a fine residential street near Columbia University, and thus near to all sorts of inexpensive eateries, bookstores, and other interesting shops. There's a subway stop less than a block away.

It calls itself a "luxury hostel," which simply means its rates are higher than those of the nearby and much larger (and, according to some, better) New York International Hostel. But by the sky-high standards of today's Manhattan, it's still quite a deal to obtain dorm beds here for $28 to $45 depending on season, or private rooms with shared bathrooms for under $135. *Note:* Credit cards aren't accepted.

An alternative to the Central Park Hostel, much preferred by my daughter Pauline, is Jazz on the Park. Here's what she says:

> Jazz on the Park (W. 106th St., btw. Manhattan Ave. and Central Park West; ☎ 212/932-1600; www.jazzonthepark. com) is the hipster's hostel, with house music blaring in the art-filled lobby, weekly barbecues in summer ($5), movie and poker nights when the weather's colder, photos of great jazz musicians in the hallways, and a color scheme in the rooms that is taken straight out of the *Wizard of Oz.* Dorm rooms come with two, three, four, five, or six bunk beds, and the numbers on the beds aren't as prominent as they should be (which can lead to some awkward situations come bedtime). Another problem here are the mattresses, which are so thin in many cases that you can feel every ridge and spring; they do vary by bed, so test-drive a couple when you check in. Those reserving private rooms (with shared bathroom only) may go 1 block

uptown to the hostel's second building, again a mural-laden, vibrantly colorful place that is generally clean. The cheapest dorm beds are the 10- or 12-bedders for $30 a night. If you're traveling with a friend, it might make the most sense to share a private room at under $100, with two twin beds (without bath).

NEW ZEALAND

SPECIALLY DESIGNED SMALL RVS IN NEW ZEALAND ENABLE CAMPING ON A BUDGET IN THAT AWESOME, CAMP-FRIENDLY COUNTRY

Traveling in New Zealand via RV—or "campervan," as the Kiwis say—is enormously popular, and thanks to the recent introduction of special minivan campers called Spaceships, the activity is cost effective and easy even for couples.

The first Spaceship began zooming around New Zealand in the fall of 2004, and now there are approximately 200 of them available for rent. The vehicles are Toyota minivans that have been custom fitted with a comfortable bed that folds out. With the rear hatch open, a special tentlike attachment can be set up for extra space and fresh air on warm nights. Sheets, duvet, and pillows are included, along with a small refrigerator, a tiny gas barbecue grill, pots, pans, cutlery, plates, cups, and a built-in DVD player that you can watch in bed.

While traveling by RV has been popular in New Zealand for decades, it has traditionally made the most sense for families or groups of friends. Spaceships are instead perfect for couples. They're priced just a bit higher than a standard car rental, they get much better gas mileage than a standard RV, and because of their smaller size, there are no worries about maneuvering a bulky vehicle through small towns or on windy mountain roads. They're a great mode of transportation for exploring New Zealand's amazing landscapes, featured so prominently in *The Lord of the Rings* film trilogy.

Rental rates, which include all taxes and standard insurance, start at $68 per day in peak summer season (when it's winter in North America). A quote for October (springtime in New Zealand) revealed that rates for Spaceships in the South Island city of Christchurch—within easy striking distance of the country's most beautiful mountains—cost only about $45 per day, and by booking a few weeks early you can save an additional 10%. Considering that during this same time period a tiny compact rental car will cost at least $35 per day, and larger traditional RVs rent for upwards of $95 daily, Spaceships are an excellent value. Call ☎ 649/309-8777, or visit www.spaceships.tv for more information.

How generally do you pull off an RV-based air-&-camping trip to New Zealand?

While the Spaceship is great for couples, the best value for families and larger groups remains a package that comes with airfare and a much larger, multiperson RV. Companies such as Sunspots International (☎ 800/266-6115; www.sunspotsintl.com) sell packages for New Zealand's springtime starting at around $1,400 per person that include flights from Los Angeles and an RV for 7 nights, though taxes are extra.

Camping in New Zealand is remarkably easy—and rewarding. Campgrounds are strewn about the country, though they're generally not called campgrounds. They're instead known as "holiday parks" because they offer much more than a simple place to sleep, and guests often enjoy pools, hot tubs, private cabins, restaurants, and shops. A night's stay at a holiday park costs around $30, about one-third the price of a basic motel. You can scout out holiday parks and plan an itinerary through sources such as Holiday Accommodation Parks of New Zealand (www.holidayparks.co.nz), which has nearly 300 members.

You may want to file away the name of another outstanding low-cost hotel for your next trip to New Zealand

Yet another promising style-minded budget hotel has made its appearance. This one, being based in New Zealand, is also deeply mindful of sustainable environmental practices. It's called Hotel SO (www.hotelso.co.nz), and it's based in Christchurch, on the South Island.

So many so-called stylish hotels use the high-design card to guarantee themselves plenty of media play in their first months of operation. Too many, such as the Hotel QT and the Dream in Manhattan, then hoist their room rates higher later on. So far, though, Hotel SO is truly affordable: NZ$69 ($53) for a single and NZ$89 ($68) for a double.

The hotel's creators, who wouldn't mind exporting their idea far and wide, have managed to come up with these low prices, in part, by cutting down on the waste that other hotels consider part of their luxury standards. A small pod-style bathroom, wireless Internet, and the by-now-ubiquitous flat-screen TV, plus plenty of biodegradable shampoos, recycled paper products, and a well-insulated room that keeps the heat in, are all part of their formula. The hotel's designers have more than given lip service to green values; each room's electric system shuts down when guests are absent, and fixtures have been selected to draw minimal energy. Rooms also come with mood lighting which guests can adjust to alter the color according to their outlook—not much of a calling card, really, but certainly a nice trend.

It makes me wonder: If the big corporate hotel brands also adopted green policies and cut down on electric and water usage, would that also mean we could pay less for hotel rooms in the future?

NICARAGUA

NICARAGUA "IN A NUTSHELL"—A THUMBNAIL SKETCH

Nicaragua (☎ 888/733-6422; www.visit-nicaragua.com and www.tours nicaragua.com) is Central America's largest nation and birthplace of its greatest literary figure, Ruben Dario. Its president, the former Sandinista leader Daniel Ortega, has been more conciliatory about tourism and foreign investment in recent years, and the country's growth seems unlikely to slacken. Many thousands of Americans are currently moving here to retire or simply get another start, amid beautiful and less expensive surroundings. Cities such as Granada (on Lake Nicaragua) and Leon (a dozen miles from the Pacific coast) are among Central America's loveliest Spanish colonial towns; San Juan del Sur on the Pacific has quite the surfing scene; and Nicaragua's Corn Islands (Islas del Maiz) still boast a barefoot, castaway vibe. The country's most popular eco-resort? That's the 5-year-old Morgan's Rock (☎ 506/232-6449; www.morgansrock.com), charging from $170 per person per day including meals.

You get to the Corn Islands, some 30 miles off the Caribbean coast of Nicaragua, either by plane from Managua (about $175 round-trip) or via a daylong trip by bus and ferry from other cities. Once there you find yourself in a different world of backpacker-like tourists living in extremely modest lodgings and enjoying nature and a laid-back form of life, to put it mildly. In addition to enjoying a pristine tropical innocence, you snorkel and scuba dive or simply enjoy the outdoors.

IT'S HARD TO KNOW HOW TO FEEL ABOUT THE FACT THAT NICARAGUA IS BECOMING THE LEAST-EXPENSIVE CARIBBEAN DESTINATION

Frequently, our ability to enjoy a luxurious vacation at low cost is brought about by the substandard wages of the people serving us. Years ago, the ultralow rates of all-inclusive resorts in Jamaica were (and to some extent still are) based on cheap labor costs in Montego Bay and Negril. The same in the Dominican Republic. But both of these modestly priced destinations are pikers compared to Nicaragua.

In a devastating article appearing in the *New York Review of Books* (June 12, 2008), Stephen Kinzer points out (in "Life Under the Ortegas") that 80% of the Nicaraguan population "subsist on less than two dollars a day." And that 27% of the population "is undernourished." Abandoned by the United States after the defeat of the Sandinista movement, left to drift without substantial aid or investment, Nicaragua is presently governed by a president (Daniel Ortega) who has limited knowledge of economics and survives only because of essentially free oil shipments from Hugo Chavez's Venezuela.

The United States, preoccupied with the Middle East, pays little attention to a nation that once worried us a great deal.

One hope for the future, according to Kinzer? Tourism. The country, he writes, has a "large potential: Nicaragua is among the safest and cheapest places in Central America, and a booming tourist enclave has already emerged around the beach town of San Juan del Sur. Some entrepreneurs also dream of creating retirement communities to attract middle-class retirees from the United States."

Elsewhere in his article, Kinzer emphasizes that the crime rate in Nicaragua is "remarkably low, nearer to the rates in placid Costa Rica than to those in Guatemala, El Salvador, and Honduras, the region's comparably poor countries."

Like many other travel writers, I have often written and spoken about the touristic appeal of Nicaragua, but without dwelling on the reason why costs there are so low. And it is perhaps fitting that we travel writers should leave unmentioned the plight of the population in such a wretched country, all in the interest of slightly improving the lot of the people through increased tourism.

Or should we? As we lie on the beach and bask in the sun and click our fingers so the waiter will bring another drink, should we travelers pay some thought to the dreadful conditions that made our vacation so pleasurable?

WANT AN EXAMPLE OF NICARAGUA'S ROCK-BOTTOM RATES? HOW ABOUT $90 A DAY PER PERSON, INCLUDING EVERYTHING, AT THE COUNTRY'S BEST FIVE-STAR RESORT?

Most observers would claim that the very best beach resort in Nicaragua is the 230-unit Spanish-owned Barcelo Montelimar Beach Hotel on 2 miles of white sands fronting the Pacific Ocean (all about 35 miles from the airport of Managua). In addition to that remarkable beach, it has the largest swimming pool in Latin America, a casino, nightly entertainment, several a la carte restaurants, a buffet, and every conceivable sea sport and associated entertainment.

For a double room off season, including three meals, unlimited drinks, unlimited sea sports and recreation, the cost is about $90 per day per person. Single persons traveling alone can often obtain a single room with all-inclusive arrangements (three meals and unlimited drinks) for about $110 a day.

Most observers would claim that these rates undercut those of any equivalent five-star hotel in Central America. You can learn more at www.barcelo.com, or at www.barcelomontelimarbeach.com.

NORTH AFRICA

THERE'S BEEN A SHIFT IN BRITISH TRAVEL PATTERNS (TO NORTH AFRICA, INCLUDING EGYPT) THAT AMERICANS MIGHT CONSIDER EMULATING

It isn't only the U.S. dollar that has fallen against the euro; the British pound has dropped against the euro as well (while maintaining its strength against the dollar). Result: British travel journals are headlining a sharp drop-off in British travel to Spain and Greece, where the euro is used, and a corresponding increase in travel to Egypt and Tunisia, where the local currency is refreshingly (to the British) weak. According to reliable travel newspapers in the U.K., British traffic to Egypt's Red Sea resort of Sharm El Sheikh is up by as much as 50%, as are passengers to Tunisia; meanwhile, travel to such former British favorites as Alicante in Spain and Corfu in Greek waters is down by about 15%.

American travelers might ponder the fact that Brits in such large numbers are going to Egypt. They, like most other Europeans, regard Egypt as acceptably safe, and Europeans currently flock there by the millions. Most Americans, by contrast, have shunned Egypt since September 11, and are thus missing an inexpensive travel opportunity. The Pyramids, the Sphinx, and other ancient sights of Egypt (Luxor, Aswan, Abu Simbel, Giza) make for an enthralling visit, as does a tour of Cairo with its ancient quarters, its cafes, and its great archaeological museum (with relics of King Tut).

Europeans have concluded that Egypt is safe to visit, and their assessment is supported by remarkable security measures taken by the Egyptian authorities. American tour operators have not yet created many low-cost air-and-land packages here, but given the low value of the Egyptian currency, independent trips can be arranged at a remarkably affordable price.

ORLANDO

FOR ORLANDO STAYS OF UNDER A WEEK, THE AIR-&-LAND PACKAGES OF SOUTHWEST AIRLINES VACATIONS ARE UNBEATABLE IN PRICE & VALUE

The least expensive way to enjoy a short stay (that is, of less than a week) in Orlando is to buy a package that includes airfare and a hotel. When your stay is for only 3 nights or so, too short a time for renting a vacation home, nothing beats the prices and value offered by Southwest Airlines Vacations, the tour operating arm of the aggressive low-cost airline, Southwest (☎ 800/243-8372; www.southwestvacations.com).

These packages are available, obviously, only from cities to which Southwest flies. Even all the way from Phoenix, the price is less than $420 per person for round-trip air and 3-night stays at a hotel within walking distance of the popular Downtown Disney shopping area. It's like getting your hotel almost for nothing, and thus freeing a significant portion of your budget for those high-priced theme park tickets.

HOW TO MATCH SOUTHWEST VACATION'S ORLANDO DEALS, EVEN IF YOU'RE IN A CITY FROM WHICH THE AIRLINE DOESN'T FLY

The cost-conscious traveler can choose among numerous tour operators, who compete aggressively for your dollar. Residents of the Midwest should never neglect to check out the offerings of Funjet (☎ 888/558-6654; www.funjet.com), which, like Southwest, sells 3-night air/hotel packages.

Vacation Express (☎ 800/309-4717; www.vacationexpress.com) operates charter jets from a number of major American cities, but also creates packages with airfare on scheduled flights to Orlando. Apple Vacations (☎ 800/517-2000; www.applevacations.com) manages similarly low tariffs and offers a wide range of hotel choices. Always check out their website for Orlando flights and packages.

Some of the best deals come from Florida-based eLeisureLink.com (☎ 888/801-8808). Here, you'll not only find air and hotel combined, but often, you'll get a rental car, too. One of its best recent promotions was for 5 nights at the Nickelodeon Suites hotel (just outside Disney, and like a theme park unto itself), plus airfare and a car, from $499 per person based on a family of four (additional travelers would pay only $249 more). The price was similar from eight major cities, including New York, Dallas, and Chicago. Deals are constantly changing, so go to the website, and keep in mind that booking deadlines are several months before the travel dates.

Walt Disney World, in Orlando, Florida, entertains its visitors with spectacular daily parades along the main streets of its theme parks.

Some general considerations: Often, in listing their air-and-land packages, the airlines and tour operators will create two categories—one for Orlando generally, the other for Orlando vacations using Disney hotels or hotels at Universal Studios. The Orlando deals are as much as 60% cheaper than the ones using the Disney-run or Universal properties. The key to saving money on an Orlando hotel is to always avoid the resort-run options, no matter what.

Finally, what about Orlando stays for a week and more? Those are best enjoyed using a vacation home (try www.evrentals.com or www.vrbo.com), which often cost less and afford you much more space and privacy.

It's important to question the "free shuttle service" that most Orlando hotels offer to the major theme parks

Most of the inexpensive Orlando hotels—and those are the ones that are not located on Disney or Universal Studios property—offer "daily shuttle service" to some or all of the major theme parks. Knowing this, many cash-strapped families cheerfully book into those establishments without fully understanding the limitations of Orlando's shuttle system—and taking the necessary action.

1. At almost all hotels, you will have to make reservations for your ride. This is easy enough, but it can happen that the departure you want is booked, leaving you to scrounge for a less desirable time. Considering that most shuttles make return trips to a given park only two or three times a day, this can constrict your schedule. You also usually are not permitted to change your reservation at the last minute, so if you're having such a good time on the roller coasters that you want to stay a few extra hours, you usually aren't guaranteed a later shuttle. Just one late-night taxi ride back to your hotel can wipe out all the money you saved using the shuttle system that day.

2. Many shuttles are run by outside companies, so they maximize profit by serving many hotels. That means they may take circuitous routes. If you're unlucky, it can take more than an hour to get home after your day at the parks, which is a huge waste of your valuable vacation time and money. It can also mean trouble for families with small children. Ask your hotel which company provides its shuttle service, and then ask that company where your chosen property fits in on the route map. You may decide to switch to a hotel closer to the park gates.

3. Some shuttles' timings don't match up with the theme parks' opening hours. It would be a shame to have to bundle your kids back to the motel an hour before the fireworks over the Magic Kingdom's castle begin, yet many people have to do just that when they rely on free shuttles. Always ask your hotel for the shuttle schedules during the days you plan to be in town (the timings change regularly), and compare them to the opening hours of the parks you plan to see.

Finally, keep in mind that many times of year, renting a car in Orlando can be reasonably priced. During lowest season (Jan, Sept–Oct), they go for as little as $22 a day through discount sites such as Priceline (www.price line.com). And you probably won't use much gas during your stay if you only plan to use your wheels to go to and from the theme parks. Also remember that if you have a car from the very start of your trip, you will not have to pay extra for transportation to and from the airport, saving you about $25 round-trip for adults and $18 for kids on the standard shuttles.

THREE GIANT ECONOMY MOTELS PROVIDE SOME 1,900 ROOMS A NIGHT IN ORLANDO AT $50 A ROOM

With admission prices soaring to those legendary theme parks, it's more important than ever that you economize on the cost of your Orlando lodgings. Three immense budget hotels will almost always have vacancies at $50 a night, and each is located close to the best mealtime bargains in Orlando.

Using these properties—whose comfort and amenities will match those of any low-cost property on the Disney grounds—is an effective first step in keeping your total costs to a reasonable level.

Quality Inn Plaza International Drive (☎ 800/999-8585; www.quality innorlando.com) has no fewer than 1,020 rooms, so it's usually ready to deal in order to fill them. While $50 is a typical price, it often rents them for $10 less, and rates drop the more nights you stay. And it operates like a tropical resort for scrimpers, with multiple pools, a lobby bar with nightly entertainment, and a free shuttle to Universal Orlando and SeaWorld. Rooms sleep four in two double beds, and there are lots of cheap chain restaurants out the front door. Downsides: The hotel abuts noisy Interstate 4, and its A Building is beside a tourist helicopter pad (so ask for the F Building).

Rodeway Inn at International Drive (☎ 800/999-6327; www.rodeway innorlando.com), the largest Rodeway in America (315 rooms), is well worn but clean, and at $40 in low season and $65 in high, it's all you could want in a budget motel. It's also close to Universal and Wet 'n Wild, within walking distance of cheap restaurants, and equipped with a heated pool and in-room fridges and microwaves. Across the street, a Ponderosa serves $4 all-you-can-eat breakfasts. And a cheap I-Ride Trolley ($1) picks you up and heads across town, with a stop at SeaWorld.

Seralago Hotel & Suites (☎ 800/366-5437; www.seralagohotel.com), which sprawls around two giant pool areas about 3 miles east of Disney, has a cheerful personality despite its low tariff. The basic motel-style place is so big (614 rooms—it was once the area's most important Holiday Inn) that staff gets around by electric cart. A $50 double rate is common, and its two-room "suites" (really, two conjoined rooms) have microwaves and fridges for an additional fee. And its van-shuttles to the Disney parks are free.

Psssst! Four other giant Orlando hotels are offering rooms in late summer & autumn for $40 per room per night.

Every year in late summer, the budget hotel king of Orlando, a certain Harris Rosen, slashes the room rates of his four large, low-cost hotels for stays during the doldrums period in Orlando: late August and the entire month of September. I phoned one of his reservations staff to learn what the price would be this summer, and was told (swearing to secrecy) that the probable rate would be $40 per room per night, at the following four giants (some have 800 rooms): the Quality Inn International (☎ 800/825-7600), the Quality Inn Plaza (☎ 800/999-8585), the Rodeway Inn International

(☎ 800/551-6327), and the mammoth Comfort Inn Lake Buena Vista (☎ 800/999-7300), the last named being my own favorite. That's for visitors calling the above numbers prior to arrival in Orlando. Specify the "late summer specials."

RENTALO.COM HAS NOW ENTERED THE HOTLY CONTESTED ORLANDO MARKET, POKING FUN AT THE HIGH COST OF HOTELS & PRAISING VACATION HOMES INSTEAD

Things are heating up in the vacation home–versus-hotel controversy for Orlando, with newcomer Rentalo.com (www.rentalo.com) offering hotel rooms for as much as $385 a night and more spacious vacation homes for as little as $99 a night.

UNIVERSAL STUDIOS FLORIDA IS A POTENT, COST-EFFECTIVE COMPETITOR TO DISNEY

Now that daily adult admission to Walt Disney World in Orlando is a whopping $67 per person (including tax), you might want to consider Universal Orlando's amazing counter-offer of only $86 for unlimited 7-day admission to Universal Studios and Universal's Islands of Adventure. It's an indication of how fierce is Universal's need to fight back against the large number of Disney theme parks in Orlando. Though Universal has only two theme parks, they are expansive and ingenious, and can support, say, 4 days of entertainment.

A FEW SUGGESTIONS FOR PLANNING A SUCCESSFUL FAMILY TRIP TO ORLANDO

It all comes down to seven simple rules.

1. Timing is everything. The least expensive times for a visit are from just after Labor Day until just before Christmas, then the first 3 weeks of January (starting just shortly after New Year's Day), and from late April up to the Memorial Day weekend. Avoid school vacation times and you'll experience smaller crowds and lower hotel prices.

2. Buy air in advance from a cut-rate carrier. Though driving is the most economical way to get there, it's not always practical if you don't live in the Northeast.

3. Book the area's modern, low-cost motels. At properties throughout the theme park area and in neighboring Kissimmee, Florida, a family of four can stay for as little as $39 a night, often including free shuttles to

theme parks. Check the rates at Wilson World in Kissimmee, Holiday Inn Sun Spree Resort Lake Buena Vista, Days Inn on U.S. Hwy. 192, Comfort Inn at Lake Buena Vista, and Best Western Plaza International on International Drive.

4. Jot down the addresses of all-you-can-eat buffets, such as the Ponderosa chain on International Drive and Hwy. 192, or Shoney's.

5. Stock up on passes and cards. Whether before you arrive or once you're here, get the Orlando Magicard from the Orlando/Orange County Convention and Visitors Bureau for discounts on lodgings, meals, car rental, and other sundries.

6. Carefully juggle theme park admissions. Spend no more than 3 days at the Disney properties and assign your remaining time to Universal Studios, SeaWorld, and Wet 'n Wild.

7. And finally, plan in advance for your meals within the theme parks. Consider bringing sandwiches in a backpack or paper bag (for lunch), and take dinner outside the theme park grounds.

To economize on food, smart families leave the Orlando theme park areas & return later

Were you aware that in Orlando, you can leave the theme park areas and return later on the same day without incurring additional expense? The tickets you've purchased are valid all day, regardless of the number of times you enter and leave. Same with parking privileges. Once you've paid to park, you can drive away from the theme park to an inexpensive eatery (such as a Denny's or any other family restaurant), and later return to the same parking lot without paying another charge.

You simply need to make sure that when you leave the park, you exit through the turnstiles devoted to people who intend to come back—they are usually called "Same-Day Return." The park may give you a hand stamp in invisible ink, but you will always need to keep your original ticket.

An additional advantage: Leaving the park can also give you a chance to hit your hotel pool during the hottest hours of the day—which can be a lifesaver if you've got weary kids in tow.

A single disadvantage: The tactic works best at all the theme parks other than Disney's Magic Kingdom. At the latter, getting to the parking lot can occasionally be so burdensome (you will either have to take a ferry or a monorail from the park) that for that one location, the hassle may not be worth it. (It could take you as long as 45 min. to reach your car.) Otherwise, parking lots are always adjacent to the front gates.

A related suggestion: Parks do not officially sanction bringing food inside, but I have never once heard of them actually preventing guests from doing so. In fact, many people do bring light meals in, which they then eat on one of the many park benches. I'd suggest not making a big production out of it—stash sandwiches here and there, and the parks will never make trouble. Just don't bring alcohol.

AS A SERVICE, HERE'S A LIST OF REPUTABLE REAL ESTATE FIRMS OFFERING VACATION HOMES IN ORLANDO

By now, most smart travelers are aware that on a trip to the theme parks of Orlando, Florida, for a family or group of four and more, the vacation home is a far better value than most hotels. But from whom do you rent those vacation homes, and who has a reliable inventory of pleasant homes? Here's a list you might want to print out and save:

All Star Vacation Homes (☎ 800/592-5568; www.allstarvacation homes.com) is a highly professional company renting three-bedroom condo units sleeping eight that start at an astonishing $119 a night per condo, which is the same price as the lowest-priced room in motel-style digs, sleeping just four, during the spring on the Walt Disney premises. Lavish private homes with screened-in pools, a barbecue, a game room, free Internet, and other perks go from $189 for a three-bedroom, two-bath house or $219 for a mammoth five-bedroom. All its properties are located within 4 miles of Disney. On stays of a week or longer, All Star will throw in a free rental car.

Oak Plantation (☎ 407/847-8200; www.oakplantationresort.com) offers one-bedroom units in condo-style buildings, shaded by trees and collected around a small pond; they are located about 6 miles east of Disney property, in an area of Kissimmee that's crammed with cheap restaurants, and cost as little as $79 a night on its website.

Alexander Holiday Homes (☎ 800/621-7888; www.floridasunshine. com) is a family-run company that has been managing and renting homes since 1989. Although most of its 200 properties technically start around $95 a night, its website spotlights deals as low as $65 for a two-bedroom condo.

Bahama Bay Resort (☎ 866/830-1617; www.bahamabayresortorlando. com), a gated development found a few miles west of Disney World's southern entrance, is a complex of pastel-colored two-and three-story condo buildings. Two-bedroom condos sleep six and cost about $99. As with any of these units, smaller groups can rent for the same price, too, and enjoy the elbow room.

ORLANDO VS. LAS VEGAS—WHICH IS CHEAPEST?

If you've been to Las Vegas lately, you've experienced the sharp rise in prices for lodgings and meals. With nationwide conventions happening there for weeks on end, the hotels are often fully booked and expensive. The same for meals. With some Las Vegas hotels currently earning more money from their restaurants than their casinos, the old policy of pricing meals as loss leaders has been jettisoned; the food of Sin City is in general increasingly pricey.

So which is the better choice for budget-minded vacationers—Las Vegas or Orlando? I say Orlando. The bargains in packages that combine airfare, hotel and car rental, and the recent competitive ticket prices at Universal Florida have created new opportunities for cost-conscious families.

The bargains begin with an Orlando offering from the Florida-based eLeisureLink.com (☎ 888/801-8808): a remarkable $499 per person for round-trip air from New York, Chicago, Cleveland, Detroit, Hartford, Philadelphia, Pittsburgh, Providence, or Washington, D.C. (with cheap add-ons from everywhere else); a two-bedroom suite with minikitchen at the Nickelodeon Family Suites Resort (kids get their own entertainment-filled bedroom and waterpark-style playground); and a 5-day midsize car rental with unlimited mileage, all based on a family of four traveling together. Add to that the admissions price of $86 per person for a full week at the theme parks of Universal Studios, and you have a record low price for a weeklong family vacation. While first-timers to Orlando will undoubt-edly prefer devoting their week to the Disney theme parks, repeat visitors seem to be well satisfied with the more contemporary attractions of Universal, whose two theme parks—a TV-oriented Universal Studios Florida and a movie-and-comic-strip-themed Islands of Adventure—provide the basis for several days of enjoyable entertainment.

A WEEK IN ORLANDO SHOULD BE SPLIT BETWEEN DISNEY & NON-DISNEY

Walt Disney World's "Magic Your Way" ticket pricing lowers the per-day cost for people who spend several consecutive days at its theme parks ("pay less per day the longer you stay"). Whereas families spending a week in Orlando used to visit Disney on days 1 to 3, and then devoted days 4 to 6 to Orlando's other noteworthy entertainments, they are now being enticed into lingering on Disney property by the considerable economy of lower ticket prices for longer stays.

I'm unhappy about that. Although Walt Disney World is a remarkable achievement in tourism, it would be a terrible mistake to spend your entire Orlando vacation on Disney property. Orlando hosts 7 of the nation's 10 most popular theme parks, and 3 of them—SeaWorld, Universal Studios, and the stunning Islands of Adventure—are not Disney properties. Neither is the stirring Kennedy Space Center, where you can see the actual Space Shuttle being readied for launch. If you refuse to leave Disney's campus, you're missing a lot.

What's a good overall strategy? In my opinion, most people will be more than satisfied with a schedule that calls for one Disney park per day for a total of 2 or 3 days. Don't let Disney pricing lure you into staying a minute longer than you really need to.

BEATING THE SYSTEM AT DISNEY WORLD

How can a family save on meal costs when they visit Walt Disney World? That's an increasing problem in a theme park where even the simplest sandwich with a soft drink now costs a minimum of $11. A trick that my daughter uses is to ask for a double cheeseburger and then to request an extra bun, the extra bun costing under $1. You then make two cheeseburgers out of the two patties of meat and thus split the total cost in half per person. An even better tactic is to buy one of those enormous $1\frac{1}{2}$-pound turkey legs at stands scattered around the parks, the legs being carved from 45-pound turkeys. One leg can easily feed two persons for less than a total of $6. I'm told that the Disney organization claims to sell 1.5 million of such turkey legs each year—probably to families desperate to save money on meals.

AMERICA'S MOST VALUABLE DISCOUNT CARD IS FOR ORLANDO—& YOU CAN PRINT IT OUT FROM YOUR COMPUTER

Most people going to Orlando are aware that the tourist office there distributes an extremely valuable discount card known as the Orlando Magicard. Trouble was that you either had to write away long in advance to get the card in time for your trip, or else pay an inconvenient visit to the tourist office to pick one up on the spot. Now, for the first time, the Orlando tourist people permit you to print out a workable version of that Magicard on your home computer. Simply go to www.orlandoinfo.com, click on "Discounts & Promotions," then "Magicard," and then on "Download a Magicard," and *voilà!* You can print out your own Magicard and save up to $500 on hotels, restaurants, shops, and attractions.

Various Disney enthusiasts are constantly looking for discounts—& posting them to the Web

TheMouseForLess (www.themouseforless.com), MouseSavers.com, and AllEars.Net (www.allearsnet.com) are sites privately owned by Disney fans who constantly search out the discounts at resort hotels in and around the theme parks, and similar reductions at restaurants and from tour operators in Orlando and Anaheim. If anyone is discounting in the big theme park cities, their offers quickly appear on these sites.

PANAMA

A day in Panama City, surrounded by scores of brand-new futuristic skyscrapers—& a perfectly preserved colonial quarter

Still reeling from the fact that our Panama City hotel had a full-scale casino of roulette wheels, baccarat dealers, craps tables, and slots (nothing had prepared us for Panama's Las Vegas–style gambling), my wife, Roberta, and I headed for our first morning in town to the city's outstanding quarter of colonial gems, the Casco Viejo district of 17th-century Spanish charm. Preserved as the conquistadors left it, Casco Viejo vies with Old Havana and Old San Juan in authenticity—but is beginning to leave the others behind with the restored beauty of its courtyards, the sparkling tiles and marble that line many of the cafes, restaurants, and shops that now occupy these historic structures. Just as Panama City's downtown across the bay is transforming itself into a totally unexpected, skyscraper-packed Hong Kong, Casco Viejo is in the process of being restored into the most tastefully attractive area of the city.

Here, the district is studded with fun gift shops selling pot holders and eyeglass cases in the strongly colorful designs—"molas"—of Panama's indigenous Indians; dolls in the ruffled long skirts of Panama's 19th-century women; and feather-light Panama hats. The cafes and restaurants are gracious and courtly. The city's skyline across the water is stunning. The Presidential Palace (currently housing the Honorable Martin Torrijos) is the center of power, surrounded by military—but friendly—guards). The chief sightseeing attraction is the Museo del Canal Interoceánico, the museum which relates the history of the Panama Canal. Though its inscriptions are in Spanish only, its many visual aids and movies are easily understood. That canal museum is an indispensable stop, a necessary prelude to your visit to the Miraflores Locks later in the day.

After a $30 lunch for the two of us (including appetizers, main course, two Panama beers, and dessert) at the elegant Mostaza Restaurant, we cabbed it to the Miraflores Visitors Center on the outskirts of town for a look at the actual workings of the canal. As we stood on a high outdoor balcony overlooking the Miraflores Locks, a live announcer speaking over a loudspeaker in Spanish, English, and French explained the intricate work-ings that lifted these giant vessels to different levels of the artificial water-way. Asian sailors stood on the deck of one enormous container ship, looking up at us tourists as we gazed at them and their ship.

From Miraflores, we visited not one but two successive marketplaces of Panama City, and bought gifts for relatives back home at prices that were a quarter of what they cost in the lobby gift shop of our hotel.

Tourism in Panama is centered not simply in Panama City, but to a far greater extent on the picture-perfect, uncrowded beaches (with several large resorts) just outside Panama City, and in the renowned San Blas Islands, Pearl Islands, and Bocas del Toro offshore islands, as well as on the Gulf of Chiriquí. It's found in the mountain stretches of Boquete housing rainforests, coffee plantations, Embera and Kuna Indians, resorts, and retirement communities.

PARIS

APARTMENTS—NOT HOTELS—OFFER THE BEST VALUES IN PARIS THIS YEAR

A recent look at the website of Paris Attitude (www.parisattitude.com), my own favorite source of Parisian accommodations, serves to remind me that in Paris and other European capitals, the short-term rental of an apartment can often cost far less than equivalent hotel rooms, especially if you are four or more persons traveling together. Paris Attitude currently lists apartments throughout the city that rent for as little as $800 a week (housing four). And that's an all-inclusive price; only the use of the phone is not included.

In such an apartment, you and your family can also save on breakfasts and occasional meals, while enjoying far more space than is usually avail-able in a hotel.

Even in a first-class hotel-apartment (apartments with the services of a hotel), the savings can be considerable. At such upscale digs in the Bastille area, cleaning is provided daily; bed linens are changed every 3 days, and towels each day. There is a 24-hour receptionist, and a bar on the premises. Yet when it's rented to four persons, the apartment costs less than $200 a night (on at least a 1-week rental), much less than you'd pay at an equivalent Paris hotel.

The apartments listed for rent on www.parisianapartmenttours.com are certainly not the cheapest available in Paris. Some are reasonable in price; a great many are through the roof. But if you'd like to experience international real estate without leaving home, you'll have fun skimming through the amazingly comprehensive photos that appear in this superelegant website. Some of the listings permit you to have a 360-degree view of the apartment; others sweep from one side of a room to the other.

To take a tour, click on "Apartments," then click on the words "Virtual Tour" where they appear beneath the photos.

YOU REALLY SHOULD KNOW ABOUT THOSE PUBLIC BICYCLES IN PARIS & SUGGEST THEM TO YOUR OWN MUNICIPAL AUTHORITIES

Paris is the latest European city to amass a fleet of bicycles (free the first half-hour, then a nominal sum) that anyone may grab for anytime use. The city has installed some 20,000 bikes at some 1,500 stations around town, and all a tourist needs in order to rent one is an American Express credit card to mainly guarantee the condition of the bike (Amex cards are thus far the only American-issued cards accepted at those bike stations).

Other cities have tried a similar idea with middling success—Vienna's version featured vehicles that were deliberately cheap and uncomfortable to discourage theft. Stockholm's system, launched with the participation of Clear Channel Communications (the multinational ad firm), now has about 1,000 bikes circulating in town, which anyone can rent for a small sum, using a card, but the system may be sunk by rampant vandalism.

The French project, called Velib (www.velib.paris.fr; French language only), began in Lyon and is also sponsored by a company (JC Decaux) that profits from advertising on the bikes. You buy a membership at ATM-like kiosks for 1 euro. The first half-hour of use is free, and rates are about 1€ per half-hour after that. You can drop your bike off 24/7 anywhere in town where there's a station.

Interestingly, because the system has been established with the full support of the city, the rental cards can be prepaid and used on traditional modes of public transportation as well.

There is an inherent risk in using these bikes: They don't come with helmets. Still, they are a major advance in the quality of life, and should be considered in your own city. How about it?

PHILADELPHIA

THE CONSTITUTION CENTER IS AN IMPORTANT ADDITION TO THE SIGHTS OF PHILADELPHIA

The comic W.C. Fields directed that his tombstone read: "Better here than in Philadelphia." A hoary joke tells of contestants winning 1 week in Philadelphia as the first prize and 2 weeks in Philadelphia as a second prize.

It isn't true. In addition to possessing extraordinary museums of art and science, top-quality restaurants, superb shopping, and venerable sights associated with the Declaration of Independence, including Independence Hall and the Liberty Bell, Philadelphia now has a giant history museum (also on the Independence Mall) called the Constitution Center, with displays that bring the Constitution to life. Its highlight is a 17-minute film.

PRAGUE

PRAGUE "IN A NUTSHELL"—THE REASONS YOU GO THERE

I am constantly asked, "What's so special about Prague? What exactly does it offer?"

You start with visual magnificence. Conventional wisdom has it that Paris is the most beautiful city in Europe, if not the world. But when you lay eyes on "Magical Prague," your jaw will drop. The central parts of the booming capital of Eastern Europe's Czech Republic are a striking mix of medieval, 19th century, Art Deco, and cutting-edge mod (check out Frank Gehry's "Fred and Ginger" building).

A stroll across the Moldau River along the Gothic Charles Bridge, with Hradcany Castle looming on the hilltop before you, is like wandering through a Brothers Grimm fairy tale. You should, first, roam Hradcany's mysterious cobblestone "Alchemists' Lane" and witness its toy soldier–like changing of the guard; marvel at the graceful Gothic tracery of St. Agnes Monastery; watch the fanciful figures in the city hall's astronomical clock dance in the arcade-lined Old Town Square every hour; explore the Jewish quarter with its spooky-cool cemetery and ancient synagogues; quaff Pilsner beer (it was invented here) or sup on goulash and roast goose under the stone barrel vaults of medieval cellar restaurants and pubs; and sip mulled wine or Becherovka herb liqueur in magnificent Belle Epoque cafes.

The Czech Republic's in the European Union but isn't converting to the euro till late 2009, so for now, while lodging has gotten generally pricier, you can still find good deals (consider apartment rentals), and in many places meals and attractions are still thumping bargains. Don't forget to schedule some time for day and overnight trips through lyrical country-scapes to magnificent castles (Konopiste, Karlstejn) and towns (such as the gracious spa city of Karlový Vary, the beer-making centers of Plzen and Ceské Budejovice, and such UNESCO World Heritage Sites as Ceský Krumlov and Telc).

Prague specialists include General Tours (☎ 800/221-2216; www. generaltours.com) and Tatra Travel (☎ 600/321-2999, www.tatratravel. com). But independent travel is a cinch, as well; there are direct flights via CSA (☎ 800/223-2365; www.czechairlines.com) and Delta (☎ 800/241-4141; www.delta.com). Get more info in the United States at ☎ 212/288-0830, in Canada at 416/363-9928, or at www.visitczech.cz.

PUERTO RICO

THAT AMERICA-LINKED ISLAND OF SPANISH-SPEAKERS MAKES FOR AN EXCELLENT CARIBBEAN VACATION

It may be a U.S. commonwealth, use the Yankee dollar, and require no pass-port to visit, but apart from some familiar Taco Bell/Blockbuster outlets in parts of San Juan, this rather large, Spanish-speaking island really does feel like another country, a touristic dream with plenty of beaches, culture, history, and exceptionally friendly locals.

Puerto Rico's "Big Apple" is of course San Juan, toward the eastern end of the north coast. The star here is its 16th-century old town, a UNESCO World Heritage Site anchored by a pair of impressive stone fortresses, El Morro and San Cristóbal, and 20-foot-thick city walls. Old San Juan is a bit touristy these days, but exploring its narrow cobblestone streets, galleries, restaurants, museums, and shops is still lots of fun. The city's nightlife, casinos, and dining are among the best in the Caribbean.

San Juan makes a good base for visiting lovely Luquillo Beach and El Yunque, the only tropical rainforest in the United States, but do try to spend a night or two "out on the island," as they say. Attractions include the city of Ponce, with its excellent art museum and charming 19th-century city center (the black-and-red firehouse is a sight to see); the surfing off the west-coast town of Rincón; the castaway offshore islands of Vieques and Culebra; the huge, dramatic Camuy caverns; the fetching little colonial town of San Germán; the Phosphorescent Bay of La Parguera (at night, tiny glowing critters light up the waters); coffee plantations; Taíno Indian ruins; and the Panoramic Route across the island's mountainous, rainforested spine. Along the way, stay in *paradores,* inns occupying historic and modern buildings.

Air Canada and most U.S. carriers operate daily flights, and most Caribbean specialists offer air-hotel packages, including Funjet (☎ 888/558-6654; www.funjet.com), GOGO Worldwide Travel/Liberty Travel (☎ 888/271-1584; www.libertytravel.com), Inter-Island Tours (☎ 800/245-3434; www.interislandtours.com), and Travel Impressions (☎ 800/284-0044; www.travelimpressions.com). For more details, call ☎ 800/866-7827 in the United States or 416/580-6287 in Canada, or log on to www.gotopuertorico.com.

LOOKING FOR A TROPICAL VACATION IN A CULTURALLY RICH AREA? TRY ONE OF THE THREE CANARIO HOTELS OF PUERTO RICO.

All three are in the Condado Beach section of San Juan, about halfway between the airport and Old San Juan, just steps from the beach. One is the 40-room Canario by the Lagoon (☎ 787/722-5058), the second is the 25-room Canario by the Sea (☎ 787/722-8640), and the third is the 25-room Canario Inn (☎ 787/722-3961), all so small and intimate as to deserve the term "bed-and-breakfast hotels" (continental breakfast is always included in the room rate). During off season (May 1–Dec 15) and for a 3-night minimum stay, all three of these charming, well-maintained properties charge $75 per single room per night, $80 per double or twin, plus taxes of about 9% and a $3 energy surcharge, which makes them a top value of Puerto Rico. High season (Dec 16–Apr 30), the same rooms go for $120.

It can't be overly emphasized that although you're in a quiet setting and able to go swimming in the sea (I've personally visited all three small hotels during multiple trips to Puerto Rico), you are also near shops and restaurants, and within walking distance (a long but interesting stroll) of the museums, fortresses, shops, and urban life of San Juan. Go to www.canariohotels.com for photographs or further information; phone ☎ 800/533-2649 for toll-free reservations at all three.

Rio de Janeiro, Brazil

You can discover the "real Rio" in a low-cost B&B

Picture yourself chatting over breakfast with a Brazilian artist in the garden of her Art Deco villa, where for $45 you've rented a double room with views of one of the world's most awesome cities flanking the beach below.

The lion's share of Rio vacationers end up staying in soulless hotel towers in the crowded oceanside neighborhoods of Copacabana. The solution? An escape into one of Rio's prettiest areas and a room rented—for anywhere from $45 to $110—through Cama e Café B&B network (www.camaecafe.com.br). Many of the 50 B&Bs in the network are in the homes of artists, writers, and other bohemian types who live in Santa Teresa, a leafy hillside neighborhood of small houses built largely between the 1600s and the 1950s (the oldest in the B&B network dates to 1860).

Cama e Café doesn't just rent rooms; it attempts to match hosts to guests. You fill out a personal profile when you sign up, and the company matches qualities in your profile to the appropriate B&B owner, one with whom you share common interests and will, hopefully, have plenty to chat about. Here's a stay that's far removed from the standard travel routine.

Rio de Janeiro, Brazil, with its unique, year-around carnival atmosphere, is one of the cities you simply have to visit.

RUSSIA

$999 (PLUS WHOPPING FEES & TAXES) CAN TAKE YOU TO RUSSIA IN WINTER. THOUGH THE WEATHER THERE IS FRIGID, A DECEMBER-THROUGH-FEBRUARY TRIP IS AN IMPORTANT CULTURAL EXPERIENCE.

In winter, $999 (plus whopping fees and taxes) will buy you a trip to Russia—and though few people may want to brave the frigid temperatures at that time, those hardy souls who do make the trip spend considerably less than they would at any other time of year. And needless to say, the cultural life of the country (the Bolshoi Ballet, theater, opera, the uncrowded Hermitage Museum, the uncrowded Kremlin, and other lightly visited attractions) is best viewed and experienced in winter.

The trip is purchased from a long-established Russian specialist, Eastern Tours (☎ 800/339-6967; www.traveltorussia.com), which offers its classic Russian itinerary combining Moscow and St. Petersburg for $999 per person in November through March. The same trip is $1,299 per person in October and April.

That price covers round-trip airfare from New York and a week in Russia. It begins with 3 nights' lodging in St. Petersburg, during which time you get an included city tour and visits to the St. Petersburg Ballet and the Hermitage, one of the world's greatest museums, up there with the Louvre, Vatican, and the Met in New York. Following an overnight ride on the "Red Arrow" train from St. Petersburg to Moscow are 3 days and 2 nights in the Russian capital, including a guided tour, visits to Red Square and the Kremlin, and a trip to the famed Moscow Circus.

Unfortunately, $999 isn't the final price you pay per person. Even seasoned travelers used to the unavoidable taxes and fees (usually associated with plane tickets) that end up tacking up to $250 onto the price tag of most trips, will be in for a shock by the massive charges—due largely to high departure taxes and visa fees—involved with a trip to Russia: up to an additional $640. That doesn't make this deal any less of a bargain—you'd have to pay that $640 in governmental and airline fees even if the trip itself were free—I just wanted you to be prepared for the wallop that's found in the fine print.

SANIBEL ISLAND, FLORIDA

I'VE JUST SPENT ANOTHER WINTER WEEK AT "DING" DARLING—& HEARTILY RECOMMEND THE EXPERIENCE

From the land of the yellow-crowned night heron and the roseate spoonbill, let me greet you. I've been writing from Sanibel Island, on the Gulf of Mexico off the west coast of Florida, where the chief attraction is the J. N. "Ding" Darling National Wildlife Refuge.

The "Ding" Darling preserve is one of several hundred national areas designed for wildlife and not for people. Although there's a road and many paths throughout the giant area, there are no accommodations or food services. You visit simply to view wildlife in the raw—consisting of some 200 species of birds that feed on fish and crabs in the estuaries scattered throughout the preserve—without interfering with their exclusive ownership of the entire domain. Just minutes ago, I saw a heron stalk, catch, and then devour a crab that had been peacefully making its way across the marshes.

J. N. "Ding" Darling was a nationally syndicated political cartoonist of the *Des Moines Register* in the 1920s and 1930s, a man violently opposed to the politics of Franklin D. Roosevelt, but also a fierce conservationist. It says something about the brilliance and character of Roosevelt that he chose Darling to head up a federal bureau that eventually became our U.S. Fish & Wildlife Service. In charge of that agency, Darling not only created scores of National Wildlife Refuges but also fought and defeated the real estate developers who were just then discovering and developing Sanibel Island.

Darling succeeded in saving a large part of Sanibel from the builders of condos, who were mainly relegated to erecting them for transient visitors along the beach, but not inland. My wife and I are enjoying one of those moderately priced condo rentals this week.

I can't imagine a more compelling National Wildlife Refuge than "Ding" Darling. Its atmosphere is magical, its lakes (estuaries) and marshes are the scene of an endless theatrical experiences as thousands of large, colorful birds (pelicans, especially) make use of the food and protection that the refuge affords to them.

January through March are the peak months here, but the wildlife is active and in attendance throughout the year, as are the lodgings, restaurants, and shops concentrated away from "Ding" Darling. An hour south of here is Naples, Florida, one of the fastest-growing cities in the United States.

But here on Sanibel the atmosphere is laid back and quiet, almost "small town" in feeling, and the big thing to do is to search for shells on the beaches after you have spent several hours at "Ding" Darling.

SICILY

PARDON THE BOAST, BUT THE RULES OF SMART TRAVEL WORKED AGAIN IN SICILY

In advance of leaving for Sicily, my wife and I read histories and art appreciations of the five basic destinations we had chosen for the trip: Palermo, Erice, Agrigento, Syracuse, and Taormina. Arriving in each city, we had no need to be herded as part of a group from place to place, nor to stuff ourselves in a motorcoach that would wall us off from the exoticism of this unique area. We knew what we wanted to see, and we walked from place to place, mixing with locals, often conversing with them, asking questions, dropping into their cafes and shops, scanning their newspapers and political posters, free from the constant jostling presence of other tourists.

We had once again applied the key rule of enjoyable travel: that advance reading in the history and culture of the destination is infinitely preferable to relying on the simplistic commentary of a tour guide.

Sicily differs in many respects from the rest of Italy, and some will claim its atmosphere is more attractive, friendly, and unassuming.

WHAT SORT OF IMPACT DO OPERATIONS OF THE MAFIA HAVE ON YOUR VISIT TO SICILY?

Call me naive, but as far as I could see, the impact of the Sicilian Mafia on the tourist is virtually nil. From arrival to departure, I heard not a word of Mafia activities, and no tourist to my knowledge has ever been targeted by a group that has every business reason to encourage visits.

Though Sicily's economic problems—it is one of the poorer parts of Italy—are sometimes "pinned" on the Mafia, just as many Sicilians will talk of the wave of foreign invasions that kept Sicily from becoming a strong nation-state for so many centuries. Its strategic position near the center of the Mediterranean made it a constant and irresistible prize for a succession of conquerors. It suffered especial damage from Allied bombardment and battle in World War II.

It is this turbulent history that provides the basis for a fascinating tour. In no other part of Europe with the exception of Malta is it possible to see so many striking remains (Greek and Roman temples, Muslim mosques, Norman cathedrals) of the key eras of human history crammed into such a small space. And all this is found in a place of striking natural beauty, of fields and rolling hills covered with such lush vegetation and agricultural richness that, by all rights, it should be one of the most prosperous areas of Europe rather than one of its poorest.

Far less developed than the rest of Italy, Sicily is also far less expensive, and rarely do you encounter the startling prices or overcharges that are sometimes found in more heavily visited parts of Europe. You also encounter a warm and welcoming local population who, in my experience, are constantly gracious towards the visitor. I'm going again.

A SELF-DRIVE CAR & A SEASIDE ITINERARY ARE THE RIGHT APPROACH TO EXPLORING SICILY

How do you undertake a first visit to Sicily? Where do you start, where do you go?

The major cities and sights are all along the sea, and the seaside highways are the routes taken by most visitors, as they were for me. You can start in Palermo, site of the international airport, and concentrate there on the 12th-century, mosaic-covered churches and structures associated with the Norman conquerors of that time. From there you might drive for an overnight stay to the medieval mountaintop city of Erice (with its awesome views of the western tip of the island), and then down the western side of Sicily to Agrigento, home to the breathtaking Greek Valley of the Temples dating from the 5th century B.C., more than six of them, including one—the Temple of Concordia—that is surely the best preserved, most fully intact Greek temple in all the world.

Most visitors then continue to the city of Siracusa (considered in its earlier time to be a more important Greek capital than Athens) and its delightful, well-restored "villagey" island of Ortygia off one side of the city, where almost all visitors go. Here, your stay must be for at least 2 and preferably 3 nights. A 5th-century Temple of Apollo is a secondary sight, overshadowed by a stupendous Archaeological Museum (a statue of Venus its outstanding feature) and a giant Greek (and later Roman) amphitheater, where plays of Euripides and Sophocles are still performed, as they were in ancient times. (The museum and the amphitheater are in the city of Siracusa proper, and not on the island of Ortygia.)

Your final stop (before returning to the airport of Palermo): the sensuous, colorful resort town of Taormina, high overlooking a breathtaking vista of sea and coastline, enlivened in the warm months by purple bougainvillea everywhere you look. Taormina is a rival to Monte Carlo, to Acapulco, to every other glittering seaside resort—and some would claim it tops them all. From Taormina, you cut through the center of Sicily and then north, back to the airport at Palermo for your homeward-bound flight.

If you seek a memorable, instructive, and yet pleasure-filled European experience at moderate cost (airfare and car rental are the major expense), think Sicily.

SOUTH AFRICA

THOUGH A NUMBER OF TRAVEL COMMENTATORS ARE CURRENTLY TOUTING THE LOW-COST PLEASURES OF SOUTH AFRICA, THE MATHEMATICS JUST DON'T ADD UP

Not long ago, the U.S. dollar bought six South African rand. When we went to press with this book, the dollar bought nearly eight South African rand. One of the few foreign currencies to actually weaken against the U.S. dollar, the rand has fallen by 25%, and prices for hotels, meals, and sightseeing are all refreshingly inexpensive in Cape Town and in the wildlife-filled national parks in easy reach of that city. As a consequence, all sorts of newspaper travel sections are touting the desirability of travel to South Africa, especially to its glittering seaside resort capital of Cape Town.

But the problem is airfare. Go to all the consolidators, aggregators, and airline sites, and you'll rarely find a round-trip ticket for less than $1,700 between the United States and Cape Town or Johannesburg. With such an initial bite at your finances, all the savings in subsequent costs can't manage to keep the total outlay to reasonable levels. Though it pains me to say it, South Africa just isn't a feasible destination for cost-conscious American vacationers flying there from the United States.

But how about a visit to Cape Town as an "add on" to a stay in London? Maybe. Using www.cheapflights.co.uk, a leading British search engine, you can occasionally find a round-trip London-to–Cape Town flight for £399 ($580), though most flights are listed for $700 and $800. If you're going to be in London anyway, you might want to consider this interesting trip.

But generally speaking, South Africa isn't currently a budget destination. It is, instead, another casualty of the sharp increase in fuel costs that has so greatly raised the cost of flying.

SPAIN

AN AMAZING TRANSFORMATION IN THE OUTLOOK & LIFESTYLE OF SPAIN

What's most impressive about modern-day Spain is the speed with which it threw off its stultifying past and became an exciting center of new ideas and humane policies. It shows what people can do when they defy the privileged nay-sayers and set about to improve their lives.

The pre–World War II–era dictator of Spain, Francisco Franco, remained in power until 1975, and his political party continued to rule for several years more. I made repeated visits to Madrid during that time, revising my guidebook to Europe, and these short stays were unbelievably depressing. Censorship prevailed. Newspapers were one note and dull. Motion picture theaters showed cowboy films, and little else. An atmosphere of repression lay heavily over the entire country.

And then in 1981, when a ridiculous army colonel burst into the parliament building, fired shots in the air, and announced that the military was again taking over, the unexpected happened: King Juan Carlos, who had been reared by Franco to be a harmless figurehead, single-handedly put down the revolt and proposed a referendum in which the Spanish were asked to say whether they wanted more of the past or a new and democratic constitution. On the streets of Malaga, where Roberta and I recently walked, bronze reproductions of newspaper front pages in 1982 announcing the turn to democracy are inlaid into the sidewalks. And in 1982, a youthful reformer—Felipe Gonzales—became premier of a liberal and democratic Spain.

This remarkable turnabout—and the almost unbelievable progress which it brought about—happened less than 25 years ago. In that short amount of time, Spain has been transformed.

The current prime minister of Spain, Jose Luiz Rodriguez Zapatero, is the grandson of a captain in the Republican Army of loyalist Spain, who was captured and executed by the army of Franco. He has made a point of educational reform, enacting laws that mandate the teaching of democratic ideals and institutions; he has greatly widened the separation of church and state. Even before Zapatero, Spain had embarked on programs of amnesty for nearly two million illegal immigrants whose presence is vital to the economy of the country, enabling—among other things—the harvesting of olives and oranges and the ever-increasing production of olive oil for a health-conscious world. Attracted to the historic capital of the Hispanic world, many of these immigrants—including several hundreds of thousands of Ecuadorians—are from nations of Latin America, and not simply from North Africa.

In addition to the overall impressions, the highlights of a trip to Madrid are its trio of world-important museums: the newly expanded Prado (with its rooms of Velasquez, Goya, and El Greco, overwhelming in their impact); the modern Centro de Arte Reina Sofía (with the *Guernica*); and the classic collection donated to the state and now known as the Museo Thyssen-Bornemisza. Your knowledge of art history is incomplete until you have visited all three and stood transfixed by paintings acknowledged to be among the greatest of all time.

The Spanish government has now pulled down the city's last remaining statue of dictator Franco. His efforts to stifle the nation's yearnings for free expression, to thwart the modern progress of Spain, have at last been defeated, and you will be exhilarated by a visit to this capital of youth and vigor. If you had thought the life of London, Paris, or Berlin was "cool," wait until you see current-day Madrid.

YOU'LL WANT TO ALERT ANY RETIRED PERSONS TO AN "EXTENDED STAY" BARGAIN IN WINTER ON SPAIN'S MEDITERRANEAN COAST

A decade ago, when oil was selling at $20 a barrel, Orlando-based Sun Holidays was able to offer a 3-week stay at a beachfront resort hotel on the Mediterranean coast of Spain, in wintertime, for as little as $999 per person, including round-trip air from the East Coast of the United States.

Things have changed, and this winter Sun Holidays is offering a shorter 2 weeks on the Mediterranean coast of Spain, including round-trip airfare from New York, for $1,325 per person, still a remarkable value.

These packages, a substitute for a winter vacation in Miami Beach or Phoenix, are available on select days in February and March.

Accommodations? They're at the big beachfront apartment-hotel known as the Sol Timor, where guests receive a studio apartment with private bath, kitchenette, and balcony. Included in the price are daily buffet breakfasts, a farewell dinner, a nonalcoholic open bar, and three sightseeing tours to communities in Andalusia. The airfare, as noted, is from New York, but there are advantageous "add-on" fares from 22 other U.S. cities.

A final lure: There's no single supplement for solo travelers on most departures.

In describing the lure of this unique program, I used to say that low-income retirees had a choice between a shabby, rusting motel in Miami Beach or Phoenix, eating in fast-food restaurants; or an exotic, high-quality stay on the Costa del Sol of Spain, eating off white tablecloths in a proper restaurant. I'm no longer confident that $1,325 per person is necessarily less than some Americans would pay to fly in winter to Miami Beach and rent a motel there for 2 weeks. But $1,325 is still a major value, and you will surely enjoy scanning the literature for this program, which has now been successfully operated for decades. Contact either www.sunholidaytours. com or phone 800/422-8000.

WANNA LEARN SPANISH? CHEAP? SALAMANCA'S THE PLACE.

Like Cambridge, Massachusetts, in the United States, the city of Salamanca (150,000 people) is the major university town of Spain. And there, in a private school charging peanuts—it's called Salmínter—some of the brightest travelers in the world learn to speak Spanish. From the moment you enter your class, weekdays from 9am to 1pm daily, all you hear is Spanish.

Salamanca is an ancient walled city whose recorded history goes back to the 3rd century A.D. It is about 2 hours by train from Madrid, for which the round-trip fare is about $30. Once there, Salmínter charges the Spanish equivalent of $383 (2 hr. a day for 20 weekdays) or $651 (4 hr. a day for 20 weekdays) for a month's worth of classes, but you can limit your participation to 2 weeks, if you wish. Living costs for that month? You can rent a flat (through the school, which will place you) for under $10 a day, or be placed by the school with a Spanish-speaking family (no English whatever) that will house you in a small room and give you three meals a day at their table, for about $27 a day.

For the full details, log on to www.salminter.com.

And why choose Spain for your language learning? Why not Mexico or Costa Rica? When that question is put to me, I answer diplomatically that Mexico is Mexico, but Spain is . . . well, Spain.

IF YOU'RE A NONSTOP TALKER, YOU CAN STAY IN SPAIN FOR FREE

Heard about the Vaughan organization? It teaches English in Spain by inviting unpaid American or British volunteers to spend entire days conversing in English with Spanish business people at various locations. You get full room and board for doing so, but no remuneration, and are expected to perform a vigorous, gregarious role by speaking at length in all sorts of classroom and social situations. Go to www.vaughantown.com for further details on an unusual vacation opportunity that costs you nothing other than your transportation to Spain.

ST. THOMAS, U.S. VIRGIN ISLANDS

ST. THOMAS HAS BEEN CALLED "A SHOPPING MALL FOR CRUISE SHIPS" IN A RECENT SURVEY OF CARIBBEAN PORTS

Kudos to *National Geographic Traveler* for speaking plainly about the current state of the Caribbean islands. If you read its story, "Island Destinations Rated" (Nov/Dec 2006; online at www.nationalgeographic.com/traveler/features/islandsrated0711/islands.html), you'll see the most startling comments on the relative success of various islands in preserving or failing to preserve their local culture and charm in the face of mass tourism. Opinions were apparently obtained from over 500 experts in sustainable tourism and historical preservation, who were bursting to vent their displeasure.

And thus, in rating the island of St. Maarten/St. Martin, *NG Traveler* opines: "The Dutch side is a mess; out of control high-rise and strip development." In talking about the former natural beauty of St. Thomas in the U.S. Virgin Islands, the magazine states that "the pressure of up to 10 cruise ships in a day (almost two million arrivals a year) erases that natural beauty. The native population is unfriendly, with a coldness that borders on outright hostility." And then the report proceeds to characterize St. Thomas as "a shopping mall for cruise ships."

As someone who visited St. Thomas recently, I can confirm that description.

In fairness to the Caribbean, it should be noted that numerous cities in the continental United States would also receive low points from a band of experts in environmental protection. Imagine the comments that could be directed at St. Louis, Detroit, Cleveland, and numerous neighborhoods of New York, Boston, and Hartford, Connecticut. The difference is that the Caribbean relies almost exclusively on tourism, and cannot afford to suffer such criticism.

By the way, among the destinations receiving favorable comments was the little island of Bonaire in the Netherlands Antilles.

STRASBOURG, FRANCE

THE HIGHLIGHT OF MY RECENT CRUISE OF THE RHINE RIVER WAS—CAN YOU GUESS IT? STRASBOURG.

It wasn't Cologne, though Cologne was awesome, and it wasn't Heidelberg, though Heidelberg was another tingling experience. On my recent cruise of the Rhine on a 140-passenger riverboat, the outstanding stop was in Strasbourg, France, where I wished we could have stayed for a much longer time than our 8 or so hours there. The architecture, the food, the culture, the history, all combined to make this charming, canal-filled, Alsatian city the biggest surprise on my most recent trip to Europe.

The city is first a visual delight, with major canals throughout, and a large medieval district known as "Petite France" lined with black-and-white half-timbered buildings preserved from the 1400s and 1500s. It is the historic home of Louis Pasteur, Albert Schweizer, Johannes Gutenberg (he printed his Bible here), and Marcel Marceau. It has a glorious cathedral, almost the equivalent of Cologne's, and sports an astronomical clock that tourists flock to see.

Its history has been a turbulent one, rotating between French and German control (though in France, it is right on the German border). It was annexed to Germany in 1940 at the outset of World War II, and then recovered by France at the end of the war by General LeClerc's French troops. As the capital of French Alsace, it presents a unique and distinctive French/German culture known as Alsatian, with restaurants specializing in such dishes as *choucroute garnie* (sauerkraut, boiled potatoes, and pork).

My wife, Roberta, and I spent the day wandering its quaint districts, enchanted by the medieval quarters and the picturesque canals, looking in on the modern headquarters of numerous agencies of the European Union (which make Strasbourg into a second capital of the E.U., after Brussels), browsing its many bookstores, drinking wine in its cafes. If you've never been there, you might want to include it on your next European visit. It is a stop on almost all cruises of the Rhine.

SWEDEN

INCLUDE SWEDEN IN YOUR NEXT EUROPEAN TRIP—& REACH YOUR OWN CONCLUSIONS

One of my most recent trips was to Sweden, where I spent an enthralling week in the awesomely beautiful city of Stockholm. You may recall that in the early 1990s, Sweden experienced an economic crisis, and numerous American newspapers leaped to proclaim that it was all over with the Swedes, that their social policies were overly generous and, indeed, ruinous. Well that economic crisis lasted, at most, for less than 2 years. Sweden recovered without altering its policies to any great extent, and nowadays you don't hear much about Sweden in the U.S. press—that's because it's doing well. I saw a nation of well-dressed people enjoying a very high standard of living, with total political freedom and cultural diversity. We can learn from Sweden, and you might want to schedule a visit.

Nearly a decade ago, Sweden overcame its own financial crisis and reassumed its path of growing prosperity.

TAMPA, FLORIDA

LOOKING FOR CULTURE IN A WARM-WEATHER STATE? YOU COULDN'T DO BETTER THAN IN THE TAMPA AREA OF FLORIDA.

I'm writing this for people who want to keep their mind active on vacation, but nevertheless want to vacation in a warm-weather state. Though the local tourist authorities in Tampa haven't done much to publicize their cultural attractions, they actually have a remarkable number of worthwhile museums in several fields and fascinating ethnic attractions—enough of them to keep you busy on a 1-week vacation (especially in the museums of neighboring St. Petersburg).

When I talk about Tampa, I really mean the Tampa Bay area, which includes the cities of Tampa (on the northern, inland side of the bay) and St. Petersburg (between the bay and the Gulf of Mexico), along with a whole host of Gulf Coast beaches and islands—from the spring break hot spot of Clearwater to the tree-shaded isolation of Fort De Soto Park.

Tampa itself has (arguably) the region's best aquarium (www.flaquarium. org), the sprawling Hyde Park residential district of 1920s bungalows and Victorian homes shaded by live oaks and palms, the New York Yankees spring training stadium (www.legendsfieldtampa.com), and the nightlife scene of Ybor City (www.ybormuseum.org), a historic Cuban neighborhood of Spanish architecture and defunct brick cigar factories, many now installed with clubs and bars (lending the area a rowdy late-night reputation).

Neighboring St. Petersburg, referred to (only half-jokingly) as the retirement capital of Florida, has easy access to the beaches and, frankly, the better museums. Its Salvador Dali Museum (www.salvadordalimuseum. org) contains the world's largest collection of works by the master surrealist; at the Florida Holocaust Museum (www.flholocaustmuseum.org) many are surprised to learn of the Sunshine State's wartime POW camps for Nazis; and the fine little Museum of Fine Arts (www.fine-arts.org) has a bit of everything from Greek vases to Monet canvases.

Since Tampa is in central Florida, it comes with the required theme park (Busch Gardens; www.buschgardens.com), but also plenty of worthier family attractions where the fun has educational value. These range from the mangrove swamp boardwalk paths of Weedon Island State Preserve (www.stpete.org) to two fantastic hands-on science museums: the Museum of Science and Industry in North Tampa (www.mosi.org) and the somewhat more commercial Great Explorations in St. Pete (www.greatexplorations. org). In this historic corner of Florida, where many of the earliest Spanish explorers of North America landed, there are also the ruins of several colonial-era forts, including De Soto (mentioned above) and Fort Dade on nearby Edgemont Key.

Tampa is a bit of an overlooked sibling lost between Florida's twin tourism powerhouses: the Orlando-area theme park juggernaut, and big city Miami and its Keys. That's a good thing. There are fewer crowds to contend with in Tampa, and it retains a bit more genuine Florida charm. Two fun-in-the-sun vacation packagers do include Tampa in their cut-rate offerings: Southwest Vacations (☎ 800/243-8372; www.southwestvacations.com) and Funjet Vacations (☎ 888/558-6654; www.funjet.com).

TANZANIA

Prior to the outbreak of widespread violence over a disputed election, Kenya was the leading destination for an African safari: Its wildlife is so massive in numbers, and its lodgings and other costs so low, that it supplied excellent, short safaris (5 nights in the actual games parks) for as little as $2,000, including round-trip airfare from the United States to Nairobi.

Though calm has been restored to Kenya, and tourists have returned, some ultracautious tourists still fear a lengthy conflict between various ethnic groups, and therefore look for a substitute. Neighboring Tanzania is regarded as the alternate (the wildlife-rich Serengeti is almost wholly in Tanzania). Most safaris in Kenya already include Tanzania.

The difference between trips to these two countries is largely one of cost. Though airfare from the States is similar, the environmentally sensitive policies of the Tanzanian government have never permitted the massive expansion of tourism that Kenya has encouraged. Fees for visiting its games parks are higher. A 1-week safari to Kenya is likely to cost about $2,500, including airfare; the same trip to Tanzania is likely to cost $3,000 and more.

If you'll go to the Web and type "Tanzania" into your browser, you'll see the available opportunities. The one assurance I can give (based on my own safari experience in Kenya and Tanzania) is that a Tanzania safari will provide the same, breathtaking, almost mystical experience of the world as it was before human beings walked upon it.

The abundance and variety of wildlife in Tanzania is even superior to that of neighboring Kenya and supports a growing safari industry.

TANZANIA IS A GRAND PLACE FOR AN AFRICAN SAFARI, BUT AT A COST SUBSTANTIALLY OVER THE PRICE OF A SAFARI IN KENYA

Two readers from Calumet, Michigan, Bob and Deloris Langseth, have written me about their very positive reactions to Tanzania, and I feel obliged to share their arguments with you:

> We have been to Tanzania on 9 occasions since 1992. It is one of the few countries in Africa that has never had a civil war. . . . You do not need to land at Nairobi. Go instead to the Mt. Kilimanjaro International Airport in Arusha, via KLM. Kilimanjaro is in Tanzania and my wife climbed it at age 72 in 2004. The Ngorogoro Crater—one of the wonders of the world—has all the big 5 animals, is a 4-hour drive from Arusha, and a gateway to the Serengeti. On the way you have Tarangire National Park which has the largest herd of elephants in any of the parks, and Lake Manyara with its vast flocks of flamingos. . . . We have been beautifully served by the Menno Travel Agency in Minneapolis (☎ 800/635-2032; www.mennotravelservice.com) and/or by Safari Makers Ltd.

(☎ **255/27-2544446;** www.safarimakers.com) out of Arusha, Tanzania. We went to the Serengeti in 2007 for our 50th wedding anniversary. The park rangers told us that more than 2 million wildebeest and zebras make the migration. We estimate we saw over a half million animals, along with 23 lions (five were in one tree) as well as a cheetah and leopard. . . . We love Tanzania and want to share this good news of a peaceful country and fabulous game parks.

TOKYO, JAPAN

THE "APARTMENT HOTELS" OF TOKYO ENABLE YOU TO LIVE IN THE JAPANESE CAPITAL AT MODERATE COST

Lots of would-be travelers to Tokyo have heard of the "capsule hotels" charging $40 a night, but aren't willing to encapsulate themselves; they've heard of *ryokan* (Japanese inns) but aren't willing to sleep on the floor.

The remaining budget option is the "apartment hotel" designed for low-spending business travelers. These are often stocked with a minikitchen (cooking for yourself enables you to save a great deal of money in an expensive town, such as Tokyo) and, usually, a washer-dryer. Maid service is slight (towels are changed and garbage is dumped daily, but thorough cleanings come weekly), which is why the rates are so affordable.

Many of these outfits court long-term business guests and have minimum stays of a month, which makes them useless to tourists, but a few welcome visitors of shorter stays. The best option, because guests may stay for as little as a single night, is Tokyu Stay (www.tokyustay.co.jp), with 11 locations sprinkled in busy neighborhoods close to the center of town (including two in neon-splashed Shibuya). Tokyu Stay charges prices starting at $79 per night for one and $123 for two. Internet access is free, and all rooms, which are snug but satisfactory, also have TV and a DVD player. Furniture is basic, but ample, and almost all rooms even have a balcony.

TURKEY

TRAVEL TO TURKEY, ANYONE?

To the surprise of everyone in travel, Turkey enjoyed a near record number of 500,000 American tourists in 2008, more than went there in the heady travel days prior to September 11. And that's as it should be: Turkey is a colorful and friendly destination that receives a grand total of more than 20 million tourists a year.

Ephesus is the Turkish city on the Aegean where Paul preached; its ancient Roman ruins are awesome, a major magnet for tourists.

Among that group, the American tourist is especially valued. Unlike the bulk of European visitors, who buy inexpensive air-and-land packages to Mediterranean and Aegean beach resorts of Turkey, the American seeks out the country's culture and history, and spends far more than the average European. And while the general decline of the American dollar has made Turkey more expensive than before, it remains a moderately priced tourist experience in which family-run boutique hotels are available for $100 to $140 a night per double room, and private "hostels" for cost-conscious tourists can often be had for $20 per person per night.

Turkey Travel Planner (www.turkeytravelplanner.com) now consists of more than 2,000 pages of informative, up-to-date commentary on every aspect of a trip to Turkey. It is a model of what a travel website should be, and I recommend it enthusiastically.

A 2-WEEK TOUR OF TURKEY BECOMES AVAILABLE AGAIN AT UNPRECEDENTED LOW RATES

When it comes to choosing the world's single best travel bargain, Turkey competes with China. The tour operators of Turkey all participate in a 17-day escorted motorcoach tour through western Turkey, with guaranteed weekly departures, all-inclusive arrangements (all meals included), no hidden costs whatsoever—and round-trip fare from the United States. Starting in late November, the price went down to $1,900 per person, which comes to about $125 a day including airfare across the Atlantic.

One of the oldest companies operating this program is Pacha Tours (☎ 800/722-4288; www.pachatours.com), which bills its deal as "Super Value Western Turkey." You'll be missing a big travel opportunity by failing to consider their trip to Istanbul, Gallipoli, Troy, Pergamum, Ephesus, Pamukkale, Antalya, Cappadocia, and Ankara, a spine-tingling assortment of places related to important eras of human history.

VIETNAM

VIETNAM REMAINS A LARGELY UNSPOILED & LOW-COST VACATION & YOU CAN ENJOY 2 WEEKS THERE FOR AN AMAZING $945 PLUS AIRFARE

The decline in American tourism to Vietnam is one of the great mysteries. While nearby China is awash with visitors from the United States, Vietnam—with the same low prices and exotic culture—is a disappointment to most of the tour operators who have ventured to promote it.

In the meantime, Canadian tour operators are continuing to offer and sell packages to Vietnam that remain popular and rival the top values of other Asian locations. G.A.P Adventures of Toronto (☎ 800/708-7761; www.gapadventures.com) operates a superb 2-week itinerary—10 nights in hotels, 2 nights on a sleeper train, 1 night on an overnight boat—that begins in Hanoi and Halong Bay and then goes sweeping down that nation's coast along the Gulf of Tonkin and the South China Sea to Hue, Hoi An (custom-made suits here!), Nha Trang, and Ho Chi Minh City (formerly Saigon). Departures are every week throughout the fall, winter, and spring, in groups limited to 15 persons but averaging 10, and including considerable sightseeing, a tour leader, local guides, and more. These are heavily booked by intellectually curious Americans. The charge is around $1,000 per person, to which you add another $1,000 in airfare from Los Angeles, booked through www.mobissimo.com.

Vietnam. If you have 2 weeks free in the months ahead—what's stopping you?

GET A SUIT MADE IN HOI AN (A LESSER REASON FOR VISITING VIETNAM)

If you're thinking about Vietnam and examining the tours there, you've probably seen a 2- or 3-night stay assigned to the port city of Hoi An, on the South China Sea. And why is everybody going there? Why is the little-known Hoi An often scheduled for the same length of stay as Hanoi or Ho Chi Minh City (the former Saigon)?

It's to permit the American tourist to buy a custom-made suit, or dress, or anything else that can be copied from the pages of *Vogue* or *GQ*. Though the picturesque Hoi An has numerous attractions dating from the medieval era (Buddhist temples and shrines, and much else), it also boasts nearly 100 tailor shops for the overnight manufacture of custom-made suits, dresses, coats, and shoes, for less than a tenth of what you'd spend in the western world ($75 for a custom-made suit). You can go there independently, or you can book an air-and-land package from such companies as General Tours (www.generaltours.com).

WASHINGTON, D.C.

TOUR THE CAPITOL WITH A CONGRESSIONAL AIDE

Although tourism to Washington, D.C., suffered greatly in the immediate months after September 11, it has now recovered with a vengeance, and when you show up at the Capitol building to take a tour, you will often find a line so long that it simply doesn't pay to wait. What many smart travelers do is write a letter to their congressperson or senator, setting forth the dates of their visit and their desire to tour the Capitol building. And lo and behold, most members of Congress will assign a staff member to take you through on an even better tour that goes on to the Senate or House floors when those bodies are not in session, or into conference and hearing rooms.

LEAST EXPENSIVE LODGINGS IN WASHINGTON, D.C.? CAMP OUT AT A VIRTUALLY UNKNOWN NATIONAL PARK.

Looking for cheap digs in Washington, D.C.? Say, something costing only $16 a night for all four of you? Camp out! Stay a night or a weekend in one of the least known of all U.S. national parks—which is Greenbelt Park in Greenbelt, Maryland. Opened to the public many years ago, it is an underused national treasure: a tranquil, wooded park of 1,100 acres, just 12 miles from the White House in downtown D.C., patrolled by the National Park Service, and offering 178 camp sites for tents and RVs (at a charge of $16 per carload of visitors).

You receive amenities other than simply a place to pitch your tent or place your vehicle. There are nature programs for the children, evening campfire events, hiking and biking trails, picnic areas, and full shower and toilet facilities for visitors. Best of all, the entrance to the park is just a few minutes' walk from a Metro stop, allowing you to leave your vehicle in the park (and thus avoid Washington's expensive garages) and take a 10-minute subway ride to all the city's top attractions.

For additional information or to reserve a spot during the park's crowded summer months, call ☎ 877/444-6777, or go to www.recreation.gov.

HEARD OF THOSE BIKES FOR HIRE IN PARIS? A SIMILAR SYSTEM IS NOW AVAILABLE IN WASHINGTON, D.C.

Ever since the capital of France installed a system of bicycle depots scattered about town—enabling visitors or residents to unlock a bike (with the swipe of a credit card) and ride it to the next depot—proposals have been made that the very same system be installed in U.S. cities.

That has now happened, in Washington, D.C., no less. And although the U.S. version isn't quite as widespread or convenient as the one in Paris, it's a start. Currently in the nation's capital, 120 bicycles are available in 10 locations. The program is known as SmartBike DC (www.smartbikedc.com), and an annual membership fee of $40 enables you to check out bikes for 3 hours at a time.

On a recent trip to Seville, Spain, I saw one of these bike systems (numerous cities all over Europe have begun to emulate Paris's Velib program) in action, and was immensely impressed by the way local residents were substituting bikes for other forms of in-city transport. The sponsors of Washington, D.C.'s system hope they will eventually have 1,000 bikes available to you. Explanations about how to use the system are posted near each depot, and as you'd expect, a valid credit card is the key.

Taking its lead from Paris, Washington, D.C., has now launched a program of short-term bicycle rentals from depots all over the city.

Chapter Thirteen

YOU'LL NEED MONEY

GETTING THE CASH, SPENDING IT
RIGHT, GUARDING IT WELL

Though the U.S. dollar has recovered a bit of its strength as I write this, it is still historically low in value against most major currencies. To keep your foreign trip affordable, you will need to be constantly on the alert for better exchange rates and fewer fees and penalties for changing your U.S. dollars into foreign currency.

That attitude of caution in changing money was unnecessary in the days when the dollar was king; everything was then so cheap that you could afford to be casual about the money-changing process. No longer.

The use of ATM machines, the selection of the right credit card for paying your bills, the process of bargaining for better rates—those are the subjects of this chapter.

ATMs

AN ATM IS THE OBVIOUS WAY TO OBTAIN FOREIGN CURRENCY OVERSEAS

It's no longer even arguable. A mass of evidence supports the wisdom of using ATMs overseas for exchange transactions—and never going to a commercial money changer, such as the kiosks found in tourist areas, airports, or railroad stations. Almost all those outlets, as many travelers have confirmed, are liable to sell currency at loan shark rates. Try to exchange British pounds at O'Hare Airport in Chicago or Heathrow in London and you'll encounter currency charges ranging from 8.4% to 16.4%. That would mean that a British pound costing $1.45 could end up costing you as much as $1.68.

By contrast, the usual exchange rate of the ATMs is a reasonable 3% over the amount shown in the newspapers or Internet currency charts. Check the more or less "official" rate of currencies as they appear at www. xe.com, add 3%, and that's approximately the amount you'll pay for your foreign currency. *One warning:* Make sure you have a four-digit PIN for use of your ATM card, as four digits are the only format recognized by most foreign ATMs.

OPEN AN ACCOUNT WITH TD BANK & YOU'LL NO LONGER PAY ATM FEES WHILE TRAVELING AWAY FROM YOUR HOME CITY

But also keep in mind that most ATMs charge a flat fee for their use, if they are not maintained by your own bank. And that fee is an increasingly hefty sum; the former $1 and $1.50 charges have virtually disappeared. Nowadays, it's common for an out-of-network ATM to add a minimum of $2, and often $3 and even up to $4 per transaction. And if you're out of town (and especially overseas), and can't easily find an ATM belonging to your own bank or network, you'll pay those hefty fees every time you use an ATM, incurring a growing expense.

To the rescue comes TD Bank (formerly known as Commerce Bank), a fast-growing chain that's out to be recognized as America's most consumer-friendly bank. It charges no fee for using its ATM card at an out-of-network machine. And if, by chance, you are nevertheless charged such a sum, it will refund the amount when you return home and present your receipt at your local Commerce branch.

BARGAINING

IN TRAVEL, ALL THINGS COME TO THOSE WHO ASK: A WORD ABOUT "BARGAINING"

It actually happened: The newlywed daughter of a friend of mine phoned home to report a tiff with her husband; could she come home right away (for a day or two)? But the cost of a last-minute ticket from her West Coast city would have been a prohibitive $800. So my friend phoned one of the hungrier, less popular airlines, asked to speak with a supervisor, and explained the problem. "We'll call it a 'family crisis fare,'" responded the airline official, who then authorized a waiver of the airline's normal advance purchase rule. And my friend's tearful daughter flew home to mommy and daddy for only $400, round-trip.

"Ask and it shall be given," says the Bible, and nowhere does that admonition work more effectively than in travel. Many thousands of Americans (but still a minority of them) receive substantial travel discounts each year by simply requesting them—from an airline, ship line, or hotel. We realists call the practice "bargaining." Others, more dignified, refer to it as smart consumerism.

To a large number of Americans, bargaining itself—let alone bargaining over travel arrangements—is unthinkable, humiliating, something done only in Persian bazaars. No other travelers regard it as such. You have only to stand in the lobby of a large Venetian hotel during off season, and you will observe one European after another engaged in bargaining. "We are looking for a room that costs no more than 80€," says a very proper Englishman to the front desk clerk. In fact, that tourist knows that there is no such thing as an 80€ room in that hotel; he is bargaining. He is saying, in effect, "We will stay in your hotel if you reduce your rate to 80€; otherwise, we will walk down the block to another hotel."

In other words, you can bargain with dignity; you do not have to act like the proverbial "screaming fishmonger," or as in a tobacco auction. Often, the smartest of travelers will simply call a hotel and bargain over rates by asking if the hotel has a teacher's rate, a student rate, a minister's rate, a civil service rate, a military rate, a corporate rate, a travel agent's rate, an airline employee's rate, whatever.

In actual fact, it does not matter what category you name, and the hotel itself couldn't care less; you could ask for a housewife's rate or a dentists' rate, and still get a discount if the hotel has gaping vacancies that night. What you are doing is bargaining. You are telling the hotel, politely, that you know it is a slow night, that they have plenty of space, and here's their chance to fill an otherwise-empty room by cutting the price to you; otherwise, you will walk down the block.

MORE ABOUT BARGAINING FOR REDUCTIONS IN THE COST OF TRAVEL PRODUCTS

Note that these tactics work only during the off season, or during slow cycles of the week. Most business hotels tend to empty out on weekends, when bargaining can be extremely effective; the same hotels tend to be fully booked from Monday through Thursday nights, when bargaining often doesn't work. And the tactic works only if you are speaking with someone authorized to discount (someone working directly for the hotel), and not with a telephone reservation agent staffing a nationwide toll-free number.

Note, too, that in the United States, where hotels tend to be widely scattered, not clustered, bargaining is best conducted from a nearby phone booth, by a phone call from the airport on arrival, or by a long-distance call from your home before you leave on the trip. The hotel then knows that you are easily able to make a call to another hotel, if they don't accede to your request. Usually, bargaining doesn't work if you are already in the hotel lobby; then the desk clerk knows it's unlikely that you will walk out and travel the long distance to another hotel if they refuse the discount.

Does bargaining work for travel products other than hotel rooms? You bet it does. Although charter flights are no longer as frequently operated as they once were, they still provide a good example of how effective bargaining can be. In my years as a charter tour operator (remember Arthur Frommer Charters, Inc.?), I sent young staff members to see off our flights at the airport; they were not simply authorized, but *directed,* to sell off, on the spot, up to minutes before departure, any remaining unsold seats, for any price that did not injure our dignity. If a bargainer, making a sudden appearance, offered $59 for the one-way crossing to London leaving in 20 minutes, we'd stamp off in righteous indignation; if they offered $99, that was another matter.

Some more prudent travelers would phone our office on the day before a charter's departure to ask whether there were still empty seats to be had for a song. While we could not also provide them with hotel space at that late date, we'd welcome the calls as a means of squeezing out a few last dollars of income from the flight. To my knowledge, a great many hard bargainers continue to make such calls to tour operators or consolidators who have committed themselves to blocs of air tickets, and would rather cut the price on unsold space than suffer empty seats.

The travel industry consists of perishable products (seats, rooms, cabins, cars) that must be sold for a particular departure or on a particular date, or else their value is lost forever. It is clearly better to receive some income for such a product, rather than none. And that is why most travel suppliers will react positively to your requests for a discount, if they sense you are "shopping" for value, and will turn to an alternative supplier if they fail to grant the requested discount.

Ask and it shall be given. More often than you'd suspect.

CREDIT CARDS

A NUMBER OF AIRLINE & HOTEL CREDIT CARDS ARE REALLY QUITE VALUABLE; WE START WITH CARDS ISSUED BY CHASE

If you're like me, you are constantly receiving offers to own an airline- or hotel-related credit card. Don't just toss them in the garbage. Signing up for such a card from such banks as Chase or Citibank is often an easy way to score a free flight or hotel stay, so long as you understand the rules.

And if you've never received such an offer, don't despair. Anyone can sign up for these cards and earn points for each dollar spent, and more importantly, get free bonuses that can be traded in for travel right away. Under "Travel Rewards" at the website for Chase (www.chase.com), Visa cards are listed with affiliations to such companies as Continental Airlines, Marriott, United Airlines, and Southwest Airlines.

The most straightforward rewards are available through Chase's hotel credit cards. After receiving approval for a Marriott Rewards Visa Signature Card, customers get one free e-night certificate, which can be traded in for a stay at one of the company's midlevel brands such as Fairfield Inn, Courtyard, or SpringHill Suites. After making a first purchase with the card, the customer receives 15,000 bonus points, which will grant another free night at similar properties. What's more, the card has no annual fee for the first year, though afterwards they tack on approximately $30 annually.

Rewards from Chase's airline-affiliated cards are more complicated, mostly because the airline reward programs themselves are more complicated. The Continental card, for example, gives 15,000 miles after the first purchase. For most domestic flights, however, Continental requires at least 20,000 miles. The United card comes with a 17,500-mile bonus, a bit short of the 25,000 miles required for a typical domestic reward ticket.

But here's a caution: All airline- and hotel-affiliated credit cards carry unusually high interest rates, often over 18%. They work only if you immediately pay your monthly charges when due and never go into debt. Got it?

A QUICK GLANCE AT THE AIRLINE- & HOTEL-RELATED CREDIT CARDS ISSUED BY CITIBANK

Chase's competitor, Citibank, is just as active in the field of airline/hotel-related credit cards.

At www.citicards.com, similar cards are available with bonuses at American Airlines and Hilton Hotels. The American Airlines AAdvantage card, which has no annual fee for the first year, comes with 20,000 bonus points once the customer has spent $750 in the first 4 months. That puts the traveler well on his or her way to the 25,000 points required for most domestic flights. A 15,000-point bonus kicks in after an initial purchase with the Hilton card, translating to a free night in many of the company's fine Hampton Inn brand properties.

But there are many things to be wary of before signing up for a new credit card. Cards with good travel rewards tend to have extraordinarily high annual percentage rates (APR), often over 18% (around 10% is more reasonable). Don't bother signing up for such a card if you're not the type to pay off your monthly bill in full and on time. The goal is to get your bonus points and redeem them on a trip as soon as possible—without incurring a high-interest-rate debt.

Finally, before signing up for a card through Chase or Citibank, visit the affiliated hotel or airline website, where sometimes the bonuses and terms are superior. A link from www.marriott.com, for instance, offered the same Chase airline card I described above, but with 20,000 bonus points, 5,000 more than at www.chase.com.

ARE THE CREDIT CARDS ISSUED BY CAPITAL ONE THE BEST FOR TRAVELERS?

Call me naive, but I'm impressed by the features relating to travel in the Capital One credit cards marketed all over the country by Capital One of Salt Lake City. At a time when nearly every issuer of Visas and MasterCards is taking a 3% chunk of every transaction for which you use the card overseas to make a foreign currency purchase (Visa and MasterCard take 1%, to which the bank issuer adds 3%, even though those banks perform no service at all), Capital One makes a point of claiming that it charges no "foreign transaction fee." In other words, it doesn't charge the 3%!

Beyond that, Capital One awards you a mile of frequent-flier privileges for every dollar you spend using the card—and those miles are yours for the life of the account; they never expire as long you use the card. And finally, all the interest and other terms of the card seem highly competitive, indeed advantageous, and you have no membership fee to pay.

Obviously, those generous policies can be withdrawn by Capital One at any time. I'm keeping my fingers crossed. If you're game to try them, you can obtain a Capital One card by writing to Capital One Card Center, P.O. Box 30284, Salt Lake City, UT 84130-9842.

REJOICE! THERE'S A FINE WEBSITE DEVOTED TO UNDERSTANDING CREDIT CARD FEES & FOREIGN CURRENCY TRANSACTIONS.

Finally, there's a site that does all the hard work when it comes to one of the most dreadfully dull yet vital subjects in travel: crunching the numbers and digging through the details of credit card foreign transaction fees, currency exchange rates, and other money-handling issues.

Travel Guide for Your Finances (www.travelfinances.com), maintained by an American expat living in Europe for more than a decade, is part resource guide and part blog about the issues of travel finances.

On the resources side, there are charts comparing the various fees for major credit card–issuing banks, links to current currency exchange information, details on dozens of different credit cards and their rewards schemes, lists of fees charged by issuers of ATM cards, and definitions of the various legal and monetary mumbo-jumbo relating to foreign charges and transactions that one encounters on credit cards and bank statements.

It could be a bit better organized, but at least it is chock-full of good information to help you make more informed decisions when choosing a credit card to use on your travels.

Chapter Fourteen

PROBLEMS, PITFALLS & CONTROVERSIES

MY TIRADES ABOUT TRAVEL, IN A NUMBER OF FIELDS

If you feel deeply about travel, as I do, then you have strong opinions about travel—and about the public policies that affect travel. From the outset of my career, I've been expressing those opinions without let-up and regarding travel as a subject worthy of serious discussion.

The people who look on travel as a mere recreation are often surprised to discover controversial viewpoints in travel journalism. I've been admonished by newspaper editors over the years to "get off the carrot juice kick," to "lighten up," to "leave the soapbox," to "go along." As you will see from the essays in this chapter, I've resisted that advice—and hope that you will appreciate a serious approach to travel, whether you agree with my particular views or not.

AMERICAN VACATION TIME

AN INCREASE IN THE AMOUNT OF VACATION TIME IS UNFINISHED BUSINESS OF OUR DEMOCRACY

The recent disclosure (in a study performed by Harris Interactive for Expedia) that only 14% of all Americans take vacations as long as 14 days, is a startling bit of news that should cause us to ponder the quality of life in our nation.

Alone among the prosperous, industrialized countries, we have no laws whatever guaranteeing a single day of vacation time to anyone. Faced with a paltry average of 2 weeks or $2^1/_2$ weeks a year of vacation granted voluntarily by our employers, we carefully divide that time into 3-day weekends scattered throughout the year. Eighty-six percent of our population never knows what it means to enjoy a sustained period of leisure, rest, and contemplation. Eighty-six percent of parents and children spend no substantial time interacting as a family.

Meantime, several European countries guarantee a minimum of 5 weeks of paid leave to their working population. And many of the people in those countries enjoy vacation time, in practice, of as many as 7 weeks each year. My nephew, who lives in France, takes as many as 3 weeks of vacation in winter, which he adds to the entire month of August when he and his family travel to an island in the Mediterranean and check into an inexpensive beachside hotel without television, telephones, computer access, or radio. And there he, his wife, and his two children enjoy a month together that undoubtedly provides the most cherished memories of their lives. Returning to work refreshed, he is one of the most productive employees of his firm.

Preceding page: Despite its considerable appeal, none of us should visit Burma (Myanmar) as long as its thuggish military regime is in power.

Now, I am aware of the arguments that are used to oppose legislation that would guarantee decent amounts of vacation time to the American people: interference with business, a blow to the sacred rights of property and contract, a burden on American productivity, a decline in our standard of living. They are the same arguments that were once arrayed against the abolition of child labor and the enactment of fair labor laws. As a young law student years ago, I had occasion to read the 19th-century arguments against abolishing child labor, and they were identical—word for word the same as today's debating points against increasing vacation time.

You may recall that the courts actually overturned statutes prohibiting child labor as "unconstitutional."

We've come a long way since those days. We now have a federal Wages and Hours Act which mandates the 40-hour week and time-and-a-half pay for overtime. We have a minimum wage law that interferes in the most beneficial manner with business and free enterprise. We have statutes requiring safe working places, and prohibiting racial, gender, and age discrimination in employment. How great a leap is it to pass a law requiring that every American engaged in interstate commerce should enjoy a minimum of 3 weeks per year of paid leave? Even that paltry an extension of our rights would bring humanity into our work lives, and cause a skyrocketing improvement in the quality of our lives.

An increase in vacation time is among the unfinished business of our democracy. It is something to propose to the new Congress that took office in January.

THE UNITED STATES IS NOW LAST IN THE WORLD (& TIED WITH CHINA) IN PROVIDING VACATION TIME TO ITS CITIZENS

Our friends at Wikipedia have recently compiled a list of the minimum vacation time guaranteed by law in various countries around the world. As you scan those names, keep in mind that in the United States, not a single statute on either the federal or state level guarantees so much as a single day of vacation time to any American.

Here's a truncated copy of the list. Read it and weep.

> Austria: 7 weeks (and 8 weeks for elderly employees)
> Belgium: 4 weeks
> Brazil: 1 month
> Bulgaria: 4 weeks
> Croatia: 3⅔ weeks
> Czech Republic: 4 weeks
> Denmark: 6 weeks

European Union: 4 weeks (and obviously more in some countries)

Finland: 7 weeks

France: 5 weeks

Germany: 4 weeks

Greece: 4 weeks

Hungary: 4 weeks

Ireland: 4 weeks

Italy: 4–6 weeks

Latvia: 4 weeks

Netherlands: 4 weeks

New Zealand: 4 weeks

Norway: 5 weeks

Poland: 4 weeks (but 5 weeks after 10 years of employment)

Portugal: 4½ weeks

Romania: 4 weeks

Spain: 4 weeks

Sweden: 5–6 weeks, depending on age

Tunisia: 6 weeks

Ukraine: Up to 5 weeks

China: It provides no guaranteed vacation time to its citizens, just like the United States. And yet China's ruling council has recently announced it is about to enact guarantees for at least a week's vacation. Here in the United States, we continue to do nothing. Hopefully, the new Congress might—it just might—bring America into step with the rest of the civilized world.

BOYCOTTS

EACH OF US—& NOT OUR GOVERNMENT—MUST MAKE A PERSONAL DECISION AS TO WHERE WE WILL TRAVEL

Throughout the many long years when Nelson Mandela was in prison, and cruel apartheid reigned, I refused to travel to the Union of South Africa, refused to write about it, refused to promote it in any way.

This was a personal decision on my part. Had our government forbidden such travel, I think I would have been on the next plane there. Travel, to me, is a First Amendment right, a vital means by which we review the foreign policy of our nation, reach our own decisions about world affairs, educate ourselves. In peacetime, our government, in my view, has no more right to tell us where we may travel than it has the right to stop us from attending a lecture or reading a book.

So each of us must reach a personal decision about traveling to particular nations. We must weigh whether such travel helps or hurts the dissidents in countries where liberties are curtailed, whether it will have an impact on the policies of other nations. In South Africa, it had such an impact and, combined with economic sanctions, it brought about a historic change in the lot of oppressed people. In other countries, and for other reasons, the opposite course can keep an authoritarian government more tolerant, less oppressive. To an outsider, such decisions may seem inconsistent. But in the last analysis, each of us must make these travel decisions according to our own lights.

Now is the time to support a touristic boycott of Burma (Myanmar)

Shockingly enough, several major U.S. tour operators continue to operate trips to Myanmar, despite pleas not to do so by the country's democratically elected leader, the Nobel Prize–winning Aung San Suu Kyi. On occasion after occasion, Kyi has emphatically stated that such visits simply support the brutal, thuggish military junta that now rules Myanmar.

Kyi has been under house arrest in Rangoon for 13 of the last 19 years and is currently allowed no access to visitors or even use of the telephone.

If you live in one of the many U.S. cities whose newspapers carry no mention of the events in Myanmar, then I urge you to go online and read about them in back issues of such magazines as the *Economist* or such papers as the *New York Times*. In a country whose citizens become more impoverished and oppressed with every year, conditions have apparently reached the breaking point, with monks leading the public in massive demonstrations, the last one being an astonishing march by many thousands, followed by the brutal repression of that movement through the jailing of thousands and the killing of many. This was the first public protest that Myanmar's grotesque military government was unable in advance to repress.

As noted above, Kyi has made it crystal clear that tourism aids the junta and helps keep them in power. She has pleaded with the travel industry not to send visitors. We should heed that persistent request. Next time you see a brochure or website advertising a visit to Myanmar, you should contact the tour operator and express your disgust over such business-as-usual greed.

The most prominent operators of tours to Myanmar appear to be Pacific Delight Tours (www.pacificdelighttours.com), Abercrombie & Kent (www.

abercrombiekent.com), Travcoa (www.travcoa.com), General Tours (www.generaltours.com), Sita (www.sitatours.com), Value World (www.vwtours.com), and Canada's G.A.P Adventures (www.gapadventures.com). I met recently with the president of G.A.P Adventures and have now sent him an urgent e-mail, pleading that he cease disregarding the pleas of the democratic opposition in Burma (Myanmar).

I would hope that readers will join me in sending similar communications to the companies named above.

SOME NATIONS ARE SO REVOLTING IN THEIR CONDUCT THAT I WOULDN'T DREAM OF VISITING THEM

Let's talk about Libya. Its supreme leader, Colonel Qaddafi, has now "accepted responsibility" for the monsters who blew up Pan Am Flight 103, causing the deaths of 270 persons, including 35 students from Syracuse University and several children under 5. For being such a good sport about it, candidly acknowledging responsibility, and paying compensation, he and his country have been readmitted to the family of nations. Cruise lines and tour operators are currently scrambling to offer visits there.

It gets worse. More than a decade ago, Libya arrested five Bulgarian nurses and one Palestinian doctor and condemned them to death for having allegedly injected the HIV virus into child patients in a Libyan hospital. Why and for what reason the nurses would do such a thing was never

I personally would never dream of setting foot in Colonel Qaddafi's Libya, and I am appalled over the decision of leading cruise lines to visit it.

explained, and yet they were kept on death row in Libya for the ensuing 10 years, all the while protesting their innocence.

Libya's Supreme Court eventually commuted these sentences to life imprisonment, which over time resulted in the nurses' release to Bulgarian authorities (the commutation was brought about through the payments of hundreds of millions of dollars by nations of the European Community). But even though they escaped execution, should the rest of us forget their 10-year ordeal? And should any of us travel within a country that is capable of such conduct? What tourist is safe from being made the object of a similar, wholly illogical trial and conviction on totally trumped-up charges?

Because Libya supports the Arab boycott of Israel, it also will not permit persons with Israeli visas in their passports to enter the country; over the years, such persons have simply remained aboard ship during port calls in Libya. Now Libya has gone further, announcing that it will not permit a ship to enter Libyan territorial waters if it is carrying passengers who have Israeli visas in their passports, whether or not they remain on board. Based on this ban, the famous P&O Cruises of Great Britain, which is now owned by Carnival Cruises, has ejected passengers from P&O cruises that were scheduled to stop in Libya on sailings through the Mediterranean. In England, there's a controversy raging in the press about British citizens Bernard and Irene Rose, who were ousted from the cruise they had booked because it was planning to stop at a Libyan port, among other ports in the Mediterranean. They were refused a refund by the line, but offered a later sailing that did not stop in Libya.

The founder of Carnival Cruises, which owns 74% of P&O, was the late Ted Arison, who retired to Israel to die. His son, Micky Arison, currently head of the line, pays enthusiastic attention to the Miami Heat, the basketball team he owns. I do not know whether he is aware of the Libyan policy and his own cruise line's acquiescence in it. Shouldn't we all send him a letter?

SHOULD KANAB, UTAH, BE ADDED TO THE PLACES WE SHOULDN'T VISIT?

The city council of Kanab, Utah, a town that lives off the tourism of Americans passing through to visit Bryce, Zion, and Grand canyons, took deliberate steps 2 years ago to announce, in effect, that homosexual Americans are not entitled to be treated like all Americans, are not to enjoy the basic human rights of which the Founding Fathers spoke when they declared "that all men are created equal."

They did this by passing a so-called "natural family" resolution that had been circulated without success to more than 240 other Utah communities, every one of which refused to adopt legislation that sent a message of hatred to the homosexuals who are our fellow citizens. Without soliciting the viewpoints of their community, or even explaining why a city council should pass judgment on such personal matters, the city council rubber-stamped a document which defined a worthy family in Kanab as solely including a child-bearing man and stay-at-home woman "with a full quiver of children." Excluded, in addition to homosexuals, were thus single mothers, adoptive parents, foster parents, childless couples, grandparents raising their grandchildren, persons who decide not to have children, and other groupings of perfectly worthwhile Americans.

I have received anguished letters from operators of businesses and other prominent residents of Kanab pointing out that they do not share the prejudicial viewpoints of the majority members of their city council. A group of business owners signed a petition to me asking that I not advocate a travel boycott of Kanab and thus injure residents who had no part in the passage of the hate resolution. All of them voice a determination to ultimately replace the city council members who voted for the "natural family" resolution.

But if the rest of us adopt business-as-usual, let-sleeping-dogs-lie attitudes towards Kanab, it is probable that the ire of Kanab's majority will subside and nothing will be done. I for one will not travel to Kanab, or stay in Kanab, until this homophobic "natural family" resolution is rescinded, and I urge all right-thinking Americans to withdraw their own travel patronage until that happens.

ETHICAL TRAVEL

IN OUR DESIRE TO TRAVEL IN A CORRECT ENVIRONMENTAL MANNER, LET'S NOT FORGET THE NEED TO TRAVEL IN AN ETHICAL MANNER

It is altogether proper that we should do all we can to prevent travel from contributing to global warming, that we should also travel in a manner that does not do ecological damage. But we should not permit these concerns to blot out the need to travel in an ethical manner as well. To that end, I'd like to quote a "Code of Ethics for Tourists" that was widely circulated several years ago, and remains valid today:

1. Travel in a spirit of humility and with a genuine desire to learn more about the people of your host country.

2. Cultivate the habit of listening and observing, rather than merely hearing and seeing.

3. Realize that often the people in the country you visit have time concepts and thought patterns different from your own. This does not make them inferior, only different.

4. Instead of looking for that "beach paradise," discover the enrichment of seeing a different way of life, through other eyes.

5. Acquaint yourself with local customs. What is courteous in one country may be quite the reverse in another—people will be happy to help you.

6. Instead of the Western practice of "knowing all the answers," cultivate the habit of asking questions.

7. Remember that you are only one of thousands of tourists visiting this country and so do not expect special privileges.

8. If you are looking for a "home away from home" when you travel, don't spend more extravagantly than you would at home.

9. When you are shopping, remember that you may be getting a bargain only because of the low wages paid to the person who actually made the product.

10. Do not make promises to people in your host country unless you can carry them through.

11. Spend time reflecting on your daily experience in an attempt to deepen your understanding. It has been said that "what enriches you may rob and violate others."

EUROPE'S LESSONS FOR TRAVELERS

WHAT RECENT TRIPS TO GERMANY & SWITZERLAND CAN TEACH THE TRAVELER

Prior to making a recent trip, I hadn't been to Germany and Switzerland for more than 5 years. I was fascinated to find many changes.

First and foremost, both nations have become multiethnic in composition to an extent that would not have been imaginable years ago. Nearly 10% of the German population is now foreign-born, something you will experience first-hand as you stroll the city streets. Yet, although certain nativist political parties have sprung up in Germany and Switzerland, I saw no clear evidence of any major anti-immigrant feelings of the Lou Dobbs/ Michael Savage/Rush Limbaugh variety.

Instead, I saw new forms of political advocacy. The Green Party in Germany and Switzerland is more powerful now, and their posters and appeals for votes are everywhere. Even more surprising is evidence of an emerging Women's Party in Switzerland—a feminist movement that has taken political form and whose vote-for-us posters were everywhere on the streets of Lucerne. Will wonders never cease!

It is clear, as well, that after considerable worry in Germany about the state of its economy—concerns that caused the defeat of the Socialists and the election of Angela Merkel—the economy of Germany is once again booming. And although Merkel has made small (almost insignificant) cuts in the welfare payments and guarantees, no one is speaking any longer of any major shift away from the strong safety net enjoyed by every German (free medical care, extraordinary retirement and unemployment benefits). The same is reportedly true in Switzerland, whose currency is now so strong that it sells at par to the U.S. dollar. Although the people with whom I spoke may not be representative of all strata of German and Swiss society (these were mainly English speaking), they all seemed somewhat smug about how well their country is doing. Germany, in particular, is now the largest country in Europe (with over 80 million people) and certainly the most influential, ousting Britain from that position.

When a speaker at a lecture I attended sought to talk about a "typical" German family (husband, wife, and two children), he cited as their average earnings: 40,000€ a year. That, dear friends, is the equivalent of $60,000, which compares favorably with the median family income in the United States of $43,000. We are no longer the richest nation in the world.

As for being on the cutting edge, Lucerne bus stops are now equipped with electric signs that tell you exactly when your bus will arrive. And when you board the bus, an electric sign tells you when you will arrive at your stop. Public facilities, even on trains, are modern, comfortable, and well maintained. Sensitive attention is paid to the environment. In many hotel corridors, hotel rooms, and even public bathrooms, the lights are out when no one is there, and the lights go on only when a person enters.

It's been interesting and instructive to return to such highly developed countries. We really should make greater investments in our own infrastructure and public facilities.

EXCESS TRAVEL SPENDING

VULGARITY KNOWS NO BOUNDS: AROUND THE WORLD FOR $114,000 PER COUPLE IN A BIG JET CONFIGURED TO SEAT ONLY 88 PERSONS

Although I am not an alumnus of Columbia University, I am on their mailing list for travel deals, and last week's delivery brought a whopper: a 3-week around-the-world trip by private jet for $114,000 per couple (or $56,950 per person, double occupancy). The trip will depart from Fort Lauderdale on February 2, 2009, returning on February 25. Columbia's alumni will share the specially configured Boeing 757 with alumni or members of the University of Georgia, the University of Connecticut, and the National Trust for Historic Preservation. (For further information, phone the Columbia University Travel Study Program at ☎ 866/325-8664.)

There are expenditures so excessive as to be grossly vulgar—and this is one of them. $114,000 would fund a year's college studies for at least three deserving young people—and still leave enough left over for a normal around-the-world trip. $114,000 would fund preschool education for dozens of deserving young children, provide considerable housing for the homeless, fund a major meals-on-wheels program in cities on the brink of discontinuing that assistance, provide thousands of AIDS treatments in a developing country, perform a dozen other worthy social tasks. Although none of us would deny well-off people the right to engage in pleasant, comfortable recreation, isn't there a point at which excessive luxury spending becomes obscene?

The eminent administrators of Columbia University, in my view, should hang their heads in shame. Or is this one of those issues that we're no longer supposed to discuss?

ISSUES

FOR WHAT CONCEIVABLE REASON DO WE CONTINUE TO PERMIT CORPORATE JETS TO FILL UP OUR DANGEROUSLY OVERCROWDED SKIES?

They account for 10% of all air traffic in the country as a whole. In certain limited areas of America, they account for nearly 30% of all air traffic. Their numbers are constantly growing, as fractional jets, charter jets, and air taxis join the fleets already owned and operated by the Fortune 500 corporations. They, the sleek private jets, are especially favored by hedge-fund executives, those privileged gents paying tax rates of only 15% on their salaries and therefore awash with money.

They are flown by people on ego trips. Each one of their two or three passengers could easily have reached their destination on a commercial flight carrying hundreds of passengers. And on those flights, they nevertheless could have traveled in the comfort they demand, occupying first-class seats and imbibing double martinis.

Even if their own company's jet could have gotten them to their destinations an hour or two earlier—so what? How many of these flights are really necessary? How many of them simply satisfy a desire to get out of the office, and play a round of golf? How many of these meetings could have been held by conference call? And even for a necessary business purpose, couldn't these corporate plutocrats have swallowed their pride and flown commercial?

The impact of the corporate jet upon the crisis of our air transportation is a taboo topic of travel journalism. I have rarely seen it discussed in any media. Among the frantic steps recently taken to ease the pile-up of planes, no one ever seems to suggest that corporate flights carrying two or three passengers should give way to commercial flights carrying 200 passengers.

An article last Thanksgiving in the *New York Times* painted a frightening picture of the perils faced in our daily air traffic. The newspaper sent a reporter to the Federal Aviation Administration Strategic Command Center in Herndon, Virginia, who witnessed the desperation of air traffic controllers as they delayed takeoffs and diverted flights, stranding thousands of passengers at airports, to reduce the numbers of planes in the sky. Among the airports saturated by air traffic were those in Teterboro, New Jersey, and White Plains, New York, "used by hundreds of corporate time-share and charter jets."

"Corporate, charter and time-share planes are smaller on the runway," reported the *Times,* "but appear nearly the same size on a radar screen."

"A plane is a plane is a plane," said an air traffic official, referring to the smaller corporate jets, "and you have to keep them separated by five miles."

When will the taboo topic be brought into the open? When will we face up to the probability that it is no longer possible to permit CEOs to enjoy their ego trips at the expense of the rest of us? When will we demand that people, regardless of their riches, should fly on efficient, commercial, passenger jets?

Enforcement of consumer rights has come to a virtual end at today's Department of Transportation

Last year at the federal Department of Transportation (DOT), the agency that enforces a great many regulations designed to protect our rights as "aviation consumers," the Enforcement Division was down to a staff of 31, 10 fewer than the already pitiful group of 41 persons who used to perform that task several years ago. Meantime, the number of annual consumer complaints directed to the DOT soared to nearly 9,000, or just about 300 for each staff member able to investigate them. With only 31 persons on duty, the number of actual cases brought against the airlines and tour operators fell to 25. And thus the airlines no longer had any reason to show a sensitive regard for passengers' rights. They knew that nothing would happen to them if they didn't.

Today, it is mainly when airlines and other travel companies have some fear of government action that they act to do right by the consumer. The consumer has become a minor cog in the equation.

If you are represented in Congress by people sensitive to these issues, you should alert them to pay attention to the budget for the Department of Transportation. Does that budget include increased funds for expansion of the department's enforcement office? A member of Congress is entitled to ask those questions—and should ask them. And an administration which occasionally makes a public point of its concern for the public should take steps to expand the D.O.T.'s bureau of enforcement—now that the flimsy nature of its consumer protection has been exposed.

A modest proposal, this time for an Airline Passenger Bill of Rights tracking a code of conduct for some friends of ours

Our air travel system is so woefully overextended, overcrowded, and technologically outdated that President Bush took the unusual step of opening up military air corridors to ease travel during the Thanksgiving holiday travel period, traditionally the most heavily traveled time of the year.

This was, of course, a temporary Band-Aid on a system that needs surgery on several fronts, from antiquated air traffic control systems to over-capacity airports.

Here is a list of measures that might well be adopted by the airlines:

- Provide transportation that reduces undue stress caused by overcrowding, excess time in transit, or improper handling during loading and unloading.
- Observe passengers to ensure that basic needs are being met.
- Provide adequate food, water, and care to protect the health and well-being of passengers.
- Promote the well-being of passengers by keeping up-to-date on advances and changes in the industry.
- Persons who willfully mistreat passengers will not be tolerated.

Now, replace each appearance of the word "passengers" above with the word "animal" or "livestock," and you have five of the nine rights enshrined in the Producer Code of Cattle Care adopted by the National Cattlemen's Beef Association.

That's right: In America we guarantee better treatment of animals being sent to the slaughterhouse than we do human passengers on airplanes. As for me, I won't even insist on still another provision of the cattle code, that our herd be provided with protection from disease and access to veterinary care.

LOOK OUT FOR TOUR OPERATORS WHO OMIT HEFTY FUEL SURCHARGES FROM ADVERTISED PRICES

Several Internet tour operators offer marvels of pricing in their air-and-land packages to Europe. And when you proceed to actually book their packages, the final sum is only slightly higher than the advertised price. That final sum has been increased by only a small amount for taxes and landing fees.

A number of other irresponsible tour companies create the appearance of competitive prices by excluding from their advertised price the hefty fuel surcharge that all airlines now impose for a transatlantic crossing. When you book the packages of these scamps, you suddenly discover that the actual price is at least $200 to $300 more than you anticipated.

Don't fall for this approach to pricing. Look immediately to learn if the fuel surcharge is included in the price that attracted you to the package. It adds significantly to the cost of your trip.

IT'S INCREASINGLY APPARENT THAT THOSE HUNDRED MILLION INTERNET VOTES CAST FOR THE "SEVEN NEW WONDERS OF THE WORLD" WERE INAPPROPRIATELY INFLUENCED

When it was announced in 2008 that Chichén Itzá in Mexico, Petra in Jordan, and the *Christ the Redeemer* statue in Rio de Janeiro had been included in the "Seven New Wonders of the World," I smelled something fishy. *Christ the Redeemer* is neither a great work of art nor even especially colossal when compared, say, with the Statue of Liberty. Chichén Itzá in Mexico's Yucatan? Petra in Jordan? Neither has the importance or monumentality of Angkor Wat in Cambodia, the Eiffel Tower, and certainly not the great Pyramids of Egypt.

An explanation was forthcoming when a reporter discovered that corporations in Brazil had spent tens of millions in rounding up Internet votes for the *Christ the Redeemer* statue by citizens of Brazil. In Jordan, which has a population of 7 million people, 14 million votes were counted for Petra. It was obvious—and the Swiss foundation sponsoring the voting has never denied—that safeguards were not in place to prevent duplicate voting.

In the years ahead, the newly designated "Seven New Wonders of the World" (Christ the Redeemer, Chichén Itzá, Machu Picchu, Petra, the Great Wall of China, the Taj Mahal, and Rome's Colosseum) will be touted to the world as absolute must-sees. We'll know better.

DO TOURISTS HAVE A RESPONSIBILITY TO SHOW RESPECT FOR THE CITY THEY'RE VISITING? VENICE SAYS "YES."

As reported by Reuters, the city of Venice—which struggles to handle 20 million annual visitors—has gotten so fed up with misbehaving tourists it has instituted an Office of Decorum to oversee new rules of behavior, fielded a squad of "hostesses" to explain and enforce them, and, if necessary, call a police officer to hand out fines to offenders ranging from $70 to $700.

Some of the rules follow common sense, such as no littering and no undressing in public. Other rules stem from Venice's unique nature: no riding bicycles in the city (narrow streets and countless little bridges make this impractical anyway), and no swimming or dipping of feet in the canals (which anyone who realizes that the canals double as Venice's public sewer system would never dream of doing).

The most worrisome rule—the direct result of tourists who have abused the hospitality of this lovely city—is that there is to be no lying down in public places and no sitting or lingering on the street. This is understandable in a city with streets barely a shoulder's width apart, where one must frequently turn sideways to sidle past oncoming pedestrians, but it's still a bit draconian. What, after all, constitutes "lingering"? How long can I admire a church facade before being asked to move along?

The saddest of the new rules is no picnicking except in designated areas. There was a time when one of the joys of Venice was to shop at the Rialto Market or from floating barges for fruits and vegetables, head to little grocery stores for delicious meats and cheeses, grab a bottle of wine, and then sit on the stony edge of a quiet canal to enjoy a picnic fit for a doge. It's apparently not the picnicking itself that the Venetians find offensive, but the littering and the fact that some visitors chose their picnic spots poorly and became traffic hazards.

Enough boorish tourists have treated Venice like a spring break beach to ruin it for the rest of us. Now, even mindful tourists who pick up after themselves cannot enjoy a canal-side picnic, and if you choose to sit unobtrusively on the steps of a Renaissance church just to watch the carnival of Venetian life spin past, you can be asked to leave or face a fine.

CAN TOURISM TO FORT LAUDERDALE SURVIVE THE PREJUDICE OF ITS MAYOR?

From an office whose walls are lined with framed photographs of Karl Rove and Ann Coulter (there's a role model!), the mayor of Fort Lauderdale, Florida, Jim Naugle, has been issuing anti-gay statements that have frightened members of his own administration into believing he is gravely damaging tourism to Fort Lauderdale. In response, the Tourism Development Council of Broward County unanimously ousted Naugle as one of its commissioners. Since approximately 10% of all visitors to Fort Lauderdale are gay, the council felt that they could not be seen as condoning Mayor Naugle's remarks, which have already caused several gay groups to call for a tourism boycott and cancel their visits to the city.

Among other statements issued by him, Naugle has said that the city should rethink its policy of marketing itself to gays because of the incidence of the HIV virus among gays. He has condemned the use of a city building for a gay library, said that homosexuals should not be called "gay" because they are "unhappy," claimed there was rampant gay sex in public restrooms, and made other remarks regarded as offensive by the gay community.

The issue here is whether all Americans are entitled to be treated with respect, free from discrimination, prejudice, or slander. I, for one, applaud the Broward County Tourism Council for distancing itself from Naugle, and suggest that the mayor of a city heavily dependent on tourism should be more respectful of the visitors who go there. Would anyone have condoned similar attacks on Jews, Catholics, Mormons, Asians, Hispanics, or Native Americans? (A bright note: Naugle leaves office in mid-2009.)

THE PREMIER OF BERMUDA DEFENDS THE RIGHT TO TRAVEL

What a leap there has been in the ability of gays and lesbians to travel openly and without fear! As recently as a decade ago, the Cayman Islands denied landing rights to a boatload of law-abiding gay vacationers, claiming that their very presence was an affront to public morals. Yet few cruise or tour operators cut back on their programs to the Caymans or supported my own argument that a destination denying access to some Americans is not entitled to receive tourism from any Americans. For years, the government of the Cayman Islands took no step to reverse its hostile policy.

Last year, in sharp contrast to the attitudes of nearly a decade ago, the prime minister of Bermuda, Ewart Brown, went out of his way to announce that Bermuda was totally receptive to gay and lesbian tourists. He made that statement after learning that Rosie O'Donnell's tour company, R Family Vacations, had canceled a cruise stop in Bermuda because various church groups had protested their presence, issuing a formal government pronouncement:

> Bermuda is a democracy that welcomes all people of all races, colors, creeds and sexual orientation. . . . We stress to the international community the Bermudian government's position of inclusion and acceptance of all who wish to visit our beautiful and friendly country.

Apparently, more and more citizens and their leaders are at last recognizing that discrimination against any group because of their sexual orientation is unacceptable.

JOURNALISM

IN TRAVEL JOURNALISM, WHAT'S REALITY, WHAT'S FANTASY?

No one can write intelligently about travel without knowing something about the incomes enjoyed by most Americans. If you truly believe with all your heart that large numbers of people earn more than $100,000 a year, then it makes sense to fill your columns and blogs with delirious raves about three-star restaurants and deluxe hotels.

But they don't. In actual fact, only 7.2% of all employed Americans earn more than $75,000 a year. (I base this and all following statistics on a recent Annual Demographic Survey of the Bureau of the Census.) That's 7.2%. Another 7.8% earn between $50,000 and $75,000. Yes, 7.8%. That leaves a full 85% of all employed Americans who earn under $50,000 a year.

Even when you group the incomes of all breadwinners in an American family, the resulting totals are still far below the dream levels of the elitist travel publications. Nearly 70% of all Americans live in families with combined incomes (husband, wife, children) of less than $70,000 a year.

Deduct income and Social Security taxes from those earnings, as well as housing, food, clothing, car, light and heating, and an occasional beer, and how much is left for $400-a-night hotels and $100 meals?

Given the actual amounts of money that Americans have, what sort of vacations do they take? Budget or deluxe? Cautious or spendthrift? How does the world of low-cost travel stand up against the Ritz-Carltons and the luxury limos, the haughty waiters and the maitre d's?

It c-r-e-a-m-s them. It overwhelms their numbers. It makes them funny. And it transforms most of the haughty commentaries and luxury magazines into narrow, special-interest rags. For every American tourist who sleeps in deluxe hotels, 10 more are staying in tourist-class hotels or economy motels. For every patron of a gourmet restaurant in vacation areas, 20 are taking their meals at budget buffets. And if you were to add up the yearly traffic of 50 high-priced tour operators, their totals would not remotely compare with the business of such popularly priced companies as GOGO Worldwide Vacations (www.gogowwv.com) or Funjet Vacations (www.funjet.com), which every year handle millions of trips—and get no attention at all in trendy travel pages.

I attempt, in all my writings, to concern myself with matters of sensible, cost-conscious travel.

THE *NEW YORK TIMES* HAS PUBLISHED ONE OF THE MOST OUTRAGEOUS ESSAYS IN THE HISTORY OF TRAVEL JOURNALISM

It filled the entire first page of the travel section of the *New York Times* on December 9, 2007, spread out over seven more pages. Its headline read: "The 53 Places to Go in 2008." But instead of citing culture, history, natural wonders, political interest, or interaction with people as the primary reason for its 53 geographical choices, it stated that the arrival of upscale deluxe hotels was the main reason for visiting most of its nominees.

- St. Lucia? You go there because "big-name resorts with $1,000 rooms are on the way."
- Verbier, in Switzerland? It "will get decidedly more upper class" when Richard Branson's latest chalet-hotel opens, charging "as little as £35,250 a week, well over $70,000."
- Courchevel in the French Alps? Developers are upping the ante with "rustic-chic apartments starting at . . . $1.95 million."

And so it read on nearly all its seven pages. You should go to Tunisia because it is undergoing a "luxury makeover" that will attract "well-heeled travelers"; to Laos for its "seriously upscale" hotels; to Prague, where the youth hostels are "being squeezed by luxe hotels"; to Munich for "cushy living"; to Playa Blanca in Panama where a "*très* chic beach club" of Miami is opening a gated resort; to Rimini, Italy, currently drawing "style-conscious Romans to its designer hotels"; to Kuwait City ("opulent hotels"); to Easter Island, acquiring its "first luxury resort"; to Virgin Gorda, where a new resort will offer "weekly rates starting at $12,500"; or to Itacare, Brazil, visited by "celebrities and the elite of Rio de Janeiro."

In no fewer than 34 of the 43 destinations listed in its printed travel section (the other 10 appeared online), luxury living was singled out as the draw of the destination. The words "luxury," "upscale," "high end," "Ritz-Carlton," "lavish," "well-heeled," "ultraexclusive," "high ticket," "chic," "upper class," "posh," "opulent," and the like, appear either repeatedly ("luxury" and "luxurious" are big favorites) or at least once in the great majority of write-ups; and the more noble goals of travel, a learning experience that expands understanding, are mainly dismissed in favor of the pleasures of discos and designer hotels.

If you, like many, are not interested in ultracostly hotels, is there anything for you to read in the travel section of the *New York Times*? Precious little. I wonder whether any major editor of the *Times* scans those pages or is even faintly aware of what that section has become. As someone with a regard for travel, who looks upon travel as a precious birthright of our generation, I want to protest against what a new team of mindless poseurs have done to the once-esteemed travel pages of our leading newspaper.

CRYSTAL CRUISES PUSHES A $1,000-PLUS MEAL (FOR ONE) WITH THE HELP OF A WEALTH-LOVING TRAVEL SECTION

Would you believe a single meal—one meal—costing $1,000 per person? It's being offered aboard Crystal Cruises (on intermittent, widely spaced sailings, mainly because of the inclusion of ultracostly wines), probably in an effort to attract hedge-fund managers to its pretentious vacations. And whom do we have to thank for revealing this information? Why, the travel section of the *New York Times,* of course, advising us without commentary or criticism (in a recent Sun travel section) that Crystal "recently began offering intimate $1,000-a-head dinners with hard-to-get wines and extravagant meals."

Elsewhere, in the same edition of the *Times*' wealth-worshiping travel coverage, the weekly review of new hotels ("Check In/Check Out") chooses to write up the Carlton on Madison Avenue in New York, which charges "from $399 to $799" per night per room. Up forward, on page 2 of the same edition, column 3, the *Times'* travel section states that readers "might be interested" in the new Emirates Palace Hotel in Abu Dhabi of the United Arab Emirates and its "394 luxury rooms, which start at about $700 a person per night."

What a pity that Marie Antoinette did not live to enjoy the current travel section of the *New York Times!*

IN THE WORLD WE LIVE IN, IS IT ACCEPTABLE FOR TRAVEL WRITERS TO SALIVATE OVER TRIPS COSTING SEVERAL THOUSANDS OF DOLLARS A DAY PER PERSON?

What is it about travel journalists that they rush to write up all the absurdly expensive travel facilities offered to a tiny number of near-billionaires? Why do they breathlessly report about pancakes with caviar selling for $700, or hotel suites costing $4,000 a night? Are they, and the publications they represent, the current-day equivalent of the court of Louis XIV? Or are they really rather ridiculous in their uncritical preoccupation with the expenditures of rich playboys?

Usually I quote from recent issues of the travel section of the *New York Times* for examples of this envious adoration of riches. Sadly, other leading publications also salivate over wealth. In a weekend edition of *USA Today* last November, dealing with "Destinations and Diversions," the editors lead their page-one coverage with the description of a pub tour costing $10,500 per person. Sharing honors is another article talking about a worldwide 3-week scavenger hunt costing $9,900 for airfare and accommodations alone. Turn to page 2 of the same issue and you find a recommendation for the Oberoi Vanyavilas near Jaipur, India, charging $872 a night for a double room. Turn to page 3 and you find a lengthy description of the San Ysidro Ranch in the San Ynez mountains of California, where room rates start at $795.

Now I have no objection to people enjoying themselves, or even splurging on a mildly expensive accommodation. But there comes a time when overspending for transitory pleasures becomes nothing short of vulgar in a world where so many people are in need. The holiday expenditures recommended by a *New York Times* or a *USA Today* could finance operations for hundreds of children suffering from cleft palates ($250 pays for one such operation in an underdeveloped country). The monies charged for an around-the-world trip in luxury style would finance a year's college education for a young person without funds.

At a time when we are supposed to pay heed to human suffering, is it right to drool over the vulgar excesses of super-rich tourists?

In a frightening case that threatens the existence of honest travel advice, a Sydney jury has found a writer guilty of defaming a local restaurant

A restaurant in Sydney, whose meals were said to be unpalatable by a newspaper restaurant critic—he ate there twice—sued the critic's newspaper for defamation and won a jury verdict. Prior to the trial, the courts of Australia had upheld the right of the restaurant's owners to maintain such an unusual lawsuit. This is a terrifying development that denies the right of a travel journalist to compose an honest opinion about restaurants, hotels, and other tourist facilities.

No one claimed that the newspaper writer had an ulterior or improper motive for criticizing the restaurant's meals. Yet an Australian jury found him guilty for rendering an honest opinion.

I am virtually certain that the courts of America would throw out any such lawsuit. Or would they? Too many of us take the right of free speech for granted. The casual way in which important elements of Australian society have trampled on free speech rights in this instance would find plenty of extremist supporters here. Imagine the state of our newspapers, magazines, and guidebooks if we could not criticize a restaurant, hotel, movie, or book for fear of being sued for libel.

I think it's important for us to let the Australians know that the world is watching, to provoke leaders in that country to confront the implications of this weird, totalitarian ruling. If you have any Australian acquaintances, shouldn't you let them know of our disappointment in their country?

A somewhat similar lawsuit is currently pending in the courts of Philadelphia, brought by a disgruntled restaurateur against a food critic for the *Philadelphia Inquirer* who had written that he had been served "a miserably tough and fatty strip steak. The crab cake, though, was excellent." We should all pray that the case will be decisively dismissed, with costs assessed against the restaurateur; otherwise, we'll all suffer the eventual disappearance of critical reviews in our press.

We all need to remain vigilant against threats to the honest expression of opinions. You may be interested in one of my own experiences in the world of guidebook writing:

More than 30 years ago, I was criminally indicted in the courts of Athens, Greece, for having published, in our guidebook to Greece, that the local English-speaking newspaper of Athens, at that time, was "practically worthless." As a result of those two words, a heavy package of legal documents arrived at my home in New York, proclaiming that I was to present myself to a court in Athens to answer charges of criminal libel.

When I called an Athens lawyer to ask what I should do, he responded that I should come to Athens and defend myself.

"But if I come to Athens to defend myself and I lose," I said, "I will be imprisoned." "Oh, chances are you won't lose," he responded.

After making fruitless visits to the Greek embassy in Washington, D.C. (whose officials were too frightened to intervene, this being a period when military colonels had seized power in Greece), and making similar pleas for help to the frightened tourist officials of Greece, all to no avail, I finally and reluctantly settled the case for a small payment, so that I could continue to travel to Greece.

And, by the way, that newspaper really was practically worthless.

THE *NEW YORK TIMES* SUGGESTS THAT YOU START A TYPICAL TOUR OF LONDON BY CHECKING IN TO THE $600-A-NIGHT CADOGAN HOTEL

The Sunday travel section of the *New York Times* gets more irrelevant and absurd with every passing week. In its edition of April 20, 2008, in an article on how to spend 36 hours in London ("36 Hours in London"), it recommends that visitors "check into the Cadogan Hotel," where rates then started at £295 ($600) for a double room.

Then, in its weekly survey of practical travel matters by Michelle Higgins, who invariably uses examples taken from the top tier of utterly unaffordable hotels, the *Times'* down-to-earth adviser doesn't disappoint. Offering a lifeline to the suffering American tourist, she eagerly points out that the organization known as Leading Hotels of the World has announced a "guaranteed dollar rate" of $490 a night for a room with a queen-size bed at the Raphael Hotel in Paris. To get this stunning bargain, you must provide a "discount code" and pay in full when booking.

I won't bore you with other examples, such as the *Times'* recent recommendation of the newly refurbished Plaza Hotel in New York, where "nightly rates start at $1,000," or its suggestion that readers stay at a small Mexican resort with 40 butlers in attendance and room rates of $695 per night.

Just when it seems that the *Times'* travel section can't get worse, it plumbs new depths. When will top editors at the *Times* restore reality to their Sunday travel section?

MYTHS OF TRAVEL
THE 10 GREAT MYTHS OF TRAVEL

Though they mean well, your friends can ruin your next vacation by persuading you to adopt all sorts of bad travel maxims. Here are 10 of what I regard as the Great Myths of Travel:

1. That you get what you pay for. Wrong. All over the world you will find expensive hotels that rip you off and bargain properties that give great value. All over the Caribbean are all-inclusive deluxe hotels claiming they have several a la carte restaurants, none of which are open when you attempt to use them. Another deluxe property I know has one of the worst beaches in all the Caribbean. Like so much in travel, you can't automatically assume that high price is a guarantee of value. You must do your homework, and check things out.

2. That the comfort of your stay increases when you spend more. It doesn't. When you close your eyes at night, and go to sleep, it doesn't matter whether you are in a luxury or a low-cost hotel; the quality of the mattress does. I've been to countless hotels whose lavish lobbies and public areas aren't matched at all in the guest rooms—a common condition of the hotel industry.

3. That someone at the destination will tell you what you're looking at. They don't, and when they do, it's too late. The traveler who arrives at a destination without any knowledge of its history or culture is unable to properly absorb the brief, rushed comments of their tour guide. Advance preparation—a few nights in the library perhaps—is the key to a rewarding trip.

4. That travel prices are fixed in stone. They are, in fact, broadly negotiable, provided you're speaking to a person with authority. The manager or assistant manager of a hotel, or the supervisor of a cruise-line reservations staff, will quite often respond favorably to a request for discounts if they have vacant cabins or rooms that have to be sold.

5. That you should stock up on foreign currency in advance of departing. You don't get a better exchange rate here at home, and you simply make yourself a prey for pickpockets or thieves. You should take only a small amount of foreign currency for immediate needs, and thereafter change—at an ATM—only those amounts you will need for a day or two at a time. Just as you would not walk around at home with hundreds of dollars in cash, or leave that amount lying around your residence, you should not do so while traveling.

6. That a guided tour is the best device for visiting a foreign destination. Touring in a group made up of your fellow citizens instantly creates a barrier between yourself and the destination, especially when that touring is in an enclosed motorcoach. An authentic experience can only be had on your own, walking about on two feet, and interacting with the people and places you encounter.

7. That you save by booking at the last minute. Though this might once have been the case, it no longer is. Generally speaking, the best travel prices are found long in advance, and fewer travel suppliers discount their rates at the last moment.

8. That shore excursions should be purchased in advance of boarding the ship. Why? The same overpriced excursions are available in the course of the cruise, when you are better able to determine whether you want to go touring with 40 fellow passengers, or whether you'd prefer to relax, wander about on your own, or tour only with someone you've met on the cruise, sharing the cost of a taxi.

9. That you should carry all sorts of devices and gadgets. The average travel product sold in drugstores and hardware shops simply clutters up your suitcase, and is rarely used on the trip.

10. That the Bahamas and Florida are reliably warm in winter. For guaranteed weather, you need to go much further south. There is nothing more boring than a so-called tropical destination when it's raining or chilly.

TO THE 10 GREAT MYTHS OF TRAVEL LISTED EARLIER, HERE ARE 14 MORE (SUGGESTED BY MY DAUGHTER, PAULINE)

1. That there's any such thing as a "free trip" (such as free accommodations in return for attending a timeshare speech, followed by unacceptable pressures).

2. That you save money by booking travel at the last minute.

3. That it's a good idea to get currency for the destination before you leave home.

4. That there are ways to avoid jet lag.

5. That the French are extremely rude to travelers.

6. That the rooms are more comfortable in expensive hotels.

7. That Las Vegas is a family destination.

8. That volunteering to be bumped from a flight is an effective money-making tactic.

9. That buying a travel agent's card gets you discounts for travel.

10. That taking a taxi will save you time.

11. That a hotel claiming to be a "spa" has extensive fitness facilities.

12. That a four-star hotel is actually "deluxe."

13. That you should order the prix-fixe meal when dining abroad.

14. That you can book a cruise from the dock a couple of hours before it leaves.

NEW YEAR'S RESOLUTIONS

IN ALL THE YEARS AHEAD:

1. I will limit myself to carry-ons, and never check a single bag.

2. I will carry sandwiches from home and never bite into a single airline snack.

3. I will use public transportation from airport into town.

4. I will never book a connecting flight; if there's no nonstop to my destination, I won't go there (with some exceptions).

5. I will share courses with my wife, ordering a single main plate for the two of us.

6. I will stop patronizing duty-free shops.

7. I will never book an uncomfortable "boutique hotel" designed by a famous fashionista.

8. I will never use a credit card that doesn't earn frequent-flier mileage.

9. I will never board a cruise ship carrying more than 700 passengers.

10. I will remain calm and unperturbed by refusing to read the travel section of the *New York Times*.

FIVE TRAVEL RESOLUTIONS FROM READERS

1. "I will leave a tip for the chambermaid, who works so hard for so little. But since she may not be on duty on the morning when I check out, I'll leave it for her every day, in an envelope, under the pillow."

2. "I will never place my luggage on a seat in the airport, thus blocking its use by other people or forcing them to ask, 'Is this seat taken?'"

3. "I will take substantial reading matter to the airport, even for short flights. Why? Because with so many delays, even a short trip may require a wait of several hours, and you may need a long-term distraction."

4. "I will never again book one of those blankety-blank, accursed, 'boutique hotels' with their tiny, podlike rooms, lack of adequate reading lamps or chairs, and futuristic (and therefore unusable) bathroom sinks."

5. "I will never again book a hotel without interrogating the telephone reservationist about any hidden fees. And if there's a single one, I will cancel my reservation."

PROBLEMS

DO AIRLINE EXECUTIVES BEAR SOME RESPONSIBILITY FOR THE SEVERE DROP IN AIRLINE SERVICE STANDARDS?

In 2006, the chairman and CEO of United Airlines, a certain Glenn Tilton, received $39.7 million in compensation. That was the year when United Airlines *lost* $152 million and also terminated the pensions of its 120,000 workers. Because the default has shifted those obligations to a federal pension guarantor, which imposes limits on its payments, the pension income of United's retirees will now undoubtedly be reduced. Is it any wonder that United's employees are not well known for their service attitudes? Or that, as *USA Today* recently reported, United had the highest rate of passenger complaints (per number of passengers flown) to the Department of Transportation?

Is it proper—or sensible—for corporations in the travel field to cut the income of their employees while raising the income of their executives to obscene heights? Should an airline losing $152 million in a single year pay $40 million in that same year to its chairman? And are we, as Americans, tolerating a radical abuse of power by corporate executives in paying themselves outsized sums that have no relation to their talents or accomplishments?

WHY HASN'T TRAVEL TO THE UNITED STATES SOARED?

I recently spent a day fielding phone calls from people who had just returned from the World Travel and Tourism Conference in Lisbon. The subject of their news: the calamitous drop in the amount of incoming travel to the United States.

Since 2000, tourism to the United States from abroad has declined by close to 20%. Though all nations lost tourism in the immediate wake of September 11, virtually all other nations have made up the deficit and forged ahead. Since 2000, tourism to Britain has increased by 13%. Tourism to Australia has increased by 21%. Tourism to France has increased by 20%.

If tourism to the United States had increased over the past 7 years, the nation would have benefited enormously. For every 1% of additional foreign travel to the United States, our country would have enjoyed $12.3 billion in additional income, 150,000 new jobs, $3.3 billion in extra payroll, and $2.1 billion dollars in additional tax revenues.

Why have we lost incoming tourism? In these days of a weak dollar, the United States has become a remarkably cheap country for most foreign tourists; by all rights, our incoming tourism should have soared. The overwhelming consensus of the World Travel and Tourism Conference was that we have made it extraordinarily difficult for most foreign tourists to obtain visas for travel into the United States. In some countries, it requires several weeks simply to make an appointment to apply for such a visa at a U.S. consulate. Let me repeat: Not only is the application process a long-term procedure, but it requires several weeks simply to make an appointment to make an application!

As in so many other areas, the situation results from the sheer incompetence of the recent administration. With so much at stake, with so much income, including tax income, to be enjoyed through added tourism, with so favorable a time for incoming tourism because of the weak U.S. dollar, the failure to create smooth and reasonably quick procedures for the issuance of visas is a catastrophic oversight, matched by so many similar oversights by the executive branch of government. Remember the response to Hurricane Katrina?

THE MISHANDLING OF FOREIGN TOURISM TO THE UNITED STATES GETS WORSE

As if the failure to issue visas expeditiously weren't bad enough, the Department of Homeland Security has proposed (as reported in the trade press) to create additional obstacles to those foreign citizens who don't need visas to travel here. Under the Visa Waiver Program, citizens of 27 countries (such as Great Britain and Ireland) don't require visas; the Department is proposing that these exempt individuals, in advance of departure, provide the United States with biographical data and their proposed travel plans within the United States. They would then receive electronic authorization to proceed with those plans. A nation that cannot issue visas on time is expected to quickly and correctly review the travel plans of millions of other would-be tourists to the United States.

In what way do these new obstacles protect us? How would such a requirement prevent a terrorist from simply e-mailing that he is planning to visit friends and relatives? Or to sightsee and attend the theater in New York? And don't such silly added steps simply discourage tourists from coming here?

CORPORATE JETS, WHOSE PASSENGERS ARE ON EGO TRIPS, ARE A MAJOR REASON FOR OUR WORSENING SKIES

The nightly news on TV, and the press in general, are full of anxious stories about our overcrowded skies. The air-control system is stressed beyond its limits, the average flight delay is more than hour, the delays themselves are historic in number, and more and more passengers are left to sweat for hours within aircraft parked on the tarmac. Complete meltdowns of our air traffic control system occur with distressing frequency.

And why? The TV commentators and the newspaper reporters will refer, vaguely, to "crowded skies"; the increased use of air transportation; the number of start-up budget airlines, the use of small, 80-passenger regional planes in place of the larger 250-passenger jets, adding to the number of aircraft that need to be cleared for flights, takeoffs, and landings.

Not a single one of them, as best I can recall, makes mention of corporate jets flying one or two exalted CEOs on ego trips to a business meeting (coupled, you can bet, with a round or two of golf). Recent reports indicate that in many urban centers of the United States, small corporate jets account for as many as 30% of the airplanes for which takeoff, landing, and flight space must be set aside. However small these corporate jets may be, however few the passengers in them, they require just as much air space as a 250-passenger jet, and just as much attention by air traffic control.

Why do we tolerate this? As Northwest Airlines and Continental Airlines are forced to cancel dozens of flights because of the overcrowded skies, disturbing the travel plans of tens of thousands, why do we permit CEOs to commandeer company jets for trips that could just as easily have been accomplished in a passenger plane?

Why do we cater to their need for luxury, for avoiding the security searches at airports that the rest of us undergo? Shouldn't Congress take up the subject before our air traffic gets totally out of control?

IT'S NOT JUST ME, BUT FAR MORE CONSERVATIVE TYPES WHO CONTEND THAT WE CAN NO LONGER TOLERATE THOUSANDS OF DAILY FLIGHTS BY SMALL CORPORATE JETS

When I spoke about the contribution made by corporate jets to the dangerously crowded conditions of our skies, several readers responded that these outlandish views were obviously a product of my notorious political attitudes. What an attack on freedom! What obvious envy of the super-rich!

And then, officials at that big, courtly, southern carrier, Delta Airlines of Atlanta, Georgia, issued a press release pointing with alarm to the same congestion of our air space by corporate jets, saying:

> Within a decade, traffic delays will cost the economy $40 billion a year, and you, the customer, a great deal of wasted time. There will be 85% more jets in the sky in the next 15 years—an increase driven largely by corporate jets, fractional jets, air-taxis and very light jets. To an air traffic controller, a jet with a celebrity or CEO takes as much effort as a commercial flight with 250 passengers.

This is precisely the point I have been making.

And what is the solution? Let me suggest an analogy. If the automobiles of America were to become so numerous as to cause total gridlock, you can bet that our municipal authorities would place the same sort of restrictions on traffic that several major European cities have imposed (in Florence, Italy, cars with odd-numbered license plates can drive into town only on odd-numbered days of the month, and so on) and that London has also adopted (a "congestion pricing" plan, requiring a heavy payment by people driving their cars into the center of the city).

And yet that gridlock is fast approaching in the air—and has already resulted in horrendous inconvenience to millions of air passengers. We will all eventually have to decide whether a rock star or the president of General Electric should be entitled to use precious air space and divert the attention of air traffic controllers, when they, the privileged few, could just as easily fly on a passenger jet.

SICKO REMINDS US ONCE AGAIN OF OUR FATUOUS EMBARGO AGAINST TRAVEL TO CUBA

Michael Moore's film, *Sicko*, ends with a trip to Cuba. After discovering that three of the "early responders" to Ground Zero apparently suffered lung ailments that their insurance plans refused to cover, Michael accompanies these heroes of 9/11 to a hospital in Havana.

Whether or not to visit Cuba is a personal decision and not for our government to determine; travel, to me, is a First Amendment right.

I have myself traveled to Cuba twice in the last several years. I went there, I am ashamed to say, legally, as a journalist, under license from the Treasury Department. I express that regret because I believe our government does not have the constitutional right to choose the countries that we, as freeborn Americans, are entitled to visit or not visit in peacetime. Travel is a learning activity, a means by which we expand our knowledge of the world; we travel, among other reasons, to reach our own judgments about the foreign policy of our nation. It follows that our government has no more right to prevent us from traveling to a particular country than it has to stop us from attending a lecture or reading a book.

I am aware of the difficulty of turning a trip to Cuba into a learning experience, of ascertaining facts in a totalitarian state. And I know full well that Cubans are less than free to express their own opinions to tourists passing through. But while those factors make information gathering difficult, they do not make it impossible, and there is much that can be learned from such a visit, just as there is in visits to Vietnam and China, to which our country not only permits but encourages travel.

It is now several years since agreement was reached between aviation officials of the United States and communist Vietnam, permitting direct flights between major American cities and Hanoi and Ho Chi Minh City. We readily permit Americans to travel to all sorts of antagonistic countries without legal hindrance, provided only that they recognize that they do so at their own risk. What distinguishes our policies towards the regime of Cuba from our policies toward Vietnam, North Korea, China, and others, other than the political influence of a community of émigrés in Florida?

It is time to stand up for our right to travel, in peacetime, to wherever we wish.

A MASSIVE NEW PROBLEM: DELAYED LUGGAGE ON CONNECTING FLIGHTS

Because most airports are today understaffed, luggage doesn't always make it to a plane on time. Passengers with only an hour or so between flights have a far less chance than before that their luggage will be transferred in time from one plane to another.

I learned that lesson on a flight from New York to Minneapolis, where I was hoping to connect to an onward flight to Billings, Montana. I left 2 hours for the connection, but learned on the day of my departure that the Minneapolis flight was canceled and replaced by a flight departing an hour later, leaving me only an hour for the transfer.

Next morning, in Billings, I had to cool my heels until 1pm when a flight arrived with my missing luggage. It was obvious that the airport in Minneapolis, as crowded as it has become, simply didn't have the necessary personnel to transfer luggage quickly from one flight to another. The painful lesson, based on similar reports I have had from others: In today's America, you take an inordinate risk when you check luggage on connecting flights, with only an hour between them.

TOO OFTEN, WE TOURISTS SEE ONLY THE CLEANED-UP AREAS OF THE WORLD'S GREAT CITIES, WITH IMPOVERISHED PEOPLE HIDDEN FROM OUR VIEW

I have been to Nairobi twice in my life, passing through to take a plane or bus out to the great games parks of the Masai Mara, the Serengeti, and Ngorogoro Crater. And although I was warned not to go wandering on my own, I was encouraged to dine at restaurants downtown, where I viewed a city not so much different from other well-developed capitals: clean streets, high-rise office buildings, apartment houses, taxis, and buses. I do recall being affected, my first morning in Nairobi, by the sight of thousands of people arriving on foot at offices, too poor for transportation, having walked for many miles from their homes to reach their places of work. And though I was mildly moved by this, my mind was really on the upcoming safari for which I had undertaken the trip.

Then, recently, I saw images on television of one of the many, giant, shanty towns of Nairobi where one million people—let me repeat that—one million people live in grinding squalor. And I realized that I had permitted myself to be shielded from reality, placed in an isolated, comfortable lodge, by the operator of my safari.

It is always thus in travel. We land in Washington, D.C., or come in to the awesome Union Station, and see an antiseptic city of gleaming office and government buildings, and all the well-dressed people who reside in or otherwise inhabit the northwest section of the city. It is only by accident that, very occasionally, we wander by mistake into parts of the city where locals live in conditions having no resemblance to the gussied-up downtown areas.

The outbreak of violence in Kenya should remind us of the condition in which at least a third—and maybe more—of the world's population live. And it should also remind us that fully 14% of our own population lives in poverty, with another 15% on the verge of poverty.

From now on, as a tourist, I will attempt to see the less favored areas of the cities I visit. And perhaps even tour companies should run visits to such places, in the same way that a New Orleans tour firm now takes visitors to the Ninth Ward there.

A MARITIME MYSTERY: ARE THOSE NEW, GIGANTIC CRUISE SHIPS TOP HEAVY?

I am concerned about whether those giant, new, 19-deck-high cruise ships carrying 3,000 passengers are top heavy and more prone to drastic tilting.

In July of 2006, the 3,000-passenger, 113,000-ton, 19-deck-high *Crown Princess*, of Princess Cruises, was moving at top speed off the coast of Florida. A junior officer on duty noticed that the automatic navigation system of the ship was executing too tight a turn. So he detached the automatic pilot, took control of the wheel himself, but in the stress of the situation, turned the ship into the direction of the turn rather than away from it. He went port rather than starboard. And the giant ship, executing an even sharper turn, heeled over by 24 degrees, causing unsecured furniture and furnishings to crash about, sending scores of passengers flying into walls and furniture, and causing severe injuries to many of them.

After an 18-month investigation, the National Transportation Safety Board issued its findings that human failure was the cause of the incident, chastising the ship's officers and the cruise line for lack of training in executing turns. The N.T.S.B., as far as I can tell, made no mention of the design of the massive ship itself, nor has anyone else (other than yours truly) raised a question about modern cruise-ship design.

You've all seen photos of these immense megavessels. They soar high into the sky, much higher than older cruise ships. And my question is: Does such height, and the weight concentrated so high from the hull, cause the ship to tilt over more when making a tight turn than a normal smaller cruise ship with only six or seven decks? Even making a turn at full speed, would a smaller ship have heeled over by as much as 24 degrees, hurling passengers off their feet? Granted that even a smaller ship would tilt over, would it tilt over that much?

That question wasn't answered by the National Transportation Safety Board, but I think it should be. Are any of our readers knowledgeable about the subject and able to allay my concerns? Any maritime engineers out there? Has anybody wondered about the radical new designs of massive new cruise ships?

Several years ago, in the wake of the *Challenger* disaster, the famous physicist, the late Richard Feynman, stumbled upon the cause of that tragedy by simply dipping a section of O ring into a glass of ice water—and found that the O ring cracked when it encountered near-freezing temperatures. He used his common sense. Heaven knows I'm not a Richard Feynman. But doesn't common sense indicate a problem here? Suppose future cruise ships were built 40 decks high. Would anyone doubt that the ship would heel over to a much-larger-than-normal extent when executing a turn? Are 19 decks too much?

DOES A NEAR TRAGEDY ON BRITISH AIRWAYS INDICATE A NEED TO OPERATE ONLY THREE-ENGINE & FOUR-ENGINE PLANES ON LONG-DISTANCE FLIGHTS?

You may remember how a two-engine Boeing 777 operated by British Airways was a mile or so away from its runway landing at Heathrow Airport when both engines failed. The plane touched down prematurely on rough terrain several hundred feet from the beginning of the runway, causing its wings and landing gear to collapse and suffer grave damage.

Fortunately, no one was hurt. But the incident reminds us of the bitter controversy several years ago when long-distance flights were first permitted on two-engine planes.

In the early years of passenger jets, and until fairly recently, all long-distance flights were made on three-engine planes (such as the DC-10) or four-engine planes (such as the Boeing 747), on the theory that if two engines failed to function, the one or two remaining engines would be sufficient to complete the flight. The airlines argued that it was inconceivable that both engines of a two-engine plane would ever fail, and therefore there was no need for the safety margin of a third or fourth engine.

Well, both engines of the ill-fated British Airways plane did fail, apparently almost simultaneously. And had this happened a few seconds earlier, the near-tragedy might have become a catastrophe.

On my own long-distance flights and transocean flights, I have always attempted to fly only on planes with four engines. This incident has bolstered my resolve. And it might be well to reopen the entire matter. Obviously, the people who denied that both engines of a two-engine plane could cease operating in the course of a flight have some explaining to do.

TRUTHS OF TRAVEL

THE 10 GREAT TRUTHS OF TRAVEL

Earlier in this chapter, I wrote about the Great Myths of Travel. There are also Great Truths of Travel—and though they aren't equivalent to the major principles of ethics and science (Einstein and the Ten Commandments are safe), they can be of importance to your next trip. Here are the Great Truths of Travel.

1. **The less you spend, the more you enjoy.** The less you spend, the more authentic is your travel experience, the more likely you are to meet typical people of the destination. You also meet a better type of traveler. In the modest B&Bs of a thousand cities, you encounter guests with a sense of adventure, an intellectual curiosity, an openness to new ideas and approaches. They are far more interesting than the pampered sorts with their stacks of luggage and arrogant demands, who flock to the first-class and deluxe hotels.

2. **The greatest rewards of travel are had from learning vacations.** The supreme activity of travel is the summer courses offered by many great universities to adults from around the world: Oxford University, University College Dublin, Cornell's Adult University, St. John's College in Santa Fe, many more that a quick look at Google will reveal. Pursuing learning for the love of learning, without grades or examinations, you use your vacation time to return to the liberal arts and improve your mind.

3. **By planning in advance to meet residents of the destination, you enliven your trip.** By making inquiries of your friends or associates, you can obtain the names and addresses of people at the destination who might accept an invitation to dinner or drinks. Those meetings are the highlight of any foreign trip, far more memorable than the standard sightseeing attractions.

4. **Listening with an open mind to people at the destination is a key to greater understanding, an exceptional reward of travel.** Smart tourists welcome the chance to encounter viewpoints or lifestyles totally different from theirs, and find that such encounters are among the great adventures of life. Above all, the smart American tourist avoids making speeches or delivering comparisons to our own life at home.

5. **The smartest travel decision is to vacation in off-season periods.** It is an exquisite experience to view the *Mona Lisa* when you alone are standing before her, to attend the opera in Sydney when only residents are in the audience, to roam through countless other venues when the tourists have fled and life has returned to normal.

6. **When undecided about your next vacation destination, choose from among those countries or cities whose currency remains weak against the U.S. dollar.** It is always especially enjoyable to vacation in places—Bangkok, Bali, Bulgaria, Buenos Aires, are currently among them—where everything is priced at less than we are normally accustomed to spend. It is always pleasant to banish the thought of expense from our travel thoughts, to enjoy the relaxation that comes from knowing that the bill you are about to receive is half as much as you would normally expect.

7. **At tourist restaurants, the decision to split courses with your travel companion will lead to better meals and huge total savings.** Order one appetizer for the two of you, and one main course for the two of you, and ask for an extra plate. You'll still send uneaten food back to the kitchen, and in the course of a trip, your total savings will be surprisingly big.

8. **The use of low-cost lodgings that were never meant to be hotels— guesthouses, B&Bs, hostels, and the like—will nearly always result in an enjoyable and memorable trip.** You will meet people in a way that doesn't happen in large, standard hotels; you will live in residential neighborhoods associated with the normal life of the city; and you will relax to a surprising extent.

9. **Packing light is another key to travel pleasure.** Restrict your luggage to one medium-size suitcase per person, lightly packed. Resolve to be a carefree traveler and not a harried clothes horse. You will cease being a prisoner of porters and taxicabs, forced to stay at the first hotel you see, unable to "shop around." If you have taken too little, you can always remedy the deficiency at the destination. But meantime, you will know a kind of travel ease that only light packing can bring about.

10. **Follow the "deals"; when you see a travel bargain, grab it!** If you follow the travel media, online and off, you will periodically spot superb bargains available for a short time at an unprecedented low price. A week in Prague for $799, including round-trip air! An all-inclusive week in the Dominican Republic for $699! A quick trip to Hawaii, and 5 nights' hotel, for $849! When you spot such an offer, rush to book it; you'll enjoy an unexpected travel bonanza, and you will rarely go wrong.

"USER-GENERATED" WEBSITES

I STILL DON'T SEE THE UTILITY OF THOSE "USER-GENERATED" WEBSITES

Last year, in a panel discussion sponsored by *Travel Weekly* magazine, I appeared with Tim Zagat of the Zagat Travel Guides (whose restaurant recommendations are supplied by the public, not by Mr. Zagat) and Steve Kaufer, the co-founder of Trip Advisor (the nation's leading user-generated site of travel opinions supplied again by the public and not by individual travel journalists). And the discussion soon developed into a heated debate between myself, on the one hand, and them, over whether their method of "polling" the public results in better travel recommendations than those supplied by veteran travel journalists.

Subsequent to the debate, I vacationed for a week in Montauk, Long Island. I casually visited several of the leading resorts in that location and later looked at the discussion of Montauk and its resorts that appears in Trip Advisor. And the views I expressed in the earlier debate are now even more strongly held by me. To put it briefly, I found that Trip Advisor was virtually useless in providing an adequate picture of the resort situation in Montauk.

To begin with, nearly every leading resort received contradictory reviews from Trip Advisor's contributors. In some cases, several people had written in that a particular resort was excellent and several other people wrote that the same resort was execrable. Which recommendation to follow? Who was a better judge?

But more important, I found that none of the write-ups gave me a word picture, an image, an impression, of the resort of the sort that you obtain from a write-up in a good guidebook written by a trained journalist. Rarely could I tell whether the property was a dignified, attractive, comfortable resort or a shabby, second-rate, oversized motel. Most contributors simply selected a single element—whether the beds were comfortable, whether the desk clerks were courteous—on which they relied for their ultimate opinion. Though I could tell that a particular visitor had disliked his or her bed, or had a run-in with staff, I couldn't discern for the life of me whether this resort would be suitable for my own stay. And although Trip Advisor tabulated all the favorable and unfavorable opinions and ranked the resorts (#1, #2, and so forth), I found that the rankings were oblivious to price or category, and again had no value at all.

So you'll have to forgive me. Though I have an obvious self-interest in touting travel guides, I will continue to use those guides, and not a user-generated poll of opinions for my own next vacation choices.

AN ADDENDUM TO MY RECENT COMMENTS ON THE ADVICE IN USER-GENERATED TRAVEL WEBSITES

I have read with great interest the response of readers to my recent slam at user-generated websites. But it seems to me that hardly anyone has dealt with the fact that these users are not making comparative judgments, but are issuing their critiques or applause based solely on their experience of one hotel—repeat, one hotel—in the community they have visited. Unlike a guidebook writer, the traveler sees only one hotel; he or she does not traipse to 20 hotels in the same price range to get an idea of what the standards are in that particular city.

In Paris, for instance, the user never realizes that there may be superior hotels in the same price category as the one they have used. Or, they are unaware that the hotel they have used is greatly superior to other hotels in the same price category. Though they are able to say that they enjoyed or disliked a particular hotel, they are never able to make a comparative judgment, which is the task assigned to the writer of a travel guide and is of enormous value to the traveler.

Isn't it important for a traveler to know that there are superior hotels to the one that traveler chose—and at no extra cost? As someone who devoted a large portion of his life to walking the streets of Europe, looking at one guesthouse and hotel after another in order to find several that I might recommend, I believe that hard work and not random chance is the key to good travel advice.

A DAILY BLOG OF MINE EXPERIENCED SOME OF THE DELIBERATE MANIPULATION THAT IS OFTEN DIRECTED AT USER-GENERATED WEBSITES

Funny thing happened when I recently ran a blog on the publication of a current best-selling book about medical and dental tourism. Almost immediately, eight or nine responses came in from readers, all of them singing the praises of the plastic surgery of a certain Dr. Carlos in Leon, Mexico. On investigation, it appeared that one of Dr. Carlos's former patients had placed phone calls to several other of Dr. Carlos's former patients, urging them to send in responses to me praising the merits of Dr. Carlos. And all of them dutifully complied.

Isn't that an apt example of how user-generated travel recommendations can be manipulated? And isn't it naive to assume that this is not happening, massively, on the most popular user-generated sites? Although our own site has now taken down the excessive tributes to Dr. Carlos, which stood out like a sore thumb, how likely is it that the giant user-generated sites can do the same? How in the world can the creators of those sites distinguish between spontaneous, honest opinions and deliberate manipulation?

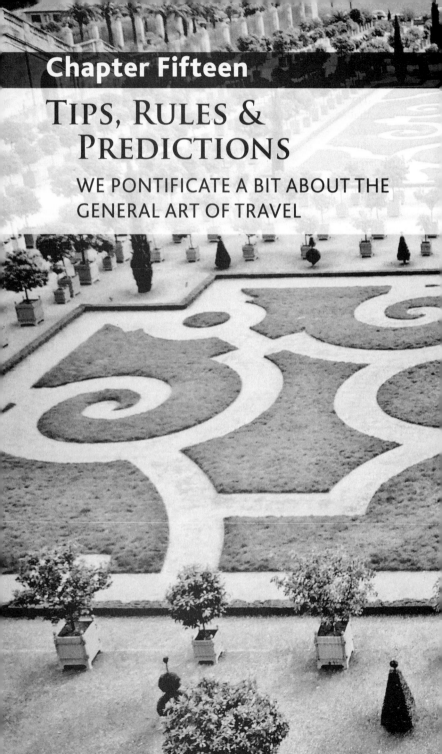

Chapter Fifteen

Tips, Rules & Predictions

WE PONTIFICATE A BIT ABOUT THE GENERAL ART OF TRAVEL

And what would an opinionated book be without Solemn Predictions about the future of travel, without Awesome Rules that govern travel, without Weighty Tips for dealing with the challenges of travel? This last chapter contains that summing-up and also sets forth a final Credo for this book, which I have phrased as follows:

May this book serve to reflect the joy of travel and the freedom that travel represents.

May it always deal with a moderate level of travel costs, so that people of moderate means can enjoy the rewards of travel.

And finally may it bring its readers, through travel, to those warm and welcoming gathering places all over the world where people of all nations and races meet in harmony and together enjoy the brotherhood of man.

BARGAINS

THE 15 TOP TRAVEL BARGAINS FOR THE YEAR AHEAD

While speaking at a newspaper-sponsored travel show, my daughter and I were asked to name what we considered the top travel bargains for the year ahead, in terms of destinations and facilities. Here's how we answered:

1. **China.** Despite a slowly strengthening currency, China remains available at unbeatable rates (including airfare there) from China Focus (www.chinafocustravel.com), Chinaspree.com, Rim-Pac International (www.rim-pac.com), Ritz Tours (www.ritztours.com), Pacific Delight Tours (www.pacificdelighttours.com), China Travel Service (www.chinatravelservice.com), and many others.

2. **Vietnam.** The basic costs for tourists are remarkably low. Shopping prices are minor miracles (such as custom-tailored suits in Hoi An for less than $100). A great many independent travelers simply book a direct United Airlines flight from San Francisco to Ho Chi Minh City (via Hong Kong), and then pick up accommodations as they move along throughout the country.

3. **Panama.** The fastest-developing country in Central America is receiving ever-growing numbers of cost-conscious vacationers, as well as U.S. retirees looking for a cheap second home. The skyline of Panama City is beginning to resemble Hong Kong or New York's financial district—except that these skyscrapers are residential condos.

Previous page: Nearly every major attraction can be reached by cheap public transportation; in Paris, a suburban train takes you to Versailles.

4. **Nicaragua and Honduras.** Both are coming up fast as favorites for adventuresome tourists. Honduras's off-shore island of Utila (for scuba diving) is the latest discovery. Nicaragua's prices for lodgings and meals are surely among the lowest in the area.

5. **Costa Rica.** It remains immensely popular, and though it's gaining swanky accommodations, it remains inexpensive for the tourist who searches out low-cost lodgings.

6. **Dominican Republic.** Home of the low-cost all-inclusive hotel. Giant crowds simply looking to laze in the sun are flocking to properties where all they do is eat three enormous buffet meals a day and doze in a chaise longue.

7. **Buenos Aires.** The amazing exchange rate for the Argentine peso—valued currently at three to a U.S. dollar—makes the city remarkably cheap. Large numbers of Americans are starting their South American stays in Buenos Aires, and then journeying further south to the natural attractions of Patagonia.

8. **The U.S. national parks.** A drop-off in foreign visitors since 9/11 and high gas prices have reduced traffic to the most famous of the parks: Yellowstone, Yosemite, Grand Canyon, Great Smoky Mountains.

9. **Bali, in the South Pacific.** Its cordial attitudes towards the visitor, coupled with its low price structure, have restarted the flow of tourism, overcoming the effects of two terrorist attacks on beachside nightclubs.

10. **Sicily.** Travel here costs much less than elsewhere in Italy. Visitors enjoy circumnavigating the island in a rental car, stopping in such places as Erice, Agrigento, Siracusa, and Taormina.

11. **Eastern Europe and Croatia.** In countries that haven't yet adopted the euro, prices remain much lower for Americans than in western Europe.

12. **Kenya.** Provided only that a political truce between warring factions remains in effect, Kenya will once again be offering low-cost African safaris to persons booking from Lion World Tours, 2Afrika, AdventureCenter.com, or G.A.P Adventures.

13. **DIY bicycle tours.** Shunning the high-priced, escorted, group bicycle tours, you enjoy inexpensive do-it-yourself biking along a prescribed route. Such healthy, spirited vacationing has become increasingly popular, and no service handles the method better than BikeToursDirect (www.biketoursdirect.com).

14. **Discount cruises.** Though cruise-line executives will deny it, a giant number of cabins are being sold at sharply discounted, rock-bottom rates. Go to Vacations To Go (www.vacationstogo.com), White Travel

Service (www.cruisewizard.com), or CruisesOnly (www.cruisesonly.com) and you'll find stunningly low fares.

15. **Newfoundland and Nova Scotia.** Though Canada has lost its low-cost appeal to some Americans due to the relative strength of the Canadian dollar, these Atlantic provinces remain moderately priced for everything from accommodations to succulent lobster dinners.

SUMMER BARGAINS

My daughter Pauline has just published her list of the world's most attractive, budget-priced destinations, and it contains a number of places that aren't well known, even among the most avid travelers.

1. **Berkeley Springs, West Virginia,** home of the Bathhouse in Berkeley Springs State Park, where you can soak in thermal waters and then receive a Swedish massage for under $50. All other activities here are similarly cheap, as are lodgings.

2. **Boundary Waters Canoe Area of northern Minnesota.** For canoeing close to 1,300 miles of navigable waters, outfitters will rent you a canoe and supply you with food at a very reasonable price.

3. **The midcoast of Maine** (Rockland, Maine), where you'll find the superb Farnsworth Museum (Andrew Wyeth, Louise Nevelson), many small galleries and restaurants, Windjammer cruises, and low-cost mom-and-pop motels. All of which makes it a fine jumping-off point for such pricier places as Kennebunkport, Bar Harbor, and the area near Acadia National Park.

4. **The Wisconsin Dells.** The "Waterpark Capital of the World" charges $30 to $35 a day for most waterpark admissions. There's fishing, golfing, rock climbing, and (with some effort at ferreting them out) reasonably priced motels for as little as $50 a night.

5. **The Oregon coast,** spectacular in its vistas, with wine areas further inland. Go, especially, to the little town of Yachats (where I've vacationed), with its excellent, reasonably priced restaurants.

6. **The Dominican Republic.** Only Nicaragua charges less for its tourist facilities, and those of the Dominican Republic are state of the art despite their cheapness. This is the budget capital of the Caribbean.

7. **Newfoundland, Canada.** Puffin colonies and caribou herds, whale- and bird-watching, hiking, and excellent camping facilities abound. Gros Morne National Park is a World Heritage Site.

8. **The Mayan Riviera,** just south of Cancun on the Caribbean coast of Mexico. Fast developing, its hotel-resorts challenge those of the

Dominican Republic as the world's least expensive. White-sand beaches and Mayan ruins are the lure.

9. **Peru.** Cuzco is a favorite jumping-off point, as is elegant Arequipa. Wonderfully low priced.

10. **Bulgaria,** Europe's budget champion, with its Black Sea beaches and well-preserved medieval villages.

Frequently Asked Questions

In any forum on travel, 10 questions are constantly asked, to which I propose the following answers

On a weekly radio program that I conduct every Sunday from noon to 2pm EST (you can hear it live via streaming video, or later via podcast, on www. wor710.com), I've been asked hundreds of varied and exotic questions about vacations. (One woman recently stumped me by asking my favorite among geological tours.) But 10 almost-identical questions are asked over and over, every week, indicating a widespread concern.

1. **Should I book my trip now or later?** Now. The days of the last-minute discount are fast diminishing, and fewer and fewer tour operators, airlines, and hotels offer reductions to persons booking late. The best travel deals are those offered long in advance.

2. **How can I, as a single person, avoid the single-room supplement?** You can't—it is an inescapable fact of hotel life, and if you refuse to share with another (an option offered by more and more tour operators), you'll have to pay the entire cost of the room you occupy. About the only way to avoid the single-room supplement is to book those institutional lodgings (hostels, university residences, and the like) that simply charge per person (often for dormlike accommodations) and not by room.

3. **How much foreign currency should I take on my trip abroad?** Only a tiny, tiny amount—the sum needed to get you from the arrival airport to your hotel. In a world of pickpockets, the last thing international travelers should do is walk around with large amounts of currency on their person. Carry your money in the form of ATM cards, credit cards and travelers' checks, and cash only a bit at a time. And obtain cash at a bank ATM machine (be sure to have a four-digit PIN), the unchallenged source of the best exchange rates.

4. **Can I, a single person without a companion, travel pleasurably on group tours?** If the tours you're considering are the standard if-it's-Tuesday-it-must-be-Belgium sort, then the chances are overwhelming that you'll be among couples, families, and other conventional types, and that you might feel alone. The answer is to book a specialty tour that focuses on a cause or special interest. In that intensely focused activity, people mix and mingle without reference to whether they are couples or singles—and a great many other single persons are usually found. Go to www.specialtytravel.com, where you'll find hundreds of special-interest tours departing each month.

5. **Should an unaccompanied woman travel alone?** This is a routine variant to question number 4. The answer is, flatly, yes. The world has grown far more sophisticated and in general no longer looks askance at the unaccompanied woman or subjects her to discrimination. Indeed, a great many feminists will argue that it is preferable to travel alone, thus becoming more sensitive in that fashion to the local culture, and having a greater chance to meet local residents.

6. **Is it safe to visit [insert destination name]?** No one other than you is able to answer that question. Terrorism and/or crime is now a statistically possible risk (though a small one) almost everywhere (such as in Egypt, Morocco, Bali), and in the last analysis, only you can decide whether you're determined to live your life free from fear or whether you'll avoid every place where an incident might conceivably occur.

7. **For a cruise I am about to take, should I buy shore excursions in advance?** Absolutely not. Wait until the cruise is underway to determine whether or not you feel on a particular day like joining a busload of your fellow passengers, or whether you've met other people with whom to share a taxi, or whether you'd prefer simply to wander the port city free of charge.

8. **Should I permit my 18-year-old to vacation in Europe?** I hedge on that question—having no way to judge the maturity of the 18-year-old in question—and suggest that the questioner look up the tour offerings of Contiki Holidays (www.contiki.com), which operates escorted motorcoach tours limited to persons 18 to 35, most of them at the younger end. Contiki is a solid organization, long in business, and generally regarded as thoroughly reliable for your adventurous kids.

9. **What's there to do in London, Paris, New York, or [here they name a large, world-renowned city]?** I answer, with barely disguised dismay, that if they have to ask that question, they haven't done their travel homework. A trip to anywhere should be preceded by a visit to the library, an evening or two in which you bone up about the city or

country you're about to visit. A failure to do that dooms you to disappointment.

10. **Should I use a travel agent?** Only if that agent possesses real knowledge of the destination you're planning to visit. Because use of a travel agent usually costs more than do-it-yourself planning (agents charge an airfare fee, now that they no longer receive commissions from the airlines), they should be able to justify the extra cost by their special familiarity with the details of a particular trip.

HEALTH

MEMBERSHIP IN IAMAT IS ESSENTIAL FOR ANY AVID TRAVELER—& CAN COST AS LITTLE AS $20

Because I sent a donation to the International Association of Medical Assistance to Travelers (which can be of any amount, however small), I recently received renewal of my membership card and a copy of the pocket-size annual directory, accompanied by several other valuable documents which I'll describe below. IAMAT was founded more than 40 years ago by the late Dr. Vincenzo Marcolongo, one of the first people to realize how urgent was the need to create a reliable list of far-flung physicians for the first generation in human history to engage in widespread international travel.

"The traveler abroad," he wrote, "is already under the psychological stress induced by change . . . and is coping with the physical conditions of different water, food, and perhaps climate and altitude. . . . There is a good chance, too, that the traveler's own immunities do not match the foreign local environment. If a medical problem arises, where does one turn for quick and effective health care?"

The answer: a directory of competent, English-speaking physicians in every destination of interest.

The 2009 directory lists hundreds of physicians around the world who are qualified in travel medicine, fluent in English, and willing to accept fees of $80 for an office visit and $100 for a visit to your hotel. Its information is awesome in its wide geographical reach. Going to Chengdu in the Sichuan province of China? Dr. Ni Rong and Dr. Sun Min have permitted their cellphone numbers to be printed in the IAMAT directory and are at your disposal.

The nations covered? They range from Algeria to Zimbabwe, and from Austria, Belgium, and Bolivia to Vanuatu and Yemen. And when you join (through a contribution that should amount to at least $20, though it needn't be that large), you receive three other publications of equal importance: a world immunization chart (required and recommended immunizations for every country in the world); a world malaria risk chart; and a pamphlet entitled "How to Protect Yourself Against Malaria." If you have ever posed a question about immunizations or malaria to your own internist (few of whom are able confidently to respond), you will appreciate the extraordinary value of this carefully prepared information.

To join IAMAT, send your contribution to International Association for Medical Assistance to Travellers, 1623 Military Rd., #279, Niagara Falls, NY 14304-1745.

Or, for further information, visit its website at www.iamat.org.

AT SOME POINT IN YOUR LIFE, YOU OUGHT TO OPT FOR A SERIOUS FITNESS VACATION

Why not devote your next vacation to health? Instead of lazing on a beach, which does very little for you, why not check into a resort that offers an intense, dedicated routine of weight reduction and physical fitness?

The Duke Diet and Fitness Center, in Durham, North Carolina, is the nation's top facility. Its weight-loss programs bring long-term results to close to 60% of the people who attend. That's because it offers no fad diet but a balanced assortment of tasty American foods, the kind you'll be eating when you return home. By limiting your daily meals to 1,000 calories—a server on the cafeteria line actually consults a computer printout of the foods you receive—and requiring active daily exercise and nutrition instruction, it brings about substantial weight loss. I dropped 10 pounds during my first 2-week stay, and maintained the weight loss for several years thereafter.

Duke's problem? Because it provides personal medical attention (by full-time doctors) and other discussions with specialists, it charges $2,700 a week for the first 2 weeks, plus the cost of accommodations in various $70-a-night condos and motels located close to the center (the price comes down sharply for a third or fourth week, or for a return stay). Don't confuse Duke's Diet and Fitness Center with the entirely separate Rice House for seriously obese people. Phone ☎ 800/235-3853, or visit www.dukedietcenter.org.

RULES

12 RULES FOR TRAVELING BETTER, AT WHATEVER PRICE LEVEL YOU CHOOSE

They're my own commandments for traveling smarter on any sort of budget, and they are based on my own travel experiences and no one else's.

1. I combat transoceanic jet lag by going to sleep immediately on arrival. Time was when I would instantly hit the streets on my first full day in London, Bangkok, or Seoul . . . and that overexertion would turn me into a sleepless zombie for the remainder of my first week abroad. No longer. I now go to bed the moment I reach the hotel. I make a relaxed transition to a new time zone and enjoy a much clearer head than ever before.

2. I prepare for my trip with works of history and art appreciation. In my early years of travel I thought nothing of flinging myself into exotic foreign cultures without first studying them. Result: I arrived as an untutored ignoramus, confused and bewildered. No more. I now read about the beliefs of Buddhism on most trips to the Far East. I refresh my memory about the evolution of the Gothic cathedral before a trip to France or Germany. And through such mature preparation, my trips become far more meaningful and rewarding.

3. I pack less and enjoy more. I no longer bring an outfit for every conceivable occasion. I've come to peace with the probability that I will not be invited to a garden party on my 2 weeks in Spain, and will not be asked to meet the queen. I bring a quarter of what I used to carry and travel with a single, medium-size suitcase half full. And that one factor has improved the enjoyment of my trips to a greater extent than any other.

4. I take one meal a day "picnic style." As I grew older, it suddenly dawned on me that no mature stomach can tolerate an endless regimen of overly rich, overly sauced meals. I now make one meal a day out of the simple, cold ingredients purchased in a foreign grocery or delicatessen. In this manner, I not only eat sensibly, healthily, and cheaply—but better, enjoying the local specialties in cold food that every country offers.

5. I bargain over the price of my accommodations. In my earlier years, I regarded the act of bargaining as beneath my youthful dignity. I learned fairly soon that all hotel rooms are "perishable," a complete loss to its owners if unsold for a particular date. I gradually realized that hotel proprietors will almost always react favorably to a request for a discount, if that's what's needed to rent an otherwise-empty room.

6. I equip myself with the names and addresses of competent, English-speaking physicians. No longer the eternal optimist about health and illness, I travel ready for the possibility of becoming ill in a foreign land. If I am unable in advance to obtain the names of reliable physicians at my destination, I obtain the list of those important doctors maintained by the International Association of Medical Assistance to Travelers (www.iamat.org).

7. In advance of departure, I acquire the names and addresses of people to look up. I pester friends, associates, or relatives for the names of their own acquaintances in the cities I am about to visit. I take pains to enjoy the most memorable events of travel, when you interact with residents of a foreign country.

8. I make use of government tourist offices and "institutes." By simply requesting literature from them, I often learn about fascinating events and activities at the destination, of which I would otherwise be totally unaware.

9. I bring along a small but select assortment of travel products. And I emphasize "small." Eyeshades to ensure sleep. Earplugs to blot out unwanted noise. A small coffee immersion heater. Tums or Maalox for indigestion. And comfortable walking shoes, however unsightly they may be.

10. I stay calm and roll with the travel punches. I accept the fact that travel is an inherently uncertain activity that doesn't always come about without glitches or delays. I no longer rant and rail when the airport announces a postponed flight time. I whip out a paperback book and savor an interlude of leisure.

11. I buy various forms of cheap travel insurance. I never did so when I first traveled, but, oh, how I learned! Travel is a complex activity in which many things can and do go wrong. Insurance can protect against many of the consequences.

12. I avoid the heavily touristed, and opt for the undiscovered. Having had my fill of all the massively popular destinations—the Londons and the Acapulcos, the Honolulus and the Orlandos—my current tastes are for the places as yet not inundated by visitors. Mature travel consists of continuing to act as a pioneer, always seeking out the new, pursuing the dreams of discovery and challenge.

THE 12 COMMANDMENTS OF SMART, COST-CONSCIOUS TRAVEL

Elsewhere in this tome, I've included (a) the 10 Great Myths of Travel, and (b) the 10 Great Truths of Travel. It's time for the 12 Commandments of Smart, Cost-Conscious Travel.

1. **Never make a phone call, change money, or send out laundry from your hotel.** Each of these activities is a hotel profit center, and hefty surcharges are added. Change money at an ATM, use a cellphone or public booth for your calls, and visit a laundromat to wash your clothing.

2. **In addition to avoiding hotel cashiers for money-changing purposes, do the same with respect to commercial money-changing kiosks and other storefront establishments.** Look instead for a bank, the biggest you can find; they offer a fair rate. Better yet, search for a bank ATM machine that honors your card—they are increasingly found all over the world—and you'll get even better rates from them.

3. **Pack the least amount of clothing your courage will allow.** People who don't pack light become money-squandering beasts of burden, needing expensive porters and taxis, unable to shop around among several hotels for the best value.

4. As a tourist, **eat one meal a day picnic-style.** Pick up bread, pâté, cheese, and wine from the foreign equivalent of a delicatessen or at the grocery section of a department store, and consume them on a park bench, alongside a river, or even in your hotel room. You'll save money and eat healthily at the same time.

5. **When eating at restaurants abroad, split, share, and divide with your travel companion.** When two of you dine, order one appetizer and one main course, and then split those dishes between you; you'll still send uneaten food back to the kitchen, and you'll save 50%.

6. **Never judge a hotel by its facade.** Some of the best lodgings values are in period buildings centuries old. Don't be deterred by the lack of an impressive lobby. Go upstairs and inspect the rooms.

7. **Visiting any large city, make a point of learning to use inexpensive public transportation.** Sample the neighborhoods. You'll not only save money, you'll discover how other people live.

8. And **sightsee on your own two feet,** without a plan, resisting the lures of city sightseeing motorcoach tours. On your strolls, you'll eventually pass the same great monuments and museums visited by the buses, but you'll see so much more, and without cost: You'll look into the courtyards of schools and hospitals, visit groceries and shops, talk with local residents.

9. **Buy your theater tickets as many residents do—on the day of performance, at half price.** On arriving in any major theater city, ask for the location of the local discount ticket booth.

10. **In any English-speaking city abroad, or here at home, haunt the university bulletin boards**—they contain the best-possible calendar of events, revealing a treasure trove of listings for free and almost

nightly lectures, concerts, workshops, and social gatherings, superior to most other forms of evening entertainment.

11. **In your travels through America, make use of tourist office discount coupons,** available at each city's main tourist information center. These handy leaflets bring important reductions in price at places you already planned to visit.

12. And finally, **never visit any destination without first purchasing a budget guidebook.** No matter how confident you may be of your own travel knowledge, you will always find in such books at least a few valuable suggestions of low-priced lodgings, meals, and activities of which you would otherwise have been unaware.

THERE'S WISDOM IN THE MOST COMMONPLACE RULES OF TRAVEL

Sometimes, the rules for saving money when you travel are so obvious, so simple minded, that I feel embarrassed to cite them. And yet some of us constantly overlook the obvious—such as shopping for your needs in the nontouristic areas of the towns you are visiting. Different neighborhoods charge different prices. In cities heavily visited by tourists, it's smart to shop for travel items, such as postcards, film, and batteries, in areas that aren't frequented by tourists—you'll save up to 50%. And sometimes, the cheaper shops are found simply 2 blocks away from the main tourist strip. And breakfast bought in a cafe located far from the tourist throngs will often cost a third of what it does in such tourist areas as Times Square in New York. And when you travel abroad this summer, keep in mind that it is almost never necessary to buy an escorted tour to such monumental sights as the Palace of Versailles, Windsor Castle, or Hadrian's Villa. Almost every major attraction near large cities can be reached by public transportation at a fraction of the cost of a commercial tour, and all you have to do is inquire. Want to visit Versailles? Take a suburban train for about $6 round-trip. When an institution is so important that it must be accessible to residents as well as tourists, public transportation there is almost always available.

TIPS

READERS HAVE SUGGESTED STILL OTHER HELPFUL TIPS FOR TRAVEL

1. Driving through Georgia on your way south to Florida, fill up your gas tank—to the very brim—just before you cross the border into Florida,

and you'll save big. Georgia has no gas tax and the prices dramatically increase once you reach Florida.

2. Before traveling by taxi in foreign (or even domestic) locations, always ask a local (often stopping in shops to question the sales staff) what the approximate taxi fare would be to a particular location. In this manner, you can be assured of paying the "locals" rate—instead of inflated tourist rates.

3. Traveling in Spanish- or Portuguese-speaking countries, you can save a great deal on meals by looking for the reduced-price *menu del día* at restaurants in Spain, the *ementa turistica* in Portugal, the *prato commercial* or *prato feido* in Brazil, and the *comida corriente* in Mexico. And limit your big meal of the day to the *comida* around 2 or 3pm, followed by a light dinner *(cena)*.

A JOB IN PARADISE

Club Med is hiring. And although most of its jobs are the standard positions in housekeeping and cooking that you'll find in any hotel, some of them are those dream opportunities to be a sailing instructor, a child-care supervisor, a dance teacher or set designer, disk jockey, or what U.S. resort hotels used to call a "social director" or "tummeler" but which the French term a *gentil organisateur*. What's best about these jobs is that they're in dream locales: Caribbean islands, the Bahamas, or Florida. You send in a written application, then attend a Club Med job fair (scattered around the country) for an interview. I'm not commenting on the pay or working conditions, but you do get room and board (and transportation to the island or beach in question), and since you probably won't devote your life to these endeavors, they may provide you with the chance to clear your head for a season or two. Go to www.clubmedjobs.com for all the details.

HOW CAN YOU MEET DYNAMIC, SPIRITED, LOCAL RESIDENTS WHEN YOU TRAVEL?

One suggestion is to visit a major museum on that day or two per week when local residents take advantage of evening hours (when they're off work) to come visit the collection. As an example, the awesome Metropolitan Museum of Art in New York City is heavily attended on Friday and Saturday nights by lively, culturally active New Yorkers of all ages, and conversations can be struck up in front of a Velasquez or Degas. The same at Los Angeles's remarkable Getty Museum (now the key attraction of that city) and dozens of other U.S. museums during their periodic evening hours, and also at London's National Gallery. In Britain, a visit to bulletin boards in the

University of London area off Great Russell Street will also reveal all kinds of free lectures attended by dynamic residents of London who are more receptive, in that setting, than in any other, to impromptu conversations.

NYROB: AN ODD SOURCE OF TRAVEL VALUES

The *New York Review of Books,* which appears 20 times a year, is one of the most erudite publications in America, devoting itself to the most serious questions of literature and politics. But it is also a superb source of short-term apartment rentals in London, Paris, Rome, Provence, Tuscany, the Hamptons, and the Berkshires. Its classified ads are full of listings of vacation properties offered by various academics for short-term rentals, and since its readership are mainly professors without much money, the properties it offers are quite sensibly priced and furnished with large supplies of books, comfortable reading chairs, and lamps. Next time you're in the market for a vacation apartment or villa, go to a newsstand and pick up the *New York Review of Books.*

PSSSST! THOSE STUDENT SPECIALS FOR AMERICAN TRAVEL PACKAGES AREN'T ALWAYS CONFINED TO STUDENTS.

Some time ago, the giant worldwide student travel operator called STA Travel offered 7 nights of hotel accommodations in Hawaii, as well as round-trip airfare there from the West Coast, for well under $500. That served to remind me that STA offers weekly travel specials on its website that are among the best in the business. Simply log on to www.statravel.com, then click on "Specials." Students and teachers get the best prices, but anyone can book through STA.

TRENDS IN TRAVEL

WHAT'S NEW & DIFFERENT ABOUT TRAVEL TODAY? WHAT ARE THE MOST SIGNIFICANT RECENT TRAVEL TRENDS?

It's always helpful to review the chief travel developments of the year. What's new and different, and how will they affect our future travels?

1. **The dollar comes first.** It has plummeted against the euro and the British pound, greatly reducing the number of Americans traveling transatlantic (a 20% drop, predicts the U.S. Tour Operators Association).

Future consequences of that? We cost-conscious travelers will now need either to consider traveling to new destinations (Central and South America, Eastern Europe, or most of Asia, where the dollar remains strong) or become more willing to use ultra-inexpensive lodgings (private homestays, weekly apartments, vacation exchanges) in western Europe.

2. **Cruise ships have exploded in size.** With the exception of a very few hyperexpensive ships, virtually every new cruise ship is being designed to carry 2,500, 3,000, or even 4,000 passengers. Cruises have thereby become an activity for crowds, and the nature of the experience is greatly altered. Persons preferring a quiet, maritime interlude will need to keep a sharp eye for the occasional discounts offered by small luxury cruise ships.

3. **Central America has soared in popularity.** In addition to Costa Rica, awash in tourism, increasing numbers of Americans are traveling or thinking about traveling to Panama, Honduras, and Nicaragua. The construction of condominiums in Panama has surpassed Miami levels, and numerous American retirees are making exploratory trips there.

4. **Medical and dental tourism have recently attracted record numbers of Americans** to health facilities in Thailand, Singapore, northern Mexico, South Korea, Hungary, Costa Rica, and Rio de Janeiro. A number of serious books favorably commenting on accredited hospitals in those countries have helped Americans overcome their former reluctance to seek low-cost medical and dental treatment outside the United States.

5. **It has become clear that a U.S. passport will become a necessity** for Americans traveling by land, sea, or air from any foreign nation back into the country. Travelers will anxiously scan the news reports for evidence that the U.S. State Department is able to issue such passports expeditiously.

6. **Passenger traffic on Amtrak has created records,** causing growing support in Congress for adequate, multiyear appropriations for the beleaguered national railway system. Attempts by anti-Amtrak forces to phase it out seem to have been thwarted—and we should all rejoice. We should also give an edge to Amtrak in our travel planning.

7. **A boom in the rental of vacation homes has occurred in Orlando** and other Sunbelt locations, as well as abroad. New online services for renting vacation homes have been launched even by hotel companies.

8. **There's been a surprising rise in the popularity of European river cruises,** a pleasant and inexpensive method of touring the Continent.

A similar jump has occurred in the rental of self-skippered boats for cruises along the canals and other nonriver waterways of Europe.

9. **Foreign airfare "aggregators"—notably, Momondo of Denmark and Mobissimo of Italy—have attracted a major U.S. audience** of technophiles who use these services even for obtaining low-cost airfares within the United States.

10. **Priceline has made a surprising comeback,** mainly in the rental of hotel rooms and cars. Apparently, large numbers of travelers feel that they are taking no risk by bidding low prices for deluxe hotels whose ratings ensure a good stay regardless of their identities.

Runners-up to these 10 most significant developments? They include: the startling rise in the number of zany Las Vegas weddings, filling the marriage chapels of that weird city; the growth of the home-exchange industry (you stay in their home while they stay in yours); the growing popularity of the repositioning cruise, in which you spend many days at sea; and the emergence of free hospitality for young people using such websites as www.couchsurfing.com and www.globalfreeloaders.com.

Appendix

LATE DEVELOPMENTS

New websites, tactics, destinations,
travel trends & choices

THE
TROLLEY

57

During the time when this book was in production, the world of travel kept madly careening—some one would say "lurching"—along. Scarcely a day went by without some frantic entrepreneur introducing a new travel website, a new service or attraction, a new and valuable tactic for travelers to pursue. A major economic slowdown required that travel companies call on every bit of cunning creativity to keep bookings strong.

These developments, which occurred too late to be inserted into the organized framework of *Ask Arthur Frommer,* are too good to waste and too important not to be brought to your attention. So we've created this appendix to serve as a last-minute grab bag, containing recent news and opinions from early 2009. It presents its essays at random and in no particular order. You are invited to glance through the pages of this appendix, stopping to read those items relevant to your own vacation planning.

In the days when printed encyclopedias were an important part of anyone's library, publishers would periodically issue small pamphlets of updated information to be inserted within the pages of the main encyclopedia. This section of late developments should be regarded as the equivalent of those supplemental pamphlets, and I very much hope they will be of value to you.

YOU MAY WISH TO KNOW . . .

NOWADAYS, FOR THE FIRST TIME, AN AIR PASSENGER MUST RECONFIRM . . . & RECONFIRM . . . & RECONFIRM

In the wake of major losses, all the big airlines have cut their flights, schedules, and destinations by as much as 15% to 20%. That 4pm nonstop to Milwaukee is about to become a 7pm departure making two stops en route. That 8am flight to Tampa is about to be canceled altogether. That crossing to London's Stansted Airport will be eliminated in favor of a flight to London's Heathrow. And you, the innocent passenger, are about to encounter big problems unless you phone up in advance to learn whether your plane really will be leaving at the time and arriving at the place you desire.

This advice to reconfirm is not just for people flying to airports that may be on the cusp of losing their service. Even service between major cities is being pared down. Orlando, for instance, is seeing many of its flights dropped; to midlevel cities, the number of daily flights may drop by as much as one third. American Airlines has scrubbed its service to London Stansted (which I wrote about last year when flights to Stansted began), so passengers will be rebooked for Heathrow, a different airport a long way across town.

Now when that happens, of course, the airlines automatically rebook passengers from the discontinued flight onto new flights. They are contracted to deliver you to your original destination, but the new journey may involve changing planes or arriving at a completely different time (resulting in the loss of a vacation day and possibly an unexpected hotel stay).

But not every airline is good at notifying passengers when their flights have been changed. E-mail addresses get lost, as do phone numbers. Unhappily, often no one is minding the store when it comes to following up with passengers about these rebookings.

So it's up to you to be proactive and to make sure that your flights have not changed. If you are not happy with the new arrangements, it is up to you to demand that the airline come up with something else. Keep checking your reservations until the time of your departure.

TRAVEL'S LATEST CONTROVERSY RELATES TO ART AUCTIONS ON CRUISE SHIPS (IT'S A BAD IDEA & YOU KNOW IT)

Among the less savory practices on cruise ships are art auctions for the sale of paintings and prints to passengers, many of them inexperienced with how art auctions work. One tip-off to the character of these questionable events is the free booze—typically a table of cocktails and wine—offered before and during the auction; tipsy cruisers get excited about the prospect of scoring deals and buy paintings for multiples of their true values. Recent newspaper articles have reported lawsuits brought against the seagoing art houses for foisting inflated, misrepresented works on ignorant travelers.

Exposés of art auctions on board cruise ships are starting to appear in newsletters circulated to avid travelers. I think you will be intrigued to read that some of the cruise lines have apparently pressured the art houses conducting these sales into allowing passengers to return their purchases for refunds. It is about time.

AN IMPORTANT NEW BOOK CALLED *TRANSPORT REVOLUTIONS* RAISES QUESTIONS FOR ANYONE CONCERNED ABOUT THE FUTURE OF TRAVEL

If the ability to continue traveling means anything to you, then you must concern yourself with questions of energy. Travel is made possible by cars, buses, trains, and planes, and those are propelled almost entirely by oil.

An important book of our time is a recently published work by two Canadian professors, Richard Gilbert and Anthony Perl, called *Transport Revolutions: Moving People and Freight Without Oil,* published by Earthscan of London and available, among other places, at Amazon.com. It makes urgent and—to some—frightening predictions about what will be required to allow persons to continue to travel (or move about) just short years from now.

According to *Transport Revolutions,* the worldwide production of petroleum—conventional oil, heavy oil (from tar sands), natural gas, deep-water oil, polar oil, oil from the continental shelf, and natural gas—will peak no later than 2012 and will thereafter decline at a rate of at least 1% a year. And this is taking into account all the possible future discoveries of additional oil fields, all the secondary recoveries of oil, all the technological advances in extracting heavy oils, every possible favorable expansion of petroleum production. No matter how much additional drilling is done, the finite supplies of oil are such that production will peak—at the latest—just 3 years from now.

Thereafter, a reduction rate of 1% per year, according to them, is devastating and will cause radical dislocations in humankind's ability to use the internal combustion engine as the major means of moving about. Our ability to travel by car, bus, ship, or plane will be gravely affected, and we will be forced to reduce the use of internal combustion engines in favor of new inventions for which we can only pray, such as efficient motors operated by electricity (if such motors can be developed).

Electrical means of transport are the only salvation, and only if they are developed can people continue to travel (or move about) in the numbers they do today. Enormous resources must thus be devoted to developing such new methods, including taxpayer-financed funds.

But while it is conceivable, barely conceivable, that electric cars, buses, streetcars, trains, and even ships can take over our means of transport, air transportation presents problems that cannot be solved through the use of electric motors. (The authors suggest that the conversion of giant passenger cruise ships into transport vehicles may permit large numbers of people to continue traveling transatlantic or intercontinental for an efficient and acceptable use of oil per person, provided they are willing to devote 5 days to the journey in each direction.)

The above is an awkward condensation of simply one of the well-argued points in *Transport Revolutions.* Its subject matter is something all of us should ponder. Its predictions are a wake-up call, a warning that we must quickly and massively adopt measures that will encourage alternative sources of power, primarily from electricity. This is a travel issue, not simply a national issue, and one that will have a direct impact on our ability to continue visiting the world.

LET ME PASS ON A FEW RECENT REACTIONS TO A CITY WE SHALL ALL BE VIEWING SOON: THE GLEAMING, MODERN, SEASIDE VANCOUVER, IN BRITISH COLUMBIA

In February 2010, the world will be watching the Winter Olympics in Vancouver, Canada, and marveling at the emergence of a metropolis that, in some respects, is comparable to Beijing in its modernity—and ethnic makeup. As amazing as it may seem, it is probable that a new census will show nearly 23% of the city's population to be of Chinese origin.

I made a recent trip to Vancouver and was immediately impressed by the city's Asian aspect. At the airport, signs are in English and Chinese. As you stroll the streets, you are struck not only by how young the population is but by the diverse nature of its origins. The initial Chinese influx came from Hong Kong, leaving that city in anticipation of the British handover to China that took place in 1997. These, in the main, were prosperous, talented business people, who immediately established a center for Chinese culture in the Vancouver suburb of Richmond and then spread to all parts of the city. It is largely their children—well dressed, cosmopolitan, optimistic, and lively—who now flock the streets of downtown Vancouver.

On Robson Street, in the center of downtown, one of the largest Chinese restaurants I have ever seen (Hon's Wun-Tun House) is patronized by hundreds of Chinese Canadians (and savvy tourists) who watch a regiment of Chinese chefs working at breakneck pace from a giant elevated kitchen at one side of the room, split into meat-preparing and vegetarian-preparing sections. The fact that Won's has been compelled to prepare vegetarian meals for half their guests is a tip-off to the attitudes of Vancouver's youthful population.

But Vancouver isn't solely Chinese; a full 50% of the population spoke a language other than English as their childhood tongue. A huge Punjabi population (Anglo-Indian) supports an immense world of Indian commerce; a large number of Somalis from Africa live here; a large number of Iraqis were granted asylum here; a significant contingent of other persons of Muslim descent include women who stroll the streets in trendy, attractive, light-silk head scarves. Vancouver is the way it is because Canada welcomes the arrival of immigrants moving here for political reasons.

One morning, the *Globe and Mail* slipped under the door of our hotel room in Banff carried a front-page announcement by the premier of Canada that the government will ease and encourage—get that, "ease and encourage"—the granting of permanent residency visas to immigrants who have come here on temporary work permits and have proved their worth to the state. Take that, Lou Dobbs! Canada is encouraging immigration as a means of adding vibrancy to its society and is preparing a path to citizenship for all the Indian, Chinese, Somali, Iraqi, and other immigrants in its midst.

From all appearances, that diverse population has brought immense prosperity to a city with low unemployment, astonishing construction activity, new convention centers, new parks, new skyscrapers rising up everywhere, and vibrant retail activity. Vancouver, I was told, is the fastest-growing city in Canada, developing at greater pace than even the cities of adjoining Alberta (Calgary and Edmonton) that are benefiting so much from the extraction of oil from tar sands in the area north of Fort McHenry.

Immigration. It was refreshing to hear the subject discussed intelligently and without ugly prejudice. And it was delightful to spend the day in Vancouver's giant Stanley Park, watching Chinese and English and Indian families all enjoying the sun and the picnics and mingling together without tension.

We shall all be watching scenes from Vancouver in February 2010.

WITH ITS RUPEES NOW SELLING AT 48 TO THE DOLLAR, YOU'LL FIND TRAVEL LUXURY AT LOW COST IN INDIA

We all continue to favor those destinations where the cost of living is unusually low—Bali and Argentina come immediately to mind. The ability to offset high airfares with cheap hotel and food costs is the obvious reason for heavy tourist traffic to those budget-priced wonders.

This is why India should be considered by travelers looking for luxury at low cost. Its hotel, food, and touring costs are among the world's cheapest, as you will see for yourself when you request quotes from the chief Indian tour operators and travel agents.

Using luxurious hotels and supplying passengers with a car, driver, and guide for their entire trip, such companies as Indian Moments (www.indian moments.com) have been quoting total prices of $3,000 for a 14-day stay in multiple destinations for two persons (not including airfare to India). And that outlay includes upscale hotel accommodations with daily breakfast for 14 nights, the private car and driver/guide, and at least one air flight within India. You travel, in effect, like a maharajah; though I personally feel that a less pretentious approach results in a more rewarding and authentic experience, it is a level of comfort that some luxury-loving Americans demand. Arriving to the bustle and exoticism of India, they take great relief in finding their drivers awaiting their arrivals, holding up signs with their names on them.

And you can greatly reduce that $3,000 charge by insisting to Indian Moments that you want a less expensive level of hotel accommodations.

Cheaper prices for your trip to India? Go to the website of Culture Holidays (www.cultureholidays.com) and note that for their Golden Triangle Tour (Delhi-Agra-Jaipur-and-Delhi) of 7 days and 6 nights, you can pay as little as $600 per person for "economy" hotels with daily breakfast, train transportation, private car sightseeing within cities, and more.

And note that G.A.P Adventures (www.gapadventures.com) and smarTours (www.smartours.net) both operate inexpensive, small-group tours to India.

If you have not been, you should go; India is fast developing into a superpower, yet its cost structure remains refreshingly low. Airfare there? Using Etihad Airways (flying via Abu Dhabi) or Air India, you'll generally pay $940 round-trip in the off season, $1,140 round-trip in the high season, between New York and either Mumbai or Delhi.

OVERNIGHTS IN INDIA FROM A WEBSITE CALLED MAHINDRA HOMESTAYS ARE A TREMENDOUS RECENT BREAKTHROUGH

If there is one destination where a Westerner could use a secure home base and some guidance and education about what they're seeing, it is India. The country, currently enjoying a touristic upsurge because of its extremely low on-the-ground costs, is a fascinating blend of people, religions, classes, cuisine, and lifestyles, and without a trained eye, it is difficult to decipher the tumult. A homestay from **www.mahindrahomestays.com**, including daily breakfast, places you with a well-heeled Indian family that is interested in reaching out to foreigners and smoothing their contact with India. All of Mahindra's hosts give travelers their own private quarters, which are air-conditioned in almost all cases, a real perk in the sweltering summer.

Most of Mahindra's 30 prospective homes range from $40 to $120 per night (about the same as a moderate-level hotel) and are found in exceptionally well-groomed, spacious homes with English-speaking hosts (it's marketed mostly to the British). At the upper price level, the homes have the appearance of lush, sprawling homes of fair size. The website has plenty of photos, which is not very common yet for online services in India, as well as descriptions and pictures of your potential hosts. Although breakfast is included, you can usually buy your other meals, too, if you want, and you can choose to eat alone or with your hosts.

The company also has representatives in London, reachable by phone at ☎ 44-20-8140-8422.

FOUR-WHEEL LUGGAGE IS CURRENTLY BOOMING IN POPULARITY, FOR REASONS SOMEWHAT DIFFICULT TO FIGURE

The addition of wheels to luggage marked a great advance in travel comfort but did not entirely eliminate the fatigue of dragging a heavy suitcase through airports. When you have to angle that luggage to permit it to move along on two wheels, a considerable effort is still required to pull it along, especially for fair distances.

And that's the apparent reason why new four-wheel suitcases are enjoying such a heavy sale. I am told that female travelers, as well as elderly travelers, are flocking to the four-wheel variety and find them much easier to pull. Why this is, I cannot quite figure out; the suitcase apparently remains fully upright and must be pushed rather than pulled; and yet everyone to whom I have spoken sings their praises.

Among the luggage manufacturers, Samsonite seems to be emphasizing four wheels to a greater extent than the others; its online catalogue refers to them as "Spinners" and devotes a number of pages to them. Another big mail-order seller of luggage, Magellan's, is offering four-wheel luggage as well.

Can any of the engineers among our readers explain why a four-wheel suitcase is easier to pull than a two-wheel suitcase? Or is a physical therapist better able to explain the phenomenon?

HOW VALID ARE THE STATE DEPARTMENT'S "WARNINGS" AGAINST VISITING PARTICULAR COUNTRIES?

Over the years, the U.S. State Department has issued what they call "advisories"—admonitions, cautions, but not necessarily flat statements, that you should not under any circumstance consider a vacation or even a short trip to the specified location.

The department has more recently adopted a sterner admonition and a more limited list, using the words "Travel Warnings" to identify 27 nations that you really should not ever visit. The 27 nations include many that all of us would instantly agree are not suitable for tourism: Afghanistan, for instance, or Iraq, Somalia, Sudan, or Yemen.

The complete list of 27 inherently dangerous places consists of: Afghanistan, Algeria, Burundi, Central African Republic, Chad, Colombia, Côte d'Ivoire, Democratic Republic of the Congo, Eritrea, the Gaza Strip and the West Bank, Georgia, Haiti, Iran, Iraq, Kenya, Lebanon, Nepal, Nigeria, Pakistan, Philippines, Saudi Arabia, Somalia, Sri Lanka, Sudan, Syria, Uzbekistan, and Yemen.

I recently published those names and immediately stirred up a hornet's nest. From all over came protests that many of the places named were eminently suitable for a look-see.

Colombia's inclusion on the list was assailed by everyone. For decades, its giant, historic, seaport city of Cartagena has been visited by innumerable cruise ships and massive numbers of tourists without mishap. Tourist industry professionals are almost unanimous in praising not only Cartagena but, increasingly, the capital city of Bogota, no longer under siege by a dwindling Colombian insurgency. European tour groups have returned in large numbers to Bogota and most other nonborder areas of Colombia.

Kenya, for the past 30 years, has been visited without difficulty by safari-bound tour groups, who are met at the Nairobi airport, transferred to overnight lodges, and then taken into the Masai Maara by bus or small plane for their encounters with the vast herds of wildlife that roam that prehistoric area. I would not hesitate to recommend a Kenyan safari conducted by one of the reputable tour companies that have safely operated there for such a long time.

Nepal, its political strife overcome and dispelled, is again being visited by large numbers of Western tourists, and recent travelers are reporting that it is now reasonably safe. The "Maoist" movement that once robbed trekkers along the trail to the foothills of Mt. Everest has now been incorporated into the political life of Nepal and, from every report, no longer threatens visitors.

The Philippines, according to some of my correspondents, should be avoided only in certain well-defined locations known to all travel professionals, but it is otherwise reportedly safe.

In general, the State Department list is for the casual tourist, not the discerning traveler who knows what he or she is doing. The fact is that difficulty in one location does not make an entire country dangerous.

THE "GREENWAYS" BETWEEN PRAGUE & VIENNA ARE AN ENCHANTING SLICE OF MEDIEVAL EUROPE & INEXPENSIVE TO EXPERIENCE

With the dollar weak and transatlantic airfares high, most Europe-bound travelers will appreciate the chance to enjoy a largely free-of-charge activity when they make a trip to the Old World this spring, summer, or early fall. I am referring to an easy, multiday hike along the well-marked and well-maintained "Greenways" of the Czech Republic, staying overnight in low-cost inns and guesthouses along the way.

The best-known "Greenway" is a 250-mile hiking and biking trail between the capitals of the Czech Republic and Austria. At intervals along the trail are small, medieval villages that have scarcely changed over the centuries. In them are tiny hotels and guesthouses, some with as few as a dozen rooms renting at most for $40 per person. Scattered about are local restaurants serving a memorable central European cuisine and the world's most celebrated beer.

It is not necessary to hike or bike the entire 250 miles. You can eliminate several 30-mile chunks by taking inexpensive buses from village to village along the "Greenways" route. Many travelers start by taking a bus from Prague to Cesky[as] Krumlov to begin their hike. They take other buses here and there, reducing the walking or cycling length of the trip to about 15 to 20 miles a day.

The trail is mainly level, through enchanting forests, alongside the foothills of low mountains, and in only a handful of instances need you walk up an incline or climb over an elevated ridge. You pass farmhouse relics of the Middle Ages or of the Renaissance, scarcely touched. In 4 or 5 days, you have one of the great adventures of travel, preceded or followed by a 3- or 4-day stay in stately Prague, where you will need to locate a hotel in an outlying neighborhood to escape the high costs of the center.

The "Greenways" of the Czech Republic, the most famous of which goes through the legendary (and inexpensive) Bohemia on the way to Vienna, are marketed by an organization accessed at **www.pragueviennagreen ways.org** and located in Brooklyn, New York, of all places. If you log on to that site, you will soon be captivated by this outstanding European opportunity. You will also find various arrangements for shipping your luggage from place to place, if you are unwilling to reduce your needs to one small knapsack.

For important new reasons, Hawaii & Morocco are strong contenders for your next vacation

Because the job of planning a visit to Hawaii or Morocco has recently become easier than ever, both should be high up on your list of worthy choices.

Chief of these is Hawaii. Suffering badly from a downturn in visitor numbers, the airlines that service Hawaii and the hotels that accommodate visitors have begun frantically discounting their prices. And the best place for discovering such deals is the website of the Hawaii Convention and Visitors Bureau, **www.gohawaii.com**.

In a radical shift in its advertising approach, the current website of the Hawaii CVB is featuring Hawaiian bargains. Because the best of those are air-and-land packages (enabling hotels and airlines to discount their rates without revealing that they are doing so), the main menu page of the site lists the icons for all the most prominent tour operators to Hawaii—Pleasant Holidays, Blue Sky Tours, Funjet Vacations, United Vacations, Liberty

Travel, Orbitz, Travelocity, Hawaii Connection, All About Hawaii, Expedia, and American Airlines Vacations. It's an impressive group. By clicking them, you will quickly discover radically reduced prices for your trip.

It is also possible to find heavily discounted airfares to Hawaii by periodically looking at a feisty website called BeatofHawaii.com, which periodically lists the sales by airlines servicing Honolulu from various West Coast cities (never including Los Angeles or San Francisco). If you are content with a deal flying out of Portland, Oregon, or San Jose, California, you will find them here—but these are usually last-minute offers valid only for a few days. The Hawaii CVB seems better suited to the traveler planning a few weeks in advance.

Morocco is also suddenly "hot." Four small-group adventure tour operators—G.A.P Adventures, of Toronto (**www.gapadventures.com**); Adventure Center, of Emeryville, California (**www.adventurecenter.com**); Intrepid Travel, of Australia (**www.intrepidtravel.com**); and Djoser, of the Netherlands (**www.djoser.com**)—offer exciting ways to visit Morocco (and other exotic or remote destinations) at moderate costs. All of them limit their tour groups to 12 persons; make use of public transportation for moving about; place their passengers in modest, locally owned accommodations (guesthouses and even private homes); and charge under $1,000 for a 2-week trip, not including airfare.

The Canadian-owned G.A.P Adventures has recently announced an especially compelling program for visiting Morocco in 2009 and 2010—10 different itineraries of 10 days' duration (usually) that are all priced at $689 per person, plus 250€ in cash, plus airfare. Actually, the price will work out to less than $689 per person if the U.S. dollar continues to buy about 1.20 Canadian dollars, because G.A.P's prices are all in Canadian dollars.

These are breathtaking journeys, especially the 10-day "Moroccan Sojourn" that crosses the High Atlas Mountains before descending into predesert countryside and reaching the UNESCO World Heritage Kasbah Ait Ben Haddou, a popular film location. From there, you ride a camel to the oasis of Nakhia and stay overnight in nomadic tents. You can also go to Marrakech and tour its historic precincts and world-famous market, then move on to the charming resort city of Essaouira. Here is a modestly priced once-in-a-lifetime travel opportunity

---

A CANADIAN TOUR OPERATOR IS GEARING UP TO HANDLE BIKE TOURS THROUGH CUBA, BY AMERICANS, THE MOMENT THE TRAVEL EMBARGO THERE IS EASED

You have probably never heard of MacQueen's Island Tours, best known for its "Independent Supported Bicycle Tours" of Prince Edward Island in the

Canadian Maritimes. It operates wonderfully inexpensive cycling trips in which you travel independently but have bikes made available to you, nightly hotel reservations made for you, transport of your luggage from place to place, and breakfast every morning.

Since 1995, MacQueen's has run similar tours in Cuba. Its 14-day "Vuelta Cuba" program from Santiago to Havana is heavily booked by Canadians of all ages. Here, you receive both breakfast and dinner (as well as occasional cervezas and mojitos) and visit historic locations ranging from villages in the Sierra Maestra mountains to Bayamo, Camaguey, the city and province of Cienfuegos, the Bay of Pigs, and more.

Because MacQueen's prices are quoted in Canadian dollars, which are discounted currently by about 20% against the U.S. dollar, the average cost for one of MacQueen's tours is about US$180 per person, per day, an entirely reasonable charge for bicycles, accommodations, two meals daily, local representatives, and other features.

Many Americans are unaware that there is already such heavy tourism to Cuba by Canadians and Europeans (the United States alone embargoes tourism to Cuba) that most hotels in Havana are fully booked for many months of the year. Thus, the ending or easing of the embargo will not be followed immediately by a torrent of U.S. visitors to Havana; it will take time for more hotels to be built or opened. And thus, such operators as MacQueen's (whose program there is called WOWCuba), creating unusual alternative methods of travel within that country, will provide one of the only programs available for immediate booking.

It thus might be prudent for you to study MacQueen's website (**www.wowcuba.com/bike/sp-tour.html**) and its several programs in anticipation of the lifting or easing of the U.S. embargo against travel to Cuba by the Obama administration. As someone who has traveled twice through Cuba (legally, as a journalist) and witnessed the damaging effects of the totally counter-productive embargo policy of our government, I can also confirm that this is an exciting travel experience. I shall be paying close attention to developments and shall leap to report them.

IF YOU ARE A FREQUENT MOTORIST ON THE ROADS OF AMERICA & YOU LOVE SAMPLING LOCAL DISHES, YOU WILL WANT TO GET A COPY OF *DINERS, DRIVE-INS AND DIVES*

I'm talking, of course, not about the interstates but about the lesser-traveled local roads that still feature diners with "fat back" and "chow chow" on the menu. Food Network host Guy Fieri has published a guidebook to the best of these locally owned, nonchain eateries, and I find it amazingly useful for adding seasoning to car trips almost anywhere in America.

HOW DESPERATE IS THE CRUISE SHIP INDUSTRY FOR LAST-MINUTE BOOKINGS? TO LEARN HOW MUCH, GO TO THE WEBSITE OF SOUTHWEST AIRLINES.

It's the last place where you'd expect cruises to be sold, and yet one gets the impression that the cruise lines rely on Southwest to sell their most desperately underbooked sailings. Log on to **www.southwest.com**, click on "Special Offers" at the top of the main menu page, click on "Cruises," and then access any number of subject matters, but especially the one reading "NCL Cruises This Winter."

You'll find 3-night cruises from Miami selling for $99. You'll find 4-night cruises from Miami selling for $100. You'll find other sailings, such as 7-night cruises from various U.S. ports, selling for $284, a full $15 less than the most amazing distress bargains offered by some of the other cruise discounters.

The economics of the cruise industry require it to fill every sailing to capacity and to maximize the revenue from such profit centers as onboard casinos, alcoholic drinks, shore excursions, and souvenirs. Cruises that have vacant cabins are offering them, as Southwest does, for as little as $25 per day per person (see that 4-night sailing for $100).

IN A VALUABLE NEW SERVICE, YAPTA WILL NOW ALERT YOU TO THE FLIGHTS ON WHICH YOUR FREQUENT-FLIER MILEAGE CAN BE USED

I have been somewhat dubious about the worth of the website known as Yapta.com. That is the service that continually tracks the price of an air ticket that you have already bought; if the price of the ticket goes down after you have purchased it, Yapta lets you know, and you can then buy a cheaper ticket. Trouble is, many of the airlines charge a fee for reissuing a ticket at a different price, and that fee can often (but not always) wipe out the savings. Yapta claims that the price reductions it is currently seeing are far larger than the penalty for changing your ticket.

Now, however, Yapta has announced a second service that seems of undeniable value. If you tell them what you are looking for, **it will periodically advise you of the flights on which your frequent-flier mileage will be accepted.** No longer do you need to place endless phone calls to the carrier in whose loyalty program you are enrolled; Yapta will tell you the date and flight on which you will be able to use those frequent-flier miles.

The exact announcement recently made by Yapta (the initials stand for "Your Amazing Personal Travel Assistant") reads as follows:

> Yapta.com today announced the launch of its frequent-flier award seat alert service, enabling travelers to be notified when they can use their frequent-flier miles to book an award seat that becomes available on a specific flight. The award seat alerts are provided in tandem with Yapta's airfare price change alerts that, to date, have notified hundreds of thousands of travelers of more than $90 million in airfare savings.

For persons wanting to use their frequent-flier miles effectively, this sounds like an excellent service.

LIFTOPIA.COM IS THE MOST EXCITING NEW SKI WEBSITE IN YEARS

A San Francisco website has apparently negotiated with ski resorts all over the nation for discounts and deals. And this year, of all years, those deals are going to be many and meaningful. If you go to Liftopia's website (www.liftopia.com), you will immediately find a simple, quick way to unearth low-price lifts and low-price ski resorts and thus plan a ski vacation that is within your budget. Enjoy.

GUESS WHICH "OPAQUE" TRAVEL WEBSITE HAS NOW MADE "FULL DISCLOSURE" OF MANY OF ITS AIRFARE & HOTEL BARGAINS?

A recent bargain-price travel website will increase your chances to fly and stay for less. Surprisingly enough, it is from Hotwire.com and reflects the increasing desperation on the part of everyone in the travel industry to off-set the current economic downturn.

Hotwire.com, as you know, is an opaque site—it does not tell you the identity of the hotels, airlines, or car-rental firms whose discounted prices it offers until you first commit yourself to buy. Hotwire.com is the fight-to-the-death competitor of another opaque site, Priceline.com, and obviously both firms are now frantic for business.

What Hotwire.com apparently has done is to take advantage of its huge inventory of bargain products and offer them a second time in a full-disclosure website, side by side with its opaque website but independent of it. The new Internet product is called Travel Ticker (**www.travel-ticker.com**). It was from Travel Ticker that I recently learned about $119-a-night suites offered at the superdeluxe Venetian Hotel in Las Vegas.

Obviously, Hotwire.com was offering those suites as mystery purchases on its opaque website, but just to make sure that you did not miss the boon, it also offered them with full disclosure on Travel Ticker.

Such is the craziness of the current travel market. From now on, when you are looking for a superbargain to anywhere, you may want to consult Travel Ticker.

When it comes to finding really expensive trips, the travel section of the *New York Times* has no peer

Guess what led the news (p. 2) in a recent travel section of the *New York Times?* It was an article called "Traveling in Style Through Rural Italy," which tells about a 5-night drive through Tuscany, not including airfare, for $9,000 per person, based on two persons traveling together. So you and your sweetie can spend only $18,000 for the two of you (5 nights, 4 days) to travel in a vintage Italian car of the 1950s, 1960s, or 1970s, plus receive luxury accommodations, "most meals" (not all of them), and various other extras, such as a mechanic who drives along in an emergency support vehicle.

$18,000 for just the two of you . . . 5 nights . . . not including airfare to Italy.

And if you think I'm making this up, see **www.vintagecartour.com**, the source of this unique deal, which actually cites a higher price (the *Times* must have overlooked it) of $10,950 per person (and therefore $21,900 per couple) for the 5-night drive through Tuscany.

The business pages of numerous newspapers and magazines are currently reporting on their decline in circulation and advertising. When a major newspaper devotes space to an absurdity like this, you can understand why the public is turning elsewhere for their travel information.

Ever heard of Points.com? It enables you to maximize your frequent-flier mileage in ways in which you might never have heard.

Points.com operates like eBay: It brings people together who want to trade assets (in the case of eBay, money for various products) and then steps aside while the two "traders" enter into their exchange. Until recently, Points.com allowed holders of frequent-flier points on a particular airline to trade those points with someone else who had frequent-flier points on another airline.

But now it has gone further. Today, Points.com permits you to trade your frequent-flier mileage (points or miles) for points entitling you to hotel stays. And that is a big advance.

There have always been frequent-flier-type programs offered for stays at the hotels of various chains. By belonging to one program, say, you could use your points for stays at Hilton hotels. But what if you preferred to use them for a stay at Hyatt hotels? Or Marriott? Or Holiday Inn? You were out of luck.

Points.com permits you to trade those points for use at a large number of hotel chains. Or for a large number of other travel privileges or assets. Or for flights on a large number of other airlines. It also permits you to supplement your privileges with a small cash payment and thus obtain either flights or hotel stays for which you might not otherwise have been entitled.

Take a look at Points.com, whose transactions are fully authorized and acceptable to the airlines. It will make your use of these privileges far more effective and satisfying.

WITH LODGINGS COSTLY IN POPULAR CITIES AROUND THE WORLD, MORE FREE-OF-CHARGE (OR NOMINALLY PRICED) HOSPITALITY SERVICES ARE EMERGING

I've reported before on CouchSurfing (**www.couchsurfing.com**) and GlobalFreeloaders.com (**www.globalfreeloaders.com**), the latter attracting largely Australian travelers. Two more have recently emerged, which you might try for your next trip.

The Hospitality Club (**www.hospitalityclub.org**) was started by a 22-year-old German (he's now 30), primarily to make free homestays available to members. Like most of these sites, it is not commercial. It exists because its founder believes in free-spirited travel divorced from money concerns and in international friendships. How does he do it? He funds the effort by accepting Google ads. And he protects your privacy by handling communication via the site's messaging system, so that your e-mail address is not posted. It is an interesting example of responsible, idealistic commerce.

RoomFT (**www.roomft.com**), which stands for "Room For Travellers," is a smaller operation that has an optional system for verifying and reviewing hosts as well as a feedback system that is similar to eBay's—a sincere but rather flimsy way to vet participants. Hosts (not the travelers) pay $2 each time they get a booking, but otherwise, the price for the room is up to them and the guest. Stays can be free, bartered, or paid for at an incredibly low rate.

VACATION HOME RENTALS IN ORLANDO ARE NOW SO POPULAR THAT TWO ORGANIZATIONS HAVE BEEN FORMED TO KEEP THEM HONEST

It is important news affecting your own next stay in Mouse Land: The major professional home rental companies have banded together to form self-policing associations for rental homes. The whole point of the enterprise is to treat customers well and boost confidence in the industry. They are all run professionally and maintain a code of ethics so that vacationers know they can be trusted.

The two websites to check are Discover Vacation Homes (**www.discover vacationhomes.com**) and the Central Florida Vacation Rental Managers Association (☎ **800/486-8302;** www.vacationwithconfidence.com). Both list available properties and smooth the reservations process.

Discover Vacation Homes reps eight different companies, which comprise 13% of the overall area market. There are strict decorating standards (furniture must be new, not ratty or old); you are almost always guaranteed in-home washer/dryers, multiple TVs, a pool or quick access to one; and so on. You can check in 24 hours a day, too.

Central Florida Vacation Rental Managers Association, another booster organization of professional renters, runs its service with similar standards. (Some companies are part of both of these groups.)

HAVING MORPHED INTO A GENERAL "DEAL" SEARCH ENGINE, PRICELINE.COM SHOULD NOW BE ACCESSED WHENEVER YOU ARE LOOKING FOR A GOOD AIRFARE OR HOTEL RATE

It used to be that Priceline.com (**www.priceline.com**) was a rather exotic service meant only for the gamblers among us, the people willing to accept the risk of a 6am flight or an out-of-town-center hotel. By featuring its bidding process ("name your own price"), Priceline.com came up with absurdly low air or hotel rates, but at the cost of sometimes providing a dawn departure, a multistop flight, or a badly located hotel.

That's all changed. Although Priceline.com still maintains its "name your own price" option—the way to get the very lowest prices imaginable—it now also offers the same full-disclosure airfares and hotel rates that such companies as Hotels.com, Expedia, Travelocity, Orbitz, and others offer.

And would you believe it? It often undercuts the prices offered by those other "full disclosure" websites. Moreover, it does not charge the same extra fees that those other websites often impose.

I hate to complicate your life, but what this means is the following: If you are simply looking for a flight or a hotel room and are not hellbent on getting the absolutely lowest price, you now have to go to Priceline.com in addition to going to such other standard services as Expedia, Hotels.com, Travelocity, and so forth. You have to add another search to be absolutely sure you are getting the best available deal.

And if you are looking for a stunning price, a price that cannot be beaten, you still have to utilize the alternate, "name your own price" feature of Priceline.com. To "bid" for a cool price is still the route to amazing savings.

A travel-publishing friend of mine was recently required to stay overnight in a hotel in Manhattan. He used Priceline.com, specified that he had to have a four-star hotel in midtown, and ended up getting a room for only $150 a night at the fancy and well-located Intercontinental Hotel (which usually charges around $450 a night).

I am also told (but have not been able to confirm yet) that the slowdown in travel has led to the reappearance of top, last-minute airfare deals on Priceline.com for people willing to take a chance. Apparently, the airlines are now, once again, heavily using Priceline.com to dispose of their last-minute unsold seats—of which there are a great many.

But the biggest news with Priceline.com is that it has also become a standard, full-disclosure search engine for airfares and hotel rates, not only in the United States but abroad. It is no secret that Priceline.com recently acquired the big European hotel search engine called Booking.com (**www. booking.com**), so if you are looking for a deal on a European hotel, you should now also go to Booking.com (in addition to Hotels.com and Quikbook.com).

Booking.com will quote U.S. dollar prices, in English, for people using U.S. credit cards.

WHO WOULD HAVE THOUGHT IT? PARIS NOW HAS A "GREETERS" PROGRAM—& IT IS BOUND TO BE A BIG SUCCESS.

The widespread indictment of Parisians as discourteous to the visitor, aloof and patronizing, has not been true for years.

It was true for a certain time in the immediate postwar years, when French chagrin over their record in resisting the Germans caused a certain bitterness toward almost every outsider. The French (and especially the Parisians) were short and abrupt with the visitor, whom they generally treated as uncouth, uneducated, and vulgarly common.

Then, as if a switch had been turned, the situation changed—and for at least the past 15 years, the French, including the Parisians, have been models of pleasantness and courtesy. Ask a Parisian for instructions and he or she will sometimes walk with you to the destination. Show uncertainty about working the coin machines at the local Metro (subway) and locals will patiently assist you.

But now the Big News. Following New York's lead (and New York has been offering this for several years now), Paris has created a "greeters' program" operated by a corps of local volunteers who will meet you at your hotel and take you on a 2- to 3-hour tour of a neighborhood designated by you or favored (and suggested) by them. The entire tour is free of charge, and you are simply to pick up the transportation expenses (like a Metro ticket), if any, of your greeter. Most tours are conducted entirely on foot.

You must, of course, provide fair notice, submitting your request for a "greeter" at least 1 or 2 weeks in advance of your arrival in Paris.

A quick look at the charming "greeter" website is enough to prove the obvious good will of the program. It has been conveyed stylishly and with great flair, as only the French can do. I predict big things for Paris's "greeters' program" and suggest that you look right away at **www.parisgreeter.org**.

Ever heard of AAE Hotels & Hostels? They can be a godsend when you are traveling alone & seeking $25-a-night digs.

When I learned that Las Vegas had a hostel on the Strip, I investigated further and discovered that it belongs to a budget chain known as AAE Hotels & Hostels.

AAE now offers centrally located hotels and hostels in nearly every major tourist location in the United States: Miami Beach, New York, Las Vegas, Santa Barbara, Anaheim, Charleston (South Carolina), Chicago, Grand Canyon, Los Angeles, San Antonio, San Diego, San Francisco, Santa Cruz, Seattle, and Washington, D.C., most of them charging around $25 a night for beds in dormlike (four to a room) accommodations. This is a growing inventory of decent but rock-bottom-priced lodgings created (mainly) from former standard hotels and made into budget hotels or hostels by simply placing four beds into what used to be double rooms. And if only two persons are around to share a room, they still pay only $25 apiece.

In Europe, AAE has budget hotels and hostels in Amsterdam, Andorra, Barcelona, Berlin, Brasov (Romania), Croatia, Kraków, and Venice. But their U.S. properties—which share a common reservations number (☎ 304/268-8981; www.aaehotels.com)—are the real finds, and you will be impressed by the photographs of rooms and public facilities found on the website.

Big news! Amtrak will now sell USA Rail Passes to U.S. residents.

Like its model, the Eurailpass, the USA Rail Pass allows you to make unlimited trips within a particular time period for a single lump sum. And because the discount it offers is so advantageous to frequent rail passengers, its sale has been restricted—until now—to persons residing abroad.

For reasons they have not yet explained (and why look a gift horse in the mouth?), the officials of Amtrak have announced that U.S. residents can now buy and use the USA Rail Pass. Details for purchase are at ☎ 800/872-7245 or at **http://tickets.amtrak.com/itd/amtrak/selectpass**.

The pass is for three different periods of use: 15, 30, and 45 days of travel. The 15-day pass offers eight different trips for $389 ($48.63 per trip). The 30-day pass offers 12 segments of travel for $579 ($48.25 per trip). The 45-day pass offers 18 segments of travel for $749 ($41.61 per trip).

Let us assume you want to make six round-trips between New York and Washington, D.C., in a 1-month period. Buying the USA Rail Pass cuts the cost of each one-way trip to $48.25.

The pass is not available for the Acela- or Florida-bound Auto Train. But it brings about remarkable savings for frequent travelers making use of other trains. This is significant news and an example of the kind of transport values that an expanded and improved, high-speed Amtrak could bring to our lives.

ARE TRAVEL AGENTS STAGING A COMEBACK? TRIPOLOGY SEEMS TO THINK SO.

When the airlines decided they would no longer pay commissions to travel agents, forcing the latter to begin charging extra fees for their services, the number of travel agents plunged. Some observers predicted that only the specialists, the persons with out-of-the-ordinary knowledge about certain destinations or modes of travel, would survive.

That belief is the basis for a new website called Tripology (**www.tripology.com**), which rounds up specialist travel agents for your next trip. You go to the website, describe the sort of trip you are contemplating, and Tripology circulates your profile among several thousand beleaguered travel agents around the country, asking whether any can help you. Tripology then advises you within a day or so of, usually, three travel agents who have suggested a particular kind of trip that meets your needs and the price at which they are able to book it. You contact the person whose services seem promising and begin discussions.

If you are simply looking for a standard trip—say, a week in Aruba—you probably would not go to Tripology. But if you are a vegan looking for a week in Aruba at a hotel that will match your eating needs (no fish, no milk products, just veggies), then you use Tripology. Or if you are a person who wants to travel only with fellow anthropologists on your next trip to Albania or Fiji, you try Tripology.

I myself have not tested Tripology, but several thousand Americans already have, and it appears that the website is succeeding. You apparently do not have anything to lose by trying it, as you are not obligated to accept the offers for help that they will forward to you.

THE DUBAI CRIMINAL CODE MAKES IT AN OFFENSE TO HAVE SEX OUTSIDE OF MARRIAGE. SUCH A HIP & HAPPY NATION!

The newspapers of Great Britain were filled with stories about the arrest of an unmarried, heterosexual, British couple (tourists) for having sex on a beach in the early hours of the morning. But the stories also pointed out that the Dubai criminal code makes sex occurring anywhere to be illegal, even in the privacy of a hotel room, if it is between people who are not married. Note that the code is directed not at homosexual encounters (which are treated much more severely) but at sex between an unmarried man and an unmarried woman. You can be imprisoned for that alone and not simply for causing a public spectacle.

What a fun place for a vacation.

As you read the hype about the glories of tourism to Dubai, with its indoor ski slope and artificial tropical islands, you might want to consider whether vacationing in a place of such hideous backwardness can ever be justified.

Not too long ago, the Royal Caribbean Cruise Line announced it was stationing a large cruise ship in Dubai to operate weekly cruises in the area. I wonder whether persons who have visited Israel and have Israeli stamps in their passports will be permitted aboard these cruises—there are conflicting reports (the situation is, at best, ambiguous) about whether Dubai will deny entry to travelers with these stamps (or ban any entry by holders of Israeli passports). It will be interesting to see whether an American cruise ship company will cooperate in direct discrimination against a large segment of their U.S. cruise ship audience.

NEW GOURMET DINING OPTIONS & SEVERAL NEW MUSEUMS GIVE PROOF THAT SIN CITY IS ATTEMPTING TO BROADEN ITS IMAGE

Until recently, there really was no reason other than gambling for visiting Las Vegas. Increasingly today, other activities are emerging to appeal to the visitor uninterested in casinos.

Food, for one. The restaurant industry is today claiming that as many visitors come to Vegas for its restaurants as for its green-felt gaming tables.

Virtually every famous chef is now represented here, including Joel Robuchon of Parisian fame, whose Las Vegas eatery charges $385 per person for its tasting menu. You can now often purchase coupons costing about $3 to get major discounts at restaurants operated by such famous names as Mario Batali, at the Venetian Hotel. (These are sold in the same kiosks that offer cut-rate admission to evening shows and entertainers.)

The Wynn Resort & Casino claims that its fish is flown in daily from Europe, already filleted to serve the presentation needs of its cooks. Elsewhere in Vegas, the top bargains and the best food are found in the off-Strip restaurants catering to residents of the city, including Lotus of Siam, which my daughter (in her guidebook to Vegas) claims is the city's single best restaurant and which *Gourmet* magazine has described as the single best Thai restaurant in all of North America (it is also cheap—you can eat for under $20).

But the best indication of the city's broadening appeal is its slew of new museums and tours having nothing to do with gambling. One tour deals with the city's mob history. A new museum, the Springs Preserve, deals with Vegas's location at a freshwater spring in the center of the Mojave Desert. Water is an increasing problem as Vegas takes on new population and needs, and the Springs Preserve can occupy several fascinating hours. It deals not only with Vegas's water problems but with water shortages all over the world, an issue that will soon be more pressing than the exhaustion of oil reserves (we can live without oil but not without water).

Add the important Atomic Testing Museum (an off-shoot of the Smithsonian), the Fine Arts Gallery of the Bellagio, and the Valley of Fire (terrific hiking); then add the water museum to the Liberace Museum and Hoover Dam to Red Rock Valley, throw in a good assortment of restaurants, and you have reasons other than mindless gaming for paying a visit to Sin City.

BECAUSE NO ONE IN WASHINGTON, D.C., IS REPRESENTING THE INTERESTS OF INCOMING TRAVEL, THE PROPOSED "VISIT USA" PROGRAM IS ABSURDLY CONTRADICTORY & SELF-DEFEATING

You are probably aware that foreign tourism to the United States has plummeted since September 11. While other foreign countries are enjoying regular and substantial increases in their incoming tourism, the United States welcomed fewer tourists in 2008 than in 2000. Late last year, a senior vice president of the Travel Industry Association testified before a congressional committee that the shortfall in incoming foreign tourism had cost America "46 million visitors, $140 billion in lost visitor spending, $23 billion in lost tax revenue . . . and 340,000 jobs."

So what is being proposed? An advertising budget to be funded by fees assessed upon foreign tourists coming to the United States. They—the foreign visitors—are to pay an extra penalty for the right to come here!

The legislation before Congress is the "Travel Promotion Act" establishing a fund of $100 million for advertising the attractions of our country overseas. Because Congress has no intention of supplying these monies, the fund is to come from private donations and a "modest fee" on foreign visitors.

The idea behind this legislation is that the foreigners are unaware of our attractions and the low cost of travel here and need to be told through ads.

In actual fact, the drop-off in foreign tourism has come about because the process of traveling here has become a grotesque nightmare for most foreigners, who must often wait months for an appointment to apply for a U.S. visa costing $131.

This year, the Department of Homeland Security has inaugurated an Electronic Authorization Program requiring most foreign visitors to send the U.S. an e-mail several days before their scheduled arrival, outlining their plans and setting forth their reasons for being admitted. Only if they then get a favorable response can they enter the country. No one at Homeland Security has revealed whether they plan to hire tens of thousands of examiners to read those e-mails and send back their rejections or approvals.

It gets worse. The Department of Homeland Security is also proposing to require that foreign tourists submit to "biometric" tests (iris scans, fingerprints) upon leaving the United States, for reasons too obscure to discuss. The airlines claim that administering these tests will compel them to spend billions of dollars, which the Department of Homeland Security itself has not the slightest intention of doing.

So while Congress seeks to encourage incoming tourism, the Department of Homeland Security takes steps to discourage it. No one has been given the authority to reconcile those conflicting aims and reach reasonable compromises; my own sense is that the new Obama administration will be reluctant to change a procedure widely touted as necessary to our security.

If you think I am exaggerating the situation, then research these programs on Google and reach your own conclusions. Try the words "Travel Promotion Act" and "Biometric Exit Procedures." You will find that I have understated the absurdity of the situation. Until new people come into the Department of Homeland Security to take care of these matters, the United States will never enjoy the healthy tourism industry that our weak dollar should long ago have created.

The good news in travel starts with an amazing feature of tourism to San Francisco

I've been meaning for some time now to write about America's most remarkable walking tour in perhaps America's most remarkable city, San Francisco. What makes it so unique is that it is entirely free of charge.

I am not referring to some minor, intermittently scheduled service that takes you past attractions that any guide book already describes ad nauseam. I am referring to the unique City Guides (☎ 415/557-4266; www.sfcityguides.org), an association sponsored by the city library that on any given day arranges at least five 90-minute walking tours, which are held rain or shine all around town. On weekends, the daily offerings rise to nearly 20.

Tourists will obviously have much to learn from seeing and learning about the city at the hands of each expert volunteer guide, who specializes in a particular route. Topics include every conceivable landmark in town (to name just a few: the Golden Gate Bridge, Chinatown, the Haight-Ashbury district, and even the considerable public spaces of the famous Palace Hotel). A visitor can learn volumes about this historic city, all without paying a penny.

Beyond such tourist-friendly staples, topics include the secret rooftop gardens hidden around the Financial District (on the "City Scapes and Public Places" tour) and the many scattered murals that have made the Mission District a famous warren of public art. There is even a selection of hikes up some of the city's most panoramic hills, such as Mt. Davidson or Telegraph Hill.

Anyone can show up without reservations (the schedule is posted on its website), and they need not spend a cent to participate—although a few dollars' donation would be thoughtful to encourage the preservation of such a terrific service. City Guides have been walking for 30 years now, and they deserve to be showcasing this richly historic city for many more.

A tribute to Canada, based (admittedly) on a limited, 2-week-long experience

All my life, I have been dipping into Canada for weekend stays, never longer than 3 days at a time. And then recently, my wife Roberta and I devoted 2 weeks to Vancouver, Victoria, Kamloops, Calgary, and the Canadian Rockies (Banff and Lake Louise). And we returned with a new appreciation for our neighbor to the north.

Canada, to begin with, has a much greater population than most of us would have thought: some 38 million people, and growing rapidly as a result of its receptive attitude toward immigration. In effect, Canada has sent word to the world that it will take in political refugees from countries where their lives had become intolerable (Iraq and Somalia among them). It has also followed a far more open policy than ours in encouraging emmigration to Canada of highly skilled scientists, technicians, and even unusually bright university students without specific accomplishments to their credit. To visit almost any large Canadian city is to be surrounded by persons of all races and ethnicities from around the world, to a much greater extent than in today's average U.S. city. Canada is creating the kind of melting-pot society that the United States was in the 1920s.

The media of Canada is especially impressive. You turn on a local radio newscast and hear reports directly from Kandahar, Aghanistan, dealing with the situation there. I cannot imagine hearing radio newscasts in the United States that would devote such attention to important world developments. Note that the broadcasts to which I refer are not NPR-type programs on nonprofit radio but on ordinary commercial radio stations.

In Canada, you do not hear an endless litany of nonstop right-wing commentators—and only right-wing commentators—of the Limbaugh-Hannity-Savage-O'Reilly variety. The Canadian temperament, it seems to me after many hours of surfing our car radio there, is simply not receptive to the brutal attacks and invented facts of U.S. talk celebrities.

The newspapers—and I scanned several of them each day—are especially impressive. The world coverage, the columnists, the editorial opinions, in Toronto's *Globe and Mail* (circulated throughout Canada) are unusually serious and well-thought-through, the kind you would find in the *Economist* or *New York Times*. During the early days of the Russian/Georgia/Ossetia war, the Canadian outlook was totally different from what you would find in the average U.S. newspaper—balanced and objective, without hysteria. I looked forward to reading each day's edition of the *Vancouver Sun,* the *National Post* (a national Canadian newspaper), the *Globe and Mail.*

The people of Canada, I concluded (admittedly based on slender experience), seem generally reasoned in their judgments; serious; tolerant toward the stranger; well educated and well read; thoughtful and reflective; and without the belief in absolutes, the dogmas, and the hatreds of our own fundamentalists and blowhards. Every cab driver to whom I directed political questions responded with details; they knew the names of Canadian politicians, their political parties, their recent histories. They were also world-minded to an extent you would not find in many U.S. states. They were up-to-date on British and even French politics, and they followed the U.S. political scene with great interest.

Let me add, as a final observation, that the social system of Canada appears to recognize the obligation of each Canadian to protect his or her fellow citizens from privation or economic disability. The Canadian single-payer medical system, similar to the Medicare program that Americans operate only for seniors, is efficient and popular.

It is quite a country, a unified and democratic nation that is ethical in its outlook and reasonable in the demands it makes of its governments. It seems to me a country that would not be capable of violating the human rights of any of the persons under its control.

I am well aware that I formed these judgments based on incomplete experience and simply a 2-week stay. And I am ready to be corrected, if I am wrong. But I gained a new respect for Canada and wanted you to know my feelings.

EXPLORING THE CANADIAN ROCKIES & THE GREAT CANADIAN NATIONAL PARKS: A RECENT TRIP

You have probably been to Yosemite, Yellowstone, and the Grand Canyon, but you have not really savored all the awesome beauty of North America until you have mountain-gazed for hours, enraptured, in Banff National Park and Lake Louise. The Canadian Rockies! These undisputed champions of soaring limestone scenery come as close to being indispensable travel visits as any I can name. And I went there following our recent stay in Vancouver.

Banff is a spectacular, gracefully maintained little town with a main, Alpine-like center street lined with shops, high-quality restaurants, small hotels, and small, 2-block-long side streets with still other Alpine-like hotels. With advance reservations, you can pick up modestly priced accommodations (including digs at a major, impressive, YWCA). Otherwise, prices in Banff are rather hefty, on the order of what you would encounter in Vail or Aspen. And the analogy is complete, because Banff in winter is a major ski resort, with *après*-ski activity offered in town.

From Banff, you make a self-drive safari. By simply motoring into the foothills of the massive limestone-and-shale, pine-covered mountains that surround, you are almost guaranteed to see bighorn sheep and elk—we made no fewer than four such sightings. There are also small-van, escorted sightseeing tours you can make of the animal activity, one of which disgorged various young tourists from Shanghai, all of them stylishly dressed and with expensive digital cameras. They were so chic in appearance we were surprised to learn they were staying at the YWCA in Banff. A funicular taking you to the top of an 8,000-foot-high mountain is another big Banff attraction.

But the main highlight is 45 minutes away: Lake Louise. This is not a town, though there is a rustic shopping mall along the highway where a town would normally be. Lake Louise is simply a lake, probably the most gorgeous in existence, almost precisely circular and of turquoise water, flanked by a couplet of mountains so symmetrical in appearance you would swear they were sculpted by hand. The lake is covered with canoeists. On one side is Fairmont's Chateau Lake Louise resort overlooking the scene, made busy in high season by the hundreds of tourists who flock through the lobby and enormous patio to enjoy the view but are themselves staying in Banff.

It would be hard to cite a single scene in all the world comparable to Lake Louise. Days later, seated in my apartment in New York, I can still recall the wondrous spectacle and the impact it had on my senses.

EASYCRUISE HAS MADE THE TRANSITION FROM ITS FORMER REPUTATION AS ONLY FOR PARTY-LOVING SWINGERS TO A RESPECTABLE, BUDGET-CONSCIOUS STATUS

Is there anyone who has not yet heard of easyCruise? Anyone who does not know that it now operates in the Greek islands? Because there is such an obvious desire for less expensive ways of touring Europe, it may be the right time to update you about this odd cruise line.

The idea behind easyCruise (**www.easycruise.com**) was to provide very cheap vacations by stripping down the oceangoing experience. Cabins essentially consist of a bed and a bathroom, with no furniture, phones, or TV. And they can usually be booked for as little as a few nights, enabling passengers to get on and off at interesting ports and catch the ship when it swings around again the next week.

Because of the ship's relatively small size and the fact its stops are just a few hours' sail apart, it is able to linger in port much longer than the typical cruise ship. Rather than piling back on board at sunset for departure, as on most cruises, easyCruise passengers can hang out in the port's bars and restaurants, sampling ouzo and fresh fish well into the night. Sometimes, you do not leave port until dawn the next day. The ship can also dock at locations close to the center of town, keeping taxi expenses low, while many of the large vessels must find berths at newly dredged harbors many miles out of town. Food is available for purchase at a decent restaurant on board (prices are decidedly sensible), but most passengers choose to eat on shore.

Critics predicted that easyCruise would turn into nothing but a floating hostel or a rowdy party boat. That apparently did not happen. Instead, the concept appears to have attracted people of all ages (mostly curious and well-behaved lovers of travel) who were interested in accessing ports that the major lines could not offer on schedules that allowed them to truly explore the islands.

After two winters in the Caribbean, the line is now centered on the islands of Greece and has added a second ship, slightly larger but as simple as the first. The value is just as strong as when the concept was new. Through early October, it offers 7-night trips of the Cyclades or the Aegean Islands, including Bodrum, Turkey, for about $400 per person. From then until mid-December, a quiet time in the region, easyCruise also runs its week-long classical Greece cruise (five ports, including Corinth, Patras, Kiato—all sites little-visited by the major lines—plus 2 days in Athens) for about $250 a week per person, including port charges.

If your goal is to get around these difficult-to-reach areas and not simply to loiter for hours in onboard casinos or at interminable meals, then you will not be able to do better than for those prices.

IF YOU ARE GOING TO LIMIT YOUR SUMMER VACATION TO A SINGLE U.S. CITY, BE SURE TO PICK UP A CITYPASS

They are described at **www.citypass.com**, and their function is quite simple. You buy a packet of entry passes to about six major attractions. When you walk up to each, you simply show the packet, and the pass is detached, granting you admission. The price paid for the packet is always less than what you would pay if you simply purchased the same number of tickets at individual box offices—a savings of 50% is not unusual.

Unlike many so-called "day passes" for sale to tourists, CityPass (☎ 800/330-5008) does not require users to race around, seeing a large number of attractions quickly in order to make their investment pay off. Instead, visitors are given about a week to see everything, and if they intend to take in four or five of the most important attractions, they will almost always benefit from the savings.

Also, unlike many other similar programs in the tourism industry, the attractions are generally not minor. They are usually the cream of each city. In New York, for example, the Empire State Building, the Museum of Modern Art, the Metropolitan Museum of Art, and the Statue of Liberty are all included. Chicago comes with the Sears Tower and the Field Museum. In San Francisco, the use of CityPass also grants unlimited free rides on city buses, trams, and even the famous cable cars (usually $4 per ride).

CityPass currently has deals in 11 important tourist locations: New York City, San Francisco, Philadelphia, Chicago, Boston, Toronto, Seattle, Atlanta, southern California, Hollywood, and Houston.

If you will be going to any of these places, look into the offerings in each packet and compare the cost to the full box-office price.

THERE IS A NEW GADGET—A "TRAVEL SCALE"—YOU WOULD DO WELL TO PICK UP IN ADVANCE OF YOUR NEXT TRIP

You attach this small, hand-held "weighing machine" to the handle of your suitcase, and when you lift the scale, it tells you the weight of your luggage. This is the new, indispensable item for travel that airline regulations have forced upon us. The penalty for going over 50 pounds (domestic) or even as little as 32 pounds (within Europe, on a cut-rate carrier), or even 40 pounds (domestic, it is rumored, on some airlines) has grown so great—travelers with heavy luggage pay as much as $100 more—that it becomes necessary to constantly weigh your luggage at various stages of your trip to insure that you are not going over the dreaded limit.

I would assume that many well-stocked hardware or drugstores carry the item, but you can definitely pick one up for $25 from the mail-order travel supply company **Magellan's** (☎ 800/962-4943; www.magellans.com).

WHEN THE COST OF AIR TRANSPORTATION RISES SHARPLY, AS IT PERIODICALLY DOES, PEOPLE TEND TO FAVOR THOSE DESTINATIONS WHERE THE COST OF LIVING IS CHEAP

Roe Gruber's tour company, **Escapes Unlimited** (☎ 800/243-7227; www.escapesltd.com), has always specialized in the island of Bali, its most popular destination. But when the cost of aviation fuel and therefore air transportation began to skyrocket, she noted a strange phenomenon. Moving into second place in terms of popularity was Argentina, the least expensive of all destinations within a 12- to 15-hour flight of most of the United States. And today her staff is handling almost as many tour passengers to Buenos Aires as to Bali.

That Buenos Aires is a suitable vacation destination for today's hard-pressed American is a point that one of our readers, Donna Cuervo, made in a response to my recent essay about "staycations" (limited to the immediate vicinity of your own home town). Her remarks are so apt that they should not be missed, as such responses sometimes are. Because her advice may indicate a good choice for your own next vacation trip, I am reprinting it here:

If a staycation is what you want, fine, but I would find it really depressing after working a whole year.

Although I hoped to return to Paris this year and take an apartment for a month, I realized that the exchange rate would take a lot of the joy out of it for me. I'll do that another time—hopefully next year.

But I won't stay home. If I can't take an expensive vacation, I'll take a cheap vacation. I'm going back to Buenos Aires.

Doing the math, I find I can have five fine meals in Buenos Aires for the price of one in Paris. A decent apartment in Buenos Aires can be had for less (often a lot less) than $1,000 a month. Go a little over that, and you have something really exciting. In Buenos Aires I can attend the theater, concerts, etc., in the best seats for low prices. In Paris I would have to sit in the balcony and bring binoculars.

In Buenos Aires I can actually shop and buy things. In Paris I could only shop for ideas, as actual buying wouldn't make sense with this exchange rate.

To Buenos Aires, frequent flyer tickets were available at a price (in addition to your frequent flyer miles) of only $37 plus tax. For Paris, there was no availability for many months.

While I could take a "staycation" and see the sights of my own New York area, a vacation in Buenos Aires will probably cost less than staying home. Prices for doing things in New York can be pretty high.

Buenos Aires, anyone? Escapes Unlimited takes you there for $859, including round-trip air on COPA from Miami, 5 nights at the centrally located Regis Hotel or similar, breakfast, transfers, and half-day city tour, with extra nights only slightly more. Add $250 from New York, $350 from Los Angeles. And for an extra $122, you can overnight on the way in Panama and take a tour of the Panama Canal.

Escapes Unlimited also goes to several other unusually cheap destinations, charging as little as:

- ◆ **$749 to Ecuador:** Round-trip air on COPA Airlines from Miami, 5 nights at a three-star hotel, breakfast, transfers, half-day city tour.
- ◆ **$679 to Panama:** Rainforests, beaches, nature, visits to indigenous people, and the Canal. Round-trip air on COPA from Miami, 5 nights at a three-star hotel, breakfast, sightseeing. Slightly higher from other cities.
- ◆ **$999 to Saigon:** Round-trip air from Los Angeles or San Francisco, with 5 nights' hotel in Saigon, transfers, breakfast daily, and a half-day city tour. Extensions to the Central Highlands, Danang, Hue, Halong Bay, and Hai On are also available.

DUBIOUS "TRAVEL AGENTS" ARE AT IT AGAIN, OFFERING ALLEGED DISCOUNTS TO THOSE TRAVELERS WHO WILL FIRST PAY THEM A LUMP-SUM FEE

To my dismay, I am continuing to hear of travel agents who charge "membership fees" for their services. They form a club or organization, claim it is capable of obtaining unusual (but unspecified) discounts and other benefits, charge a fee of $1,500 to $3,500 for "membership," and then proceed to book you into various flights and resorts at what they claim are preferential prices.

Of course, the prices they obtain are no lower than many Internet services or other non-fee-charging travel agents would obtain for you. I am astonished at the gullibility of the public in responding to these "club" offers. And I am shocked at the so-called "bonuses" and "discounts" that these fee-charging travel agents offer.

Often the benefits are coupons entitling the bearer to a free 2-night stay at a resort hotel in a sunbelt location. These are almost always timeshare properties that subject the coupon-holder to intense marketing sessions pressuring them to buy a timeshare. Alternately, the coupons and certificates simply entitle the bearer to a discount that they could have obtained from numerous other marketing organizations without paying a "membership fee."

I know our readers will respond with extreme skepticism to the offers of these scattered, fee-charging "travel agents." The moment you hear of an agency offering benefits only if you will first pay an upfront fee, make a wide detour around that snake oil company and scurry away.

TO SETTLE FOR A "STAYCATION" IS TO STOP ENJOYING ONE OF THE GREAT ADVENTURES OF LIFE

The ditziest word in current use in travel reporting is "staycation." That's the shameful second-rate substitute for travel that various pundits are currently recommending. Shocked by the cost of transportation, unwilling to offset it with cheaper accommodations, they are advocating, in effect, that we all return to an earlier era (like the 1800s) and explore the towns in which we live.

In earlier times, most people had no alternative to a "staycation." They did not enjoy the extraordinary privilege of moving easily between regions of the United States and countries of the world.

Things have obviously changed, and so have the goals we seek on a vacation. Today we have discovered that the chief benefit of our nonworking interludes is not simply rest and relaxation but the chance to expose ourselves to different ways of life, different settings—through travel. We travel to experience the new and the novel, deliberately placing ourselves in situations where our most cherished opinions are confronted by diametrically different beliefs, where we reassess our assumptions and witness different ideologies and theologies, different attitudes and lifestyles, different responses to social and urban needs.

The personal growth that results from those confrontations is exhilarating beyond measure. It is part of the adventure of life and cannot be acquired through a "staycation." We must keep it in our sights by adopting a different type of travel.

Rather than bemoan the cost of transportation, the smart traveler makes the effort to offset those higher costs by reducing the expenses of accommodations, meals, and sightseeing. By lowering your requirements, by living in less pretentious settings, by making use of public transportation, local cafes and groceries, free sights and activities, you can continue to travel despite the high cost of gasoline.

By opening your mind and your eyes to other regions of the United States and to foreign countries, you experience, in effect, the "actions and passions" of our time. The late Oliver Wendell Holmes once wrote it is required of a man that he share those actions and passions, "at the peril of being judged not to have lived." Most of us will reject the boring, enervating, vapid "staycation."

THE SECOND EDITION (JUST PUBLISHED) OF JOSEF WOODMAN'S *PATIENTS BEYOND BORDERS* HAS ADDED HOSPITALS & DENTAL CLINICS IN MANY MORE COUNTRIES

I wrote earlier about the first full-length book to take up the subject of medical and dental tourism in a serious and scientific fashion. The book, *Patients Beyond Borders*, by Josef Woodman, carefully and soberly lists and describes those hospitals overseas that provide competent medical treatment in various fields at highly affordable prices—and those that do not. For the first time, Americans who have no medical insurance or whose medical insurance does not cover the treatment they need have a way of learning where they can go to obtain that care at a price they can handle (even considering the cost of travel).

Woodman's book was the first to point out, as far as I know, that many of these overseas hospitals are accredited by the very same organization that accredits U.S. hospitals, employing exactly the same criteria. It goes on to point out that many of these overseas hospitals actually have better success rates, lower infection rates, and more comprehensive comfort and care than the average U.S. hospital. Photographs of hospitals in Singapore and

Thailand, as one example, are eye-openers, revealing the most modern facilities imaginable and an unusually high ratio of staff to patient (you can see some of those photographs on **www.patientsbeyondborders.com**).

Thus, in Thailand's famed Bumrundgrad Hospital, a veritable army of nurses and attendants surround you with the most careful attention.

Recently I placed a phone call to Woodman in Hong Kong, where he was on an Asian tour visiting still other hospitals (Hong Kong itself is not one of the places he recommends, because of its high medical fees).

Woodman advised me that the revised second edition of *Patients Beyond Borders* has added appraisals of hospitals in Israel, Jordan, South Korea, New Zealand, Panama, the Philippines, Taiwan, and Turkey. He was particularly enthusiastic about the low cost and high level of medical care in Taiwan. He pointed out that each of these new destinations excels in a particular medical specialty.

I asked him whether the U.S. medical profession has attacked the book; whether, in particular, U.S. doctors have been asked to write critical reviews of it. This has not happened, he responded; in fact, at a recent Harvard conference, some participants complained that *Patients Beyond Borders* had succeeded too well—that by revealing the availability of low-cost medical care overseas, it had removed pressures on the U.S. medical system to reform itself! So careful and guarded are the book's factual assertions that apparently U.S. doctors have thus far found nothing to attack.

The new edition is in bookstores now and can also be purchased through Amazon.com. Or you can write directly (enclosing $23) to Healthy Travel Media, P.O. Box 17057, Chapel Hill, NC 27516. Or call ☎ **919/370-7380.** If you have little or no medical or dental insurance and need treatment, you might consider obtaining a copy of a book that has clarified the way to a new form of travel: medical or dental tourism.

ONLY A CHUMP BUYS THEME PARK ADMISSIONS AT THE THEME PARKS. BUY THEM AT HOME BEFORE YOU LEAVE & YOU WILL SAVE BIG.

Important, breathless advice: Visitors heading to Orlando should always book their theme park tickets online, ahead of time. Like many of the more grungy local amusement parks, which pack the house using a variety of two-for-one promotions available at grocery stores and in area newspapers, the glossy Orlando parks have steady deals, too, which they reserve for web reservations. Only a chump pays the box office price for park tickets.

For example, if you step up to the ticket booths at the two parks at Universal Orlando on the day you attend, you will pay $72 for adults and $60 for children (which across Orlando means ages 3–9). That buys access to a single park, with no option of being able to enter the second park on the same day.

But if you book on Universal's website (www.universalorlando.com/tickets.php), you will have access to a variety of better deals. For example, you can visit both its parks for a day for $80 adults and $70 kids, enabling you to see much of the attractions in a single day. Or you can stick to a one-park ticket offered at the gates, but pay $2 less for it. During the slow season, Universal has been known to sell online a full week of access for around the price of 1 or 2 days' tickets. All you have to do is buy your tickets at least 48 hours ahead of time and either print them at home or extract them from ATM-like machines at the front gates, the way you do for reserved movie tickets.

Likewise, while a 1-day price for SeaWorld costs $70 adults and $60 kids at the gate, online (www.seaworld.com/orlando) you can get it for $60 with a free second day at the park. You can also get a pass that admits you to both SeaWorld Orlando and Busch Gardens Tampa for $90, as opposed to about $70 per park if purchased at the gates (you have to buy these at least 7 days ahead online). So if you want to see more than one park, and almost every family visiting Orlando does, you will save considerably by purchasing passes in advance.

SUDDENLY, THE WEIGHT OF YOUR LUGGAGE HAS BECOME A BIG DEAL. PACK LIGHTLY.

In years past, if you walked up to the airline check-in desk with luggage that was reasonably over the posted weight limits, you could often talk the clerks into checking it anyway.

But now that the airlines are desperate for cash, people with heavy bags will find themselves slapped with an extra expense. Airlines are uniformly enforcing these policies to the ounce so that they may glean extra funds from overweight baggage fees. Even some conveyor belts at the check-in desks have been reprogrammed to stop moving if they sense heavy luggage.

On British Airways, the coach passenger's allowance is just 51 pounds. Anyone who goes over pays the equivalent of $50. If the bag weighs more than 70 pounds, the airline says it may not even be allowed on board. The charges on American Airlines, to cite another example, are almost identical, and Delta charges $80. Worse, fees are almost always for each way, so double them for a round trip.

Although it might seem at first like the simplest of vacation advice, "pack lightly" is not always so easily accomplished. We all have a sense of when our luggage is becoming overstuffed, but we do not always know how close to the weight limits we actually are. Packing your bags is ultimately guesswork, especially when you are on vacation and about to return home with your souvenirs. Despite the fact that these overweight fees are hitting flyers in their pocketbooks, I do not know of any hotels that maintain scales for the purpose of weighing outgoing customers' luggage before it is brought to the airport for the flight home.

So it is imperative that you know how much your luggage weighs when empty. Get out the bathroom scale and rest your empty suitcase on it. Once you have that base weight, you will have a greater sense of how much more you can put into it before reaching the limit.

Simply knowing the weight of your empty luggage will go a long way in helping you avoid any unpleasant and expensive surprises when you show up at the airport and anxiously watch the numbers climb on the airlines' own equipment.

New York's famed Museum of Modern Art is free of its hefty admission charge on 1 night each week

Visitors to New York City will obviously consider the city's famed Museum of Modern Art (an overwhelming collection of the past century's master-works) to be a must-see, but many are deterred from stepping in by a hefty $20 per person admission fee. Other great museums of Manhattan theo-retically charge as much but also advise that the fee is simply a "suggested" donation, and I know a great many residents who simply drop a single dol-lar bill into the admissions box at such institutions as the Metropolitan Museum of Art and then saunter gaily inside without being challenged by the ticket takers.

That cannot be done at the Museum of Modern Art (MOMA), which is a privately owned, and not city-run, attraction. There, $20 means $20.

But, Friday evenings at MOMA from 4 to 8pm are "Target nights," when the nation's Target stores pick up the tab, and admission is free of charge. That policy is known to a great many parsimonious New Yorkers, but cer-tainly not to all, and it is unknown (as best I know) to almost all out-of-town visitors. So I feel good about alerting you to the fact that Fridays from 4 to 8pm, you can visit one of the world's great museums for free.

Do not fail to take advantage of this big opportunity.

For visitors to Orlando, the "Disney Dining Plan" strikes me as a poor way to arrange your meals

If you are an adult traveler to Orlando who would not dream of purchasing a prearranged dining plan, you can skip this essay. Read no further. But if you are a family going to Mickey Mouse Land and have booked a room at Orlando's Walt Disney World Resort, you have undoubtedly been offered the chance to opt into the Disney Dining Plan. In its basic version costing $38 per day for anyone over 10 ($10 ages 3 to 9), it grants guests credits good for one table-service meal, one meal from a fast-food counter, and one snack at Disney-operated eateries.

Because of the plan's apparent convenience, it has become an extremely popular add-on. Let me point out the following:

The dining plan's popularity has created difficulties. So many people use it that the advance reservations systems for restaurants are clogged for weeks ahead of time. Dining plan users often find they have to do hours of homework and advance telephone work to eat where they want to eat. Booking sit-down restaurants involves an opportunity loss in that it keeps you from enjoying the rides and shows you presumably went to Florida to enjoy.

Whereas last year, the dining plan included appetizer, dessert, and tip, in 2009 Disney stripped the appetizer and tip from the plan. So your "paid-for" meal is not really paid for; if you want a starter, you must pay, and there are still gratuities to consider.

Without the plan, you will pay $10 to $12 at a counter-service restaurant anywhere at the resort, which includes a drink. No tipping is required there. Simple math proves that if you stick to counter-service locations, as a majority of Disney guests do, you will spend about $24 (plus the price of snacks, if you eat or drink any) as opposed to $38 (before tips) for the same period with the dining plan. That is not a savings.

THERE ARE MULTIPLE WAYS TO CUT YOUR THEATER COSTS IN LONDON—YOU SIMPLY DO NOT HAVE TO PAY THE PUBLISHED RATES

The West End in London rivals Broadway in New York for its high-quality, big-budget stage performances. But currently (and for the foreseeable future), you pay $1.50 for just £1. Because tickets for London's musicals cost about £50 to £60, accessing much of that world-class entertainment is problematic.

But you do not have to pay that much. Exactly as in New York, most London productions (save the ones that are sold out for weeks on end) offer discounts, if only you know where to find them. Several websites round up the going deals, present them to you, and then give you the necessary discount codes and links to book them yourself.

One of those sites is Theatremonkey.com (**www.theatremonkey.com**), which lists half-price promotions and meal-and-a-ticket packages. The site BroadwayBox.com (**www.broadwaybox.com/london**), which is mostly about New York, also brings some West End discount codes to the masses. Some other ways to save?

◆ Given a lead time of a few weeks, lastminute.com (**www.lastminute. com**) sells many shows for half-price, as does LOVEtheatre.com (**www. lovetheatre.com;** click "Special Offers"). Booking fees of a few pounds usually apply.

◆ Matinees are often slightly cheaper than evening shows.

◆ Ask at box offices about standing room tickets. Not all theaters have them, but the Donmar, the National, and the Old Vic, to take three examples, do, and they sell for under £10. These are usually available only if the show's seats are sold out.

◆ Seats at the very back of the theater might cost a quarter to a third of what the seats in the front do—but bring opera glasses.

◆ Some older theaters sell what are called restricted-view seats. You may have to crane your neck at times to see around the edge of the balcony or a pillar, and if the staging has actors at the extreme sides of the stage you might not be able to see them momentarily, but you will be in the theater. Such seats cost about a third of what top-price seats do. Theatremonkey.com posts audience members' opinions about which theaters have decent restricted-view seats and which are too terrible to consider.

◆ If you are a student and can prove it with I.D., some box offices may offer you discounts of 20% to 40%.

Finally: You can always choose to see a show mounted in a smaller theatre away from the West End, which Londoners call the "Fringe." There, prices can start as low as £5 and go to around £30. Many of Britain's top talents make Fringe performances a part of their careers; in fact, many playwrights test their work there before the big time of the West End.

If all else fails, you can buy same-day, half-price tickets to a range of shows (including dance) at the TKTS booth (**www.officiallondontheatre. co.uk/tkts**) on the south side of Leicester Square. Like the Manhattan booth that inspired it, tickets are half-price there, but unlike the New York booth, it accepts credit cards, not just cash, adding to its convenience.

Happy theatergoing, mates!

SOME MID-YEAR MUSINGS, OF VARYING TRAVEL SIGNIFICANCE

Last July, I got to thinking about the fact that my nephew and his wife and two children, who live in Paris, were preparing for their month-long vacation, like a good French family should. They spend all of August at a small seaside hotel in the Greek islands, where they receive three meals a day and inhabit a room that has no English-language television and no access to the English-language press. For 1 month, this family is together, getting to know each other and enjoying some of the most memorable moments of their lives.

Meantime, here in the United States, a recent poll by the Opinion Research Foundation found that two thirds of all American workers enjoyed vacations of considerably less than 2 weeks last year. Sixty-nine percent of them would favor a federal law establishing a guaranteed minimum of vacation for all Americans, and only 27% were opposed. When will we take this step toward a more humane America? Perhaps in 2010, if a more progressive Congress is elected?

Recently, US Air eliminated the showing of movies as the latest in its frantic, cost-saving efforts. That was a wake-up call to bring books, good books, on your next flight. Some recent readings of mine: Karen Desai's *The Inheritance of Loss* (a juxtaposition of life in northern India with the experience of illegal Indian immigrants in New York), Amos Oz's *A Tale of Love and Darkness* (Israel in 1948), J. M. Coetzee's *Disgrace* (South Africa), and Barack Obama's impressive *Dreams from My Father*. And I reread Kurt Vonnegut's *Cat's Cradle*. What movie could possibly compare?

In a response to one of my writings about the imposition of pesky fees and charges by the airlines, one reader chortled that I had finally awakened to the beauty of the marketplace, the ability of unfettered supply-and-demand to solve all problems (I had asked readers to shun the airlines that had led the charge to impose new fees and thus cause them to change their policies; he found that free-marketplace approach to be just dandy). I wondered what that same reader felt when reading about our government's bailout of Fannie Mae, Freddie Mac, AIG, and Bear Stearns—the exact opposite of letting the marketplace solve all problems.

Recently, the euro settled at a level of 1.40 to the U.S. dollar, which means that most travelers will be paying nearly $1.60 for a euro when fees and commissions are taken by the money-changers who supply you with euros. In the immediate future, all of us who want to continue traveling transatlantic will need to become happy-go-lucky, unpretentious, informal, comfort-shunning people, patronizing hostels and guesthouses, cafes, groceries, and pubs. And that is not a bad idea.

I HAVE A MONUMENTAL SPLURGE TO SUGGEST: A ONE-WAY CROSSING OF THE ATLANTIC ON THE *QUEEN MARY 2*

It may be time to consider that once-in-a-lifetime transatlantic crossing between England and New York City on the Queen Mary 2, one of Cunard's grand ocean liners and the last ship to ply this legendary route.

That is because the price of airfare to London has shot up so much that it is approaching the luxury level you would pay to take the ship instead. In high season, round-trip, midweek airfare to London from America's East Coast costs around $1,000. But a one-way ocean crossing from Southampton to the United States is being sold for as little as $1,400 (that's for an inside cabin in summer).

If you take a one-way transatlantic ship crossing, that still leaves a one-way flight (either to London or back) to complete a round-trip journey. The cheapest one-way airfare available from New York to London, when we went to press, was that of Air India midweek (about $450 including taxes), while Aer Lingus charged $570 and Virgin Atlantic charged $830. Those prices, plus $1,400 for the ocean crossing, will total around $1,900 to $2,300 for a trip of a lifetime. (Add about another $250 for a water view.)

In the winter, airfares are much lower, but the ship does not cross the Atlantic Ocean then.

Cunard's *Queen Mary 2* is a liner cut from the classic mold. Picture a lofty, old-fashioned 6-day journey full of evening banquets at which diners wear tuxedos and gowns, couples ballroom dance until late, and chefs serve as much food as you can eat—it is a cruise, of course.

Yes, it is still more expensive than the plane, but the plane does not give you that grand experience, and now that we are finally in a period where both airfare and the cruise are priced in the same ballpark, is it not worth splurging on a ship crossing?

HOSPITALITY CLUBS CONTINUE TO EXPAND IN NUMBERS & IMPORTANCE. EVER HEARD OF GUESTROOM NETWORK?

With the cost of lodgings continuing to soar, it behooves us all to consider searching for alternatives to standard accommodations. A great many avid travelers find that membership in a "hospitality club," enjoying the spare room or cot that members offer to one another, is not simply a means for saving money but actually enhances the trip by introducing you to local residents. And no such organization—until now—has been more successful in offering free hospitality throughout the United States than the Evergreen Club (**www.evergreenclub.com**). It attributes much of its success to its policy of not offering completely free hospitality but charging a nominal fee of $15 a night for the use of a member's spare room or cot. This, apparently, makes members more serious about honoring reservations (and also serving a tasty breakfast to their guests).

I said that Evergreen has been successful "until now." Recently, it has been reported to me that Evergreen's organizers include on their application form a place where prospective members can opt out of hosting someone because they are gay. I find that disturbing. If you do not want to meet someone based on their totally private sexual preference, what are you doing in the Evergreen Club to begin with? Evergreen, after all, is about meeting people.

So some Americans will begin looking for an alternative to Evergreen, and they may find it in Guestroom Network (www.guestroomnetwork. com). It works in the traditional manner of hospitality organizations, except that its fee for an overnight stay is only $4.

THE NEW "THEME CRUISE FINDER" IS A SUPERB INSTRUMENT FOR CHOOSING A CRUISE THAT CATERS TO YOUR OWN SPECIAL INTERESTS

History and world affairs. Music and photography. Liberal and conservative. Jewish and Catholic. Sports and performing arts. Gospel and bluegrass. TV and wellness.

And hundreds of others . . .

As broad as life itself, as varied as the world, as full of special themes as has ever been found in travel, a new website called Theme Cruise Finder (www.themecruisefinder.com) attempts to inject excitement and variety into a cruise industry that, until now, has grown more and more uniform. It lists all the specially themed cruises—the ones led by celebrities who have made their names in various disciplines, from astronauts who have walked on the moon to rejected candidates for the U.S. Supreme Court. You click on the topic that interests you, and up come departure dates for cruises catering to that topic. It is an excellent idea that has been well executed, and I think you will enjoy the well-designed site. I also think that, perhaps for the first time, you may be tempted to book a cruise that focuses on one of your own special interests.

PO CHAI PILLS ARE COMING ON STRONG AS A REMEDY FOR ALL KINDS OF TRAVEL ILLNESSES

More and more mentions of the potent Po Chai are appearing in travel and other literature (see, for instance www.gadling.com). And what are they? They are Chinese medications that supposedly work wonders on such travel-associated discomforts as indigestion, heartburn, vomiting, diarrhea, and bloating. Po Chai (which are also known as Curing pills or Bao Ji pills) can be purchased at many pharmacies in U.S. Chinatowns and are an example of the herb-based remedies so highly prized by Asian cultures.

Large numbers of U.S. travelers are renting apartments for their stays in major European capitals—for instance, Rome

Eight Internet services are currently advertising the availability of short-term (like a week) apartment rentals in Rome, Italy. If you ever needed proof of the explosion in European apartment rentals, you have it here.

Note that far more than eight such Rome-renting companies are found on the Internet; these are simply the ones that advertise. The rents (usually about $150 a night for an apartment housing up to four persons) are somewhat higher than those of the many nonadvertising websites simply found by using a search engine.

The eight rental websites for Rome are RomePower.com (**www.rome power.com**), Under the Roman Sun (**www.undertheromansun.com**), Rental in Rome (**www.rentalinrome.com**), SleepingItaly (**www.sleepingitaly. com**), Romerenting.com (**www.romerenting.com**), BestRentRome.com (**www. bestrentrome.com**), and The Smart Cactus.com (**www.thesmartcactus.com**).

If three or more of you are traveling together, renting an apartment is the way to go. You not only spend less than at hotels of similar quality, but you enjoy far more comfort and space and the ability to prepare an occasional meal at low cost (spaghetti and meatballs, anybody?). The only "disadvantage"? The need to spend at least a week per European city, which is probably the smartest decision you could ever make. It is certainly an antidote to the weak dollar.

INDEX

PHOTO CREDITS

484 Photo Credits